Paul Schalow—
February 18, 1997

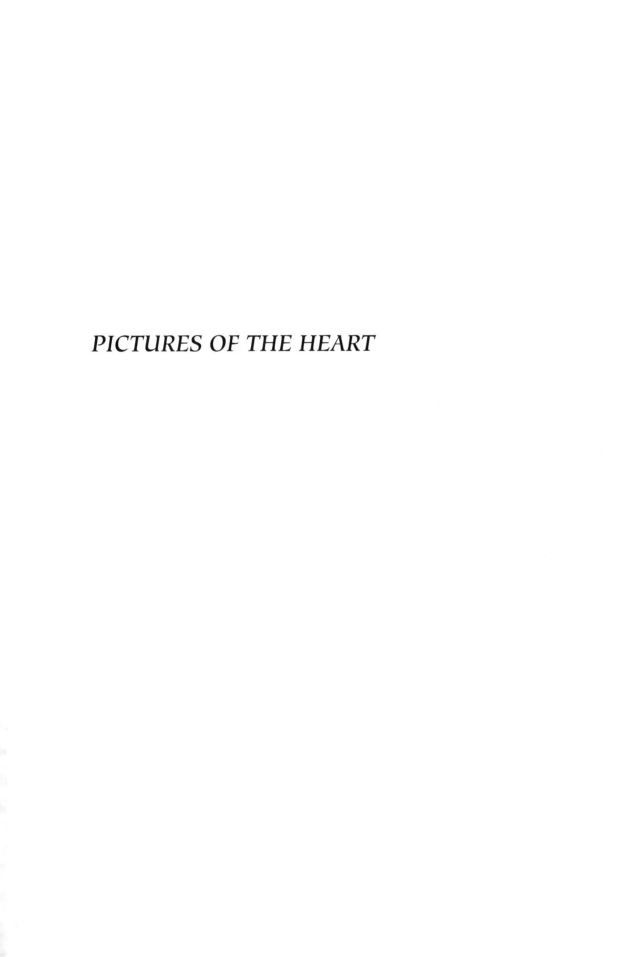

PICTURES OF THE HEART

PICTURES

 UNIVERSITY OF HAWAI'I PRESS
HONOLULU

OF THE HEART

THE *HYAKUNIN ISSHU*
IN WORD AND IMAGE

J OSHUA S. M OSTOW

01 00 99 98 97 96   5 4 3 2 1

Library of Congress Cataloging-in-Publication Data

Mostow, Joshua S., 1957–
    Pictures of the heart : the Hyakunin isshu in word and image / Joshua S. Mostow.
      p. cm.
    Includes bibliographical references and index.
    ISBN 0–8248–1705–2 (alk. paper)
    1. Ogura hyakunin isshu. 2. Waka—History and criticism.
3. Japanese poetry—To 1600—History and criticism. 4. Waka—Translations
into English. 5. Japanese poetry—To 1600—Translations into English. 6. Waka—
Illustrations. 7. Japanese poetry—To 1600—Illustrations. I. Ogura hyakunin isshu.
English & Japanese. II. Title.
PL728.5.04M64 1995
895.6'1108—dc20   95–30185
                                                   CIP

Publication of this book has been assisted by a grant from the Japan Foundation.

The excerpt on pp. 90–91 is from *The Tale of Genji* by Murasaki Shikibu, trans.
E. G. Seidensticker. Copyright © 1975 by Edward G. Seidensticker. Reprinted by
permission of Alfred A Knopf Inc.

The excerpt on p. 78 is from *The Ink Dark Moon* by Jane Hirshfield and
Mariko Aratami. Copyright © 1990 by Jane Hirshfield and Mariko Aratami. Reprinted
by permission of Vintage Books, a division of Random House Inc.

Book design by Kenneth Miyamoto

Writ in a language that has long gone by . . .
And every margin scribbled, crost, and crammed
With comment, densest condensation, hard . . .
And in the comment did I find the charm.
                    —Tennyson, *Idylls of the King*, Bk. VI

To my mother
Gloria Margaret Swan Mostow Pelletier

CONTENTS

Color plates follow page 126

ACKNOWLEDGMENTS

It seems appropriate that it should be an image of Princess Shokushi that graces the cover of this work, as it was in connection with her poem that I first considered the idea of looking at pictorializations as evidence for a reception history of *waka*. This connection occurred while I was working on my dissertation on Heian period *uta-e* at Mukogawa Joshi Daigaku, under the direction of Professor Tokuhara Shigemi. The Mukogawa library had a small collection of *One Hundred Poets* editions, which were catalogued by Professor Tokuhara and his students during my tenure there and it was he who first brought this topic to my attention and encouraged my research of it. It was also at Mukogawa that I wrote the first version of what appears in the present work as a study of the history of English translations of the *One Hundred Poets*. In this connection I would like to thank the Department of English and American Literature of Mukogawa in general, and Professor Honda Masahide in particular.

I touched on Moronobu and his pictorializations of the *One Hundred Poets* very briefly in my dissertation, as I touch briefly on *uta-e* in the present volume. Portions of the section on the history of *uta-e* first appeared in article form in *Monumenta Nipponica,* and I gratefully acknowledge permission to reprint them here, with thanks to the editor, Dr. Michael Cooper. The topic of *Hyakunin Isshu* pictorializations, however, was placed on a back-burner after my return to North America in 1987. It was not until a chance encounter with Professor Stephen Addiss in 1990 that I began to turn my attention to the subject again, and it was due to his encouragement that I presented my first paper on the topic at the Association for Asian Studies annual meeting in 1992. Further encouragement was offered by Professor Sandy Kita, and Dr. Donald Jenkins of the Portland Art Museum. I would also like to thank Professor Edward Kamens for inviting me onto an AAS panel in 1994, my paper for which forms part of the present work's introductory chapter.

While I did not pursue the topic of the poems' pictorializations steadily, I was fortunate to be able to teach the *One Hundred Poets* in seminars a number of times. I would like to thank the institutions and students who made that possible, at the University of Minnesota at Minneapolis/St. Paul; the University of California, Berkeley; and the University of British Columbia. I would also like to thank my colleagues in the Department of Asian Studies at UBC, and especially those of the Japanese section, for allowing me an environment in which to pursue my research. Thanks in this regard are also owed to the two heads of the department during this time, Professors Daniel Overmyer and Michael Duke. Nor can I omit the department's administrative assistant, Mrs. Enid Graham, whom I must thank for the countless ways she made my academic life at UBC easier, despite my unreasonable requests and unconventional methods.

As will become apparent in the reading, this study would have been all but impossible if not for the extremely generous cooperation and assistance of Atomi Gakuen Tanki Daigaku Toshokan, with their unsurpassed collection of *Hyakunin Isshu* materials. I would like to thank in particular Ms. Nakai Toshie, and above all Mrs. Takahashi Mieko, for her constant assistance and kindness.

I would like to thank the anonymous readers contacted by the University of Hawai'i Press for their careful reading of the original manuscript—their corrections, queries, and suggestions have helped strengthen the final version. Professor Sharalyn Orbaugh was also kind enough to read portions of the original manuscript. I would like especially to acknowledge and thank Professor Maribeth Graybill, whom I think of as my *senpai,* for her encouragement and assistance not only on this particular project, but over the last decade. Robert Khan was also of great help during the final manuscript preparation.

Others I would like to mention in thanks are Dr. James Ulak and the staff of the Art Institute of Chicago, Messieurs David Caplan, Komatsu Shigemi, Maruyama Nobuhiko, Matsubara Shigeru, Nagasaki Iwao, and Tokugawa Yoshinobu, and Professors Akiyama Terukazu, Amano Shiro, Sonja Arntzen, Ii Haruki, Ikeda Shinobu, Kobayashi Tadashi, Peter Kornicki, Kuwabara Hiroshi, Earl Miner, Gene Phillips, Tom Rimer, Paul Schalow, Uchida Kinzō, Yoshida Kōichi, and Yoshikai Naoto. Unfortunately, the listing of an individual's name here cannot be taken as an indication of his or her endorsement of the final product, and the errors that inevitably remain in the present work are my sole responsibility.

Funding for this study was provided by the University of British Columbia (HSS) and the Canadian Social Science and Humanities Research Council. A Japan Foundation Fellowship allowed me to go on leave and be in Japan during the final stages of manuscript preparation. While in Japan during the 1994–1995 academic year, I benefited from seemingly innumerable people's goodwill and assistance, some of whom have already been mentioned above. In addition, I would like to thank Professor Michael Watson and Midorigawa Machiko for their hospitality and guidance, as well as the Faculty of International Studies at Meiji Gakuin University, for the use of their facilities and their support. I am also extremely grateful to Professor Chino Kaori and the faculty of the Department of Philosophy at Gakushūin University for inviting me as a Visiting Researcher and providing me office space and facilities.

Karen Wilson has been an unfailing companion throughout, patient and understanding, and I can only apologize for the neglect that writing this book has entailed.

Although perhaps not as obvious, several other people have left their mark on this work, and I hope they will recognize their influence—Barbara

Ruch, Barbara Herrnstein Smith, Peter Steiner, and Wendy Steiner. I would also like to acknowledge an even more fundamental influence, my mother, to whom I dedicate this book. Her interest in my work on translation history encouraged me to develop it further, and it is my hope that her life-long professional involvement in the fashion industry, and innate sense of curiosity, will make other parts of the book of interest to her as well.

Finally, I would like to thank my copy editor, Don Yoder, and, at the University of Hawai'i Press, Cheri Dunn and most especially Patricia Crosby, for her unflagging enthusiasm for this project, which made what seemed an endless series of daunting tasks far more manageable.

A NOTE ON TRANSLITERATION

The romanization system used in this book requires explanation. All names and titles (of works and people) and modern Japanese terms are romanized according to the standard Hepburn transcription system used in *Kenkyūsha's New Japanese-English Dictionary*. The classical Japanese poems quoted in the text, however, since they are included primarily for students of classical Japanese, represent a transliteration (not transcription) of the Japanese texts. I have used the Hepburn equivalents for each *kana* but have kept a distinction between *he, we,* and *e,* between *wo* and *o,* and between *wi* and *i;* and I have added *dzu* for づ and *jhi* for ぢ. Moreover, as a transliteration, the romanization follows the historical spelling of words *(rekishi-teki kana-zukai)* rather than post-1946 modernized spellings.

I have adopted this unusual system for a number of reasons, but primarily I wish to allow students to look up words in a classical Japanese dictionary: if one does not know that the modern *kyō* ("today") was spelled *ke-fu,* rather than *ki-yo-u* or even *ki-ya-u* (also possible in classical orthography), one will not be able to find it in a classical dictionary. Historical spelling also tends to make both pivot words and line counts more apparent. My concern, then, has been for the student of classical Japanese rather than some mythical common reader who is going to intone the romanizations out loud in the hopes of "directly experiencing" the poem—presumably the belief that underlies the inclusion of the romanized poems in modern transcription.

My word division also follows *Kenkyūsha:* where a lexeme can stand as an independent word (such as *in,* "cloister"), it is romanized as a separate word; where it cannot, it is made part of a compound (as in *Kokin*); when it is a nonindependent prefix, the first letter of the following lexeme is capitalized (as in KoShikibu and *ShinKokinshū*). In the titles of works, *Shū* ("Anthology") and *Shō* (rendered "Commentary") are treated as independent words unless part of an abbreviated title (thus *Man'yō Shū* and *Kokin Waka Shū* but *Kokinshū*).

Hyphens are used in the following cases: words that have a grammatical relationship to each other are divided, but compound Japanese substantive pairs are hyphenated (thus *shiroki tahe* but *shiro-tahe*); between a verb in the *ren'yōkei* and the conjoined verb (as in *oki-mayofu*); to indicate a prefix in a common, rather than a proper noun (thus GoToba but *sa-mushiro*).

Finally, an apostrophe is used to distinguish between *ni + y* and *n + y* (as in *Man'yō*); to indicate a voiced laryngeal between two like vowels (as in GoMizuno'o); between strings of three or more short vowels (thus Kane'ie, but Shōi-chi); and finally between vowel clusters that might be misread as diphthongs by an English speaker (thus Sane'akira).

CHAPTER 1

Introduction: A Poetics of Interpretation

The *Hyakunin Isshu,* or *One Hundred Poets, One Poem Each* collection, is a sequence of one hundred Japanese poems in the *tanka* form, selected by the famous poet and scholar Fujiwara no Teika (1162–1241) and arranged, at least in part, to represent the history of Japanese poetry from the seventh century down to Teika's own day. The *One Hundred Poets* is, without a doubt, the most popular and most widely known collection of poetry in Japan—a distinction it has maintained for hundreds of years. As such, it has had a tremendous influence on Japanese literature, visual art, and culture, both "high" and "low." Since at least the sixteenth century it has been the most important primer of classical Japanese poetry in the *tanka* form, and it was this genre that in turn served as the foundation of the other major medieval literary forms, such as linked verse *(renga)* and *nō* theater. By the early modern period (1600–1868), Teika and his *One Hundred Poets* collection had come to define the classical poetic tradition. The *One Hundred Poets* became the subject of ever more popular and widely circulated commentaries, illustrations, adaptations to clothing and furnishings, parodies, and appropriations. For instance, virtually every major woodblock *ukiyo-e* artist at some time or other tried his hand at illustrating the entire set. It also became the basis of a popular card game, which in turn became a regular part of the new year festivities. Today as well, students study the poems of the *One Hundred Poets* in school, and many Japanese still memorize them in the context of the card game. Moreover, the *One Hundred Poets* was one of the earliest complete poetic texts to be translated into English, and since then it has served as a textbook for foreigners as well, leading to at least a dozen complete translations in English alone.

A Question of Historicity

The *One Hundred Poets* collection is a compact history of Japanese poetry from the seventh to the mid-thirteenth century. Yet even when it was first put together, in the 1230s, there was confusion about the meaning of poems written in earlier periods. Not surprisingly, then, Japanese poets and scholars have been writing commentaries on the *One Hundred Poets* since at least the late thirteenth century, and Japanese readers have long read the poetry of the *One Hundred Poets* through such commentaries. While an individual poem might take only seconds to recite, readers were used to analyzing and savoring every word and phrase. Despite the number of English translations of the *One Hundred Poets,* however, since the beginning of the twentieth century most have included as little annotation as possible. Apparently this custom can be traced to a belief that poetry should, and should be allowed to, "speak for itself" without pedantic footnotes and commentaries. Regardless of the value of such an idea, no translator since the nineteenth century has provided English readers the chance to read the *One Hundred Poets* as the Japanese do: aided by commentaries, alerted to differing interpretations, or informed about the historical background.

Almost fifty years ago, the Czech scholar F. X. Šalda wrote:

> Literary history very wrongly limits itself to describing only the *genesis* of a work, by which is meant its creation from the first impulses and initiatives up to its material embodiment. A second and often greater and more difficult part of the task awaits it: to describe how the work has changed in the minds of those following generations who have dealt with it, who have lived on it, fed on it, and nourished themselves on it. This is the second part of the biography of a work—and it is frequently, even usually, neglected.[1]

It is precisely this kind of reception history of a literary text that is still usually neglected by European and English-speaking scholars of Japanese literature.[2] And even in more recent studies that do attend to issues of reception, no one has questioned how reception history might influence *translation*—scholars still seem to see the text as essentially the self-same over time.

In other words, scholars continue to work within an Ingardian phenomenological framework. This approach was ensconced in literary New Criticism in the bible of the same, entitled *Theory of Literature,* by the Czech René Wellek and the American Austin Warren, published originally in 1942. In Part Four, "The Intrinsic Study of Literature," Wellek and Warren include a chapter on "The Mode of Existence of a Literary Work of Art," making explicit reference to the "Polish philosopher, Roman Ingarden, [who] in an ingenious, highly technical analysis of the literary work of art, has employed the methods of Husserl's 'Phenomenology.' "[3] Rather than "reception," Ingarden and his fellow phenomenologists speak of the "concretization" of a work of art. As Felix Vodička put it: "Ingarden . . . finds the source of the difference in concretizations primarily in the schematic and indefinite nature of some strata of the work, while other strata maintain their identity. . . . He insists that the changing concretizations of the work do not violate its identity in its nonschematic parts, for otherwise the artistic essence of the work would be violated. Ingarden [also] presupposes an ideal concretization that would fully realize *all* the esthetic qualities of the work" (p. 110). In the same way, Anglo-European scholarship on Japanese literature has, at best, seen posterior interpretations of a work such as the *Genji* as "readings" of a constant, self-same text and, at worst, have cited, for instance, Edo-period interpretations of such works as the *Tales of Ise* only to dismiss them.[4] I know of no case in which the issue of reception has been considered relevant to translation or been seen to challenge the essential identity of the literary work.

All this is perfectly consonant with an orientation toward literature that views poetry either as the best thoughts great men have ever thought or as a timeless time machine that always works the same way (when properly operated), no matter in what century its button is pushed. In Archibald MacLeish's oft-repeated words: "A poem should not mean / But be." "Being," of course, excludes interpretation: something simply is, or it isn't.[5] Accordingly, translations of poems are thought of as either "right" or "wrong," and the issue of interpretation is often not broached at all. This is not to say that most translators are unaware of interpretive controversy; rather, they seem to believe that their primary obligation, as translators, is to provide a text through which the reader can intuit the unchanging structure of the work.

The poems that Teika anthologized date from at least as early as the seventh century up to his own day: a span of some five hundred years. This collection, as noted, has long been popular as a textbook, and thus the poems can be treated individually and interpreted according to the most recent knowledge of their original contexts. The *Hyakunin Isshu Zen Yakuchū*, or *The One Hundred Poets, One Poem Each Collection, Completely Translated [into Modern Japanese] and Annotated*, edited by Ariyoshi Tamotsu, for instance, exemplifies the textbook approach to the *One Hundred Poets*.[6] Ariyoshi uses as his base text the oldest extant manuscript copy of the *One Hundred Poets*, copied by Gyōkō (1391–1455), the grandson of the Nijō poetic school adherent Ton'a, and owned by the Imperial Household Agency. But the *One Hundred Poets* has undergone some changes during its transmission from Teika's day. For instance, in the case of the poem by Murasaki Shikibu (Poem 57), Ariyoshi gives the poem as it is written in the Gyōkō manuscript but notes that this poem is included in the *ShinKokinshū*, the *Nishidai Shū*, and the *Murasaki Shikibu Shū*, all works edited by Teika; and in each of these, as well as in other copies of the *One Hundred Poets* such as the *Ōei Shō* of 1406, the wording is slightly but significantly different. In other words, the poem as it appears in the Gyōkō manuscript, while it may reflect the way Gyōkō knew the poem, probably does not reflect either the poem as Murasaki Shikibu, its author, wrote it nor as Teika, the compiler of the *One Hundred Poets* collection, knew it. Accordingly, some Japanese editors emend their base text. In contrast to Ariyoshi, for instance, Shimazu Tadao offers an edition of the *One Hundred Poets* that is based on the oldest extant printed version, the *Soan-bon*, but emended to reflect his conclusions about how Teika designed the work.[7]

Some Anglo-American translators have accepted the necessity for such emendation, presumably because it is also understood to be in accord with the poet's original intent—that is, what, in the preceding example, Murasaki Shikibu herself meant. Yet they seem unwilling to apply the same principle when Teika's reading of a poem is no longer accepted as correct by modern scholars. In fact, the most recent American translator of the *One Hundred Poets* dispenses with any actual text at all but relies on a virtual one: he draws his text of the individual poems from the original imperial anthologies from which Teika collected them, rather than any extant copy of the *One Hundred Poets* itself, and translates them according to the best modern information of their meaning at their time of composition, whether Teika seems to have read them in the same fashion or not.[8] The *One Hundred Poets,* in this case, exists only as an excuse to collect together one hundred particular poems from various imperial anthologies, and the translator's interpretation of the whole reflects the historical understanding of no period but his own.

In contrast to the standard approach, this book attempts to present, and represent, what Louis Montrose has called "the historicity of texts"—that is, "the cultural specificity, the social embedment, of all modes of writing" and, I would add, all modes of reading.[9] Such an approach, however, still remains within the circle of what I would call "the conceit of the modern," puns intended. In other words, the reception history I have just outlined remains positivistic albeit plural: *we* know what Murasaki Shikibu *actually* intended, and we know that Teika got it wrong.[10] But Montrose also draws our attention to what he calls "the textuality of history," the idea, "firstly, that we can have no access to a full and authentic past, a lived material existence, unmediated by the surviving textual traces of the society in question—traces whose survival we cannot assume to be merely contingent but must rather presume to be at least partially consequent upon complex and subtle social processes of preservation and effacement; and secondly, that those textual traces are themselves subject to subsequent textual mediations when they are construed as 'documents' upon which historians ground their own texts, called 'histories' " (p. 20).

In other words, not only should we recognize that the survival of texts such as the *One Hundred Poets* is not "merely contingent" but must be "at least partially consequent upon complex and subtle social processes of preservation and effacement," which we should try to reveal and explain, but we must also recognize that the very effort to reveal and explain these processes is historically mediated and every bit as much "consequent upon" the very same kind of "complex and subtle social processes" of our own time. Objectivity, in other words, or "the truth," is not available to us. Our readings and our interpretations remain just that—readings and interpretations—and while we may avail ourselves of the work of our predecessors, that is no reason to believe our results will be any more correct. While many argue the necessity of appreciating the historicity of the past, fewer seem willing to consider the historicity of the present. Such a perspective is, however, essential. To quote Montrose again:

> Integral to . . . a . . . project of historical criticism must be a realization and acknowledgement that our analyses and our understandings necessarily proceed from our own historically, socially and institutionally shaped vantage points; that the histories we reconstruct are the textual constructs of critics who are, ourselves, historical subjects. If scholarship actively constructs and delimits its object of study, and if the scholar is historically positioned vis-à-vis that object, it follows that the quest of an older historical criticism to recover meanings that are in any final or absolute sense authentic, correct, and complete is illusory. Thus, the practice of a new historical criticism invites rhetorical strategies by which to foreground the constitutive acts of textuality that traditional modes of literary history [and, I would argue, translation] efface

or misrecognize. It also necessitates efforts to historicize the present as well as the past, and to historicize the dialectic between them—those reciprocal historical pressures by which the past has shaped the present and the present reshapes the past. [pp. 23–24]

To exemplify this issue, I want to consider a bold and recent reading of the work of Murasaki Shikibu that appears in a book called *Murasaki Shikibu no Messeeji* by Komashaku Kimi, a scholar of modern Japanese literature and an openly lesbian feminist.[11] In one section of this work, Komashaku asserts: "Murasaki Shikibu wa dōsei ni ai o kanjite ita," which one might provisionally translate as "Murasaki Shikibu experienced love homosexually." Komashaku's thesis has been met with stony silence by Japanese scholars of classical literature. One suspects that many of them found Komashaku's interpretation the most egregious example of the ahistorical and anachronistic application of a new "discourse" and modern concerns to a classical text.

Komashaku draws particular attention to Murasaki Shikibu's relationship with another lady-in-waiting, her roommate KoShōshō. Here is one exchange of poems between them:

> I was writing a reply to a letter sent by Lady Koshōshō from home, when suddenly it clouded over with the autumn rains—the messenger too was in a hurry. "And the sky too looks like it's unsettled again!" I wrote, and it must have been, because I added some clumsy poem and later, when it had become dark, the messenger returned with this, written on dark purple paper with a graduated cloud-pattern:

kumo-ma naku	Like the clouds without a break
nagamuru sora mo	I gaze at the sky that has
kaki-kurashi	grown dark—
ikani shinoburu	how should it be the autumn rains
shigure naruramu	that let fall tears of longing?

Not remembering even what I may have written, I replied:

kotowari no	While there may be breaks
shigure no sora ha	in the clouds in the sky of the seasonal
kumo-ma aredo	autumn rains,
nagamuru sode zo	there is never a break to dry
kawaku ma mo naki	the sleeves of she who gazes out.[12]

What is particularly intriguing about the example of Komashaku reading Murasaki Shikibu is that it can be shown to be so clearly a product of its time and place. The best proof of this is the English translation of the *Murasaki Shikibu Nikki* and *Shū* published by Richard Bowring. Despite considering in great detail almost every other aspect of this work—whether Murasaki Shikibu had an erotic relationship with Michinaga, her attitude toward religious retirement and life at court, and more—Bowring does not for one minute suggest there might be anything erotic in the exchange of poetry between two women.[13] This is not to blame Bowring, really—Bonnie Zimmerman complains

of the same blindness among feminists, including earlier work by Elaine Show-
alter.[14] It is simply to point out how our preconceptions make certain interpre-
tive possibilities invisible to us.

In fact, the case of lesbian criticism is an exemplary instance of what one
might call "blindness and insight." This is because the blindness to lesbian
interpretations of texts has also entailed denial—an explaining away of the sim-
plest interpretation of a text in favor of a more complicated, but heterosexually
normative, reading. This tendency to explain away can be seen in the following
discussion by Edward Kamens about another Heian-period exchange of poetry
between two women in "The Collected Poems of the Great Kamo Priestess," or
DaiSai In GyoShū:

> The *kotobagaki* of poem 39 in *Daisaiin gyoshū* introduces it as one Senshi sent to
> an absent attendant, "Kodaifu," on a night when a bright moon was intermit-
> tently obscured by clouds *(tsuki no kumorimi harezumi suru hodo ni)*, and hence
> unable to fulfill its most conventional *waka* role, that of nocturnal companion:
>
> > *kumogakure sayaka ni mienu tsuki kage ni*
> > *machimi matazumi hito zo koishiki*
>
> The moon obscured by clouds *(kumogakure . . .)* sheds a light *(tsuki kage)* that
> barely allows the poem-speaker to see into the night *(sayaka ni mienu,* "I can-
> not see it [the moon] clearly"); nevertheless, she peers into the darkness,
> waiting for the reappearance of the moon from behind the clouds, then giv-
> ing up in impatience, then looking out in hope again *(machimi matazumi,*
> "waiting, then not waiting"). Similarly, she waits anxiously for the return of
> the absent Kodaifu, yearning for her companionship *(hito zo koishiki)* as much
> as or perhaps even more than for that of the unhelpful moon. The juxtaposi-
> tion of a similar construction in the *kotobagaki (kumorimi harezumi,* "the moon
> clouding over, and not clearing") in the setting of the scene accentuates the
> sense of the discomfiture of the moment and the reflexive relationship
> between the moon, here a failed companion, and Kodaifu, an absent one.[15]

Let us, in passing, note the similarity of phrasing between this poem and the one
by Murasaki Shikibu in the *One Hundred Poets,* also addressed to a woman, with
the shared expressions *kumo-gakure* and *tsuki-kage,* as well as the semantic similar-
ity of *mishi ya* ("did I see it?") and *sayaka ni mienu* ("I cannot see it clearly").

Kamens follows this poem with another example from the *DaiSai In
GyoShū:*

> On another night, one on which the full moon shone in all its splendor *(tsuki
> no kumanaki akaki ni),* another absent attendant, "Taifu," was sent this poem
> by her colleague "Ukon" *(Daisaiin gyoshū* no. 121) . . .
>
> > *kokoro sumu aki no tsuki dani nakariseba*
> > *nani o ukiyo no nagusame ni semu*
>
> Were there not at least this autumn moon that calms the heart,
>   what would be my solace in this sad life?

—a suggestion that, in Taifu's absence, the luminous moon will serve amply as substitute and solacing companion. . . . Taifu's response (*Daisaiin gyoshū* no. 122) to Ukon is a claim to the same moon as her own substitute companion:

> *kaze ni sou mugura no toko no hitorine mo*
> *tsuki yori hoka no nagusame zo naki*

> For one who [also] sleeps alone on a windblown pallet of grass,
>   there is no solace other than the moon. [pp. 33–34]

And it is here that Kamens remarks that "the unmistakably erotic subtext of this exchange is part of its poetic character: the two women are playing with images and sentiments that, *in another context,* would readily be read as explicit tropes of sexual desire" (p. 34, emphasis added).

As scholars and members of our society, we have of course been trained either to ignore (that is, be blind to) or deny (that is, explain away) what would appear to be homosexuality. Yet there is increasing evidence that female same-sex erotic relationships were hardly unknown at the Kamo Shrine in the Heian period.[16] It is only thanks to our present political and intellectual moment that we are able to "see," that is, consider, these texts as homoerotic. Indeed, such readings are part of a growing trend to explore the possibility of an erotic interpretation of love poems written between women, a trend that ranges from consideration of poems written to singing girls by the Ming-period "gentry wife" Xu Yuan (1560–1620)[17] to the adaptations of Horace by the seventeenth-century Aphra Behn.[18]

Komashaku's interpretation comes in no small part from her own sexual identity, and her discussion of Murasaki Shikibu's *dōsei'ai,* or "homosexual love," is punctuated by references to the current state of women's rights in Japan and the current rights of "sexual minorities" in the rest of the world. In fact, Komashaku's very conception of "homosexuality" owes much, I suspect, to the definitions of Adrienne Rich and Rich's idea of a "lesbian continuum" that frees definition from the phallocratic genital fixation.[19] Above all, a "lesbian" interpretation problematizes the very definitions of "lesbian," "homosexual," "homosocial," *dōsei'ai,* indeed the very terms "sexual" and "erotic" themselves. The issue is really what we—now, today—mean by these terms. Is this erotic poetry, or were the terms of erotic poetry the only ones available to poets, even to express friendship? One does not, then, apply new "critical discourses" to classical texts; rather, one applies them to one's own understanding of the world. In a way, the "classics" do embody what Nicolai Hartmann has called "das Stehenbleiben des Monumentalen," or the "stand-still of the monumental." This is not to champion what Vodička labels "aesthetic dogmatism," which "has sought eternal and constant aesthetic values in a work or has conceived the history of reception as a path toward a definitive and correct understanding" (pp. 107–108). Rather, it is to suggest that the classic serves as an Other by which we measure our own reflection. Classics remain vibrant only if we continue to "deautomatize," as Šalda puts it, the "concretizations propagated in schools and popular handbooks" (Vodička, p. 128). Šalda contends that boredom with automatized concretizations is the initiative for new concretizations; Vodička argues that the initiative lies in "the needs of new literary movements" (p. 129), what he calls "the contemporary development of the literary norm" (p. 130). Today we are further away from these art-for-art's-sake orientations, and there is an increasing tendency to see literature and canonization as part of a system that has helped to perpetuate dominant ideologies, racial, sexual, and colonial. Accepting that all scholarship is ideological, scholars and translators of Japanese literature may find themselves echoing Montrose's words: "By choosing to foreground in my readings of Shakespeare or Spenser such issues as the politics of gender, the contestation of cultural constraints, the social instrumentality of writing and playing, I am not only engaged in our necessary and continuous re-invention of Elizabethan culture but I am also endeavoring to make that engagement participate in the re-formation of our own" (p. 30).

A New Approach

Writers and artists of Japan's medieval, early modern, and modern periods too were engaged in a "necessary and continuous re-invention" of the "classical" past of the Heian court, and those engagements were crucial to the reformation of their own culture and time. It is the traces of these engagements, particularly with the canonical text of the canonical genre par excellence—the *One Hundred Poets*—that I attempt to limn in Part Two of this work. The evidence for such engagements is various, and I have eschewed any totalizing or narrative interpretation of the poems themselves or the commentaries, both verbal and visual, that surround them. Each of the *One Hundred Poets* poems is presented in a romanization of its historical spelling *(kyū-kana-zukai)* in the form that the best evidence suggests Teika established for it; this version is paired with a translation into English (the principles of which will be elaborated shortly). Listed too are the imperial collection *(chokusen shū)* in which the poem was first anthologized, as well as other exemplary collections *(shūka shū),* by Teika and others, in which it appeared. This strategy allows the reader to see when the poem was first canonized (some poems were selected shortly after they were written, others not for hundreds of years) and how often it was presented as an exemplary composition, especially by Teika in the numerous teaching collections he assembled over his lifetime. This information gives us an idea why a particular poem appealed to readers of a particular time. Moreover, as both imperial and exemplary collections were organized by themes, the placement of the poem in different contexts provides important clues as to how the poem was interpreted by its anthologizer. (For instance, was it read as a love poem or as a seasonal poem? Was it read as a poem of early or late winter?)

The poem is followed by a brief biography of its putative author. While the evidence (discussed in Part One) suggests that Teika chose the poems of the *One Hundred Poets* for their value as individual poems, and not as representative of a poet's entire oeuvre, the image of the poet "behind" the verse was always important to Japanese readers. Brief biographies of the poet's genealogy (that is, aristocratic pedigree), rank achieved, and offices held appear as early as the

Satake-bon Imaginary Portraits of the Thirty-Six Immortal Poets (Sanjūrokkasen-e), pro-
duced in Teika's lifetime. In the Heian and Kamakura periods, court status and
poetic accomplishment were understood to be mutually reinforcing and were
rarely considered divorced from each other.[20] Likewise in the early modern
Edo period, there was a renewed attention to lineage, as those newly come to
power attempted to justify and consolidate their position as well as to inhibit
the social mobility they themselves had benefited from.

With the biographical sketch of the poets I have also included information
on how many of their poems were chosen for imperial anthologies and from
what date. Like the information on when and where each *One Hundred Poets*
poem was anthologized, knowing the relative number of poems by a particular
poet selected for imperial anthologies can give us some idea of his or her repu-
tation over the years. This in turn indicates whether Teika's selection of the poet
was conventional or must be explained as the result of Teika's idiosyncratic taste
or some particular needs of the *One Hundred Poets* collection itself.

It is in the commentaries to the *One Hundred Poets*, of course, that we find
the most specific information on how the individual poems have been inter-
preted over the centuries. The exegetical tradition behind the *One Hundred
Poets* is long and verbose, and an annotated translation could easily run to a
thousand pages. Not all this commentary seems of particular interest, however,
and even less of it may seem pertinent to someone reading in translation. I
have attempted to sharpen the focus of the commentary by concentrating on
four points: what modern scholars believe the poem meant when it was first
composed; what modern scholars believe Teika thought the poem meant;
major interpretive differences that appeared in the Muromachi (1338–1573)
and Edo (to 1868) periods; and finally any interpretations that seem to be
reflected in extant pictorializations of the poems.

Notice should perhaps be given about what is not provided in the section
on the commentaries: the reader will not find what are known as "close read-
ings"—the hallmark of New Criticism, the formalistic critical approach that
held sway virtually unchallenged in North American colleges and universities
after World War II. As suggested earlier, texts were both dehistoricized and
depoliticized, while attention was paid to their intrinsic formal features, which
were believed to be primarily responsible for a literary text's greatness. This
critical method was first applied to Japanese poetry in the late 1950s by Earl
Miner and the late Robert Brower, most significantly in their landmark *Japanese
Court Poetry* (1961). New Criticism subsequently formed the foundation of most
American students' training in Japanese literature, and especially poetry, con-
tinuing up to the present. Much of this work can still be read with great profit,
and similar modes of analysis have been adopted by Japanese scholars as well,
such as Ariyoshi Tamotsu. Nonetheless, this approach is not at all representa-
tive of how Japanese readers themselves have analyzed or evaluated poetry for
most of their history, and it is to the more indigenous and traditional modes of
interpretation that the present study turns its attention.

It is my contention, and one of the major theses of this book, that one of
these traditional modes of interpretation is to be seen in the many pictorializa-
tions of the *One Hundred Poets* that appeared primarily as woodblock prints dur-

ing the Edo period. These, I argue, are not mindless designs but represent specific readings, uses, and appropriations of the classical canon. In the earliest extant example of such pictorializations, the famous *ukiyo-e* artist Hishikawa Moronobu writes that he has "indicated the heart of the poems in pictures." It is these pictures of the hearts of the poems that have led to the present work. Nonetheless, analysis of this kind is very much in its infancy and can only be presented here in the guise of a preliminary effort. Here, too, hermeneutical issues concerning the constraints of interpretation raise their heads. Robert Graves, for instance, suggests that the misreading of pictures inspired many of the Greek myths. The story of Tereus, Procne, and Philomela, as an example, "seems to have been invented to account for a series of Thraco-Pelasgian wall-paintings, found by Phocian invaders in a temple at Daulis," he writes. "The cutting-out of Procne's tongue misrepresents a scene showing a priestess in a prophetic trance, induced by the chewing of laurel-leaves; her face is contorted with ecstasy, not pain, and the tongue which seems to have been cut out is in fact a laurel-leaf, handed her by the priest who interprets the wild babblings."[21] In the same way, we need some sort of evidence when we offer the interpretation of a visual image. Such support may be iconological—that is, it may have an explicit textual basis; or it may only be circumstantial—that is, the meaning of an image or gesture may be extrapolated from its repeated appearance. In any case, such evidence must be offered if we are to avoid completely unsubstantiated "readings." Accordingly, my interpretations of the pictures may seem tame or obvious, but they are the most that can be responsibly made with the information presently available—there is much that we still do not understand of the Edo visual vocabulary.

The entries on the individual poems, which comprise Part Two of this work, are preceded by the study that makes up Part One. In Chapter 2 I offer a brief examination of the history and function of exemplary collections in the Japanese poetic tradition in general and Teika in particular. This review shows that such collections were always designed for specific purposes and frequently for specific individuals. Consequently, they do not necessarily represent what the compiler thought were the unqualifiedly "best" examples of poetic art—they represent, rather, what the compiler thought would be most appropriate for the person or occasion for which the collection was created.

I then consider the history of the exegetical efforts that surround the *One Hundred Poets*. We see how such commentaries were transmitted along hereditary lines and served to support the claims of these lineages to poetic authority. A consideration of extant commentaries shows some of the differing attitudes among these varying lineages. The history of the exegetical tradition also shows the dramatic changes that occurred in the transmission of knowledge between the medieval and early modern periods, as this cultural expertise was made available to different strata of society. As the *One Hundred Poets* entered these strata, it was adapted to a variety of uses from women's education to nationalist ideology.

I proceed to an examination of interpretive problems posed by the *One Hundred Poets* as a whole. Included in this discussion are Teika's principles of selection and organization, as well as the problem of reading the *One Hundred*

Poets as an "integrated sequence." I first argue that the *One Hundred Poets* represents an extreme instance of decontextualization—that is, the removing of poems from their original context and functions. This decontextualization is counterbalanced by Teika's emphasis on *yōen*, or "ethereal beauty," an aesthetic concept, I argue, that relies on a kind of ur-narrative of a man's brief meeting with a mysterious and beautiful woman of divine nature. This emphasis in turn influences Teika's selection of poems and leads us to consider whether the *One Hundred Poets* should be read as an "integrated sequence" that is structured according to the principles of "association and progression" enunciated by Konishi Jin'ichi and demonstrated by Brower and Miner in the translation of Teika's *Superior Poems of Our Time (Kindai Shūka)*. I argue that the extrinsic historical evidence does not support a reading of the *One Hundred Poets* as a sequence "integrated" with the degree of formality and to the extent that Konishi and Brower and Miner would suggest. Yet this is not at all to argue that the choice of poems, or their order, was in any way haphazard, and I end my discussion of the sequence per se with a demonstration of the kinds of linkages that can be made with the evidence available to us.

In Chapter 3 the discussion turns to the ramifications these interpretive decisions have on the translation of the poems, and I use this occasion to trace the fortunes of Japanese poetry in English translation from the late nineteenth-century to the present. This chapter touches briefly on the role of translated Japanese poetry in the mutually fashioned orientalist construct of Japan created by the Japanese and "Westerners" in the late nineteenth and early twentieth centuries. We see also the role of "culture" and literature in Japan's new relations with North America and Europe after the Pacific War. Again the discussion insists on the historical nature of poetry, seeing its production and reception as constituted by specific historical forces of which we ourselves are a result and a part.

In Chapters 4 and 5, I examine the poem-picture tradition in Japanese culture and analyze the historical positions of both Teika's *One Hundred Poets* and the Edo-period pictorializations in that tradition. It is here that I argue for the concept of pictorialization as interpretation or, put more trendily, "picturing as reading." In the process I demonstrate some of the uses "classical" culture was put to in the early modern period—including its appropriation by the new military government, as seen in the work of the official Kanō artist, Tan'yū, as well as in two different works by the plebeian woodblock artist Moronobu. The discussion considers media as diverse as robe decoration and as recent as the comic-book versions of the classics produced today.

Most of these topics are deserving of full, monograph-length treatment. Here I have simply attempted to lay out some of the problems and issues. Such an approach risks oversimplification, of course, and invites myriad errors of both commission and omission. Nonetheless, it is my hope that the present work will encourage others to refine or extend or challenge the ideas explored here.

This introductory chapter concludes with a brief outline of the basics of Japanese poetics. Those readers already familiar with the essentials of *waka* may wish to move directly to Part I.

Japanese Poetry and Its Techniques

The *One Hundred Poets* is a sequence of verses written in the genre known as *tanka,* also called *uta* and *waka. Waka* is the Sino-Japanese pronunciation of two graphs that literally mean "Japanese song." *Waka* stood in contrast to *kanshi,* or "Chinese poetry," which the Japanese also wrote—much as Europeans before the Renaissance wrote poetry in Latin. The distinction between *waka* and *kanshi* was reinforced by the decision, early on, to eliminate from the vocabulary of *waka* almost all the Chinese loanwords Japan had adopted for use in other contexts, such as government and religion. Poetic diction, therefore, was defined as the indigenous "words of Yamato" *(Yamato kotoba),* Yamato being an early name for Japan. When the second graph of *waka* is read as a "Japanese," rather than Sino-Japanese, word, it is pronounced *uta. Uta,* however, can refer to any of a number of Japanese poetic forms, the major two of which were *chōka* (also read *naga-uta),* or "long poems," and *tanka,* or "short poems." *Tanka* are, in principle, thirty-one syllables long, divided into five lines, or *ku,* with an alternating length of 5–7–5–7–7 syllables.[22] Each *tanka* can be divided into two halves: the upper hemistich, or *kami no ku,* is comprised of the 5–7–5 lines; the lower hemistich, or *shimo no ku,* is the final two lines of seven syllables each.

Grammatical Techniques

Taking a cue from Mark Morris, we can think of *tanka* as an "attempt [at] the transformation, or deformation, of a single Japanese sentence. A good waka was the successful struggle with a virtual line of prose."[23] At its simplest a *tanka* can be little more than a single sentence with a subject and predicate divided between the upper and lower halves of the poem, as is seen in Poem 32 of the *One Hundred Poets:*

yama-gaha ni	Ah, the weir
kaze no kaketaru	that the wind has flung
shigarami ha	across the mountain stream
nagare mo ahenu	is the autumn foliage that
momijhi narikeri	cannot flow on, even though it would.

The basic grammatical structure of this poem is *shigarami ha . . . momijhi narikeri,* or "the weir . . . is the autumn foliage," a grammatically straightforward construction of a subject followed by a predicate.

To some extent, such a statement is read as a *tanka* because it fulfills the *tanka*'s metrical pattern of 5–7–5–7–7. Once this form was accepted as standard, the first stylistic variation possible was a violation in the number of syllables, either too many *(ji-amari)* or too few *(ji-tarazu).* While *ji-tarazu* is almost never seen—there is no example of it in the *One Hundred Poets—ji-amari* was not infrequent.[24] Such a technique is often interpreted as a case where an excess of emotion has broken free from metrical constraints, as in Poem 21 by Priest Sosei:

ima komu to	It was only because you said
ihishi bakari ni	you would come right away

naga-tsuki no	that I have waited
ariake no tsuki wo	these long months, till even
machi-idetsuru kana	the wan morning moon has come out.

Here, according to at least one scholar, the extra syllable in the last line "strongly charges it with the feelings of disappointment and bitterness."[25]

The simplest grammatical technique would, of course, be some kind of inversion—that is, reversing the subject and predicate of a sentence, as if we were to say "the autumn foliage is . . . what the weir is." This technique is called in Japanese *tōchi-hō*. One of the most frequently anthologized examples of this technique is Poem 23, by Ōe no Chisato:

tsuki mireba	When I look at the moon
chi-jhi ni mono koso	I am overcome by the sadness
kanashikere	of a thousand, thousand things—
wa ga mi hitori no	even though it is not fall
aki ni ha aranedo	for me alone.

Grammatically speaking, the first half and the second half of the statement have been reversed in this poem, and the concessive *aranedo* ("although") should start, and not end, the sentence. Such inversion also requires caesuras, or line breaks, in what would otherwise be viewed as an undivided whole. In Chisato's poem there is a break at the end of the first hemistich, a placement called *san-ku-gire,* or "third line break." Line breaks can be inserted as well after the first line (*shoku-gire,* as in Poems 12 and 19), second line (*ni-ku-gire,* as in Poems 2 and 9), and fourth line (*shi-ku-gire,* as in Poems 11 and 14).

If the poem ends in its fifth line with an uninflecting word, such as a noun, it is called *taigen-dome* ("noun end-stopping"). Since Japanese sentences grammatically end with verbs, perhaps the simplest way of achieving noun end-stopping is to elide a final copula. This technique appears in Poem 2 of the collection, attributed to Empress Jitō:

haru sugite	Spring has passed, and
natsu kinikerashi	summer has arrived, it seems.
shiro-tahe no	Heavenly Mount Kagu
koromo hosu tefu	where, it is said, they dry robes
ama no kagu-yama	of the whitest mulberry!

Since in Japanese relative clauses precede the nouns they modify, the second half of this poem actually reads: "where, they say, they dry robes / of the whitest mulberry—Heavenly Mount Kagu (it is)!" This noun end-stopping is considered to give the line a mild exclamatory quality (hence the exclamation point in the translation).

Lexical Techniques

Moving beyond the mere rearrangement of words, the most fundamental technique of Japanese poetry at the lexical level is the *uta-makura,* or "poem-pillow." As its name suggests, this is a word on which the entire poem may depend, or rest, as on a pillow. Since the twelfth century the term has been used to refer to place-names famous through poetry. Sometimes such place-names are used because of what the place signifies in history or myth. Take, for instance, the *uta-makura* "Kasuga" in Poem 7 by Nakamaro:

ama no hara	As I gaze out, far
furi-sake-mireba	across the plain of heaven,
kasuga naru	ah, at Kasuga,
mikasa no yama ni	from behind Mount Mikasa,
ideshi tsuki kamo	it's the same moon that came out then!

Kasuga Shrine at Mount Mikasa was where envoys such as Nakamaro prayed for a safe return home before leaving on their missions. Thus it is not at all strange to see it appear in a poem of homesick longing composed in China. However, *uta-makura* usually functioned in a more complex manner. In fact, a great number of famous place-names have embedded or double meanings that anchor the entire verse. The most famous of these is without a doubt "Afusaka," (pronounced / ōsaka / and not to be confused with the modern city). *Afu* is the verb "to meet," and thus "Afusaka," normally taken as a proper noun about whose meaning one gave no more thought than one would to the name "Oxford," for instance, in poetry was taken to mean "meeting hill," just as a poet might remind us that "Oxford" originally meant "a place to ford oxen."

Another example is Poem 8, by Priest Kisen:

wa ga iho ha	My hut is to
miyako no tatsu-mi	the capital's southeast
shika zo sumu	and thus I live. But
yo wo ujhi-yama to	people call it "Uji, hill
hito ha ifu nari	of one weary of the world," I hear.

Here the lines *yo wo ujhi-yama to / hito ha ifu nari* contain two sentences—*yo wo u* ("the world is bitter") and *ujhi-yama to hito ha ifu nari* ("I hear people call it Uji Mountain")—that are joined only by the "pivoting" syllable *u* (which can mean "gloom"), which is part of both sentences. This kind of wordplay (not necessarily thought of as humorous) is called *kake-kotoba,* or "pivot words." Note that there need be no logical connection between the two phrases—much as if we said in English "I love [you] / yu / [ewe]s run through the forest."

This technique of pivot words is related to the far broader technique known as *engo,* or "word association." In *engo,* words are considered to be semantically related to each other, usually based on some pivot word that creates two semantic fields that intersect like a Venn diagram. We can use as an example Poem 55 by Kintō:

taki no oto ha	Although the sound of
taete hisashiku	the waterfall has ceased,
narinuredo	and that long ago,
na koso nagarete	its name, indeed, has carried on
naho kikoekeri	and is still heard!

To attempt a formal definition of *engo*, we can say that when A, a word in a poem, and B, another word in the poem with which A does not have a direct grammatical relationship (for instance, as a grammatical subject or modifier), do have a semantic relationship based on an association of ideas or based on convention, then it is possible for A to be B's *engo*, or its "associated word." In this case A always carries two meanings, both of which are semantically related to B. In Kintō's poem, *nagaru* ("to flow, to be carried along") is an *engo* of *taki* ("waterfall") because, while it is not grammatically connected to *taki* (the grammatical subject of *nagarete* is *na*, or "name"), it refers to both the idea of the waterfall "flowing" and the idea of the fame of the waterfall being "carried on" to the present. In the same way *oto* ("sound") and *kikoe* ("to hear") are *engo*, or "associated words," because, again while not connected grammatically, together they convey the sense both of hearing the sound of the waterfall and of hearing of its fame.[26]

Some word associations are so conventionalized that they have become frozen. These are called "pillow words" *(makura-kotoba)*, usually described as fixed epithets "on" which specific words lay, much as in Homer dawn is always introduced as "rosy-fingered dawn." In Jitō's poem we have "robes of the whitest mulberry" *(shiro-tahe no koromo)*; the expression *shiro-tahe no* typically modifies "cloth *(nuno)*," "robes *(koromo)*," and such. This technique was most productive during the earliest period of Japanese court poetry, represented by the first anthology of *waka*, the *Man'yō Shū* (compiled mid-eighth century). As time went on, however, poets no longer knew exactly what many of these pillow words meant, yet they continued to use them to give a sense of grandeur or antiquity to their verse. Today most pillow words are of uncertain meaning, and some translators ignore them entirely.

Pillow words are typically five syllables, or one line, in length. When a modifying phrase exceeds this length (and is nonformulaic in nature), it is called a *jo*, or "preface." Prefaces can be based on a metaphoric relationship, as we see in this overly literal translation of Poem 3, attributed to Hitomaro:[27]

ashi-biki no	(Long like) the tail,
yama-dori no wo no	the drooping tail of the pheasant
shidari-wo no	of the foot-dragging mountains,
naga-nagashi yo wo	these long, long autumn nights
hitori kamo nemu	must I sleep all alone?

Here the phrase "the tail, the drooping tail of the pheasant of the foot-dragging mountains" modifies "long, long night"—and we are meant to understand that the night seems as long as the long, drooping tail of the pheasant. Such prefaces can also be introduced by pivot words, as well as by sound reduplication—something we might call "unrealized pivots," where phrases are linked by sound repetition rather than the semantic double-reading of *kake-kotoba*. We see this use of simple repetition in Poem 18 by Toshiyuki:

suminoe no	Must you so avoid others' eyes
kishi ni <u>yoru</u> nami	that not even at night,
<u>yoru</u> sahe ya	along the road of dreams,

> | *yume no kayohi-jhi* | will you draw nigh like the waves |
> |---|---|
> | *hito-me yokuramu* | to the shore of Sumi-no-e Bay? |

Here we have the lines *kishi ni yoru nami* ("the waves that approach the shore") immediately followed by *yoru sahe* ("even at night"). *Yoru* can mean both "to approach" and "night," but rather than using it as a pivot word, Toshiyuki has repeated it, as if the sounds of the first meaning have suggested the sounds of the second (something like "the waves have *drawn*—not even before *dawn*"). There is also the word reduplication called *kasane-kotoba*—such as *naga-nagashi* ("long-long") in Hitomaro's poem above—thought simply to serve for emphasis.[28]

The final technique to consider under the lexical rubric is *honka-dori*, or "allusive variation." This technique involves the explicit borrowing of phrases or concepts from earlier poems. While earlier poets may have based certain verses on yet earlier poems, the term *honka-dori* is reserved for the *ShinKokinshū* period (late twelfth to early thirteenth centuries) onward. Hence it should not be surprising that four of the last ten poems in the *One Hundred Poets* are allusive variations. One of these is Poem 91 by Yoshitsune:

> | *kirigirisu* | When the crickets |
> |---|---|
> | *naku ya shimo-yo no* | cry in the frosty night, |
> | *sa-mushiro ni* | on the cold reed-mat, |
> | *koromo kata-shiki* | spreading out my robe just for one, |
> | *hitori kamo nemu* | must I sleep all alone? |

This poem in fact draws on two earlier poems, one of which is the poem by Hitomaro that we examined earlier: from it Yoshitsune has taken his last line, "must I sleep all alone?" The second, anonymous, poem Yoshitsune uses is from the *Kokinshū* (Love 4): 689:

> | *sa-mushiro ni* | On the cold reed-mat |
> |---|---|
> | *koromo kata-shiki* | spreading out her robe just for one, |
> | *koyohi mo ya* | this evening too |
> | *ware wo matsuramu* | is she waiting for me— |
> | *ujhi no hashi-hime* | the goddess of Uji Bridge? |

From this poem Yoshitsune has taken the first two lines, making them his third and fourth lines.

Note that the "foundation poems" *(honka)* are never explicitly identified—they were presumed to be apparent to an educated audience. As time passed, however, the education of the audience changed. In the case of Yoshitsune's poem, no fewer than four other poems were averred to be the "foundation poems" by early modern commentators, including one in the *Man'yō Shū* and one from the Chinese *Classic of Poetry (Shih Ching)*. "Allusive variation," then, is another matter of interpretive debate among later readers.

Figural Techniques

Two rhetorical techniques frequently encountered in the *One Hundred Poets* transcend the grammatical or lexical and work instead on the figurative plane. The first of these is *mi-tate,* or "conceit," sometimes called "elegant confusion" in English discussions of *waka.*[29] This technique is exemplified in Poem 31 by Korenori:

asaborake	So that I thought it
ariake no tsuki to	the light of the lingering moon
miru made ni	at dawn—
yoshino no sato ni	the white snow that has fallen
fureru shira-yuki	on the village of Yoshino.

In this poem, the poet wakes to see the bright white snow on the ground shining to the extent that he pretends to have mistaken it for moonlight reflecting off the ground.

The second figural technique is *gijinka.* *Gijinka* is frequently translated as "personification," but this is not meant in the sense of "personifying Beauty." Rather, *gijinka* is closer to Ruskin's concept of "pathetic fallacy," where the poet gives human thoughts and feelings to objects in the natural world, such as birds or flowers. The most influential poem using this technique is Poem 30 by Tadamine:

ariake no	Ever since our parting,
tsurenaku mieshi	when the morning moon looked
wakare yori	so cold-hearted,
akatsuki bakari	there is nothing as depressing as
uki mono ha nashi	the very break of day.[30]

There are, of course, a number of other techniques that poets used to make their verses effective—parallelism, assonance, consonance, hyperbole, and sarcasm—but those surveyed here are the ones most often discussed.

Pragmatics: The Occasions for Poetry

The nature of *waka* was of course determined by the occasions for which it was typically produced. One of its oldest functions was in courtship, for instance, where a man and woman would exchange poems, called *zōtōka* ("exchanged poems"). Convention typically required that the man initiate the exchange; the woman would then base her reply on the man's poem, usually playing on its basic conceit or employing some of its imagery in a sarcastic rebuff. Poems not written in response to another poem, or not intended to elicit a response, are called *doku'ei-ka,* which we might translate as "soliloquies."

In court society, poets were often called upon to compose verses for their masters. Sometimes a poet was required to compose in the place of his or her master; sometimes the lord or lady would set the poet a topic *(dai)* on which to compose. Both these possibilities combined in the case of *byōbu-uta,* or "poems for screens," where poets would typically assume the persona of a human figure depicted in a landscape painting and compose a poem from the viewpoint of that figure. These poems would then be inscribed on decorated poetry paper and affixed to the screens.

"Composition on topics" *(dai'ei)* also occurred when poets pitted their works against each other in poetry contests *(uta-awase)*. Poets might be required to submit a group of poems during the planning stages of either a poetry contest or the production of a poetry screen. As early as the late eleventh century, poets were composing in hundred-poem sequences, or *hyakushu*. These sequences might be devoted to one or two specific topics—such as "Hawks" or "The Moon and Cherry Blossoms"—much like the topics used in poetry contests. They might also follow the format of an imperial anthology, as does one of the oldest extant *hyakushu*, by Minamoto no Shigeyuki (d. 1001?) (see Poem 48), which has twenty poems on each of the four seasons and ten poems each on "Love" and "Miscellaneous." Hundred-poem sequences became much more common in the twelfth century, a trend signaled by the "Horikawa Hundred-Poem Sequences" *(Horikawa Hyakushu)* of 1105–1106. Here a number of poets composed on set, detailed topics ordered in the fashion of an imperial anthology—for instance, twenty poems on spring, running from "First Day of Spring" *(risshun)* to "The End of the Third Month"; fifteen poems on summer topics, starting with "Seasonal Change of Clothing" *(koromo-gahe);* and so on. In later times this set of topics became a model for poets, who now tended to practice their art by composing in hundred-poem sets.[31]

The most prestigious place for a poem to appear was in an imperially commissioned anthology, or *chokusen shū*, twenty-one of which were compiled between the years 905 and 1439. As presented in such an anthology, a poem usually consisted of three parts: a "headnote," or *kotoba-gaki*, which described the occasion for which the poem was composed (or the phrase "occasion unknown," *dai shirazu*); the name of the poet (or the phrase "poet unknown," *yomi-bito shirazu*); and the text of the poem itself. Following the lead of the first imperial anthology, the *Collection of Ancient and Modern Japanese Poetry (Kokin Waka Shū*, hereafter *Kokinshū*) of 905, most imperial anthologies comprised twenty books *(maki)*, in the following categories:

1. Spring	11. Love
2. Spring	12. Love
3. Summer	13. Love
4. Autumn	14. Love
5. Autumn	15. Love
6. Winter	16. Grief
7. Felicitations	17. Miscellaneous Topics
8. Parting	18. Miscellaneous Topics
9. Travel	19. Miscellaneous Forms
10. Names of Things	20. Traditional Songs

As can be seen by the number of books dedicated to each category, love poetry by far predominated, followed by poems about spring and autumn. Later imperial anthologies made minor modifications of these categories. The eighth collection, for instance, puts "Grief" after "Felicitations," includes three books on "Miscellaneous Love" in lieu of the two on the simpler topic "Miscellaneous Topics," and replaces the "Traditional Songs" category with one book each on "Buddhism" and "Deities."

Individual poets also made collections of their verse, or that of their relatives, and these were known as "house collections," or *ie no shū*. These might follow the same pattern as the imperial anthologies, or the poems might be arranged chronologically, even serving as the framework for a narrative self-representation, or autobiography. It was often from submitted house collections that the editors of imperial anthologies made their selection.

PART ONE

THE *HYAKUNIN ISSHU*
ITS FORMATION AND RECEPTION

CHAPTER 2

Historical Context

In the same fashion as imperially commissioned anthologies, individuals made their own personal anthologies of other people's verses, called *shisen shū,* or "privately edited anthologies." Poems could be collected together for educational purposes, though in a society where almost everyone who read poetry also wrote it, the distinction between collections put together to illustrate the correct way of writing poems, and those put together for the pleasure of reading, is heuristic at best. The earliest extant treatise on Japanese poetry is the *Uta no Shiki,* or *Rules of Poetry,* written by Fujiwara no Hamanari (724–790) in 772.[1] It contains some thirty poems meant to illustrate Kamanari's ideas about "poetic ills" *(kahei* or *uta no yamahi).* While every illustrative poem is attributed to a named individual, Hamanari offers no general assessment of the poets as poets. For this kind of criticism we must wait until the Japanese preface to the first imperial anthology, the *Kokinshū,* written by Ki no Tsurayuki. In his preface Tsurayuki gives a history of Japanese verse from the "age of the awesome gods" down to "recent times" *(chikaki yo).*[2] The recent times appear to be thirty to fifty years before Tsurayuki's day, and he represents this period by six poets, whom he discusses by name, in the manner of the Chinese poetic treatise, the *Shih P'ing.*[3] Of Narihira, for instance, Tsurayuki says: "Ariwara no Narihira has too much feeling, too few words. His poems are like withered flowers, faded but with a lingering fragrance."[4] While this may not sound complimentary, the fact that Tsurayuki valued these six poets enough to mention them by name in his preface led to their being called the "Six Poetic Immortals" *(rokkasen)* by later generations.

Exemplary Collections

Individual collections of the Six Poetic Immortals' verses were circulating by the late ninth century. Somewhere between 1009 and 1011 the editor of the third imperial anthology, the *Shūishū,* Fujiwara no Kintō (966–1041), put together a collection of poems by those he considered the best thirty-six poets of the Japanese tradition. The *Sanjūrokunin Sen,* or *Selections of Thirty-Six Poets,* contains ten poems each by Hitomaro, Tsurayuki, Mitsune, Ise, Kanemori, and

*Nakatsukasa and three poems each by Yakamochi, Akahito, Narihira, Henjō, Sosei, Tomonori, Sarumaru, Komachi, Kanesuke, Asatada, Atsutada, *Takamitsu, *Kintada, Tadamine, *Saigū no Nyōgo, *Yorimoto, Toshiyuki, Shigeyuki, Muneyuki, *Sane'akira, *Kiyotada, *Shitagō, Okikaze, Motosuke, Korenori, *Motozane, *Kodai no Kimi (also read O-ō no Kimi), *Nakafumi, Yoshinobu, and Tadami. (Names with asterisks do not appear in the *One Hundred Poets*.)[5] A hundred years later, more extensive collections of verses attributed to each poet were made and copied out in a deluxe edition now known as the *Nishi Honganji Sanjūrokkasen Shū* (ca. 1112). Kintō also produced two poetic treatises: the *Shinsen Zuinō*, or *The Newly Compiled Essentials of Poetry,* and the *Waka Kuhon,* or *Nine Stages of Poetry.*[6] In each of these treatises, a small collection of eighteen poems is given to exemplify fine poetry. By at least the Kamakura period (1185–1333) such collections were being made by poetry instructors for specific students. Teika's father, Shunzei, compiled the *Korai Fūtei Shō,* or *Poetic Styles Past and Present,* in 1197 for his student, Imperial Princess Shokushi. Here we also see the idea of presenting a *history* of poetry—indeed, it is in this very work that Shunzei says: "It is a dubious practice to discuss ancient poetry by standards that are not its own."[7]

Teika was perhaps the most prolific compiler of exemplary anthologies. But this followed naturally from his position as editor of two imperial anthologies. Teika was a member of the editorial board for the eighth imperial anthology, the *ShinKokin Waka Shū,* or *New Collection of Ancient and Modern Japanese Poetry* (hereafter *ShinKokinshū*), commissioned in 1201. Almost thirty years later, he was given the signal honor of being appointed sole editor of the ninth imperial anthology, which he entitled the *Shin Chokusenshū,* or *The New Imperially Commissioned Anthology.* Since such anthologies were designed to glean previously unanthologized poems from the past as well as the present, they required both extensive reading and a thorough familiarity with the contents of the previous imperial anthologies. Teika applied this knowledge to the teaching of poetry. While there is considerable debate about the exact dates of many of his exemplary collections, let us trace one plausible chronology. Only a year after the first version of the *ShinKokinshū* was completed (1205), Teika grouped some 286 poems, predominantly from the *ShinKokinshū,* under ten styles, creating a work known today as the *Teika Jittei,* or *Teika's Ten Styles.*[8] His next treatise-cum-exemplary collection seems to have been the *Kindai Shūka,* or *Superior Poems of Our Time.* This is a collection of eighty-three poems, ordered along the lines of an imperial anthology, that Teika compiled for his student, the shogun Sanetomo. Around 1215 Teika compiled his personal anthology of anthologies, the *Nishidai Shū* (literally, *Collection of Twenty-Four Reigns*), a collection of 1,811 poems culled from the first eight imperial anthologies. The poems of all of Teika's later exemplary collections would be drawn from this master anthology.

By Teika's day, students were typically taught poetry by writing hundred-poem sequences, what Hiroaki Sato has called "format compositions,"[9] which they would send every month to their teacher for grading. If these *hyakushu* followed the format of imperial anthologies, the student would naturally get more practice in composing the more important kinds of verses, such as love poetry and seasonal poetry, and less practice in the lesser anthologized forms, such as laments or travel poems. Accordingly, it made good sense for the teacher's exemplary collections to follow the same format, which is what we see in the *Eiga no Taigai,* or *Essential Outline for Composing Poetry,* compiled by Teika, probably for his student the Imperial Prince Sonkai, around 1222.[10] This was followed by another collection of a little over one hundred poems, the *Shūka no Daitai (Essential Outline of Superior Poems),* for Retired Emperor GoHorikawa sometime after 1226.

Teika's next exemplary collection took a very different form: the poems of the collection today called the *Hyakunin Shūka (Superior Poems of One Hundred Poets)* were in fact originally inscribed individually on sheets of decorated poetry paper and affixed to the sliding doors of the villa of Teika's son's father-in-law, Utsunomiya no Yoritsuna. We find a record of this in Teika's own diary, the *Meigetsu Ki,* under the entry for the twenty-seventh day of the Fifth Month of the Second Year of Bunryaku (1234):

> I have never had good handwriting. But the Novice [Yoritsuna] has been asking that I write out some cartouches for the sliding doors of his villa at Saga. Even though I knew they were unsightly, I halfheartedly dipped my brush and sent them off. They are one verse each by poets since antiquity, starting with Emperor Tenji and coming up to Ietaka and Masatsune.[11]

There are a number of interpretations of this passage and its relationship to either the *Hyakunin Shūka* or *Hyakunin Isshu.*[12] That offered by Ariyoshi Tamotsu seems the most probable. According to Ariyoshi, this passage refers to the *Hyakunin Shūka,* which has ninety-seven poems in common with the *One Hundred Poets* but no poems by either Emperor GoToba or his son Juntoku, both of whom had been sent into exile after the Jōkyū Rebellion of 1221. Sometime after GoToba's death in 1239, Teika, using the *Hyakunin Shūka* as a basis, produced a new set of cartouches to decorate his own villa at Ogura.[13] It is these that comprise the *One Hundred Poets.* In fact, the oldest title by which the *One Hundred Poets* is known is the *Ogura Sansō Shikishi Waka,* or *Poems from the Cartouches of the Ogura Mountain Villa.*[14]

After Teika, authority over the *waka* tradition largely became the hereditary possession of his descendants, the only people considered appropriate to edit imperial anthologies. This potentially moribund state of affairs was enlivened by the fact that Teika's grandchildren ended up fighting among themselves, resulting in a division of the poetic world into three schools: the main line, Nijō, and its two rivals, the Kyōgoku and the Reizei (see Figure 1). These descendants fought over real estate, prestige, and, perhaps most important, the ownership of family documents—that is, poetic treatises and anthologies inherited from Teika. The influence of Teika's major treatises, the *Maigetsu Shō,*[15] *Eiga no Taigai,* and *Kindai Shūka,* can be seen in the treatise written by his son, Tame'ie (1198–1275), the *Yakumo Kuden* (also called the *Eiga no Ittei*).[16] Quotations from the same texts run throughout *Lord (Kyōgoku) Tamekane's (1254– 1332) Notes on Poetry,* or the *Tamekane-kyō Waka Shō,* written between 1285 and 1287.[17] Since theoretical prose plays no part in the *One Hundred Poets,* its transmission is harder to trace. One of the earliest references to it seems to be in the

Figure 1. Branches of the Mikohid.

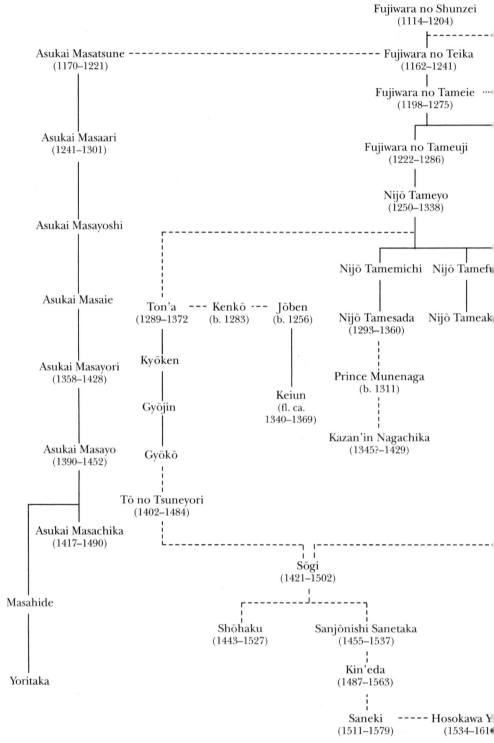

Figure 1. Branches of the Mikohidari House and Their Artistic Offshoots.

House and Their Artistic Offshoots

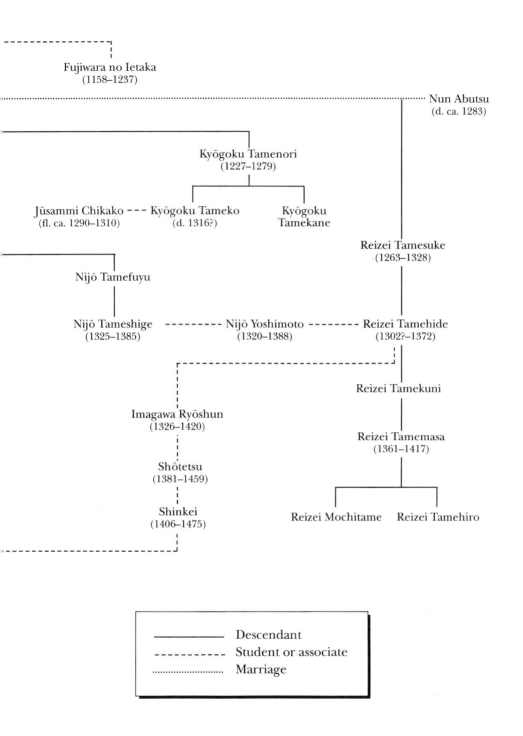

Fujiwara no Ietaka
(1158–1237)

Nun Abutsu
(d. ca. 1283)

Kyōgoku Tamenori
(1227–1279)

Jūsammi Chikako   Kyōgoku Tameko   Kyōgoku
(fl. ca. 1290–1310)   (d. 1316?)   Tamekane

Reizei Tamesuke
(1263–1328)

Nijō Tamefuyu

Nijō Tameshige ---------- Nijō Yoshimoto -------- Reizei Tamehide
(1325–1385)   (1320–1388)   (1302?–1372)

Reizei Tamekuni

Imagawa Ryōshun
(1326–1420)

Reizei Tamemasa
(1361–1417)

Shōtetsu
(1381–1459)

Shinkei   Reizei Mochitame   Reizei Tamehiro
(1406–1475)

———————— Descendant
- - - - - - - - - - Student or associate
.... Marriage

Sui'a Ganmoku (ca. 1361–1364), written by the Nijō adherent Ton'a (1289–1372). The oldest extant complete manuscript of the *One Hundred Poets* is in the hand of Gyōkō (1391–1455), Ton'a's grandson.[18]

Commentaries on the *One Hundred Poets*

In addition to copies of the *One Hundred Poets* per se—that is, copies of the poems alone—annotated copies from the early fifteenth century also exist. The most influential exegetical lineage stems from texts known as the *Sōgi Shō*, or *Sōgi Commentary*. These are notes of the lectures the famous *renga* poet Sōgi received from Tō no Tsuneyori (1401–1484) in 1471 and are believed to represent the teachings of Ton'a and the Nijō poetic house. The *Sōgi Commentary* exists in two versions, the earliest copies of which date from 1478 and 1490, respectively. The earliest extant *One Hundred Poets* commentary dates from the thirteenth year of the Ōei era (1406) and is known, therefore, as the *Ōei Commentary (Ōei Shō)*. The contents of the later draft of the *Sōgi Commentary* are largely identical to the *Ōei Shō*. The *Sōgi Commentary* became the basis of many other commentaries, especially that by Hosokawa Yūsai (1534–1610), of which many printed editions were produced from 1631 on.

Despite the dominant influence of the *Sōgi Commentary* and the Nijō house interpretive tradition, the other main poetic houses, the Reizei, Asukai, and Sanjōnishi, had their own traditions. There are also extant commentaries that seem to derive from no tradition and appear to represent individual interpretations. Generally the *Kaikan Shō (The Rectified Commentary)* of Keichū, first written in 1688, is taken as the dividing line between the medieval commentary traditions and the new philological, scientific approach that characterized the early modern period.[19] As we shall see, such a view is an oversimplification.

To get a sense of the exegetical tradition, let us look at what several commentaries have to say, in their entirety, about the first poem of the *One Hundred Poets*, attributed to Emperor Tenji:

aki no ta no	In the autumn fields
kari-ho no iho no	the hut, the temporary hut,
toma wo arami	its thatch is rough
wa ga koromo-de ha	and so the sleeves of my robe
tsuyu ni nuretsutsu	are dampened night by night with dew.

The *Ōei Commentary* (Figure 2) gives the poet's name (with diacritical marks to note voiced consonants), then the poem in one line, set off as a kind of header, then the following commentary:

> *Kari-ho no iho:* one explanation is "hut of reaped ears of grain" *(kari-ho no iho).* Another is "hut, a temporary hut" [*kari-iho no iho*]. It is said that even if it is taken as "reaped ears," it is to be read /kariwo/. But, still, isn't "hut, a temporary hut" the best interpretation? In old poems reduplications *(kasane)* are common.
>
> Now, the meaning of the poem is: the time for the huts in the autumn fields is over and autumn itself has come to an end and the thatch and such

are decayed and can no longer keep out the dew; my sleeve is wet just as if the dew were falling on it. This is a poem of grievance *(jukkai)* over the decline of imperial authority [literally, the "royal way," *ōdō*]. This lord, when he was in Kyūshū, was afraid of the world[20] and set up a barrier of cut reeds and announced himself to those who would go to and fro, only then letting them pass through.[21] What he was troubled by was his feeling that the age of imperial authority had already passed. It is said that he was able to perceive the truth of this by means of the temporary hut whose season had passed. Nonetheless, one should inquire about this. This poem is in the ancient style. In the ancient age, since people put their thoughts into the meaning, they did not need detailed words. The "overtones" *(yosei,* i.e., *yojō)* are something that one should carefully consider, it is said.[22]

We can compare this passage with the *Ogura Sansō Shikishi Waka,* a commentary attributed to Asukai no Yoritaka, a nephew of Masachika (1417–1490). This is one of the few Muromachi-period commentaries extant and is believed to represent the Asukai family teachings:

> *Kari-ho* is a temporary hut *(kari naru iho).* Again, it is the ears *(ho)* of rice on the fields. *Kari-ho no iho* is word repetition *(chiuten).* When Emperor Tenji was going down to Tsukushi, he saw a hut in a wasted field and, fiercely missing the capital, he composed this poem expressing his own feelings. The thatch of the hut was torn, the dew was unbearable, so he compared it to the dewy condition of his own sleeve.[23]

Notice that this commentary allows both interpretations of *kari-ho* without choosing between them. But rather than a moral or political interpretation, the Asukai commentary associates Tenji's poem with the conventions of travel poetry, making it about the poet's longing for the capital. Hence we can see how the Asukai commentary touches on many of the same points as the Nijō commentary but has different things to say about them.

The *Yūsai Commentary* of 1596, however, is based, literally, on the *Sōgi Commentary.* In other words, the *Yūsai Commentary* repeats the *Sōgi Commentary* verbatim and then adds the following comments, creating the effect of a layered text:

> Even though there is an explanation that *kari-ho* is "ears of grain," it is to be read simply as /kariho/. Sōgi says: "Nonetheless, one should inquire about this"—referring to the fact that this prince by nature paid the greatest attention to the troubles of his people. Thus he cared for the people all the more and was saddened. When he saw the people exhausting themselves guarding the fields in rundown temporary huts, he thought what an unpleasant task it was. Tears fell on the emperor's sleeves and he sang, "My sleeves are dampened each night by the dew." Through the emperor's poem one senses deep feeling.

aki-ta karu	I build a temporary hut
kari-ho wo tsukuri	to reap the autumn fields
ware oreba	and as I keep watch
koromo-de samushi	my sleeves are so cold
tsuyu wokinikeri	that the dew has settled on them![24]

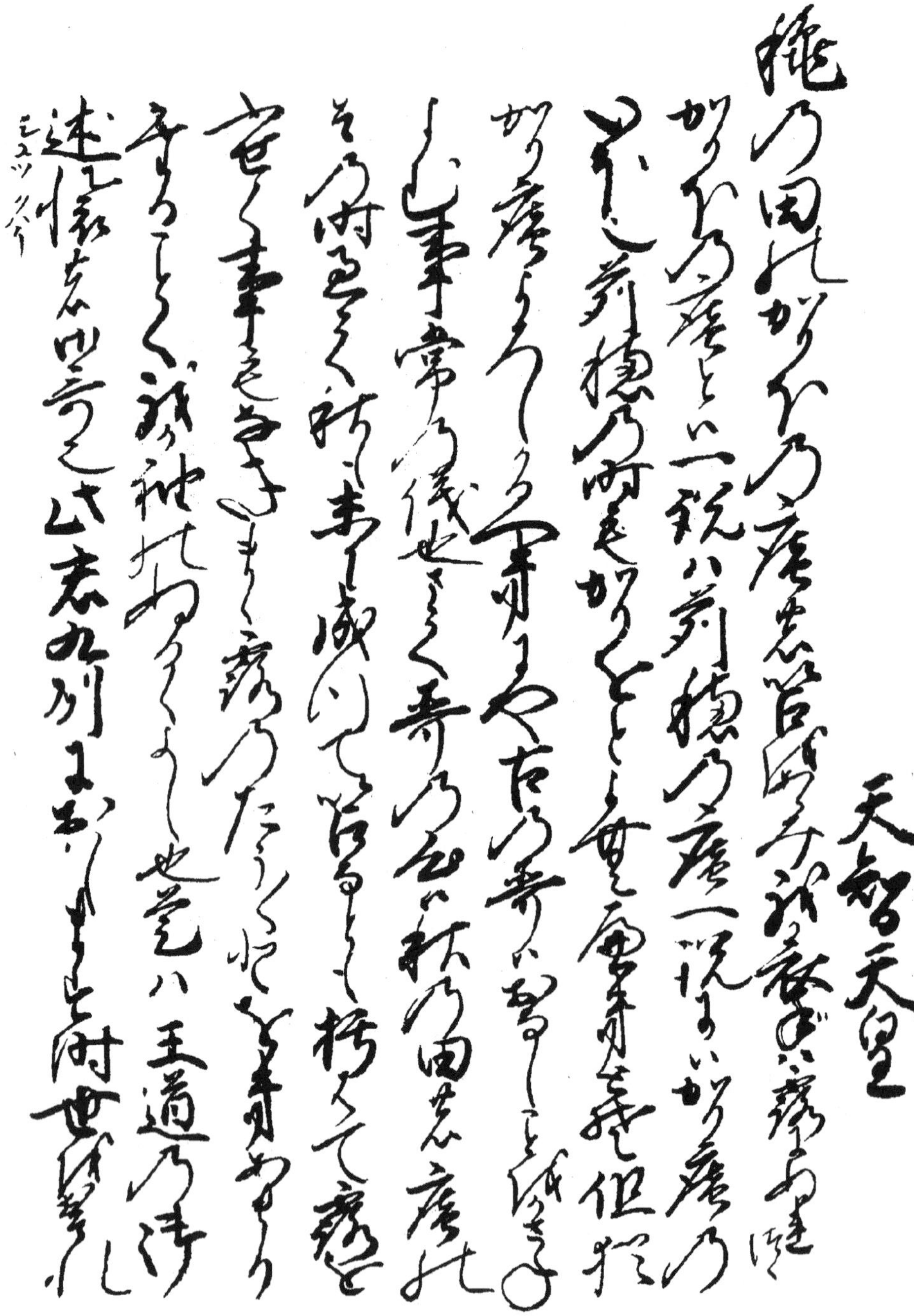

Figure 2. *Ōei Shō*, entry on Emperor Tenji, 1406.

Kari-ho is a temporary hut. In the *Man'yō* it is written [with the two graphs] "temporary hut." This was Sōgi's explanation. The matter of Emperor Tenji being in Kyūshū is not seen in any of the imperial histories other than the *Nihongi*. It is unclear. The hidden meaning behind this poem is that it is a song of mourning by the emperor. Just as for commoners, there is a temporary hut in which the emperor secludes himself when mourning his mother or father. When an emperor mourns his father, on the day the previous emperor passes away, the new emperor builds a temporary hut, avoids the spaces between the planks, hangs curtains of reeds, lies down on thatch, and makes a pillow out of earth, it is said.[25] Based on the saying "exchanging the months for days," he stays in the hut twelve days. Although he should be there twelve months, he condenses it into twelve days. This is what is called "exchanging the months for days." This poem is an imperial composition that Tenji made while thinking about the rural cottages and becoming sad and careworn like the huts of the autumn fields.

It was in order to make the Way of Filial Piety the foundation of the myriad people, both high and low, that Lord Teika put this poem at the head of the *One Hundred Poets*. It is with Empress Saimei that national mourning for the mother of an emperor began. It was this part that Sōgi concealed and did not explain! Still, among those things about which one should inquire, one can see places where there are things left out concerning the deeper truths. Sōgi's commentary was made just as lecture notes, from the one time that the lectures were transmitted from Tsuneyori. In the past, secret teachings were given orally and transmitted only once.

Concerning the national mourning for the imperial mother: since death struck while Empress Saimei was on the throne, the mourning observance of later imperial mothers was not patterned on the national mourning for Saimei. Of course there should have been a national mourning [for an Empress]![26]

As can be seen, the issue of *kariho* is brought up yet again. In fact, Yūsai's commentary is actually a commentary on the *Sōgi Commentary* and not a direct treatment of the *One Hundred Poets* itself.[27] And commentary Sōgi's notes do need, as Yūsai makes clear: they are notes taken during one set of lectures, which apparently left no opportunity for questions or any return to unclear points.

Included in Yūsai's commentary is a family tree of Tenji, something that would become a common feature in *One Hundred Poets* commentaries. But the most conspicuous addition is the "revelation" of "hidden meanings" *(ōgi)*. The story is often repeated that the siege of Tanabe was lifted at the request of Emperor GoYōzei (r. 1586–1611) to save Yūsai, who was the sole inheritor of the tradition of secret poetry teachings related to the *Kokinshū*.[28] Perhaps it was this experience that persuaded Yūsai to commit such "inner teachings" to writing. Certainly he could not have imagined the public diffusion that resulted from their printing in the Edo period. In any event, one can see the level of minutiae to which such secrets descended. Nor is logic the strong suit here: if it was to establish the "Way of Filial Piety" that Teika put this poem at the head of his collection, then keeping the fact that it was a poem of mourning a secret would have completely frustrated that noble aim. Indeed, even Yūsai notes that the period of national mourning for Saimei could not have set the precedent of such periods for the mother of an emperor because Saimei herself, at the time of her death, was the reigning monarch and thus would have been due the national mourning appropriate to an emperor, not the lesser rites held for an emperor's nonreigning mother.

Although one gets a sense of debate and correction in these traditional commentaries, the philological approach that we begin to see in Keichū's *Kai-kan Shō*, or *Rectified Commentary*, (1688), is something of a shock:

> Found in the *Gosenshū*, Autumn 2, topic unknown. In the *Kokin Rokujō* it appears in the second book, under the topic *kari-ho*. *Kari-ho* in the *Man'yō Shū* is written with the Chinese characters "temporary hut." It is an abbreviation of what should be said as *kari-iho*. It is just like *omohi-ide* ("recollection") being pronounced *omohide: Kariho no iho* is the usual word-reduplication. The *Wamyō Shū* states: "In the *Book of Odes* it says: 'The farmers make huts so as to be convenient to their fieldwork.' "[29] Again, in the *Man'yō Shū* the word that is written with the Chinese graphs "field hut" and read *ta-fuse* is the same thing. It is not just farmers: *kari-ho* are also made as travel huts. There are many of these in the *Man'yō Shū*. Although the character 菴 is read the same in Japanese, its meaning has changed. The explanation that [*kari-ho*] means "cut ears" is a benighted conjecture that is not seen in the *Man'yō Shū*. Since deer and boar feed on mountain fields, in the *Man'yō Shū* they sing of "protecting the fields from the deer and boar of the small mountain fields." [*Kari-ho*] is a place where they keep guard over the fields, as well as do such things as hull the rice. "Its thatch is rough and so": the rushes with which the hut has been thatched are thin, and there are many gaps. From these gaps the dew leaks in, and there is no time when his sleeves dry. "My sleeves": due to the fact that since long ago they have persisted in making this "my" the emperor *(tenshi no ware)*, who is thinking about the people and composing, they have erred in explaining this poem. Just as in Tanabata poems in the *Man'yō Shū*, the *Kokinshū*, and elsewhere, composed in the persona of either the Herd Boy or the Weaver Maid, so this poem is in the persona of the peasants *(domin no ware)* and the emperor has put himself in the place of the peasants and completely become them—it is a wonderful thing that he composes while identifying with their hardship. It is in accord with the following. The *Kuan Tzu* says:
>
> > The king achieves heaven's will by means of the people;
> > The people achieve heaven's will by means of food.[30]

The *Chou I* says: "When one descends to what is base by means of what is noble, greatly will one win the people."[31] The *Lao Tzu* says:

> Dignity finds its root in meanness;
> what is lofty finds its foundation in what is low.[32]

Again, with this meaning, when the emperor is of a nature to deign to lower himself from his status of sovereignty to that which is base, then all the people surrender themselves up to him and the realm is at peace. There is nothing so wonderful as the realm at peace. This must be why this imperial composition was placed at the head of the collection. That being the case, interpretations which claim that this is a lament over the decline of imperial authority, or that it is a poem of grief, are all mistaken suppositions with no evidence in either the poem's classification, its topic, or the poem itself. Since both laments and grief are inauspicious matters, how could they be placed at the head of a collection? This all arises from seeing "I" *(ware)* as the emperor *(tenshi no ware),* as every previous commentator has maintained. This emperor matched rank with feeling, punished Soga no Iruka with death, and beyond that was a lord of myriad restorations. . . .[33]

Man'yō Shū 10 [*2235, anon., "Composed on Rain"*]

aki-ta karu	In my travel hut
tabi no ihori ni	amidst the autumn fields they reap,
shigure furi	the late rains fall and
wa ga sode nurenu	soak my sleeves, there being
hosu hito mo nashi ni	no one to dry them. . . .

Man'yō Shū [*10:2174, anon.*]

aki-ta karu	I build a temporary hut
kari-ho wo tsukuri	to reap the autumn fields,
ware oreba	and as I keep watch
koromo-de samushi	my sleeves are so cold
tsuyu wokinikeri	that the dew has settled on them!

Kokinshū (Autumn 2) [*307, anon., topic unknown*]

ho ni mo idenu	When I guard the mountain fields
yama-da wo moru to	where the grain has not yet come out
fujhi-goromo	—my coarse wisteria robes—
inaba no tsuyu ni	there is no day when they are not dampened
nurenu hi mo nashi	by the dew of the rice-plant leaves.

These poems are of the same type as the emperor's composition.

ShokuGosenshū, Izumi Shikibu

aki no ta no	The rushes with which
ihori ni fukeru	the hut of the autumn fields
toma wo arami	has been thatched are rough,
mori-kuru tsuyu no	and so the dew that leaks in
iya ha neraruru	makes it difficult to sleep.

The Hosshōji Regent [*Fujiwara no Tadamichi*]
Country House in Late Autumn Rain

kari-fuki no	The grass hut
kusa no ihori no	of cut thatch—
suki wo arami	its gaps are wide, and so

shigure to tomo ni	it is together with the autumn rains
yama-da wo zo moru	that I guard the mountain fields.

These are based on the emperor's poem.[34]

Keichū is viewed by some as the immediate forerunner of the *kokugaku*, or "National Learning," movement.[35] This movement founded itself on the critical examination of the oldest texts of the Japanese language. The methodology seems derived, at least in part, from the *kogaku*, or "ancient learning" of Itō Jinsai (1627–1705), who rejected the various commentary traditions that had grown around the basic Confucian texts and called for a return to the texts themselves, establishing the meanings of particular words and concepts by comparing their usage in a number of specific contexts, rather than relying on the definition or explanation supplied by later exegetes.[36] This method, when applied to the *Man'yō Shū*, allowed Keichū and others to understand the text to a degree unknown for centuries. In fact, study of the *Man'yō Shū* became the backbone of the National Learning movement. Nonetheless, all the major *kokugakusha* first learned the *One Hundred Poets*: Keichū, for instance, was credited with having memorized the entire collection in the space of ten days, when he was only five years old.[37]

Keichū's familiarity with the *Man'yō Shū* is of course quite evident in his commentary on Tenji's poem. But his insistence on relating the poem to Chinese classics shows that he is not really part of the later *kokugaku* movement that would attempt to expunge all Chinese influence from the Japanese texts. For Keichū the poem remains an imperial composition expressing the sentiments of a sage-king, a concept derived from China. The true National Learning style, and the startlingly untraditional conclusions it could lead to, can be seen in Kamo no Mabuchi's *Uimanabi* (*First Lessons*, 1765):

> *Gosen* (Autumn 2), topic unknown. Although there are many matters to discuss in this poem, what I will first say is that since this poem is of the type that is called "composed on rice fields" in the *Man'yō*, it is composed from the viewpoint of a peasant who is in a rice field.
>
> [Paraphrase:] The hut in the rice field, since the rushes that were temporarily thatched together are rough, the dew of the long nights drips in and my sleeves get extremely wet.
>
> The first thing that must be discussed about this poem is the line *kari-ho no iho*. Although in one explanation they say it is word reduplication (*kasane-kotoba*), in old poems there is a principle of substantive-and-inflectional (*taiyō*) in word reduplication. The meaning differs but the words are the same—the word is set up and then reduplicated. In such poems as *Man'yō Shū* 10 [2248, anon., "Love Songs of Autumn"]

aki-ta karu	Staying in
kari-ho wo tsukuri	the temporary hut I build,
ihori shite	in the autumn fields they reap,
aruran kimi wo	how I wish I could see my lord
min yoshi mogamo	who must be near!

or [10: 2100, anon., "Composed on Flowers"]

aki-ta karu	Lodging in the temporary hut
kari-ho no yadori	in the autumn fields they reap,
nihofu made . . .	till I am imbued . . .

the upper *iho* is a substantive and the subsequent *ihori shite* or *yadori* are the inflectionals that mean "to enter and stay in a hut." As for the meaning differing and the words being the same—in other words, *aki-ta karu kari-ho* ("the temporary hut in the autumn fields where they reap")—it is of the same type as *kishi ni yoru yoru sahe ya* ("approaching the shore, even at night"). To set up and then reduplicate is the same type as in *Man'yō* 1 [27]: *yoki hito no / yoshi to yoku mite* ("good people / found it good and had a good look"). Accordingly, the *kari-ho no iho* under consideration reduplicates words to no purpose! If that is the case, then even if it is understood as "hut of the reaped ears of grain," there is no precedent in the old poems. Although there is, surprisingly, in the *Gosenshū* the following poem:

aki no ta no	In the autumn fields,
kariho no ihori	the hut, the temporary hut,
nihofu made . . .	till I am imbued. . . .[38]

it is a misreading of *aki-ta karu / kari-ho no yadori / nihofu made,* cited above, and therefore not worth mentioning as evidence.

Second, in the *Man'yō,* Book 10, there is in fact the following:

aki-ta karu	I build a temporary hut
kari-ho wo tsukuri	to reap the autumn fields
ware woreba	and as I keep watch
koromo-de samuku	my sleeves are so cold
tsuyu okinikeru	that the dew has settled on them!

Since both the meaning and the words of this poem are exactly the same as that under consideration, the *One Hundred Poets* poem is a corruption of this last poem.

Third, in the *Nihongi* (entries on Empress Saimei), when the empress went to the province of Chikuzen, she died at the Asakura Palace. In the entry for winter, tenth month, it says the following:

The Empress' funeral train, returning, put to sea. Hereupon the prince imperial, having come to an anchor in the same place, was filled with grief and longing for the empress. So he sang to himself, saying:

kimi ga me no	Longing as I do
kohoshiki kara ni	For a sight of thee,
hatete kite	Now that I have arrived here
kaku ya kohimu mo	Even thus do I long
kimi ga me wohori	Desirous of a sight of thee![39]

In the first book of the *Man'yō,* there are poems on three mountains by Prince Naka-no-Ōe [Tenji]. These are truly poems he composed when he was Prince

Imperial, and they are in the style of the ancient age. When we compare it with these poems, we see that the *aki-ta karu kari-ho wo tsukuri* poem is in a slightly later style; and compared to that, the *aki no ta no* poem is far later, having the style of the Kōnin era [A.D. 810–823] Consequently, the *One Hundred Poets aki no ta no* poem is, from the outset, not a poem by Emperor Tenji; moreover, it cannot be taken as a correct poem, since it is a corruption of the *aki-ta karu / kari-ho wo tsukuri / ware woreba / koromo-de samuku / tsuyu okinikeri* poem.

Kari-ho is a field hut in a field far from the village. It is a dwelling where villagers stay, when autumn has deepened, to do such things as reap and dry the rice until the harvest is over. Consequently, to take *aki-ta karu kari-ho* ("the temporary hut of the autumn fields where they reap the ears of grain") as the *One Hundred Poets* version, *kariho no iho*, is incomprehensible, and since there is no other example of such diction, we must realize that it is something that has been corrupted.

The explanation that attaches special meaning to the phrase *wa ga koromo-de* ("the sleeve of my robe") is bad as well. In *Man'yō Shū* 10 [2235, anon., "Composed on Rain"]:

aki-ta karu	In my travel hut,
tabi no ihori ni	in the autumn fields they reap,
shigure furi	the late rains fall and
wa ga sode nurenu	soak my sleeves, there being
hosu hito mo nashi ni	no one to dry them. . . .

Just see, by means of this similar poem, the relative insignificance of the word *ware* ("I")! Again, in Book 10 [2185, anon., "Composed on Autumn Leaves"]:

ohosaka wo	When I arrive,
wa ga koe-kureba	crossing Osaka,
futa-gami ni	at Futagami
momijhi-ba nagaru	the showers keep falling
shigure furitsutsu	with autumn leaves washing down.

And even later, in a poem by the Lord of Kamakura:[40]

hakone-jhi wo	When I arrive,
wa ga koe-kureba	crossing the Hakone Road
izu no umi ya	—the Sea of Izu—
oki no o-shima ni	I see the waves approaching
nami no yoru miyu	the islets in the offing.

In these poems, it does not matter who the "I" is—indeed, if it is thought of as someone special [an emperor or shogun], then how will one interpret these poems? There are those who do not go back to look at the style of the times and instead try to interpret forcibly just this one poem, saying it is an imperial composition. Yet since it seems to be about nothing more than a hut in a field, it becomes difficult to comprehend. Some say it is about a time when the emperor was thinking about the decline of imperial power—although this was the age when the law codes were formulated and great government was arising and day after day the imperial power was blossoming! Others say it is a song of mourning, although it is in the middle of the Autumn section of the *Gosen.* Even if one says that it disregards the classification, is this not still an interpretation that twists the meaning? On top of that, if Lord Teika thought of it as a poem of imperial mourning, there are many other poems he could have chosen—would he have written out this one first to send in response to [Utsunomiya no Yoritsuna's] request?

Again, as far as the third line, the meaning of the field hut continues—there are no dividing words and it is not in the form of a preface poem—and then to say that suddenly, from the fourth line, it is about the emperor himself, is not in accord with what it means to be a poem.

As for *toma wo arami,* it is wrong to say that it means that autumn has deepened and so the thatching has become thin. The *mi* of *arami* is an abbreviation for *mari,* and the whole phrase is *aramari. Mari,* in turn, is an abbreviation of *araku mo ari.* Consequently, it is similar to the simple *araku* ("it is rough") and not *araku narite* ("it has become rough").[41]

Careful comparison and wide reading in the *Man'yō Shū* allowed Mabuchi both to date particular poetic styles and to identify certain poems as versions of older texts. Thus he is led to the bold conclusion that the first poem of the *One Hundred Poets* is not by Tenji at all and in fact dates from the ninth century. Mabuchi is not really interested in a reception history, of course, and he does not ask himself what the poem meant to Teika or readers of any other period. Mabuchi's concern is with the "authentic" poem and what it can tell us about Japan before the introduction of Chinese. Nonetheless, Mabuchi provides a painstaking analysis of each element of the poem and provides documentary evidence for his conclusions.

If modern readers find such detail tedious, they are not alone: the beginning of the nineteenth century saw a spate of simplified commentaries produced by the students of Mabuchi's successor, Motoori Norinaga (1730–1801). The popularity of the *One Hundred Poets,* and the need for popular commentaries, is summed up in the colophon to the *New Commentary (Shin Shō)* by Ishihara Shōmei, published in 1804. In his postscript, Shōmei notes that the *One Hundred Poets* is memorized by high and low, men and women, even the young. And while there are many commentaries in circulation, not one provides an easy-to-understand explanation of the basic text. The old commentaries (such as, presumably, the *Ōei Shō* or the *Yoritaka-bon*) are crude and of no value, while later ones (such as the *Yūsai Shō* perhaps) talk about "hidden explanations" *(ura no setsu)* and are of no use. Only Keichū's *Kaikan Shō* and Mabuchi's *Uimanabi* are of any value. Yet Shōmei says Keichū is too high-class, referring, perhaps, to his emphasis on Chinese learning, and Mabuchi is just too detailed. Shōmei's book is designed to be useful for learning the basics—putting courtly words and sentiments into the everyday words of the present. In line with this intention, Shōmei declares, he has left out all the discussion of the etymologies of place-names and poets' family trees that can befuddle readers.[42] The result is a much-pared-down text:

> *aki no ta no kari-ho:* a contraction of *kari iho* ("temporary hut").
>
> *no iho no:* a small guard hut where someone stays to stand guard so that the

rice fields will not be ruined by animals. The continuation in *kari-ho no iho* is of the same type as *mikka no hi yokka no hi* ("the day of the third [day], the day of the fourth [day]").

toma wo: not thatching as on a usual roof, but piling up rushes to thatch temporarily.

arami: mi corresponds to the phrase *sa ni* ("due to the -ness") in the vernacular: due to the roughness of the thatch's mesh.

wa: in the vernacular means "one's" *(jishin ga).* It indicates the viewpoint of the person who is standing guard. It is the same as in the present day when, to indicate oneself, one says "oneself" *(wa ga mi),* "one's own" *(te-mae),* "oneself" *(onore),* "one" *(ware),* and so on.

koromo-de: as for his sleeve.

tsuyu ni nuretsutsu: -*tsutsu* is "while"; it is the same as "while -ing." All poems that end with -*tsutsu* include some extra meaning underneath.

The meaning of the whole poem is: the dew is dripping through the gaps, due to the roughness of the netlike thatch on the roof of the small temporary guard hut in the autumn fields, and the sleeves of the peasant who is keeping guard in the hut get dampened by the dew throughout the night while he keeps guard—how lonely it must surely be!

Shōmei's text is part of the diffusion of the *One Hundred Poets* to a larger urban populace. A significant element in this popularization was the use of the *One Hundred Poets* as a text specifically for female education. In fact, as Ronald Dore has shown, Japanese literature was seen in the Tokugawa period as the appropriate curriculum for women, while men were trained in the Chinese classics.[43] The first edition of the *One Hundred Poets* specifically for women seems to have been the *Manpō Hyakunin Isshu Taisei,* published in 1707. *Karuta,* the card game based on the *One Hundred Poets,* was already flourishing by the early eighteenth century; Ogata Kōrin's lovely set dates from some time before 1716. Copies of the *One Hundred Poets* done in exemplary calligraphy became the standard textbook for writing classes, and by 1722 more than eight hundred writing teachers were reported to be operating in Edo alone.[44]

Two other highly influential commentaries must be mentioned. In 1823 Kagawa Kageki (1768–1843) published his *Hyakushu Iken,* or *Differing Opinions on the One Hundred Poems.* It is every bit as contrary a work as its title suggests: Kageki was from a line of poets that rejected the archaisms of Mabuchi and the poets of the National Learning movement. His *Iken* specifically attacks interpretations by Keichū and Mabuchi. Yet, more than for his criticism, Kageki became famous as the founder of a style of clear, easy-to-understand *tanka,* named after his residence, Kei'en-ryū. It was this style of *tanka* that became dominant in the late Tokugawa period and became the model for the state-sponsored poetry of the Meiji court in the nineteenth century.[45]

The most widely distributed version of the *One Hundred Poets,* outside of the card game, was Ozaki Masayoshi's *Hyakunin Isshu Hitoyo-gatari,* or *One-Night Stories About the One Hundred Poets* (1833). This text gives the usual biography of the poet, the poem, and a brief discussion of the poem, largely following Keichū. Yet by far the most space is given over to stories about the poets—in

Tenji's case, five stories about the emperor, including how he assassinated Soga no Iruka at court (Figure 3).[46] Commentaries on the *One Hundred Poets* continued to be written in the modern period, and today new scholarly editions, as well as new textbook editions, continue to appear. While the collection as a whole is no longer memorized by every schoolchild, it remains a central part of the secondary school curriculum.

Reading the *One Hundred Poets*

As we have seen, the *One Hundred Poets* has had a long tradition of commentary, and not all commentaries accord with one another. How did Teika himself read the poems he selected? This is a question that will inevitably entail the additional question of his criteria for selection.

Decontextualization and Narrative in the *One Hundred Poets*

Teika's exemplary hundred-poem sequences can be seen as an extreme point in a trend toward the decontextualization of *waka* inaugurated by Tsurayuki in the *Kokinshū*. Previous to the *Kokinshū*, the *waka* was appreciated almost entirely as what we would call "occasional poetry." In other words, individual poems were evaluated on the basis of how well they fulfilled a specific function at a specific moment—for example, as a retort to an unwanted suitor.

Figure 3. Ōishi Matora, "The Assassination of Soga no Iruka." In Ozaki Masayoshi, *Hyakunin Isshu Hitoyo-gatari* (1833).

By collecting poems into an anthology arranged by seasonal and thematic top-
ics, the editors of the *Kokinshū* divorced the poems from their original context
and asked readers to consider them as aesthetic objects, emphasizing their for-
mal properties. The contrast between the *Kokinshū* way of reading and the pre-
vious way can be seen by comparing the headnotes to poems that appear in
both the *Kokinshū* and the *Tales of Ise.*[47] In the *Tales* the poem is part of a specific
narrative; in the *Kokinshū* it must stand much more on its own.

Nonetheless, there are still a fair number of narrative headnotes in the
Kokinshū. In addition, the progression of poems by season, as well as the sugges-
tion of a movement from the first stirrings of love through to the falling out of
love, provide a general narrative cast. Such vestigial narration was completely
eliminated by Tsurayuki in his final distillation of the *Kokinshū*, the *Shinsen
Waka,*[48] where the headnotes have been entirely omitted and the poems paired
in such antithetical and atemporal pairs as "Spring and Autumn" and "Felicita-
tions and Laments." In the *One Hundred Poets,* too, the contextualizing head-
notes that originally introduced the poems have been excised, leaving the
reader to guess the circumstances of the poem's composition.

Two historical trends tended to counteract this decontextualization. One
was the trend toward composing, compiling, and reading poems in sequences.
The second trend was the use of allusion in the poetry of Teika's day (as noted
in the foregoing discussion of *honka-dori*). Such allusion was not limited to ear-
lier poems but included reference to famous narratives, most especially the *Tale
of Genji*. In fact it was Teika's father, Shunzei, who first insisted that a thorough
knowledge of the *Genji* was essential for a poet.[49] And in Teika's poetry of the
ShinKokinshū period we can see the predominant influence of narrative allu-
sion in his poetry: of his six poems in the Spring books of the *ShinKokinshū*, for
instance, half contain an allusion to a literary romance (one to *Genji* and two to
Tales of Ise).

It seems that a narrative quality is fundamental to the aesthetic concept
many scholars claim was Teika's chief concern: *yōen,* or "ethereal beauty."
Brower and Miner define this term as follows:

> The esthetic ideal of a romantic, unworldly beauty, like that of "a heavenly
> maiden descending to earth on a hazy moonlit night in spring." Advocated by
> the mid-classical poet Fujiwara Teika during his early manhood. Character-
> ized by complexity of technique and tending to express subtle shades of
> pathos, the poetry of yōen typically combined elements of more sombre styles
> with "beautiful" imagery and an ethereal atmosphere.[50]

Wayne Lammers cites a group of five poems "frequently noted by scholars and
critics for their *yōen* qualities."[51] Let us look at two by Teika from the *ShinKokinshū:*

1 (Spring 1): 38

haru no yo no	The floating bridge of dreams
yume no uki-hashi	in the short spring night
todae shite	comes to an end and,
mine ni wakaruru	in the sky, a bank of clouds
yoko-gumo no sora	parts from the peak.

1 (Spring 1): 44

ume no hana	The plum blossoms
nihohi wo utsusu	transfer their scent
sode no uhe ni	to my sleeves
noki moru tsuki no	and fight with the light of the moon
kage zo arasofu	that has leaked through the eaves.

Konishi Jin'ichi describes these poems as manifesting "a bright, positive beauty," which he claims is in fact different from what Teika and his contemporaries meant by the term *yōen,* a style that Konishi claims "conceals *en* ["refined beauty"] within a superficially gloomy, subdued, negative setting."[52] To exemplify what Teika and others meant by *yōen,* Konishi cites numerous judgments from the poetry contests of the time in which the term *yōen* is explicitly used. Again, let us restrict our attention to those poems with judgments written by Teika (translations by Gatten and Harbison):

The Poetry Contest at the Residence of the Kōmyōbuji Regent (Kujō no Michi'ie), Round 4, "Clothing and Love," 282, Right, Tadatoshi:

omohi-shire	Know that my underrobes
mune ni taku mo no	Are scorched by a breast as hot
shita-goromo	As burning seagrass:
uhe ha tsurenaki	On the surface, coolness reigns,
keburi nari tomo	Although inside I smolder.

The ethereal beauty in the last four lines of the poem is of especially high quality.
Round 48, "Pillows and Love," 289, Right, Tadatoshi:

nageki-waki	In grief and sorrow,
sate furu hodo no	I lapse into remembrance
omohide ni	Of times now gone,
musubi mo hatenu	But I cannot recapture
yume no ta-makura	The dream of that pillowing arm.

Several participants remark that *yume no ta-makura* ("the dream of that pillowing arm") has ethereal beauty.
Round 81, "Bedclothes and Love," 293, Right, Tadatoshi:

hakanashi ya	How ephemeral!
sono yo no yume wo	That of that night's now vanished dream
katami nite	Only this for memory:
utsutsu ni tsuraki	A reality so cruel,
toko no sa-mushiro	The cold matting of my bed.

Although several of the participants maintain that the Right's poem has ethereal beauty. . . .
The Poetry Contest at Wakamiya, Iwashimizu Shrine, Round 1, "Haze by the River," 272, Right, Lord Shunzei's Daughter:

hashi-hime no	The Lady of the Bridge—
sode no asa-shimo	The morning frost upon her sleeves

naho saete	Makes them yet colder,
kasumi fuki-kosu	And the spring haze is swept along
ujhi no kaha-kaze	By the Uji river wind.

The Right wins because "The Lady of the Bridge— / The morning frost upon her sleeves" truly reveals the *yōen* mode.

Round 18, "Cherry Blossoms in Darkening Mountains," 275, Right, Lord Shunzei's Daughter:

tsuki-kage mo	The moonlight, too,
utsurofu hana ni	Like fading cherry blossoms
kaharu iro no	Makes all seem white
yufube wo haru mo	Even as evening is seen in spring
mi-yoshino no yama	On the fine peaks of Yoshino.

The Right's poem may be said to produce a *yōen* effect.

The Poetry Contest Held on the Fourth Day of the Eleventh Month, in the Fifth Year of Kempō, Round 33, "Snow on a Wintry Sea," 258, Left, Emperor Juntoku:

kaze samumi	With the wind so cold
hi-kazu mo itaku	The many days pass heavily
furu yuki ni	In falling snow:
hito ya ha oran	Is he indeed gathering
ise no hama-ogi	The shoreside reeds of Ise?

The windswept snow scene is portrayed through diction of truly ethereal beauty.[53]

Despite the difference Konishi perceives between these two groups of poems, I believe they evoke a common response in the reader—namely, to imagine a narrative context in which such poems would be appropriate. The first poem, *ShinKokinshū* 38, requires us to imagine the speaker waking from a brief dream about a love from his past: the man and woman met for one equally brief spring night, and then the woman left, like a cloud leaving a peak. This poem alludes to a poem about unrequited love in the *Kokinshū*, as well as to the last chapter of the *Tale of Genji*, which relates the interrupted love affair between Kaoru and Ukifune and the latter's disappearance. Most importantly, this poem has a Chinese subtext in the *Kao-t'ang Fu*, which tells of a king meeting and lying with a heavenly maiden on Mount Wu, who is described as coming and going like a morning cloud from a mountain peak.[54] It is this dense web of narrative allusion that leads Kubota Jun to describe this poem as "tale-like" (*monogatari-teki*).[55]

The second poem, *ShinKokinshū* 44, borders on the surreal. Indeed it is only through a narrative setting, such as the following provided by Minemura, that it is intelligible:

The plum blossoms that bloom near the eaves transfer their scent to the sleeves which are wet from tears of longing for days past, and the light of the moon that leaks through the dilapidated eaves is reflected in those tears as if competing with the scent of the plum.[56]

Minemura, too, describes the speaker of the poem as "a character in a tale" (*monogatari-chū no jinbutsu*).

In fact, Lammers relates Teika's interest in *yōen* to his interest in writing fiction—specifically, to the literary romance attributed to Teika, the *Tale of Matsura* (*Matsura no Miya Monogatari*). The main romantic situation of this tale revolves around the protagonist, Ujitada, being repeatedly visited by a mystery woman during his stay at the Chinese imperial court and his growing inability to hide his feelings by day while in attendance at court. It is precisely this kind of setting that is depicted in the first poem above by Tadatoshi *(omohi-shire):* while indifferent on the surface, the speaker burns with love underneath. (Compare this, as well, with Poem 49 of the *One Hundred Poets*.) The next poem, from Round 48, is specifically about remembering a love now past. Particular attention is paid to the "dream of that pillowing arm," which suggests the brevity and ethereal quality of the lovers' meeting. This motif is even clearer in the next poem, from Round 81. Moreover this poem, and the next by Lord Shunzei's Daughter, allude to a famous poem from the *Kokinshū* 14 (Love 4): 689:

sa-mushiro ni	On the cold reed-mat
koromo kata-shiki	spreading out her robe just for one,
koyohi mo ya	this evening too
ware wo matsuramu	is she waiting for me—
ujhi no hashi-hime	the Goddess of Uji Bridge?

This poem, and the image of the Goddess of Uji Bridge, is a Japanese version of the goddess of Mount Wu, suggesting the same kind of brief, ethereal romance. The Goddess is explicitly named in Lord Shunzei's Daughter's poem, as well as adding a kind of white-on-white (haze over frost) that Teika is known to have particularly liked: the wind blowing the white spring haze over the white morning frost. This white-on-white is simply a "colder" version of the same trope we see in the poet's next poem (from Round 18), where both fading cherry blossoms and moonlight merge in the darkening spring night. It is this same white-on-white that Teika praises in Juntoku's poem, where snow is falling on the white sands and the wind is blowing it onto the whitecaps. In addition, the poem marks the passing of time (*hi-kazu . . . furu,* literally, "the number of days . . . pass") and asks the reader to imagine the relationship between the speaker of the poem and the absent man in Ise.

We see, then, that despite apparent disagreements over the definition of *yōen,* the term can be consistently related to a kind of ur-narrative that involves a confusion over the remembrance or experience of a brief meeting with a mysterious woman, identified with the heavenly maidens of Chinese and Japanese myth. While one should not expect to relate this ur-narrative to every poem Teika wrote or anthologized, it is to be expected that, to the degree that he formulated *yōen* as an aesthetic criterion, it might be involved in both his interpretation and his selection of the poems in the *One Hundred Poets*.

Teika's Principles of Selection

Given the centrality of *yōen* to Teika's aesthetics, one might well expect that it was an important criterion in his selection of poems for the *One Hundred*

Poets. This assumption is borne out by the evidence we do have of how Teika interpreted specific poems within the collection. Let us look at one example, Poem 21 by Priest Sosei:

ima komu to	It was only because you said
ihishi bakari ni	you would come right away
naga-tsuki no	that I have waited
ariake no tsuki wo	these long months, till even
machi-idetsuru kana	the wan morning moon has come out!

There are two basic interpretations of this poem: the "one night" interpretation *(ichiya-setsu)* and the "many months" interpretation *(tsuki-goro-setsu).* The meaning of this poem in the *Kokinshū* follows the first interpretation—that is, the poem is a complaint by a speaker who has waited through the night (one night) for her lover to come. The second interpretation—that the woman has waited many nights through the spring and into the Ninth Month of autumn— makes the poem seem part of a longer literary romance *(monogatari)* and hence closer to the *yōen* spirit. And in fact it is just this interpretation that we see recorded in the *Kenchū Mikkan,* a commentary on the *Kokinshū* compiled by Teika. Such examples in turn encourage one to interpret other poems in the collection from this literary romance perspective. However, this is not at all to suggest that the entire *One Hundred Poets* collection can be read as a unified sequence related to some overarching narrative. I will return to the issue of "integrated sequences" in due course. At this juncture my aim is simply to examine the criteria Teika might have used to select *individual* poems contained in the *One Hundred Poets.*

Beyond the admittedly circular hermeneutics of *yōen,* one can specify other concerns that seem to have motivated Teika's choice of poems. Are the poems chosen for their own intrinsic value, or are they meant to represent, synecdochically, the entire oeuvre of the poet? Unlike Kintō's *Sanjūrokunin Sen,* Teika seems to have been choosing poems rather than poets. For instance, it seems reasonable to suspect that Teika realized that the attribution of Poem 5 to Sarumaru was spurious—it is presented in both the *Kokinshū* and the *Shinsen Man'yō Shū* as anonymous. Nonetheless, it is obviously a poem Teika greatly valued: he included it in his own copy of the *Superior Poems of Our Times* and in his *Eiga Taigai.* Since none of Teika's exemplary collections contains any other poems attributed to Sarumaru in the apocryphal *Sarumaru Shū,* we must conclude that Teika included this poem on the merits of the poem itself and not those of its putative author. In the same way, Abe no Nakamaro has only one poem in imperial anthologies through Teika's time—clearly it was the poem that was important to Teika, not the poet's entire body of work.

But are we in fact reading the same text as Teika? This question is concerned with two possible situations: in the first case, there is a difference between the earliest example of a poem and Teika's version of it; in the other situation, the form of the poem has changed during its transmission from Teika's day. Let us start with the second situation first, as it is more easily dealt with. There are several poems in the *One Hundred Poets* in which actual words were changed sometime between Teika's day and the Edo period. One example is Poem 57 by Murasaki Shikibu. In standard editions of the *One Hundred Poets*, the last line of this poem reads *yoha no tsuki kana*, or "ah, the moon at midnight!" Yet the line appears as *yoha no tsuki-kage*, or "the face of the midnight moon," in the *Collected Poems of Murasaki Shikibu* (*Murasaki Shikibu Shū*), the *ShinKokinshū*, and the *Nishidai Shū*—all works that Teika was involved in as editor. In fact, the line still appears unchanged in the *Ōei Commentary*. Consequently, it is clear that the line was altered in the process of transmission after the early fifteenth century. Thus if one is interested in the *One Hundred Poets* as Teika designed it, one will change the standard text back to the original form of the poem.

While changes such as these are fairly easy to establish, the first situation is not. Unlike modern Japanese, traditional Japanese orthography did not make distinctions between voiced and unvoiced consonants. Thus the grapheme *ka* was used to represent both /ka/ and /ga/. On the one hand, this convention supported the word play of pivot words. On the other, however, there are a few poems where real confusion results. The most significant example is Poem 17 by Narihira. Here again it is the last line that is in dispute—specifically whether it is to be read *midzu kukuru*, "the water tie-dyed," or *midzu kuguru*, "the water flowing under [the leaves floating on the surface]." Although scholars have established that *kukuru* is the original meaning, we know from the *Kenchū Mikkan* that Teika read the word as *kuguru*. Again, if one wishes to read the *One Hundred Poets* as Teika conceived it, one will follow his reading of this poem and not the original *Kokinshū* version, even though Teika's version is not the poem Narihira wrote.

Once we have established the form of the poems actually chosen by Teika, we can return to the question of his criteria for selection. We have already seen that he seems to have been choosing poems rather than poets. In fact, the situation is more complicated. It is clear that another principle of selection was heredity. In other words, Teika's selection shows a marked emphasis on the blood relationships between poets, especially through generations. This factor is immediately apparent in the first two poems, by Emperor Tenji and his daughter, Empress Jitō. In total, thirty-four of the hundred poets are related to each other through direct lines of descent. Given that the *Hyakunin Shūka*, which has ninety-eight poems in common with the *One Hundred Poets*, was originally compiled for Teika's father-in-law, this attention to the hereditary aspect of Japanese poetry should not perhaps be surprising. It would also explain the inclusion of otherwise rather minor poets such as Emperor Yōzei (father of Prince Motoyoshi, Poem 20).

The specific purpose and setting of the *One Hundred Poets* can also be used to explain the choice of certain poems, if not poets. It is no surprise, for instance, to see Fujiwara no Kintō, the arbiter elegantiarum of his age, included among Teika's *One Hundred Poets*. What needs some explanation, however, is why Teika chose the particular poem of Kintō's that he did (Poem 55). This poem appears in none of Teika's other exemplary collections (or in those of anyone else, for that matter). But when we remember that the poems of the *One Hundred Poets* were chosen to decorate Teika's villa at Ogura, the choice of a poem composed on a famous nearby temple seems understandable.

Finally, we can explain Teika's choice of certain poems based on his known predilections. For instance, it is well known that Teika had a special fondness for the color white,[57] especially its use in situations of white-on-white—a point already noted in connection with the concept of *yōen*—which we see again in Poem 29 by Mitsune:

kokoro-ate ni	Must it be by chance,
woraba ya woramu	if I am to pluck one, that I pluck it?—
hatsu-shimo no	white chrysanthemums
oki-madohaseru	on which the first frost
shira-giku no hana	lies bewilderingly.

The fact that Teika included this poem in several of his exemplary collections testifies to his fondness for it.

Reading the *One Hundred Poets* as a Sequence

There is one final factor to consider when we examine Teika's inclusion of any particular poem, and that is the poem's function in the whole hundred-poem sequence. Did Teika give any consideration to the movement from one poem to another or to a poem's influence when placed before or after another? To answer these questions, we must review American scholarship on Japanese poetic anthologies and sequences for the last thirty years. In America, the idea that poems were arranged as integrated sequences has come to be accepted as a matter of fact.

At first glance, the question of sequence in the *One Hundred Poets* seems fairly obvious: the poets are placed in historical order, starting with Emperor Tenji of the seventh century and concluding with Retired Emperor Juntoku of the thirteenth century. But even such a simple principle breaks down upon closer inspection. For instance, Teika's interest in parent-child continuities has Murasaki Shikibu (Poem 57) followed by her daughter Daini no Sanmi (Poem 58), and he presents all of Empress Akiko's salon as a group, from Izumi Shikibu (Poem 56) through to Ise no Tayū (Poem 61), but this places their older contemporary Sei Shōnagon (Poem 62) after both Murasaki Shikibu's daughter and Izumi Shikibu's daughter, KoShikibu no Naishi (Poem 60). Teika's order, then, is not strictly chronological.

Yet even if we accept that the collection is in generally chronological order, the question remains whether any attention was paid to the placement or selection of poems as they related to each other. There is some evidence that such attention was paid. In fact, although the *Hyakunin Shūka* and the *One Hundred Poets* have ninety-eight poems in common, their order and arrangement are very different. In the *Hyakunin Shūka,* for instance, Teika chose the following poem of Minamoto no Toshiyori:

yama-zakura	Since the mountain cherries
saki-someshi yori	have started to bloom:
hisakata no	the white threads of a falls
kumowi ni miyuru	that can be seen in the clouds
taki no shira-ito	of the wide heavens!

This poem has been replaced by the following in the *One Hundred Poets:*

ukarikeru	"Make that heartless
hito wo hatsuse no	woman, O mountain storm
yama-oroshi yo	of Hatsuse Temple,
hageshikare to ha	crueller still!"—this is not
inoranu mono wo	what I prayed for, and yet . . .

In the *One Hundred Poets*, Toshiyori is preceded by the following poem by Masafusa:

takasago no	Above the lower slopes
wonohe no sakura	of the high mountains, the cherries
sakinikeri	have blossomed!
toyama no kasumi	O, mist of the near mountains,
tatazu mo aranamu	how I wish you would not rise!

Higuchi Yoshimaro suggests that if Teika had used Toshiyori's "mountain cherries" poem, two poems with very similar conceptions would have been placed right next to each other. Moreover, Poem 76 contains the expression *hisakata no kumowi* ("clouds of the wide heavens"), which would appear unduly repetitious.[58]

There appears to be some evidence, then, that Teika did pay attention to the succession of poems in the *One Hundred Poets*. In fact, a whole genre of linked verse, called *renga*, with detailed rules for the succession of stanzas, was coming into vogue during Teika's time. The question naturally arises whether Teika used *renga* or *renga*-like rules to order the succession of poems in the *One Hundred Poets*. The origins of *renga* stem from the practice of "capping" verses— that is, one poet would compose half a *tanka* and invite (or challenge) another poet to complete the verse. Examples of this practice are found as early as the eighth-century *Man'yō Shū*. The idea of continuing such capping through a succession of verses *(kusari-renga)* seems to have arisen in the twelfth century,[59] and by the thirteenth century the *hyakuin*, or hundred-stanza form, seems to have become standard (although the oldest extant complete *hyakuin* date only from the early fourteenth century). These early *renga*, however, were of a particular type known as *fushimono renga*. To quote Steven Carter:

> This early variety of *renga* composition involved a technique of weaving hidden words and images from certain specified categories into the syntax of each verse in a sequence. There were many different kinds of these *fushimono;* in a "Five Color Sequence," to offer one example, the first verse was designed to include a reference to the color green, the second to yellow, the third to red, the fourth to white, the fifth to black and so on in that order through the entire *hyakuin*.[60]

In fact, Carter argues that the development of true *renga*, as practiced in the Muromachi period (1333–1573), required the abandonment of the *fushimono* format. Carter suggests that "this drift away from a principle of coherence and toward more desultory forms of progression is complemented by similar trends in *waka* poetry":

A move away from temporal and thematic organization and toward more "associational" modes of integration in the imperial anthologies is, as Japanese and Western scholars agree, one of the identifying characteristics of *waka* history in the thirteenth and fourteenth centuries. Robert Brower and Earl Miner have shown how series of poems in the *Gyokuyōshū* (Collection of jeweled leaves, 1314) and the *Fūgashū* (Collection of elegance, 1346) in particular are linked together as much by conventionally associated words, images, concepts, and rhetorical techniques as by dramatic, chronological, or temporal factors.[61]

Let us take a moment, then, to review the history of the concept of "association and progression" in the writings of Brower, Miner, and the Japanese scholar Konishi Jin'ichi.

Patterns of Association and Progression

In 1958, *The Harvard Journal of Asiatic Studies* published an article by Konishi Jin'ichi, translated and adapted by Robert Brower and Earl Miner, entitled "Association and Progression: Principles of Integration in Anthologies and Sequences of Japanese Court Poetry, A.D. 900–1350."[62] This article proposes that, in Japan, "the anthology and sequence [are] lyric forms integrating numerous short poems into a unified series" (p. 61). In 1961 Brower and Miner incorporated this theory into their *Japanese Court Poetry,* where it was, in Donald Keene's words, "perhaps the most striking single feature of the book."[63] In 1967, Brower and Miner gave what is perhaps the strongest presentation of this model in their translation of Teika's *Kindai Shūka (Superior Poems of Our Time),* where each link of association and progression is pointed out in notes between the poems. Since the appearance of these works, the association and progression model has not only been accepted by English-speaking students of Japanese court poetry almost as a matter of course, but it has proved to be an attractive model to scholars working on other genres, such as collections of didactic tales[64] and *nikki,* that is, diaries or memoirs.[65] In Konishi's model, "association" and "progression" refer to two distinct methods for linking *waka.* "Progression," he says "is essentially temporal and chronological, with poems following the changing of the seasons, or more specifically, the annual calendar of court festivities *(nenjū gyōji)*"; or the "dramatic plot structure" (p. 101) of a typical love affair at court. "Association," by contrast, is atemporal and achieves integration through a juxtaposition of imagery, spatial progression, rhetorical techniques, and allusions.

The idea that poems in the imperial anthologies, at least those in the seasonal books, were arranged according to seasonal "progression" is not open to debate. In fact, the position of poems in such groups is used by scholars to establish how the compilers interpreted specific poems. Perhaps the best-known example of this interpretive use of a poem's position in connection with the *One Hundred Poets* is Poem 5:

oku-yama ni	When I hear the voice
momijhi fumi-wake	of the stag crying for his mate
naku shika no	stepping through the autumn leaves

> *kowe kiku toki zo*   deep in the mountains—then is the time
> *aki ha kanashiki*   that autumn is saddest!

This poem appears in about the middle of the first of two books of autumn poems in the *Kokinshū,* in a group of five poems on deer. After these five poems come three poems on deer and bush clover *(hagi).* Clearly, then, the poem is set in mid-autumn and the "autumn leaves" are the yellowing leaves of the bush clover (in the *Shinsen Man'yō Shū* the word "autumn leaves" is written with the Chinese characters for "yellow leaves") that the stag is brushing through. Yet Teika, when he included this poem in his *Nishidai Shū,* placed it in a group of late autumn poems. Accordingly, medieval commentators interpreted the "autumn leaves" of the poem as fallen maple leaves (written with the characters for "scarlet leaves") that the stag was trampling on.

Brower and Miner argue that "techniques of progression seem gradually to have led to techniques of association":

> When a compiler had several poems to fit into a progressive sequence—several poems whose chief constituent was imagery—the order he gave the poems would naturally take into account something of the force of the images so as to capitalize upon rather than to violate their associations. If he had, for example, three poems on the topics of "Love at Sea," "Love on the Coast," and "Love with a Distant View of the Sea," he would arrange them in this order, or in reverse; the order of the sea, the sea from a distance, and the sea from the shore would have been too abrupt in its near-far-near relation to the central image of the sea.[66]

As Brower and Miner state, concern for the order of the poems would be something that a compiler "would naturally take into account." The question is whether such concerns were formalized into a set of rules or explicitly specified by Teika's day. Certainly the techniques seemed very explicit as they were presented in Brower and Miner's application of them to sequences, in their translation of Teika's *Kindai Shūka, Superior Poems of Our Time,* which, they asserted, was "not only, or even preeminently, an anthology of so many poets and poems, but a poetic whole of 415 lines, in 83 stanzas." They explained that "the integration of the *Kindai Shūka* is achieved by the techniques of progression and association: temporal and spatial progression through subgroups in the sequence, and association of poems with related diction, images, rhetorical techniques, or motifs."[67] To aid "in making the pattern of association and progress clear at every point in the sequence," Brower and Miner provided notes under each poem with the rubrics "Time," "Space," and "Motifs," the last, especially, presumably relating to the techniques of association. An idea of how this all worked together can be gleaned from their translation of the first three poems:

> 1. *haru tatsu to*   Is it just because
>   *ifu bakari ni ya*   They say this is the day which marks
>   *mi-yoshino no*   The coming of the spring
>   *yama mo kasumite*   That even the mountains of fair Yoshino
>   *kesa ha miyuran*   Are veiled this morning in a haze?

Time progression: first day of spring
Space progression: mountains viewed from afar
Motifs: haze

2. *yama-zakura*   Since first they flowered,
    saki-someshi yori   The mountain cherries have seemed to be
    hisakata no   The white cascades
    kumowi ni miyuru   Of a celestial waterfall that streams
    taki no shira-ito   From the distant cloudland of the sky.

Time: from beginning of spring to cherry-blossom season
Space: mountains viewed somewhat more closely
Motifs: celestial imagery continued—haze of poem 1 is now clouds; cherry
blossoms

3. *sakura saku*   Even through a day,
    toho-yama-dori no   A day as long as the flowing tail
    shidari-wo no   of the mountain fowl,
    naga-nagashi hi mo   The cherries flowering white on distant hills
    akanu iro kana   Possess a beauty that can never pall.

Time: cherry blossoms at their height
Space: hills or mountains at a distance
Motifs: cherry blossoms and hills, continued; *iro* (color, beauty) is associated
with *shira-* (white) of 2

Here we see the suggestion that poem 2 is linked to poem 1 by the same "cate-
gory of phenomenon,"[68] what later in *renga* would be called "Rising Things"
(sobikimono), including Haze, Mist, and Cloud.[69] Poem 3 is then associationally
linked to poem 2 through the concept of color, in the fashion of *engo,* or "word
association," where *iro* suggests first "beauty" (in poem 3) and then literally
"color" (in relation to poem 2).

Brower and Miner's association and progression paradigm became widely
disseminated and proved a productive framework for students. But just as a
new generation of scholars was enthusiastically embracing the idea of "associa-
tion," Brower, at least, seems to have been having second thoughts. In his 1973
translation of Teika's *Hundred-Poem Sequence of the Shōji Era* (*Shōji Hyakushu,*
1200) we read:

> With respect to association and progression, once the general principles are
> understood, their functioning can be more or less readily discerned, and
> readers can work out a scheme for themselves if they choose, without having a
> detailed and perhaps too arbitrary analytical apparatus imposed upon them.
> Therefore, I have commented only here and there upon particular problems
> or points of interest, dispensing with the lists of associated images, delinea-
> tions of movements through space, time progressions from morning to
> evening, or from day to day, and the like. Besides, it is well to remember that
> the relationships between poems in a sequence are to some extent fortuitous:
> when two poems on winter are placed side by side, for example, some associa-
> tion of imagery is virtually inescapable. And in Teika's age, such relationships

were also to a large degree probably a matter of instinct—at all events not painstakingly worked out according to fixed structural rules or an elaborately articulated theory. In the reader's response, too, there could be a degree of latitude within conventional limits. Indeed, perhaps the worst mistake is by working out the details in too schematic a fashion to slight the potentiality, even the likelihood, of alternative "readings" of the same passage in a sequence, depending upon the multiplicity of possible unspoken implications, imagery, and subtle nuances—the *yojō*, or "overtones," which are the essence of the characteristic of the *Shinkokin* period.[70]

This statement represents a significant modification of the method used in the *Superior Poems of Our Time.* In fact it is more than that, since it was the rigorous and systematic application of the techniques of association that Konishi claimed distinguished the *ShinKokinshū* from its predecessors.

Where does this leave us, then, especially in regard to the *One Hundred Poets?* The reader should be aware that the collection was meant to have some coherence as a whole. Readers may also note that techniques used within individual *tanka,* such as word association and allusive variation, historically led to a form of linked poetry, *renga,* which employed many of the same techniques and recall, too, that this genre of poetry was developing during Teika's lifetime. Thus it is reasonable to assume that some of these techniques may have been operating in either Teika's or his readers' minds when they read the *One Hundred Poets.* Yet it is equally important to note there is no historical evidence to suggest that these techniques were explicitly recognized (unlike, for example, the explicit recognition of the function of pivot words). Moreover, as we shall see, when discussing the pictorializations of the *One Hundred Poets,* the book format had a profound effect on the reading of this collection: the poems typically appeared one to a page, paired across the binding. This format, along with the influence of the poetry contest and *renga's* attention to linked couplets *(tsuke-ku),* encouraged one to read the poems in pairs, reinforcing a tendency that seems apparent in the original selection.

The most important thing to realize, however, is that once we posit some kind of association between individual poems in the *One Hundred Poets,* we will inevitably find it. As Stanley Fish has written in another context: "These facts and intentions emerge when a text is interrogated by a series of related questions." In other words, "it is not because the [theory] has been shown to be in accordance with the facts but because it is from the perspective of its assumptions that the facts are now being specified."[71] In cases ranging from Keats to Wordsworth, once critics have asked whether there is a reason for the order in which the poet has presented his poems, they inevitably "discover" that there is.[72] The advantage of the Konishi model of association is that it is at least to some extent based on indigenous methods, such as *engo* and *renga* techniques.

Teika and the "Simultaneous Order"

With these caveats in mind, let us look at the first four poems of the *One Hundred Poets,* and examine how their relationship to each other may explain certain of their individual features. The collection starts with a poem by an emperor, followed by one by his daughter, an empress. This beginning pair is balanced by Poems 99 and 100, by two emperors who are also parent and child. Moreover, it was the emperor of Poem 1, Tenji, who bestowed on Teika's forebears the surname "Fujiwara," so in a sense, this beginning of the collection, which itself is a history of *waka,* is not only the beginning of *waka* but the beginning of the Fujiwara family as well.[73] The poem attributed to Tenji reads:

aki no ta no	In the autumn fields
kari-ho no iho no	the hut, the temporary hut,
toma wo arami	its thatch is rough
wa ga koromo-de ha	and so the sleeves of my robe
tsuyu ni nuretsutsu	are dampened night by night with dew.

As noted earlier in discussing the exegetical tradition of the *One Hundred Poets,* the most widely accepted interpretation of this poem is that Teika read it as expressing the emperor's concern over the hard life of his peasant subjects. Such an interpretation makes the poem eminently suited to start a collection of poetry long associated with imperial rule.[74]

Poem 2 is by Tenji's daughter, Empress Jitō:

haru sugite	Spring has passed, and
natsu kinikerashi	summer has arrived, it seems.
shiro-tahe no	Heavenly Mount Kagu
koromo hosu tefu	where, it is said, they dry robes
ama no kagu-yama	of the whitest mulberry!

This poem originally appears as *Man'yō Shū* 1:28:

haru sugite	Spring has passed
natsu kitarurashi	and summer has come, it appears,
shiro-tahe no	for they are drying robes
koromo hoshitari	of the whitest mulberry
ame no kagu-yama	on heavenly Mount Kagu.

The original *man'yō-gana* transcription gave rise to many different readings in the Heian period, such as *koromo hoshitaru* and *koromo kawakasu,* so that the *ShinKokinshū* editors had to choose one from several possible readings.[75] It is generally agreed that the version they chose is not as forceful as the original—*kinikerashi* contrasting with the more definite *kitarurashi.* Yet the biggest problem is in the fourth line: *koromo hosu tefu,* "they dry robes, it is said," contrasting with the original's simple "they dry robes." The original poem is presumed to have been written from Jitō's palace, the Fujiwara no Miya, which is only about a mile to the northwest of Mount Kagu—in other words, the Empress is writing about a scene before her eyes. The *tefu* of the *ShinKokinshū* version, however, makes the robe-drying a matter of hearsay, not direct observation. The confusion this change entailed is seen clearly in the commentary to this poem in the *Hyakunin Isshu Hitoyo-gatari* of 1833:

This poem was originally in the *Man'yō Shū* as follows:

haru sugite	Spring has passed
natsu ha kinurashi	and summer has come, it appears,
shiro-tahe no	for they are hanging out the robes
koromo saraseri	of the whitest mulberry
ama no kagu-yama[76]	on heavenly Mount Kagu.

In the *ShinKokinshū* version it is hard to know whether the words were corrected to conform to the writing of the period [the *ShinKokin* era] or whether an error was made during the transmission and they were written this way. If we were to interpret this poem as its words appear in the *Man'yō Shū* we would have: "Has spring passed and summer come? Well can I see the peasants drying their white clothing on heavenly Mount Kagu." It is a poem composed on a view that can be seen from the palace. . . .

However, it is a mysterious matter that, in the *ShinKokinshū* and *One Hundred Poets,* the line *koromo hosu tefu* is written. The word *tefu* means *to iu* ("they say"). . . . Yet there is no way that the drying of garments before the empress' very eyes could be spoken of as *koromo hosu tefu*. Thus while there are many complicated explanations found in the many commentaries to the *One Hundred Poets,* one finds none that can clearly explain the matter.[77]

We will discuss the interpretation of this author, Ozaki Masayoshi, in more detail later. For the moment we might note that this poem in the *ShinKokinshū* is placed at the beginning of the summer section and was no doubt taken to refer to the seasonal changing of clothes. Moreover, as Katagiri notes, Mount Kagu was used in poems celebrating the sovereign's longevity, as in the following poem from the imperial anthology that preceded the *ShinKokinshū*, the *Senzaishū* (Felicitations): 608 (presented 1188):

kimi ga yo ha	During my lord's reign
ama no kago-yama	I pray there be no limit
idzuru hi no	to the shining of the sun
teramu kagiri ha	that emerges from
tsukiji to zo omofu	heavenly Mount Kago![78]

The reason for this association is that Mount Kagu was the location of the stone door which Amaterasu, the Sun Goddess and ancestor of the imperial line, closed behind her when she withheld her light from the world; thus these poems forge a specific link between the light of the Sun Goddess and the rays of beneficent rule of her earthly descendant, the mikado. Likewise Teika's placement of this poem in the *One Hundred Poets* may well have been meant to suggest such celebratory poems, connecting it to the imperial concern expressed in Poem 1. Moreover, Emperor Tenji was best known as a poet for his *chōka* on the "Three Mountains of Yamato," of which Mount Kagu was one.[79]

Yet this still does not explain the strange "it is said" phrasing. The interpretation offered by the *Hyakunin Isshu Hitoyo-gatari* continues:

Here is a thought: in Regent GoKyōgoku Yoshitsune's *Gessei Shū* there is a poem composed for the retired emperor's second hundred-poem sequence. Among the winter poems, he composed:

kumo haruru	The brightness of the snow
yuki no hikari ya	once the clouds have cleared!
shiro-tahe no	Heavenly Mount Kagu,
koromo hosu tefu	where they are said to dry robes
ama no kagu-yama	of the whitest mulberry.

This Lord GoKyōgoku was a person of the same era as Lord Teika, and so there can be no question of his thinking to steal three lines of Empress Jitō's poem to pass them off as his own. The meaning of Lord GoKyōgoku's poem is: When Empress Jitō composed her "Heavenly Mount Kagu / where they bleach robes" that is in the *Man'yō Shū*, it was for a scene set at the beginning of summer. Right now, the light of the snow after the clouds have cleared appears pure white—did the scene of Mount Kagu, which in the past Empress Jitō described as [pure white like] the "bleaching of robes," appear like this too?

So he thought and composed his poem echoing that of Jitō.[80]

Ozaki goes on to suggest that Yoshitsune's and Jitō's poem somehow became mixed during transmission. This seems unlikely. Rather, it would appear that Mount Kagu, preceded by the descriptive phrase "where they are said to dry robes / of the whitest mulberry," becomes a kind of fixed epithet indicating "pure white." Moreover, as Ariyoshi writes, in place of the *Man'yō Shū* version's direct observation is the *ShinKokinshū*'s sense of a transmitted, traditional image that conceals a longing for the ancient age.[81] Extending this idea, one might even say that the speaker of the poem is no longer Jitō but Teika in the act of quoting Jitō—an idea I will elaborate shortly in connection with Poem 4.

Poem 3 is attributed to Hitomaro, the "patron saint" of *waka*:

ashi-biki no	Must I sleep alone
yama-dori no wo no	through the long autumn nights,
shidari wo no	long like the dragging tail
naga-nagashi yo wo	of the mountain pheasant
hitori kamo nemu	separated from his dove?

Given Hitomaro's reputation as the first great Japanese poet, his position as number three, right after two emperors, is hardly surprising. In fact, not only does this poem appear in the same position in the *Hyakunin Shūka*, but it is the foundation poem *(honka)* for the poem by GoToba that appears as poem 3 in the *Superior Poems of Our Time,* and an equally famous poem by Hitomaro is the foundation for poem 2 in the *ShinKokinshū*. Note also that in the *Superior Poems of Our Time,* GoToba's allusive variation is preceded by a poem that can be read as a metaphor for a lord's munificence. In terms of context within the *One Hundred Poets,* Hitomaro's verse of unrequited love invites us to reread Tenji's poem as one about an equally solitary lover—an interpretation encountered often, as seen in the commentary of the *Ogura Sansō Shikishi Waka* cited above. Sandwiched in this way, Jitō's poem, in turn, can be read as cheerful contrast between two forlorn men—one might even suggest that it is the wet sleeves of Poem 1 that "dry" in Poem 2 (*sode, tsuyu, hosu, nuru,* and *koromo* associated through *engo*).[82]

Poem 4 is by the poet ranked by Tsurayuki as the equal of Hitomaro,[83] Akahito:

tago no ura ni	As I set out on
uchi-idete mireba	the beach of Tago, and look,
shiro-tahe no	I see the snow constantly falling
fuji no taka-ne ni	on the high peak of Fuji,
yuki ha furitsutsu	white as mulberry cloth.

Like Poem 2 by Empress Jitō, there appear to have been many different readings of the *Man'yō* script of this poem in the Heian period. The accepted modern reading is conveyed in the following translation by Ian Levy:

tago no ura yu	Coming out
uchi-idete mireba	from Tago's nestled cove,
ma-shiro ni zo	I gaze:
fuji no taka-ne ni	white, pure white
yuki ha furikeru	the snow has fallen
	on Fuji's lofty peak.[84]

Of the three differences between the *Man'yō Shū* source poem and the *One Hundred Poets* version, two have received attention. The *One Hundred Poets* version has the first line reading *tago no ura ni,* that is, "at / on Tago no Ura," which in turn forces the *uchi-idete* to mean "setting out on," while the original clearly has "coming out of/from *(yu)* Tago no Ura," with *uchi-idete* then meaning "coming out [from the shadow]." Thus Tago no Ura itself was in Akahito's time some spot in mountain shadow where Fuji could not be seen, probably somewhere around present-day Yubi, Nishi Kurazawa, or Mount Satsuta.[85] Under the influence of the *One Hundred Poets* reading of this poem, the location of Tago no Ura was relocated to a place where Fuji could in fact be seen, with *ura* being understood as "beach" rather than "bay."

For our purposes here, however, the important problem is the last line, where *One Hundred Poets* has *furitsutsu* for the original's *furikeru.* The latter simply means "the snow is falling (and has been falling, but I just became able to see it)," while the former's *-tsutsu* indicates the repetition of an action (as in Poem 1's "my sleeve keeps getting wetted repeatedly by the dew"). Yet even if Akahito is walking along the beach, he would not be present long enough to be able to assert that the snow "keeps" falling.

The locus classicus of the *yuki ha furitsutsu* line would seem to be the *Kokinshū,* where it appears three times in the early Spring section, poems 3, 5, and 21 (the last is the source for Poem 15 in the *One Hundred Poets* as well). In the first two usages, the point is that while certain signs of spring have arrived, the snow is still falling. Consequently, as in Jitō's Poem 2, the *One Hundred Poets* version gives a traditional feeling and the standpoint seems to be Teika's rather than Akahito's. In a way this is similar to what we saw in Poem 2 by Jitō: both the falling snow and Akahito's composing of his poem "keep on" happening in a timeless space created by poetic tradition and the canon.

What has been generally disregarded is the third difference between the *Man'yō Shū* and *One Hundred Poets* versions—that is, the replacement of *ma-shiro ni zo* with *shiro-tahe no*. The latter, of course, is the way the poem appears in the *ShinKokinshū*, but this fact does not make its appearance in the *One Hundred Poets* any less surprising. Teika has set himself the task of representing the entire six-hundred-year tradition of Japanese poetry in chronological order in no more than one hundred poems. One might naturally suspect that he would want to show as much of the variety and range of that tradition as possible. Instead he includes as the fourth poem in the collection one that repeats the same pillow word as in the second poem *(shiro-tahe no)* and one that has a grammatical construction identical to the first *(-tsutsu)*.

Nor can this be explained away by suggesting that tradition dictated that this particular poem was Akahito's "signature verse" or most famous poem. In fact, this poem was not included in Kintō's *Sanjūrokunin Sen* or Shunzei's *Korai Fūtei Shō;* nor did Teika vote for its inclusion in the *ShinKokinshū* or include it in many of his own earlier anthologies. Kintō chose *Man'yō Shū* 6:919:

waka no ura ni	In the bay of Waka
shiho michi-kureba	when the tide comes in full
kata wo nami	the lagoons disappear, so
ashi-be wo sashite	toward the banks of reeds
tadzu naki-wataru	the field cranes, crying, cross.

And Shunzei chose this apparent variation on *Man'yō Shū* 10:1883 (*ShinKokinshū* spring 1:104):

momoshiki no	Are the officials
ohomiya-hito ha	of the hundredfold palace
itoma are ya	at leisure, then?
sakura kazashite	They stick cherry blossoms in their hair
kefu mo kurashitsu	and spend the day, again, in play.

Indeed, Teika is in fact weaving an incredibly dense intertextual web, juxtaposing poems so they allude to other, *unincluded* poems. Poems 1, 2, and 4 of the *One Hundred Poets*, together, clearly suggest *Kokinshū* 3:

haru-gasumi	The spring mist,
tateru ya idzuko	where is it that it's rising?
mi-yoshino no	On the hills of Yoshino,
yoshino no yama ni	Fair Yoshino,
yuki ha furitsutsu	the snow keeps falling.

First, the place-name Yoshino is distinctive for frequently appearing with *jūgen* repetition *(mi-yoshino no yoshino no)*.[86] "Where" the mist is rising is clearly in the *One Hundred Poets* Poem 2, and Mount Fuji in Poem 4 takes the place of Mount Yoshino, where the snow is typically spoken of as "always falling" *(furitsutsu)*. If we imagine the poems inscribed on the sliding doors surrounding Teika as he sat in his villa, we get a literal manifestation of the "simultaneous existence" of which T. S. Eliot spoke in "Tradition and the Individual Talent":

> Tradition . . . involves, in the first place, the historical sense, which we may call nearly indispensable to anyone who would continue to be a poet beyond his twenty-fifth year; and the historical sense involves a perception, not only of the pastness of the past, but of its presence; the historical sense compels a man to write not only with his own generation in his bones, but with a feeling that the whole of literature . . . has a simultaneous existence and composes a simultaneous order.[87]

The poet's sleeves are "dampened night by night" *(nuretsutsu);* Mount Kagu is where, "it is said" (since ancient times), they dry robes; the night is long like the long tail of the mountain pheasant; and the snows "keep falling" on Mount Fuji, a mountain whose very name can be taken to mean "undying."[88] All these poems at the beginning of the *One Hundred Poets* can be read to suggest the length, continuity, and eternity of the poetic tradition Teika saw himself inheriting and perpetuating.[89]

CHAPTER 3

Waka in Translation

All the issues we have discussed have an impact on the *One Hundred Poets* as a translated text. Because the *One Hundred Poets* is still used today as a school text for the history of Japanese poetry, the vast majority of Japanese and English editions interpret the poems according to scholars' conclusions about the poems' original meaning, rather than interpreting them either as Teika read them or as they were read in the Edo period, for instance. Even if we are not going to try to read the *One Hundred Poets* as an "integrated sequence," if we are going to read it as one work, rather than as a fortuitous amalgam of one hundred works, we must read it as Teika seems to have conceived it.

The translating of *waka* into English has itself become something of a tradition by now. In fact, the earliest complete translation of the *One Hundred Poets* into English appeared in 1866. To date, some fourteen translations of the entire *One Hundred Poets* (and close to forty selected translations) have appeared in English.[1] It might be a kind of poetic justice, then, to use some of these translations to trace the history of English translation of Japanese classical poetry. In her informative introduction to *Translation Studies,* Susan Bassnett-McGuire defines translation as follows: "What is generally understood as translation involves the rendering of a source language (SL) text into the target language (TL) so as to ensure that (1) the surface meanings of the two will be approximately similar and (2) the structures of the SL will be preserved as closely as possible but not so closely that the TL structures will be seriously distorted."[2] It is the second of these provisos that is particularly problematic when translating poetry. We have already encountered Mark Morris' suggestion of viewing *tanka* as the deformation of a prose sentence. And in fact all modern approaches to the understanding of poetry can be seen as finding their way back to the Russian formalist concept of *ostraneniye,* "making strange," or defamiliarization: the idea that poetry foregrounds the medium rather than the message and that this is done primarily by using language in a different or "strange" way, at any of a variety of levels, as we saw in our discussion of basic *waka* techniques.[3] Certainly it could also be said that much modern poetry in English "distorts" the normal communicative structures of the language.

What the small group of readers of contemporary poetry are willing to be subjected to, however, appears to be far different from what the readers of translated poetry will bear. As Nakai Yoshiyuki has written: "Readability was not a virtue in the tradition of Asian literature, especially not in Japan where students were trained to read the incomprehensible Chinese classics in Japanese and where it was not considered excessive to spend years to understand one page of text. By contrast, readability is a fundamental requirement for modern English-language readers. Even compared to other European linguistic traditions such as French, let alone Japanese, contemporary English stands out for its intolerance of any obscurity in language."[4] If the poetry is difficult in its original language, then English translators tend to simplify it and make it more transparent, always emphasizing its paraphrasable surface meaning. Even without the concept of defamiliarization, there is the fundamental question of whether the translator is trying "to make Virgil speak such English as he would himself have spoken, if he had been born in England, and in this present age,"[5] or to say "what Dante says, and not what the translator imagines he might have said if he had been an Englishman."[6]

To consider these issues, I want to look at a number of translations of one poem from the *One Hundred Poets:* Poem 9, attributed to Ono no Komachi. As this poem is drawn from the *Kokinshū*, we might begin by looking at how it is presented to a modern Japanese audience as exemplified by the Nihon Koten Bungaku Zenshū edition of the *Kokinshū*, edited by Ozawa Masao (Figure 4).[7] A transliteration and translation of the poem will aid our discussion:

hana no iro ha	The color of the flowers
utsurinikeri na	has faded indeed
itadzura ni	in vain
wa ga mi yo ni furu	have I passed through the world
nagame seshi ma ni	while gazing at the falling rains.

The poem appears in the middle register of the page. It is preceded by the poet's name and followed by a list of other early works in which this poem appears—in this case in three different textual lines of the *Komachi Shū*. The transcription of the poem uses historical spelling *(rekishi-teki kana-zukai)*, but the editor has added several ideographs *(kanji)* to make the poem easier for the modern Japanese reader. The *kana* used have also been limited to those employed in modern *hiragana* (in other words, no *hentai-gana* are used.) The poem is surrounded by an upper register of notes and below by a modern translation and commentary. The notes are as follows:

1. [*hana:*] Superficially it is "flower," but underneath it points to the author's looks.
2. *Utsuru* [which in modern Japanese usually means "to move to"]: the fading of the flowers' color. *Na* means the speaker is speaking to herself, overcome with emotion *(Ayuhi Commentary)*. It is attached to the conclusive form *(shūshi-kei)* of inflecting words.
3. [*Wa ga mi yo ni furu:*] My body has gotten old in this world. *Yo ni* can also be taken as an adverb meaning "extremely." *Furu* means "to grow old," to become chronologically late. It is the conclusive form of an r-line *kami-*

nidan verb. (For other examples of *mi ga furu*, see poems 398, 445, 736, 782, and 1065.) If *furu* is taken instead to mean "to pass time," it becomes an h-line *shimo-nidan* verb in the attributive form *(rentai-kei)*, ornamenting "the long rains" of the following verse, which is trite. Here it is a pivot word with "[rain] falls *(furu)*."

4. [*nagame:*] While I was sunk in thought. *Nagame* probably includes the idea that she is gazing at the scenery of her garden; it is also pivoting on "(the spring's) long rains *(naga-ame)*."

Ozawa, the editor, points out some of the ideas implicit in the poem, explains unfamiliar words or usages and also adjudicates between different interpretations. These latter he defends partly through grammatical analysis, partly through comparative examples, and partly through taste. The issue of the editor's taste is even more apparent in the lower register, where a modern Japanese translation of the poem is followed by a short "appreciation":

> Both the color of the flowers and my beauty have already faded away and vanished. When I think about it, my body has completely aged and wasted away in vain. Just as, while I was gazing out, lost in haughty thoughts, the flowers have been battered by the long spring rains and fallen.
>
> The skillfulness of the wording is great, but it is a poem that is completely divided between the second and fourth lines. It is something that has been composed by combining the idea of her beauty, which has come to ruin, with a bit of imagination, and there is a suggestion of deeper feeling. It is a representative work of Komachi, but it was not particularly appreciated up to the time of Shunzei; it was from Teika's time that it began to draw attention.[8]

Ozawa reads the poem as a quiet meditation, not a heartfelt cry of grief. He attributes the poet's loneliness to "haughtiness" *(kyōman)*. Although he is quite explicit about his own estimation of the poem, he also notes the changes in its reputation over the years. Nonetheless, a North American reader would probably find these editorial comments intrusive.

Let us now turn to the most thorough explication of the poem to appear in English to date: Helen McCullough's commentary in her study of the *Kokinshū:*

> KKS 113. Ono no Komachi. Topic unknown

hana no iro wa	Alas! The beauty
utsurinikeri na	of the flowers has faded
itazura ni	and come to nothing,
wa ga mi yo ni furu	while I have watched the rain,
nagame seshi ma ni	lost in melancholy thought.

The compilers have assigned KKS 113 to the Spring category, for reasons the translation attempts to indicate. But Komachi's wordplay poems contain much more than can be conveyed in English paraphrases of the same length. Almost every noun and verb in the poem has at least two potentially relevant meanings:

hana: flower; feminine beauty
iro: color; circumstances, situation; beauty; sexual passion

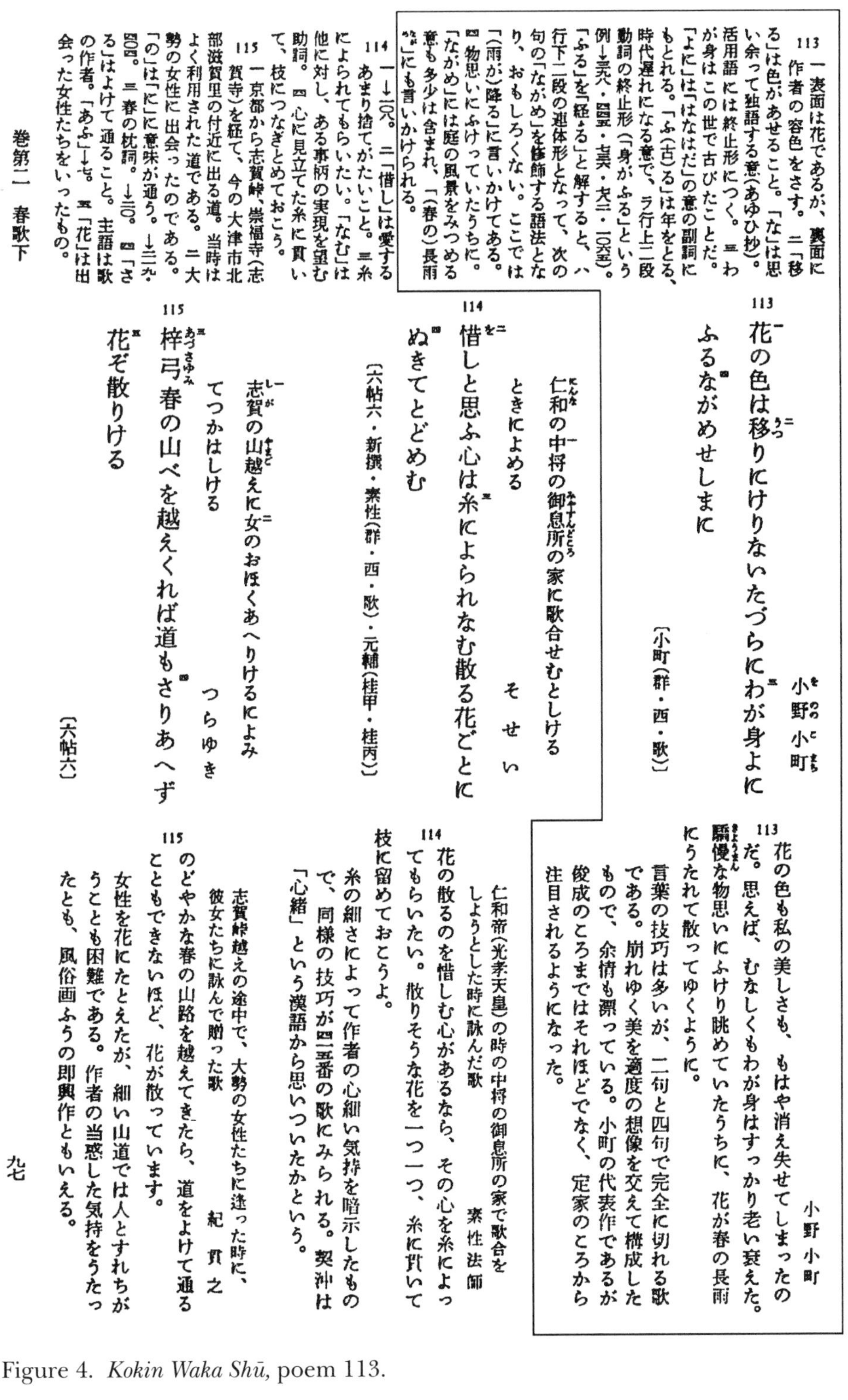

113 花の色は移りにけりないたづらにわが身よにふるながめせしまに

小野小町

〔小町(群・西・歌)〕

114 仁和の中将の御息所の家に歌合せむとしけるときによめる

そせい

惜しと思ふ心は糸によられなむ散る花ごとにぬきてとどめむ

〔六帖六・新撰・素性(群・西・歌)・元輔(桂甲・桂丙)〕

115 志賀の山越えに女のおほくあへりけるによみてつかはしける

つらゆき

梓弓春の山べを越えくれば道もさりあへず花ぞ散りける

〔六帖六〕

113 一 表面は花であるが、裏面に作者の容色をさす。二「移る」は色があせること。「な」は思い余って独語する意(あゆひ抄)。活用語には終止形につく。三 わが身はこの世で古びたことだ。「よに」は「はなはだ」の意の副詞にもとれる。「ふ(古)る」は年をとる、時代遅れになる意で、ラ行上二段動詞の終止形(「身がふる」という例→三六八・四四五・七三六・九六二・一〇六五)。「ふる」を「経る」と解すると、ハ行下二段の連体形となって、次の句の「ながめ」を修飾する語法となり、おもしろくない。ここでは「(雨が)降る」に言いかけてある。四 物思いにふけっていたうちに。「ながめ」には庭の風景をみつめる意も多少は含まれ、「(春の)長雨」にも言いかけられる。

114 一 ↓一〇八。二「惜し」は愛するあまり捨てがたいこと。三 糸によられてもらいたい。「なむ」は他に対し、ある事柄の実現を望む助詞。四 心に見立てた糸に貫いて、枝につなぎとめておこう。

115 一 京都から志賀峠、崇福寺(志賀寺)を経て、今の大津市北部滋賀里の付近に出る道。当時はよく利用された道である。二 大勢の女性に出会ったのである。「の」は「に」に意味が通う。↓三二九・四四四。三 春の枕詞。↓二〇。四「さる」はよけて通ること。主語は歌の作者。「あふ」↓七。五「花」は出会った女性たちをいったもの。

113 花の色も私の美しさも、もはや消え失せてしまったのだ。思えば、むなしくもわが身はすっかり老い衰えた。驕慢な物思いにふけり眺めていたうちに、花が春の長雨にうたれて散ってゆくように。

小野小町

言葉の技巧は多いが、二句と四句で完全に切れる歌である。崩れゆく美を適度の想像を交えて構成したもので、余情も漂っている。小町の代表作であるが俊成のころまではそれほどでなく、定家のころから注目されるようになった。

仁和帝(光孝天皇)の時の中将の御息所の家で歌合をしようとした時に詠んだ歌

素性法師

114 花の散るのを惜しむ心があるなら、その心を糸によってもらいたい。散りそうな花を一つ一つ、糸に貫いて枝に留めておこうよ。

糸の細さによって作者の心細い気持を暗示したもので、同様の技巧が四一五番の歌にみられる。契沖は「心緒」という漢語から思いついたかという。

志賀峠越えの途中で、大勢の女性たちに逢った時に、彼女たちに詠んで贈った歌

紀貫之

115 のどやかな春の山路を越えてきたら、道をよけて通ることもできないほど、花が散っています。

女性を花にたとえたが、細い山道では人とすれちがうことも困難である。作者の当惑した気持をうたったとも、風俗画ふうの即興作ともいえる。

巻第二　春歌下

九七

Figure 4. *Kokin Waka Shū,* poem 113.

utsuru (dictionary form of *utsurinikeri*): scatter; fade; change

yo: world; life; relations between the sexes; with *ni,* extremely

furu: fall (as of rain). The verb can also be construed as the attributive
   form of *fu,* go through life, spend time, or of *furu,* get old.

nagame su (dictionary form of *nagame seshi*): rain a long time; stare pen-
   sively into space

   We can make the poem purely seasonal by treating *wa ga mi* ("I," "my per-
son," "my body") and *yo ni* as a semantically unrelated *jo* introducing *furu:*
"Alas! The flowers have bloomed in vain [i.e., unobserved] and scattered dur-
ing these long rains." Alternatively, we can translate the first three lines as
"The situation as regards my beauty [or youth] is that it has passed to no avail
[i.e., I have been unlucky in love]." Line 4 can become "growing old," "grow-
ing very old," "spending time," or "growing old [growing very old, spending
time] in this relationship," with the speaker as subject. Line 5 can mean
either "while long rains fell" or "while I was lost in pensive thought." There
are, consequently, numerous possible combinations, in most of which *furu*
will function as a kakekotoba and in all of which an associate relationship will
exist between *iro* and *yo.* But to choose a single one is to run the risk of losing
the overtones so beautifully abundant in the original—on the one hand, the
rich Chinese literary associations of the lonely lady in springtime, and on the
other, the implied comparisons between the flowering tree and the woman's
youth (two especially poignant examples of the transitoriness of beauty),
between human sorrow and the dark moods of nature, and between rain and
tears. Komachi's poem is neither metaphorical nor symbolic; rather, it is
wordplay of the highest order, with almost every word functioning to some
extent as engo; and we must interpret it accordingly if we are to avoid viola-
tion of its artistic integrity.[9]

While it is not clear what "artistic integrity" would mean in such a polyvocal
context, McCullough's explication is enormously useful. It is particularly
instructive to compare it with Ozawa. Unlike the Japanese editor, McCullough
does not really discuss grammar, nor does she really reject any interpretation.
She also mentions a Chinese literary subtext that the Japanese editor does not.
Indeed, following the lead of Konishi Jin'ichi, much of McCullough's book,
from which this passage has been drawn, is concerned with how Japanese poets
of the ninth century adapted Chinese poetry to their own native verse.[10] Now
let us see where McCullough's treatment fits into the history of *waka* translation
in English.

Nineteenth-Century Translations

   The first two English translations of the *One Hundred Poets* date from the
nineteenth century. These works were intended for students of the Japanese
language. Due to the nature of this audience, the translator concentrated, as
one put it, on the "process" as much as the "product." In other words, the trans-
lator let the student read over his shoulder and gave as much information
about his sources as possible so that his reader could benefit from his experi-

ence and carry on the project of learning about the alien culture. This approach is most evident in the first translation by Frederick Victor Dickins, published in London in 1866 and entitled *Hyak Nin Is'shiu, or Stanzas by a Century of Poets, Being Japanese Lyrical Odes, Translated into English, with Explanatory Notes, the Text in Japanese and Roman Characters, and a Full Index.* As the title so amply reveals, this is an amazing work. Its title page includes a quote from Horace; its dedication is Latin. Dickins tells which modern commentary he used,[11] includes catalogs of court titles and works mentioned,[12] and offers a completely indexed "vocabulary for students of Japanese."

Although Dickins' preface to this work is a scant five pages long, the contradictions peculiar to orientalist logic can already clearly be seen. He explains that while the poems of the *One Hundred Poets* "are familiar in every Japanese household, high and low, . . . few even among tolerably well-educated persons can understand perfectly the ancient dialect in which these Odes are written." As Edward Said has shown, this division between the glories of an Eastern culture's past and its present degraded state is a typical orientalist move that allows the Western scholar to usurp the alien culture's past.[13] As we shall see, the orientalist stance dovetailed perfectly with the views of the Japanese Nativists *(kokugakusha)* who were devaluing the centuries of Chinese influence in their culture. Likewise, Dickins explains that the poems "are written in the old Yamato language, free from any intermixture of Chinese derivatives, a very noble and harmonious tongue, but much disfigured now by the introduction of . . . ill-sounding Sinico-Japanese syllables" (p. vii).

While Dickins has clearly acquired the Nativists' nostalgia for a "pure" Japanese language, he has not yet apparently become familiar with the entire *kokugaku* program and its devaluation of Heian poetry. Nonetheless, the degraded state of the modern Japanese language is for Dickins evinced by the "crowd of commentaries" surrounding the *One Hundred Poets.* These he explains not as differences of interpretation so much as the inability of modern Japanese to "understand perfectly" the ancient language. Finally, Dickins disclaims any "high poetic merit" for the poems themselves—they are, he says, "but prettily and somewhat cleverly-rendered metrical expressions of pretty but ordinary sentiments." Dickins excuses his translation of these pseudopoems, however, because "they are extremely popular with the Japanese"—those same Japanese who, we were earlier told, cannot really read or understand them.

Dickins' translation of Poem 9 reads:

> Thy love hath passed away from me
> Left desolate, forlorn—
> In winter-rains how wearily
> The summer past I mourn!

In the footnote to this translation Dickins places Komachi in "the early part of the 5th century," an error of four hundred years. His entry for this poem in the appendix, where we are given "literal" versions of the poems along with a romanization, is much fuller, as he glosses *hana no iro* as "lit. 'colour of flowers,' here 'love'"; and "'yo ni furu' is explained as equivalent to 'nan jo katarai suru'" [literally, "for men and women to converse together"]—an explanation that would clearly be meaningless to anyone other than a student of Japanese. Dickins gives a "literal" translation (" 'As to love, it has faded away, alas! for me: the time of my loving intercourse with thee has become the time now of the long rains.' She laments her lover's desertion of her"), noting that this is the interpretation preferred by his commentator, Koromogawa. Nonetheless, Dickins' own interpretation seems, to himself at least, "equally correct," and it is his gloss that he gives in the main body of his translation and repeats yet again in the appendix. While Dickins' several versions translate the pivot words in a variety of ways, he does not remark on them as pivot words at all. And although the poem comes from the Spring books, Dickins sets it in winter, balanced by the "summer past."

The second English translation was originally published in 1899: *Hyakunin-Isshu (Single Songs of a Hundred Poets), Literal Translations into English with Renderings According to the Original Metre by Clay MacCauley, A.M. D.D., Ex Vice-President of the Asiatic Society of Japan: Author of "An Introductory Course in Japanese;" "Japanese Literature"; "The Japanese Landscape"; "Japan's Present Dangers and Need"; etc., etc.* In the preface MacCauley explains that he first became familiar with the *One Hundred Poets* when he saw it being played as a card game at the house of a Japanese friend. A little later he asked one of his students to translate the poems for him. Like Dickins, MacCauley first translated the poems into English metrical quatrains; but upon seeing Dickins' work he determined to attempt "literal translations that should, at the same time, follow the metre of the Japanese originals."

The idea of following the meter of a foreign language when translating seems to be a Romantic one, seen, for instance, in August Wilhelm Schlegel's use of terza rima for his translations of Dante.[14] This adoption of foreign forms has historically been of profound importance to the growth and development of many literatures—without it English would not have Shakespeare's sonnets, originally an alien form. But linguistically, such forms must be adapted to the phonological rules of the target language. Even when the verse forms of two languages are superficially similar, their relationship to their languages and their function within each language's literature will be very different. Writing about iambic poems in both Russian and Czech, Roman Jakobson noted: "The Czech and identically-named Russian meters are so fundamentally different in their structure, function, and effect, that this is merely a case of homonymity. Thus if a Russian iambic poem is translated by Czech iambs (or vice versa), we have, as a matter of fact, a mere convention, and not an approximation of the original."[15] This is even more true for English and Japanese. Japanese verse, as we have seen, is based on quantity—the number of syllables—while English is based on stress. An English reader is likely to notice, not how many syllables a line has, but how many stresses. Thus nothing is to be gained, linguistically speaking, from using a metrical pattern based on an alien language.

Returning to MacCauley, we note that he also records in his preface that he had at his disposal the notes of Ernest Satow "made by him during his reading of the poems in 1872, 'with a very good teacher,' " as well as the German translation of the poems by P. Ehmann, which appeared in the German Society's *Natur und Völkerkunde Ostasiens.* We see, then, the *One Hundred Poets* again being used as a textbook, but this time for foreigners learning Japanese. In fact, MacCauley himself notes in his introduction that the *One Hundred Poets* served as "a text-book for private female education" in the Genroku period (p. xvi). Likewise, for Westerners, "there is no other gathering of Japanese poems so manageable for a single course of study" (p. x).

The first *History of Japanese Literature* was written by W. G. Aston, the former secretary to the British Legation in Tokyo, and published in New York in 1899. Although MacCauley refers to this work in his preface, his attitudes toward the history of Japanese poetry are distinct from Aston's and somewhat anticipate Dickins' writings from 1906. We can perhaps do no better to convey a sense of MacCauley's perspective than to quote in full the first paragraph of his introduction:

> Japanese poetry, regarded as part of the world's literature, is individual and unique. It had its origin in a prehistoric age; its form and context were of its own kind and were practically fixed at the time it first appeared in written speech; and it reached its culminating excellence nearly a thousand years ago. At the present day, when the Japanese people have been released from their long held seclusion from the other peoples of the world, there is the probability that their poetry will come under the same stimulus that has vivified and started forward their sciences and their other modes of mental energy; but, so far, there has appeared little sign of promise for any noteworthy poetic development. A study of Japanese poetry, therefore, carries one far back in the centuries, and into a literary realm that lies as isolated in the world of letters as the Empire of Japan has lain in the world of nations.[16]

The intellectual imperialist assumptions of this passage are conspicuous by their matter-of-factness. Japanese poetry is now "part of the world's [that is, the West's] literature." The Japanese and their literature are portrayed not as victims of colonialism's need for ports and "free trade," but as captives whom the Western powers have released from (presumably feudal) bondage. There is the suggestion, too, that this isolation was somehow coeval with the origins of Japan itself, rather than a relatively recent policy of the last two hundred years. In any event, Japanese poetry is portrayed as a literature without history, frozen in time, and not yet awake to the scientific progress of the West. Curiously, a few contradictory views about Japanese poetry exist side-by-side in MacCauley's introduction. For instance, while we see the suggestion, which will be elevated to a central thesis in Dickins, that the *chōka* of the Nara period "once promised much for the future of Japanese poetry" (pp. ix–x), we are later told that the pinnacle of Japanese poetry was reached with the *ShinKokinshū*—despite the fact that "the frugal and industrious habits of the Nara age by degrees disappeared" during the Heian period, when "the ruling class entered upon a career of high culture, refinement and elegance of life, that passed, however, in the end, into an excess of luxury, debilitating effeminacy and dissipation" (p. xxvi). Here again we see the ideas of Nativist discourse merge with Western fantasies about "oriental decadence."

As for MacCauley's translation (Figure 5), as late as 1967 Brower and Miner were recommending it as the best complete version in English. The left-hand page gives a trot for the student (note, however, the elision of the expletive *na*), while the right gives accurate information about the poet and explains the poem's basic conceit. MacCauley felt obliged to give each poem a title (here "Vanity of Vanities"), while his "metrical" translation falls, to my ear at least, completely flat, in addition to necessitating ungrammatical constructions such as "Color of flower." It should also be noted that unlike more recent translators using this style, such as McCullough, MacCauley does not "correct" his original: the first line of the Japanese has six, not five, syllables, and so too does MacCauley's.

The final work of the orientalist period is Dickins' *Primitive and Mediaeval Japanese Texts,* published by Oxford University Press in 1906. The second volume of this work is a transliteration of all the texts translated in the first volume: 255 pages of romanized text (followed by an 80-page glossary). But it is in Dickins' lengthy introduction that we see the near-complete triumph of Nativist discourse. This Nativist orientation is clear in the very scope of Dickins' project: his choice of translations are all the *chōka* from the *Man'yō Shū,* the "Story of the Wicker-Worker" *(Taketori Monogatari),* and Tsurayuki's preface to the *Kokinshū,* all of which, Dickins claims, "are the earliest of the categories to which they respectively belong, and have been followed, more or less closely, as models, in the production of most of the purely Japanese—as distinct from Japano-Chinese—literature of later times."[17]

In fact, Dickins' translation of the *Man'yō Shū* poems is based on the magnum opus of Kamochi Masazumi (1791–1858): the *Man'yō Shū Kogi Chūshaku,* or *An Annotated Commentary on the Ancient Meaning of the Man'yō Shū.* Kamochi was a *kokugakusha* in Tosa and died before the *Kogi* saw print. However, in 1879

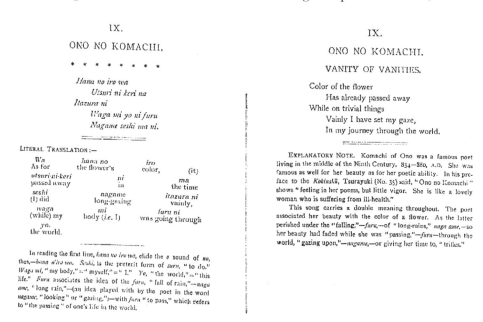

Figure 5. Poem 9: Ono no Komachi. From *Hyakunin-Isshu (Single Songs of a Hundred Poets), Literal Translations into English with Renderings According to the Original Metre* by Clay MacCauley (1899).

it was published in a 124-volume de luxe edition by the new Imperial Press, under the direction of the Imperial Household Agency, with a dedicatory inscription by Imperial Prince Taruhito. While Dickins identifies Kamochi with "the rather unreal Shinto revivalism of the eighteenth century" (p. xlviii), he makes no explicit connection between it and the imperial restoration of the Meiji period. Instead he translates verbatim, and without comment, Kamochi's Nativist defense of the *Man'yō Shū*, which includes the following:

> Thus the ancient spirit of Dai Nippon was fully alive in the *Manyōshiu* age. But from that period onwards a gradual change took place. Foreign ideas more and more predominated, and the poetic impulse found a less and less perfect expression in accordance with the pure primitive genius of the people. The poems of the *Kokinshiu* (Songs Old and New), and of later collections, departed in an increasing degree from the temper and form of the *Manyōshiu*, to which we must look if we wish to know what was the true spirit of the earlier time.
>
> What was that spirit? . . . It is in the sixty-second of the long lays of the *Manyōshiu* that we meet with the following pithy description of the true duty of a Japanese:

> > Heavenwards mounting,
> > thou might'st thine own will follow,
> > but earth thou dwell'st on
> > where ay the Sovran ruleth,
> > and sun and moon 'neath,
> > as far and wide as hover
> > the clouds of heaven,
> > down to the tract so scanty
> > the toad's realm is,
> > wherever sun or moon shines,
> > allwhere the land
> > our Sovran's sway obeyeth.

> The philosophy of China teaches that any one who is sufficiently virtuous may become the chief of State. Not only is this not the Japanese ideal, but our doctrine is directly opposed to it. The Mikado is Sovran because he is Sovran by divine right, not by divine appointment, nor by the grace of God, but by right of divine descent, and his people owe him loyalty because of his descent, not because they appreciate his virtue. Such is the true motive of all Japanese feeling and action. In their exposition and praise of this motive our poets show their patriotism; patriotism is loyalty to the Sovran, for Sovran and country are one. So it has ever been from the beginning of our land—the Sovran is born one and the people are his servants. This is the unique character of the land and people of Japan. [p. xcvii]

It is fascinating that Dickins, even after the Sino-Japanese War of 1894–1895 and the Russo-Japanese War of 1904–1905, saw no threat in this ideology.[18] In fact, not only does he quote it in extenso but he has completely internalized it and founds his entire discussion of the history of Japanese literature on it.

Thus the introduction of the Chinese language is held responsible for the stunting of the poetic growth of the Japanese languages. Indeed:

> The development of the language in the direction of imagery or rhetorical expression was almost destroyed. One can neither be witty nor pathetic in the current language of educated Japan, save so far as recourse is had to the remains of Old Japanese.... The modern literature of Japan, as such, is nearly worthless. Not a line of power or beauty, it is scarcely too much to say, has been penned since the last *monogatari* was written [late twelfth century?]. [pp. xxv–xxvi]

Without such interference, Dickins suggests, "Old Japanese" might have developed into a true "literature":

> With an enlarged vocabulary, a somewhat extended use of pronouns, and a more frequent expression of the subject of the sentence, Japanese might have become a vehicle of literary expression not much less inferior to Greek than, in many respects, such a language as French is to the tongue of Homer and Sophocles. [p. xxvii]

That it did not so develop is due to the "progressive sinicization" of the language. With the *Man'yō Shū,* "the production of true poetry ended in Old Japan" (p. xxxi).

Nonetheless, Dickins' book includes "Short Lays from the *Hiyakunin Isshiu,*" one of which is a new rendition of the Komachi verse:

> The tint of flower,
> alas, how soon it fadeth!
> how soon, too, beauty
> the rain and storm of time,
> as pass the years by, wither.

Now, as indicated by McCullough's "purely seasonal" translation of this poem, despite its pivot words and word associations, it is grammatically fairly simple and, ignoring its double (or triple) meanings, can superficially be translated in a rather straightforward fashion. Dickins here has adopted MacCauley's idea of translating in the "original meter," but he has done more violence to the English grammar than can be explained away by the needs of his metrical scheme. Offhand one suspects that what has been called Dickins' "almost compulsive inversion"[19] is due to the influence of William Morris (1834–1896) and his "translations," such as that from the Icelandic. In any event, Dickins' 1906 translation can be seen as an example of what has been called Victorian "archaicizing."[20]

The Popularization of Japanese Poetry in Europe and America

The fate of MacCauley's translation exemplifies the transition from the orientalist period of translation to the more popular. In 1917 his translation was reprinted by Kelly & Walsh of Yokohama, Shanghai, Hong Kong, and Singapore. In the prefatory note to the new edition, MacCauley observes that his work "has received an unexpectedly cordial consideration from scholars, not only in America and in England, but in other countries, especially in Japan" and that "in recent years, I have been often asked to give the whole work a reprint in popular form"—hence the publication by Kelly & Walsh, who seem to be an early example of English presses set up in Japan for the expatriate Anglophone population.

In fact, popular translations started appearing as early as 1909, which saw William N. Porter's *A Hundred Verses from Old Japan*.[21] Porter makes the popular, and popularizing, nature of his translation very clear in his introduction:

> [The translator] makes no claim his verses have any merit as English poetry; nor . . . does he claim that his translation is in all cases the correct one. In two or three instances the original has been purposely toned down somewhat, to suit English ideas. He has, however, tried to reproduce these Verses from Old Japan in such a way, that a few of the many, who are now unfamiliar with the subject, may feel sufficient interest in them to study a more scholarly translation, such as . . . Professor MacCauley's literal translation . . . and may thus learn to appreciate a branch of Japanese art which has been far too much neglected up to the present.

In other words, Porter is out to inspire area specialists—men, like himself, who might be of service to the political and commercial interests of the British Empire. While one might be tempted to concur with Porter's own assessment of his verse, he is of course being disingenuous. Yet his aims are not unreasonable: his audience was upper-class English gentlemen among whom he could readily expect to find some who, their appetites whetted, would indeed turn to "more scholarly" translations and, ultimately, to the original itself, just as they might have done with Portuguese, Italian, Persian, or Chinese, having been trained in an educational system that had already taught them Latin and Greek. Such an approach may be condemned as "élitism . . . where the translator appears as a skillful merchant offering exotic wares to the discerning few,"[22] but too quick a dismissal will overlook the important role such "exotic wares" had in interesting future merchants, missionaries, and colonial administrators.

Porter is also very clear about his choice of form: "A *tanka* verse has five lines and thirty-one syllables, arranged thus: 5–7–5–7–7; as this is an unusual metre in our ears, I have adopted for the translation a five-lined verse of 8–6–8–6–6 metre, with the second, fourth, and fifth lines rhyming, in the hopes of retaining at least some resemblance to the original form, while making the sound more familiar to English readers" (pp. vii–viii). Unlike Dickins' 1866 translation, Porter attempts to use one consistent verse form for all the *tanka*. His choice of a form that is appropriate to English prosody is linguistically valid (except that he has reversed the alternation of long and short lines, making the two shortest lines of the original the two longest in his verse). Nonetheless, adoption of target language prosody is no guarantee of success, as we see in Porter's translation:

> The blossom's tint is washed away
>   By heavy showers of rain;
> My charms, which once I prized so much,
>   Are also on the wane—
> Both bloomed, alas!, in vain.

While McCullough may be right in stating that this poem is not metaphorical, grammatically there is no direct connection between the exclamation of the first two lines and the rest of the poem, except the temporal: "the color of the flowers has gone!, while I was . . ." As in Dickins' 1906 translation, Porter creates a direct causal relationship (it is the rains that have "washed away" the flowers' color) and makes explicit what is implicit in the original (the equating of the flowers' color with the woman's beauty).

By the first decade of the twentieth century, Asian responses to the West had found support in the Western world itself: Swami Vivekananda had established the Vedanta Society in the United States after his success at the World's Parliament of Religions in Chicago in 1893; Okakura Tenshin had inaugurated an aesthetic pan-Asianism with his *Ideals of the East, with Special Reference to the Art of Japan* (1903); and Nitobe Inazō had recast *bushidō* in the form of Christian chivalry (*Bushido: The Soul of Japan*, 1905). We should not be surprised, then, to see a book such as Clara Walsh's *The Master-Singers of Japan* (1910) appear in the "Wisdom of the East" series, whose objectives are spelled out by the editors:

> The object of the Editors of this series is a very definite one. They desire above all things that, in their humble way, these books shall be the ambassadors of good-will and understanding between East and West—the old world of Thought and the new of Action. . . . They are confident that a deeper knowledge of Oriental thought may help to build a revival of that true spirit of Charity which neither despises nor fears the nations of another creed and colour.[23]

Walsh's translations are reworkings of the "literal" translations of Dickins and Aston—and as in a game of "telephone," we can see the results move farther and farther away from the original verse:

> Swift fade the hues of hill and wold,
> Glories of Spring and Fall depart,
> More evanescent still, behold
> The fading blossoms of the heart!

"Hill and wold" suggest something between Wordsworth and Anglo-Saxon; Dickins' "winter-rains" and "summer past" have turned into "Spring and Fall"; and, finally, the flowers have been made into a metaphor for a fickle lover, rather than for the poet's own beauty.

Translations Before the Pacific War

Due to the influence of Impressionism and Whistler, English poets of the early twentieth century were taken most with the shorter haiku, rather than

with the *chōka* or *tanka*. By the 1920s, however, new translations of *tanka* appear.
First came Arthur Waley's *Japanese Verse: The "Uta,"* which manages to be schol-
arly, exotic, artistic, and popular all at the same time. Though Waley includes
poems from the *One Hundred Poets,* he declares the collection to be "so selected
as to display the least pleasing feature of Japanese poetry."[24] The earliest com-
plete English translation of the first imperial anthology, the *Kokinshū,* appears
to have been by T. Wakameda: *Early Japanese Poets: Complete Translation of the Kok-
inshiu.* Its introduction, by Ichiro Kobayashi, helps us to situate it both within
the intellectual traditions of Japan and in the history of Japan's response to the
West. Kobayashi starts by dating the *Kokinshū* to "the fifth year of Yengi in the
[reign] of the Emperor Daigo, viz, in the year 905 A.D., and fifteen years after
the founding of Oxford University."

Although Kobayashi's topic is the *Kokinshū,* he in fact spends a full one-
half of his essay on the *Man'yō Shū* and the causes for the decline of the *chōka*
form. The *chōka* form is of central interest to him because a "shorter poem will
be sufficient to express a bit of thought, but many words will be needed to con-
vey complicated thoughts" (p. xvi). Kobayashi attributes the decline of the
chōka to four causes. The first three are the "indolent atmosphere" caused by
the Fujiwara usurpation of imperial power, the attendant "corruption" of man-
ners, and the "progress" of prose. While Kobayashi attributes the refinement of
prose to the influence of Chinese, it is this same Chinese, and the popularity of
writing verse in that language, that is the fourth cause of the decline of *chōka.*
In the context of such a thesis, one is not surprised to see the name of the
famous Nativist scholar Kamo no Mabuchi, who, we are told, "took pains to
revive the longer poem."

In fact, Kobayashi presents the standard Meiji state ideology of the con-
nection between the emperor, poetry, and the "Japanese spirit." We are told
that the "Emperor Daigo was an excellent versifier—nay, and many other Japa-
nese emperors excelled in poetry," including the first emperor, Jimmu, who
composed a poem when he had "subjugated the natives in the neighbourhood"
of his capital at Kashiwara. That poem, "handed down to posterity . . . was com-
posed in 662 B.C." The Nativist *(kokugaku)* approach to *waka* is clearly set forth
in the remainder of his paragraph:

> In such ancient days, of course, they used no special art in making poems, but
> sang what they actually thought. So these poems have little or no poetical
> merit, but the elegancy of national spirits can be traced up to such an ancient
> age. In days of yore, there was little strict distinction between the high and the
> low. Some emperors were of so plebeian taste that when they went out hunt-
> ing they often talked in verse with peasants. When Chinese learning was
> imported in abundance and people imitated Chinese institutions, trouble-
> some ceremonies arose by degrees, and the distinction between high and low
> began to assert itself. In the Heian period the emperors and court officials
> were called "kumo-no-uwabito" or "men above clouds." This was contrary to
> the intrinsic national traits of Japan, which were simplicity and homeliness,
> with both of which the emperors treated their people generally. These good
> qualities later revived among the samurai: the so-called spirit of the samurai

was merely the revival of the national traits of the Japanese nation. It will be most interesting to study these national traits by means of Japanese poetry.

Ancient Japan is depicted here as a communal democracy where king and subject speak to each other in verse. The role of the snake in this Garden of Eden is played by Chinese, and *bushidō,* the "way of the warrior," is seen as a return to traditional values of the Japanese people. This role for the samurai dovetails nicely with the portrayal of Jinmu as an imperialistic sovereign who subjugates "the natives" of a land that is, after all, Japan. Nonetheless, the contradiction inherent in Kobayashi's introduction is readily apparent, and it is clear that he would much rather be writing an introduction to a translation of the *Man'yō Shū,* a task accomplished by the governmental Nippon Gakujutsu Shinkōkai (Japan Society for the Promotion of Scientific Research) in 1940.[25]

In Wakameda's *Early Japanese Poets,* the *tanka* are translated into a variety of English metrical forms. While other poems are rendered into heroic couplets, Komachi is given in five lines of tetrameter, an attempt to reflect the five-line *tanka* form:

> The colours of the blossoms fair
> Are faded now and gone for e'er,
> While the long rain is falling on;
> The beauties of my looks are gone
> Now that I grow old, left alone.

The rhyme scheme here is rather confusing: one suspects that we are to see "gone" and "alone" as rhymes, making the final two lines function something like the final couplet in a Shakespearean sonnet. Yet "gone" in fact rhymes with "on," disrupting the division between the Japanese hemistiches, which would have suggested, if anything, the same end rhyme for the first three lines (fair, e'er, . . .). In terms of content, the idea that the poet has spent her time brooding over her love affairs is missing, and while it may be fair to extrapolate "left alone" from "in vain, uselessly" *(itadzura ni),* one suspects rather an influence from the Komachi legend, found especially in *nō* plays, that she lived to an extremely old age, poor and alone.

It is again in the 1920s that the image of the emperor as poet reemerges—this time, rather than singing songs of martial victory, instead composing paeans to the new, post–World War I international peace. Thus, only two years after the Washington Conference of 1921, where Japan reluctantly agreed "to abide by a status quo of defenses in the Pacific and reaffirmed the 'Open Door' policy in China,"[26] we find Curtis Hidden Page, an American translator, concluding his *Japanese Poetry: An Historical Essay,* with an assessment of contemporary *tanka* that begins: "From the beginning of the twentieth century a new note has become dominant in many of the tanka—the note of a thoroughly modern social consciousness; and strangely enough, this note is heard first and oftenest from the Court." Poems by the Emperor Meiji, Page suggests, "may help us to understand his patient statesmanship, which finally succeeded in bringing Japan, politically, socially and industrially, as well as in the arts, to a leading place among nations."[27] Page includes poems by Empress Dowager Shōken, by the reigning Emperor Taishō, and finally one, with "an almost Homeric expression," by the Crown Prince and Regent Hirohito:

> Vast spaces of the untilled noble sea
>> Lying serene beneath the morning sun,
> Would that all nations of the world might be
>> Like you forever, peaceful and at one.

Page concludes: "If these poems truly represent—and I feel sure they do—the ideals and character of the Japanese people today, as summed up in their present rulers, then there certainly is no need to fear from them any unprovoked attack on the peace of the world" (p. 169).

Obviously Page had missed the following poem by Empress Dowager Shōken, published in English translation in 1919 by Wadagaki Kenji, a professor at Tokyo Imperial University:

asashi tote	The still and silent water of a stream,
seki ka ha afururu	Shallow as it may be, does swell and rise
midzu-gaha no	And flows o'er the land, if abruptly stemmed:
kokoro ha tami no	Likewise with the most peaceful People, too.[28]
kokoro narikeri	

Page's translations are chiefly revisions of work by earlier scholars.[29] His version (p. 47) reads:

FINALITY
(By Ono no Komachi)

> The fairest flowers most quickly fall,
>> Beaten with rain . . .
>> And yet more vain,
> My beauty fadeth once for all
>> And will not bloom again.

Of the *One Hundred Poets,* Page says: "I know nothing so artificial, even in the French Renaissance or in Elizabethan England" (p. 59). Although he compares the collection at its best with Emily Dickinson and the *Greek Anthology,* he claims that "I find it the least valuable poetically among the more important anthologies; for the poems in it were chosen in an epoch when poetic taste had grown excessively artificial, long after the great early period of Japanese poetry had passed its height" (p. 53)—an assessment with which the next generation, raised on T. S. Eliot's rehabilitation of the Metaphysicals, would surely take issue.

In fact, while Wakameda was still promoting *chōka* as the greatest example of Japanese verse, Waley had dismissed the form as "an unsuccessful experiment." Waley explains: "The Japanese poets quickly realized that they had no genius for extended composition." Thus the very qualities that Dickins had identified as the pernicious influence of Chinese on the original genius of the Japanese language and the poetry of the *Man'yō Shū* were now identified as the main attraction of Asian poetry. Dickins complained that "Chinese is a skeletal tongue, . . . brief without being terse, for the reader is left largely to guess the relations between the ideas expressed, and depending very much upon the visual comprehension of the characters. . . . A Chinese poem, in a word, is rather a collection of notes for a poem, or a telegraphic summary of one, than a completed work."[30] But to Ezra Pound and the other Imagists, this "telegraphic" quality was a great attraction, and the visual nature of Chinese characters would be hailed in Pound and Fenollosa's *The Chinese Written Character as a Medium for Poetry.*[31]

The 1930s are remarkable for the emergence of a type we might call the Japanese professional academic translator. The motivation behind this change is clearly expressed in the preface to the Nippon Gakujutsu Shinkōkai translation of the *Man'yō Shū:*

> The importance of rendering Japanese classics into foreign languages as a means of acquainting the world with the cultural and spiritual background of Japan cannot be overemphasized. Few Japanese, however, have ventured into this field, the work so far having been largely undertaken by foreigners. It is in view of this regrettable fact that the Japanese Classics Translation Committee was appointed in 1934. [p. ix]

The two most conspicuous Japanese translators of the period are Miyamori Asatarō and Honda Heihachirō, both of whom translated several volumes of Japanese literature. What is most distinctive about their translations, however, is that their choice of texts is clearly dictated by native constructions of the canon and not necessarily by foreign interest. Thus Miyamori's two-volume *Masterpieces of Japanese Poetry Ancient and Modern* is devoted almost exclusively to *tanka.* Moreover, his introduction gives a history of Japanese poetry that traces the continuous tradition of this form from its beginnings through to the "Tōkyō Period." Nonetheless, Miyamori states that he has chosen poems that he "thought suitable for introducing abroad . . . which serve to illustrate national traits."[32] And while these volumes are "intended principally for foreign readers who have no knowledge of Japanese language and literature," Miyamori includes not only the poems printed in Japanese but also a romanization, both "for those foreign readers who have some knowledge of Japanese literature, and also for Japanese students of English" (p. ii). Moreover, he gives a paraphrase of the poem, a brief discussion of its pivot words, and an alternate translation—that by Wakameda (quoted earlier).

Another interwar Japanese edition is H. H. Honda's 1938 translation:

> As in the long and weary rain
>   The hue of flowers is all gone,
> So is my young grace spent in vain
>   In these long years I lived alone.[33]

Honda has used a far more natural meter (iambic tetrameter) than Porter and an *a/b/a/b* rhyme that is far less intrusively bouncy than Porter's *x/a/x/a/a.* Yet Honda too has created a causal link between the rain and the flowers' vanishing color and has turned the metaphor into an explicit simile ("As in . . . , so . . ."). Further, it is not that the speaker has lived alone—on the contrary, she has wasted time in many affairs that have all ended in disappointment. Honda's translation presents us with a shy wallflower—caused, one suspects, by the exigencies of the rhyme. Fortunately, English readers no longer demand that poetry rhyme.

But it was not just assumptions about the nature of verse that led Honda to use rhyme. The *One Hundred Poets* is perhaps best known to the Japanese through a card game based on it: a reader sings out the first half of the poem while the competitors try to find the second half, written on cards spread before them. Honda's intention was to make his translation of these poems amenable to the same sort of game in English. The *a/b/a/b* rhyme scheme and the regular meter thus aid in identification and memorization. If we take this "translation" of the Japanese card game to be Honda's primary aim, then we may say that he has succeeded. In fact, Honda's rhyme scheme makes the card game perhaps easier than it would be in Japanese, which has no rhyme. Nonetheless, Honda's primary motivation in translating the *One Hundred Poets* would seem to have been because it was there—in the canon. Here we see a tendency, first manifested by Wakameda and still apparent in such scholars as McCullough, to translate in toto—that is, complete works rather than selections. Thus Honda produced complete translations of the *Man'yō Shū*, the *ShinKokinshū,* and the *Sanka Shū,* among others.

Translations After the Pacific War

Translations that appeared immediately after the Pacific War present themselves, not surprisingly, primarily as aesthetic objects rather than scholarly works or nationalist tracts. The change is perhaps symbolized by a work called *Introduction to Classic Japanese Literature* (1948). While this work clearly follows in the footsteps of the 1940 *Man'yō Shū* translation, the latter was produced by a group called the "Japanese Classics Translation Committee" of the Japan Society for the Promotion of Scientific Research (Nippon Gakujutsu Shinkōkai), whereas the new work is by the Kokusai Bunka Shinkōkai, or "Society for International Cultural Relations." The new committee's translation of the Komachi poem reads:

> Long continuing rain
> The beauty of the flowers
>   Has painfully marred;
> So has age stolen on me,
> As I brooded pensively.

According to the committee, Komachi's poems "strike the elegant note characteristic of a poetess, showing purity of feeling." Moreover, contrary to the assessment of prewar translators, "there is no unnatural artificiality in these poems, but a spontaneity with no conscious effort at artistic expression."[34] It is interesting to note that, among Japanese, the scholars responsible for presenting Japanese literature to the English reading public have changed from professors of English, such as Miyamori, to scholars of classical Japanese, such as Sasaki Nobutsuna. Many of these scholars, in turn, were conservative *tanka* poets. In fact, the *tanka* form was closely associated with "patriotism" during the war years—indeed, many Japanese after the war held *tanka* to be complicit in the militarism that led to the nation's devastation.[35] It is against this background that the committee was attempting to rehabilitate the *tanka* tradition.

The primarily poetic approach is also evident in Kenneth Yasuda's translation of the *One Hundred Poets,* entitled *Poem Card,* which appeared with a foreword by the English poet and longtime resident of Japan, Edmund Blunden:[36]

> Ah, the sweet and gay
> > hues are faded from the flowers
> > in the long night-rain
> While I squandered time away,
> > gazing on this world in vain.[37]

Here the upper hemistich *(kami no ku)* and the lower are distinguished through indentation. Yasuda has kept the Japanese syllable count but has added a rhyme scheme of *a/x/b/a/b,* which enforces on the poem a kind of rhythm. Although Yasuda later became a professor of East Asian languages and cultures at Indiana University, his translation is clearly for the general reader: it includes no notes or introduction, not even an explanation of its title. Thus one must conclude that the inclusion of the Hepburn transcription is to allow the reader to attempt a recitation of the poem, while the inclusion of the poem in *kanji* and *kana* is meant to be largely decorative and visually intriguing.

In Yasuda's translation we hear a trace of what Miner calls Blunden's "sturdily Georgian" style as well as the neo-Metaphysical poetry influenced by Eliot. In the following decades, it was the Beats who attempted to recast Japanese poetry in their own image. One of the major figures of this movement was Kenneth Rexroth, who in 1955 published his *One Hundred Poems from the Japanese.* While this is not a translation of the *One Hundred Poets,* we do find Komachi's verse included:

> As certain as color
> Passes from the petal,
> Irrevocable as flesh,
> The gazing eye falls through the world.

Rexroth describes his process of translation as follows:

> A few of these translations date back many years, one to my adolescence (it happens to be perfectly literal) so there is a certain amount of inconsistency in degree of literalness. Over the years the relationship to the Japanese poem was always a personal and creative one, and in some cases the mood of the moment led me to develop slightly certain implicits or suppress certain obvious explicits. Hardly ever are there many more syllables in the English poem than in the Japanese original, and in ninety out of a hundred examples the translation is as accurate and brief as I could manage. I have never tried to explain away the poem, to translate the elusive into the obvious, as has been, unfortunately, so often the case with translators from the Japanese in the past.[38]

It would appear that Rexroth's translation of Komachi is one of the ten out of a hundred. It would certainly be wrong to believe that he has simply "developed slightly certain implicits or suppressed certain obvious explicits"—his rendition is entirely "a personal and creative one."

Indeed, there are questions about Rexroth's competence in classical Japanese and what commentaries or informants he used. His "retranslation" of this poem in 1977, however, was done with the assistance of a Japanese cotranslator and may legitimately be called a translation:

> The colors of the flowers fade
> as the long rains fall,
> as lost in thought,
> I grow older.[39]

The repetition of "as" seems, at first glance, awkward. Yet upon closer inspection one sees its purpose: Rexroth is not translating *ma ni* twice, rather the first "as" serves as a conjunction, while the second introduces the simile and serves as a conjunction simultaneously. In other words, Rexroth has made "as" a kind of pivot word. Further, looking at both his productions, certain characteristics become clear. Rexroth avoids the past tense and, in the first poem, eliminates the personal pronoun, even though both a past tense marker *(shi)* and a pronoun *(wa ga mi)* are clearly in the original. What we are seeing here, I suspect, is the influence of Zen-colored translations of haiku: Japanese poetry (and culture) are in this period valued for their simplicity and their Zen-inspired impersonality and tranquility—qualities largely introduced by Rexroth into his renditions of Komachi's poem.

This second translation appears in a collection entitled *The Burning Heart: Women Poets of Japan,* a publication that augurs a significant postwar development in the reception of Komachi. The postwar period in Japan saw the rise in importance of the term *joryū bungaku,* or "women's-style literature." While the term *joryū bunshi,* or "feminine literati," dates from the Taisho period,[40] it was the marked increase in the publication of women's writing after the Pacific War that gave currency to the categorization of "women's literature." This concept was in turn read back into the classical past, and scholarly works on *ōchō joryū bungaku,* or "court-centered women's-style literature," written by male scholars, became increasingly prevalent. The importance of this categorization was linked to a general feminization of the literary canon—perhaps a backlash in response to the stress on the masculine and martial during the war years.

On the other side of the Pacific, the Beat movement was coinciding with the so-called sexual revolution and the American occupation of Japan. This conjunction encouraged the ever-present orientalist tendency of feminizing/eroticizing the "Orient," so that white men's fascination with Asian women could now be more freely displayed, under the aegis of sexual "revolution." The results of this trend are apparent in Rexroth's *One Hundred More Poems from the Japanese* (1976) and its prominent inclusion, along with examples by the famous Meiji poet Yosano Akiko, of several poems by a woman identified only as "Marichiko":

> I hold your head tight
> Between my thighs and press

Against your mouth and
Float away forever in
An orchid boat
On the River of Heaven.

Anata no atama wo watashi no
Mata ni shikkari hasami
Anata no kuchi ni watashio [sic] *tsuyoku*
Oshitsukeru to, watashi wa
Ran no hana no fune ni notte
Tokoshie ni Tengoku no Kawa wo
Tadayotte yuku.[41]

In *The Burning Heart,* however, Rexroth has moved from an orientalist pruri-
ence to the cause of feminism: poems by Marichiko are replaced by a useful
essay on "The Women Poets of Japan—A Brief Survey" and the inclusion of
many modern poets from Hayashi Fumiko (1904–1951) to Kanai Mieko (b.
1947). The growing importance of feminism on both sides of the Pacific has
seen a steady stream of books aimed at (re-)constructing a specifically femi-
nine literary canon. Dissertations have been written about Komachi, and we
find the *hana no iro* poem in *The Ink Dark Moon: Love Poems by Ono no Komachi
and Izumi Shikibu, Women of the Ancient Court of Japan,* translated by Jane Hirsh-
feld with Mariko Aratani, the preface of which declares: "In the history of
world literature there is only one Golden Age in which women writers were
the predominant geniuses"—the Heian period. Hirshfeld and Aratani's trans-
lation reads:

While watching
the long rains falling on this world
my heart, too, fades
with the color
of the spring flowers.[42]

One notes that this translation conveys no sense that the poet is mourning the
loss of her physical beauty; apparently it is her affections that have faded.

Let us return, however, to the more immediate postwar era. The year 1955
saw the appearance of the "first anthology of Japanese literature," Donald
Keene's *Anthology of Japanese Literature from the Earliest Era to Mid-Nineteenth Cen-
tury.* Almost all the translators in this work were trained by the military during
the war—indeed, some have ungenerously called the result the "GHQ
approach to Japanese literary texts,"[43] that is, an exclusive concern with *what* is
said rather than how it is said. Certainly Keene's translation of Komachi's poem
is rather prosaic:

Hana no iro wa	The flowers withered,
Utsurinikeri na	Their color faded away,
Itazura ni	While meaninglessly
Wa ga mi yo ni furu	I spent my days in the world
Nagame seshi ma ni	And the long rains were falling.[44]

Keene's principles are clearly stated in his preface: works that translate into "interesting and enjoyable" English have been chosen while those that defy "artistic translation" have been excluded. Nonetheless, Keene has aimed for a representative sampling of all periods and genres. As the translations are "literary and not literal," Keene tells us that "puns, allusions, repetitions, and incommunicable stylistic fripperies have also been discarded." Finally, he says, "extracts have been made with the intent always of presenting the work in as favorable a light as possible, even though it might at times be fairer if the book were presented as rather uneven." Keene's anthology is clearly a proselytizing text, out to make Japan and its culture better known to the general public of its vanquishers. And in all fairness, Keene specifically refers to other works for those of a more scholarly inclination. Keene's anthology is meant to have "as wide an appeal as possible."

Japanese Court Poetry, by Brower and Miner, is clearly intended for the academic reader. The writing and publication of this book can be seen not only as part of the postwar boom in Japanese studies (enabled by a number of wartime-trained intelligence officers entering academia), but also part of the rise in this period of comparative literature and what was called world (or general) literature.[45] Earl Miner, in particular, was suited to such a moment, having published scholarly work both on Japanese poetry and on English poets such as Dryden. It is to be expected, then, that Brower and Miner's translation of Komachi's poem should embody the kind of ambiguity and paradox prized by New Criticism:

> The color of these flowers
> No longer has allure, and I am left
> To ponder unavailingly
> The desire that my beauty once aroused
> Before it fell in this long rain of time.

Brower and Miner comment:

> The "color of the flowers" *(hana no iro)* is clearly a symbol for "my physical being" *(wa ga mi),* and the natural imagery is sustained to the end by pivot-words. *Furu* means both to "grow old" and to "fall" as rain. *Nagame* means to "gaze" or to "think abstractedly," and "long rain." By establishing a symbol and developing it at length by means of pivot-words, Komachi has managed to suggest—in the very act of statement—the relation between nature and herself. Her view of nature and her attitude of what might be called passionately resigned despair are part of one brilliant poetic whole.[46]

In the original the flowers have faded *while* the speaker gazed pensively; but in Brower and Miner's rendition the speaker is "left / to ponder unavailingly" *after* the flowers have faded. The treatment of the pivot word is interesting: it is translated twice and seems to risk losing the idea that the speaker is gazing at the rain, but her gazing is instead suggested by the use of the index "this." The exclamation has been eliminated, suggesting a more contemplative poem. And while the diction of the original is completely unremarkable, the construction "my beauty . . . fell" seems unnatural. (Does beauty "fall"?) Generally we see Brower and Miner approaching the poem through the Western poetic concept of symbol, and their reading puts a premium on the "sustained" development of that "symbol" into a "poetic whole." The poem is clearly thematized as being about "self and nature," and that relationship is found to be, paradoxically, "passionately resigned." One can well imagine how such a reading of Komachi's poem would make it possible to include it in the company of such other "world" poets as Marvell.

Accordingly, translated Japanese poetry was also appearing in trade publications for the educated "common reader"—that is, the college graduate of the new comparative and world literature courses. One sure sign of this trend is the appearance of *The Penguin Book of Japanese Verse* (1964), the very year the summer Olympics were held in Tokyo. Here again it is instructive to quote the foreword of the general editor of the series—in this case from the selected verse of Baudelaire, not the Japanese volume:

> The purpose of these Penguin books of verse in the chief European languages is to make a fair selection of the world's finest poetry available to readers who could not, but for the translations at the foot of each page, approach it without dictionaries and a slow plodding from line to line. They offer, even to those with fair linguistic knowledge, the readiest introduction to each country's lyrical inheritance, and a sound base from which to make further explorations.
>
> But these editions are not intended only for those with a command of languages. They should appeal also to the adventurous who, for sheer love of poetry, will attack a poem in a tongue almost unknown to them, guided only by their previous reading and some Latin or French. In this way, if they are willing to start with a careful word-for-word comparison, they will soon dispense with the English, and read a poem by Petrarch, Campanella, or Montale, by Garcilaso, Gongora, or Lorca, straight through. Even German poetry can be approached in this unorthodox way. Something will, of course, always be lost, but not so much as will be gained.
>
> The selections in each book have been made by the various editors alone. But all alike reflect contemporary trends in taste, and include only poetry that can be read for pleasure. No specimens have been included merely for their historical interest, or to represent some particular school or phase of literary history.[47]

There is much of interest here. One wonders what a "fair" selection is, for instance. And note how quickly we move from "the chief European languages" to "the world's finest poetry." The metaphors of conquest are conspicuous: "the adventurous . . . a command of languages . . . attack a poem . . . guided only by. . . ." The editor's assumptions about his readers' education speak of a time with a very different market than that educated after the curricular reforms of the 1970s. Most interesting, perhaps, is the boldly anachronistic approach that insists on "contemporary trends of taste"—not only must Virgil speak like an Englishman, but if he doesn't, we will ignore what he has to say. It is ironic that it was this very insistence of the "contemporary" that led to the demand for "relevance" in school curricula and the eradication of the editor's readership.

In any event, unlike the volumes of French—or even German!—poetry, the Penguin volume of Japanese verse does not include any version of the originals. The Komachi verse reads:

> The lustre of the flowers
> Has faded and passed,
> While on idle things
> I have spent my body
> In the world's long rains.[48]

Here again *utsuri-keri* is translated twice, as if the translators could not make up their minds which way to render it—literally as "passed" or, as it is glossed by Ariyoshi, as "faded" *(aseru)*. The adverb *itadzura ni* is turned into a noun phrase, "idle things," and *yo* and *nagame* are conflated into "the world's long rains." Finally, the phrase "I have spent my body" is very strange and not a little awkward; it might be justified if it were attempting to duplicate something in the original, but in fact it is at complete variance with *wa ga mi . . . furu* ("I/my body grows old" or "I spent my time"). All this may be the result of the process by which the Japanologist Bownas and the poet Thwaite produced their text: as explained in the preface, Bownas did a literal, nonliterary translation of the poems and then "passed them on" to Thwaite to turn them into English poetry. To what extent Bownas checked the final product is not mentioned.

We have already seen Helen McCullough's most recent translation, with which we began this chapter. It was preceded in 1968 by an earlier version in her translation of the *Tales of Ise*. Let us put her two versions side by side:

Alas! The cherry blossoms	Alas! The beauty
Have flowered in vain and faded	of the flowers has faded
During these long rains	and come to nothing,
Interminable as my own	while I have watched the rain,
Melancholy reveries.[49]	lost in melancholy thought.

McCullough's new translation (the right-hand version) adopts the 5–7–5–7–7 format as well as a staggered lineation that visually indicates the "length" of the lines—as the difference in metrical length would be imperceptible to an English reader otherwise. Gone too is the capitalization of each line: now there is a greater sense of continuity. The specification of "cherry," added in the first translation, has been removed from the second. Gone too is the "have flowered"; in its place is the far more linguistically defensible "has faded" and "come to nothing"—a plausible rendering for *itadzura ni*. The fourth line manages only six syllables (though visually seven if we count "watched" as two) and uses the compound past ("have watched") to represent *nagame seshi*, literally, "I did gaze." Moreover, in both translations McCullough has felt obliged to add explicit melancholy, though the melancholy of the poem would certainly seem clear enough. Nonetheless, McCullough's most recent translation seems a sound rendition.

In fact, the translations of the 1980s and 1990s have typically appeared in books designed for college classes or published by university presses. Let us compare McCullough's new translation of the Komachi verse (the right-hand version just quoted) with that by Laurel Rasplica Rodd and Mary Catherine Henkenius:

113 * Topic unknown

hana no iro wa	the colors of the
utsurinikeri na	blossoms have faded and passed
itazura ni	as heedlessly I
waga mi yo ni furu	squandered my days in pensive
nagame seshi ma ni	gazing and the long rains fell

Ono no Komachi

The complex rhetoric, including two kakekotoba, "furu" (to grow old; to rain) and "nagame" (long rains, pensive gazing), and the comparison of the beauty of the blossoms and of youth mark this as a poem by Komachi, the famous poetess of love and longing.[50]

The translation by McCullough quoted at the beginning of this chapter does not in fact come from her complete translation of the *Kokinshū* but from her book-length study of *Kokinshū* period poetry, *Brocade by Night.* Her separate translation of the *Kokinshū* provides no notes or discussion of this poem. From this aspect, Rodd and Henkenius' translation, as a complete translation of the *Kokinshū*, is far preferable to McCullough's, which seems to derive from the mistaken notion that the poetry should be allowed to "speak for itself" and can somehow magically do this without the aid of notes. All this relies on a concept of translation as the transparent medium of a stable and fully recoverable meaning—what we might call the logocentrism of translation.[51] For other poems McCullough does include some notes, but for Komachi she has presumably decided that her reader will also consult her companion volume. The question is whether, having read *Brocade by Night,* any reader would find it worthwhile to read the bare translation from cover to cover. And this in turn raises further questions: is there any sense in translating large anthologies as such, or should they be presented in some kind of interpretive or narrative context?

Nonetheless, the 1980s and 1990s have seen the production of more of these bare anthologies of Japanese poetry—texts that learned professors presumably elaborate in lecture classes after students have read the text uncomprehendingly in preparation as homework. The major textbook of Japanese poetry has been, until recently, *From the Country of Eight Islands* by Burton Watson and Hiroaki Sato. This text includes two translations of the Komachi verse—one by each of the translators. Watson's reads:

The beauty of the flowers faded—
no one cared—
and I watched myself
grow old in the world
as the long rains were falling.[52]

Although a longtime resident of Japan, Watson is best known for his translations of Chinese texts, and certainly his rendering of Komachi has the feel of the more simply declarative and uninflected quality one might associate with Chinese poetry. While the speaker of the original poem is startled by what has happened to the flowers while she was not looking, Watson has a simple declarative sentence: "the beauty of the flowers faded." "No one cared" seems an unnecessary extrapolation for "in vain." Most critical, however, is the addition of a kind of visual reflexivity: "I watched myself." Given all the contemporary discussion of the "gaze," a student in a women's studies class, for instance, might be led to believe there was something in this poem that simply is not there. In the original, it is the flowers that have faded "as the long rains were falling," not as the poet was watching herself grow old.

Sato's poem is perhaps one of the most graphically distinctive to appear:

> The flower's color has passed, I gazed on it in vain, while I was trying to
> live my life[53]

Sato's translation reflects his conviction that a *tanka* is a one-line poem.[54] Sato seems to confuse the prosody of poetry with its graphic lineation. Many scholars have rebutted his thesis, but he remains unconvinced. Having used his translations in the classroom, I can second William LaFleur's assertion that "a one-line poem—at least in Western languages [or, better, in Western-language translations]—is willy nilly at the same time a no-line poem."[55] Beyond the issue of lineation, Sato's translation seems weak: the Komachi poem does not say that the poet gazed at the color but intransitively gazed "out"; nor is it clear where Sato got the idea of "trying to live my life."

In the Watson and Sato textbook there are no footnotes, no comments, just the bare translation. Nor is there any Japanese text. Worst of all, there is no Japanese bibliography, and thus the student has no idea where the translators got the poems or what edition they used. Yet as Eric Rutledge has stated: "the only way to determine the accuracy of a translation is to compare it with the edition on which it is based."[56] With no Japanese text, and no bibliographic source listed, a student would have to scan the entire *Man'yō Shū*, for instance, to try to find the original of an anonymous poem such as:

> Let me die now,
> love,
> for once in love
> not for one night, not one day
> of peace is mine![57]

The same criticism must unfortunately be leveled at the most recent college textbook: Steven Carter's *Traditional Japanese Poetry*. While the companion volume by McCullough, *Classical Japanese Prose,* does in fact note which Japanese editions she used, Carter lists his source for the *Man'yō Shū* and all the imperial anthologies as the *Shinpen Kokka Taikan,* an index-like collection that is entirely unannotated. Is one to believe that this is the only text Carter relied on? Carter's translation reads:

> Behold my flower:
> its beauty wasted away
>   on idle concerns
> that have kept me gazing out
>   as the time coursed by with the rains.[58]

Again no notes about pivot words. The direct address to the reader ("Behold") is startling. While *hana* in the poem clearly refers to cherry blossoms, Carter's singular "flower" suggests something larger, such as a rose—certainly he has made the identification between the poet and the flower quite explicit, almost sexual. "Idle concerns," too, seems unfortunate, suggesting there were other concerns the poet should have been more profitably engaged in. Yet, as we shall see, the conceit of this poem is that of a woman abandoned by her lover or lovers—she has played the game of love "in vain," and lost, by being left alone. There is little suggestion that she is contemplating any other sort of game, as Carter's translation might lead one to think. To Carter's credit, the line "its beauty wasted away" does give the impression of a woman exhausted by waiting for a lover who does not come, and the final line is an innovative solution to the pivot word *furu*.

If the textbooks currently on the market give little reason for optimism about the state of translation, the revolution of desktop publishing may offer new hope. Perhaps the reduced costs of such technology will, like cable television, allow a wider range of publishing options targeted to more specific audiences. This hope is suggested by the appearance of *Ono no Komachi: Poems, Stories, Nō Plays,* by the family of Roy, Nicholas, and Rebecca Teele.[59] This book seems to be coming out of the cross-Pacific interest in *nō* theater and performance. The Teele children are active in *nō* theater and teaching in Japan, and the main body of this text is translations of the *nō* plays about Komachi. The translations are scholarly but accessible; those of the plays include diagrams of stage movements for both the Kanze and Kongō schools of performance. While the poem translations are essentially background to the plays, they are thorough and pay particular attention to intertextuality with Chinese literature:

113.

Theme unknown. Ono no Komachi

hana no iro wa	The color of the blossoms
utsuri ni keri na	has faded
itazura ni	vainly
waga mi yo ni furu	I age through the rains of the world,
nageme seshi ma ni	watching in melancholy.

Notes: Line one: *iro* means "color" but is at the same time a word for "passion." Lines four and five contain two *kakekotoba, furu* (meaning both "to rain" and "to become old") and *nagame* (meaning "to look at a scene," "to feel melancholy," and "long rain").

Use of convention or allusion: This poem makes use of the convention of comparing the brevity of a woman's beauty to that of a flower. Here are two examples of the use of this convention in Chinese poetry. First, the fourth of a series of six poems titled "Thoughts in the Apartments," by Hsü Kan (171–218 A.D.), from Chapter One of the *Yü-t'ai hsin-yung.*

> Sad, sad the season is exhausted,
> fragrant flowers wither, then fragment.

> I heave a very long sigh . . .
> There was a time you soothed my feelings.
> Turning it over and over in my mind, I can't sleep.
> Long nights . . . why are they so drawn out?
> I step, walk, rise up and go out the door and
> look up at three stars joined together.
> Disturbed by the fact that what I want to happen won't
> I weep silent tears like a bubbling spring.

Second, the relative [*sic*] lines from a poem by the early T'ang poet Liu Hsi-i (ca. 651–78 A.D.; *Complete T'ang Poems,* Bk 82:886–7).

> The girls of Lo-yang have beautiful faces,
> they sit and watch the flowers fall, and heave long sighs.[60]

In the translation of the Japanese poem, as mentioned earlier in regard to McCullough's renditions, *nagame* does not in fact mean "to feel melancholy," but simply "to be sunk in thought." As the translated subtext makes clear, the speaker is clearly unhappy, but whether this is melancholia is another matter. Regrettably the original Chinese texts are not included, even though the Japanese is. This lapse is especially frustrating as the Teele translation of the Hsü Kan verse differs significantly from Anne Birrell's more polished version.[61]

Historicizing the Lyric

Having examined and criticized previous translations and translators, it is now incumbent on me to explain my own choices in translating. Let us begin with the issue of "what" to translate. I have chosen to translate the *Hyakunin Isshu* because its poems are arguably some of the most influential in Japanese literature. Although Steven Carter has included a complete translation of the *Hyakunin Isshu* in his anthology, *Traditional Japanese Poetry,* the present effort differs from Carter's in one important respect: I have attempted to translate the poems according to a historically specific interpretation—that is, to translate them to reflect our understanding of how Teika himself read the poems. This strategy has led me to include discussions of how the individual poems have been interpreted in different historical periods. The explanation of such interpretations has, in turn, led me to discuss specific words and phrases of the poems—in other words, to provide notes and annotations.

The assumptions behind this approach are, first, that there are no native speakers of classical Japanese poetry. As will be seen in the main body of this work, there is almost no interpretation of a poem so seemingly outlandish that it has not been suggested and defended by someone over the course of the last six hundred years. Probably no Japanese reader since Teika's days has simply sat down and read the *Hyakunin Isshu.* Rather, it has been studied, analyzed, taught, and learned, and it is only after such a process that readers could feel they had appreciated the poem. It seems strange to me that we should assume that the reader of a translation can somehow dispense with such aids. Moreover, for hundreds of years readers of Japanese poetry have been approaching the *One Hundred Poets* as a puzzle: what does the poem mean, and why has it been so highly esteemed? Translators and their readers approach the text with the same questions—we should not assume that the text is transparent, its meaning clear and fixed. But to appreciate how different interpretations have arisen, the translation must maintain as many of the ambiguities of the text as possible.

These considerations are especially true with respect to the Komachi poem. Mark Morris has repeatedly insisted on the "mythic" nature of Ono no Komachi: "Ono no Komachi has been for eleven-hundred years an effect produced by a handful of ninth-century waka texts, mediated through later tales and plays." He argues that insistence on personal lyricism is an adaptation of *waka* "to certain Western conventions of interpretation at the cost, however, of philological frankness about the alien and intractable differences of the waka form."[62] These "intractable differences" also fight against attempts to read the *One Hundred Poets* as an integrated sequence. Since at least the fifteenth century, readers have come to the text one poem at a time, studying and mastering one before moving on to the next. While it may be unrealistic to ask the nonacademic reader of the translations to devote similar time and effort, it is nonetheless necessary for the translator to convey some of the complexities of the poem and not suggest that its meaning is wholly contained in a fluent paraphrase.

Nor, I think, should a translator be interested in producing "the definitive translation." As I hope the foregoing survey has shown, every period finds something new, something of itself, in the poem. A definitive translation is a murdering translation, one that claims there is nothing more to be said. The translations in Part Two, then, are offered as just one more in what we have seen is a long chain of receptions of the *One Hundred Poets.*

CHAPTER 4

The Poem-Picture Tradition

One of the aspects closely associated with the popularization and diffusion of the *One Hundred Poets* is the inclusion of pictures in the printed editions of the Edo period. These pictures are essentially of two types: pictures related to the poets (that is, imaginary portraits of the poets, called *kasen-e*) and pictures that seem to relate in some fashion to the poems themselves.

Imaginary Poet-Portraits *(Kasen-e)*

Kasen-e can be traced back to the late twelfth century, concurrent with a more "realistic" style of secular portraiture that arose at the time and that is associated with the name of Fujiwara no Takanobu (1142–1205), a half-brother of Teika. The earliest mention of a group of portraits of thirty-six poets is found in a "record" of an imaginary poetry contest, the *Jishō Sanjūrokunin Uta-awase*, dating probably from 1178–1179. In the preface to this collection, conjectured to have been written by Kamo no Shigeyasu (1119–1191), we read:

> I persuaded thirty-six poets, monks and laymen, who have been skilled at Japanese poetry in recent days, to allow me to copy down ten of their outstanding compositions. Moreover, as these poets are all persons of great sensitivity, I drew their portraits as mementos for later generations. Limiting the number of poets to thirty-six emulates Lord Kintō and the thirty-six verses, and the selection of three hundred and sixty poems recalls Tsurayuki's [*Shinsen waka*] and represents the three hundred sixty days.[1]

From another anthology firmly attributed to Shigeyasu, the *Tsuki Mōde Waka Shū*, we learn that a few years later he "drew the forms of poets on partitions, and for each one, he requested the poets to submit a *shikishi* [square of decorative paper] inscribed with their compositions."[2] The idea of making imaginary portraits of poets from the past, rather than portraits of contemporaries, seems to have been born in the circle that included Teika's son and heir, Tame'ie, and Takanobu's son, Nobuzane (1176?–1266?), to whose portraits the new term *nise-e*, or "resemblance pictures," was applied.[3] Predictably the thirty-six poets chosen were those of Kintō's selection, and it is such sets that are properly called *kasen-e.* The oldest extant version of these sets that can be traced back to the style of Nobuzane is the so-called Satake version dating from the 1240s at the earliest.[4] A very different iconographic style is represented by the Narikane version dating from the second half of the thirteenth century.[5] Maribeth Graybill has argued that the Narikane version shows the influence of illustrated versions of Emperor GoToba's *Jidai Fudō Uta-awase* (Poetry Competition Between Different Eras), the earliest extant examples of which have traditionally been attributed to Tame'ie.[6] In any event, virtually all Kamakura-period *kasen-e* are attributed to lineages stemming from either Takanobu or Teika,[7] and it is the Narikane version that was used as the model for all Muromachi (1333–1573) and Edo-period versions.[8] In the Muromachi period, *kasen-e* painted on plaques as votive offerings, called *hengaku kasen-e,* began appearing; the earliest extant example dates from the 1430s.[9] Graybill suggests that a *Thirty-Six Poets* set made for the shrine of Taga Taisha in 1569, attributable on stylistic grounds to the Kanō school, represents the compositional formula that also became the standard for Edo-period portraits of the *One Hundred Poets.*[10]

Pictorializations of Poems and the *Uta-e* Tradition

While the origins and lineages of poet-portraits can be fairly clearly mapped out, the case for pictorializations of the poems themselves is much less clear and has been almost entirely ignored by Japanese scholars. In fact, there is no general agreement on what even to call these pictures: some speak of them as "illustrations" *(sashi-e),* others as "pictures of when the poem was made" *(sakka bamen no zu).* It is my contention that these pictures are pictorializations of the poems—that is, visual equivalents of the verbal texts. As early as the tenth century such pictures were called *uta-e,* or "poem-pictures."

Screen Poems and Poem-Pictures

The most common pairing of poem and picture in the Heian period seems to have been *byōbu-uta,* or "screen poems"—poems inscribed on squares of decorative paper *(shikishi)* that were then pasted onto the screens themselves as cartouches. The best extant example of such a screen and its cartouches is the *Jingoji Landscape Screen (Jingoji Senzui Byōbu)* dating from the thirteenth century but believed to represent Heian-period styles.[11]

Scholars still debate whether in general it was the screens that were painted to match the poems, the poems written to match the screens, or both created separately and later joined by a third hand. It is clear, however, that in at least some cases poets would base their poems on wordplay suggested by images in preexisting screens. Elsewhere I have labeled this technique "visual pivot words" *(shikaku-teki kake-kotoba),*[12] a good example of which is a poem by Ōshikōchi no Mitsune (fl. 898–922), written for a screen depicting activities of the twelve months *(tsukinami byōbu)* belonging to Emperor Daigo (r. 897–930):

The Day of the Rat [First Month]

netaki ware	If only I, who am so vexed,
ne no bi no matsu ni	were the pines of the Day of the Rat!
naramashi wo	Ah, I am envious—
ana urayamashi	For they are pulled up and taken along
hito ni hikaruru[13]	by people, but I am not.

Here the screen undoubtedly depicted courtiers pulling up young pine saplings in the snow, an annual new year observance. Mitsune puns on the word *hikaruru,* which means "to be pulled up" but also "to be taken along"—the speaker of the poem complains that he was not taken along to the festivities.

This technique of visual punning moved from large-scale screens to smaller-sized drawings, and poet/calligraphers began to compose poems and illustrate them simultaneously or, at least, compose poems with their possible pictorialization in mind. The best example comes from *The Collected Poems of Murasaki Shikibu (Murasaki Shikibu Shū):*

Uta-we ni, ama no shiho yaku kata wo kakite, kori-tsumitaru nageki no moto ni kakite, kaheshi-yaru

As a poem-picture, I drew the figure of a fisherman burning off seawater for salt, and just below the pile of cut-up firewood I wrote the following poem and sent it back in reply:

yomo no umi ni	To the seas' four corners
shiho yaku ama ni	the fisherman, who burns off
kokoro kara	seawater for salt,
yaku to ha kakaru	says he "burns" with all his heart,
nageki wo ya tsumu	but isn't it he himself who stokes the fire like this?[14]

Here the pivot word is *nageki,* which can mean both "firewood" and "griefs" or "sighs." The poem also includes the deictic, or index, *kakaru,* "like this," actually pointing to the drawing that was meant to accompany it. Thus poem and picture work together as an integrated whole.

The surviving literary evidence suggests that *uta-e* gradually moved from being pictures designed in conjunction with original poems and tended instead toward pictorializations of well-known classic verses. The best surviving visual example of this is the *Kanfugen-kyō Sasshi-e* (ca. 1120) (Figure 6).[15] A transcription of *Kokinshū* 6 (Winter): 331 by Tsurayuki also appears in this booklet:

fuyu-gomori	Winter seclusion:
omohi-kakenu wo	unexpectedly
ko no ma yori	from between the trees
hana to zo miru made	snow falls so that
yuki zo furikeru	it looks like blossoms.

On the left of the painting is a single plum tree in blossom, despite the poem's "from between the trees." On the right, five figures are gathered around a sunken brazier. The man is asleep and covered to his nose with a cloak; the woman in the background too seems oblivious to the scene outside. The woman on the left, however, is turning her head to look behind her. The relatively larger size of the woman on the right suggests that we are meant to take her as the speaker of the poem. There are no pivot words in this poem by Tsurayuki, yet evidence from several Heian-period texts suggests that the painter, much like earlier *byōbu-uta* poets, has seized on a potential pivot word, *ko*, which can mean both "tree," as in *"ko no ma yori,"* and "child," such as the one depicted next to the fire. In other words, both the image of the tree and particularly the image of the child are serving as visual pivot words in this pictorialization of Tsurayuki's poem.

We find literary evidence of such visual pivot words being used by painters to take advantage of potential *kake-kotoba* in the "Trefoil Knots" *(Agemaki)* chapter of *The Tale of Genji*. Prince Niou is visiting his older sister:

> On a quiet day of heavy winter rains he went to call on his sister, the First Princess. She and a few attendants had been looking over a collection of paintings. He addressed her through a curtain. . . . By way of distraction he picked up several of the pictures that lay scattered about. They had been painted, and very skillfully, to appeal to womanly tastes. There was, for instance, a lovelorn gentleman, and there was a tasteful mountain villa, and there were a

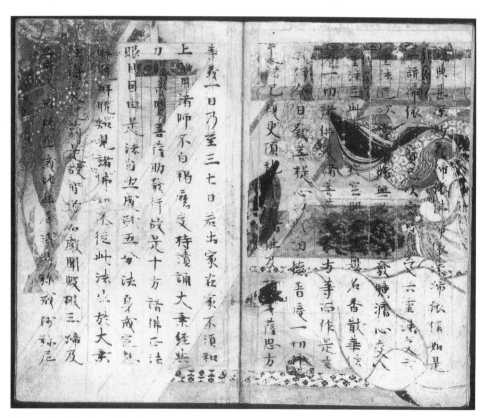

Figure 6. *Kanfugen-kyō Sasshi-e.* Ca. 1120. Booklet (eight sheets), pigments on decorated paper. 18.5 × 11.5 cm.

number of other scenes that seemed to have interested the artists. . . . The illustration for the scene from *Tales of Ise* in which the hero gives his sister a koto lesson brought him closer to the curtain.

"'A pity indeed if the grasses so sweet, so inviting,'" he whispered, and one may wonder what he had in mind. "I gather that in those days brother and sister did not have to talk through curtains."[16]

Niou's quotation of a line from the poem clearly indicates that the episode illustrated is number forty-nine. In the *Teika-bon* text of the *Tales of Ise* this episode reads:

Once a man, stirred by the beauty of his younger sister, composed this poem:

Ura wakami	How regrettable it is
Neyoge ni miyuru	That someone else
Waka-kusa wo	Will tie up
Hito no musubamu	The young grass
Koto wo shi zo omofu	So fresh and good for sleeping.

She replied,

Hatsu-kusa no	Why do you speak of me
Nado medzurashiki	In words novel as the first
Koto no ha zo	Grasses of spring?
Ura naku mono wo	Have I not always loved you
Omohikeru kana	Quite without reserve?[17]

The problem here is that the *Teika-bon* version of this episode makes no mention of a koto lesson. There is a variant text (the *Saifukuji-bon*), however, in which the line reads: *ito okashiki kin wo shirabekeru wo mite* ("seeing his sister playing on a very beautiful *kin*").[18] Accordingly, many scholars assume that this was the version known to Murasaki Shikibu.[19] After a thorough examination of the textual history of this lineage, however, Katagiri Yōichi concludes that this variant is of later origin and was, in fact, inspired by *The Tale of Genji*. In other words, some later editor, noticing the discrepancy between the extant *Tales of Ise* and the description in the *Genji*, concluded that the original text had been altered, and accordingly rewrote the episode to bring it in line with the *Genji*.[20] But assuming for the sake of argument that Murasaki Shikibu was referring to a type of illustration of this scene that did in fact exist in her day, how do we explain it?

The answer lies in the man's poem, where the words *koto* and *wo* appear. Both these words can function as pivot words: *koto* meaning both "matter" and the musical instrument of the same name; *wo* serving as an object marker and also meaning "string" (of an instrument). Katagiri further suggests that with such a meaning in mind, the phrase *neyoge* ("having the appearance of being good for sleeping"), which already suggests the pivot word *ne* ("sleep"/"root") in association with the grasses, would become triply layered since *ne* can also mean "sound" (of the koto). Thus the main point to be drawn from the *Tales of Ise* example is that artists used visual pivot words in their pictorializations of poems even when, in fact, the words so pictorialized did not originally function as pivot words in the poems. Were *uta-e* merely "illustrations" of poems? I think not: the evidence suggests that *uta-e* were, rather, pictorializations *(kaigaka)* of poems and moreover were thought of as such by the Japanese of the period. "Pictorialization," of course, suggests there is some basic equivalency or identity perceived between word and picture—that is, a verbal artifact has been transformed into a picture, and yet both visual and verbal artifact represent the same poem.

Scholars have long been searching for something distinctive in *uta-e*, something unique that would justify the existence of a specific term for one subgroup of poem/picture combination in a culture where such combination was ubiquitous. To this point it may seem that visual pivot words provide the unique criterion by which we may identify *uta-e*. Yet this clearly is not the case—not only are there *uta-e* that do not use visual pivot words but visual punning itself was rampant, not only in *byōbu-uta*, but in poems for *suhama* (decorative landscape trays, something like modern bonsai) and any other gift or object to which a poem was tied or attached. A notable example appears in the *Hatsune*, or "The First Warbler," chapter of *The Tale of Genji:*

> From the Northern Mansion were given bearded baskets and food-boxes apparently gathered especially for the occasion. The superb [artificial] *uguisu* that had moved onto the pine branch must also have meant something:

> | *toshi tsuki wo* | Let she who had the pine |
> | *matsu ni hikarete* | pulled from her, while time passed, |
> | *furu hito ni* | oh, let her hear today |
> | *kefu uguhisu no* | the very first notes |
> | *hatsune kikaseyo*[21] | of the *uguisu!* |

Here the visual pivot word is not in a picture but is the artificial pine branch and bird, which represent two pivot words: *matsu*, meaning both "pine (tree)" and "to pine," and *hatsune*, meaning not only "first sound" but also "first day of spring."

It would be tempting to take another term from the Heian vocabulary, *monogatari-e*, or "tale-picture," and imagine it as the natural contrastive term to *uta-e*—that is, "narrative pictures" in contrast to "lyrical pictures," the metonymic in contrast to the metaphoric.[22] Our present understanding of *monogatari-e* (and another term, *e-monogatari*), however, is not firm enough to permit this assumption.[23] Nonetheless, contemporary documents clearly show that the people of the time saw at least two distinct modes of pictorialization, one of which was *uta-e*. What the other was labeled we cannot say, but we get a crucial idea of the differences between these two modes from "The Former Lady Reikeiden Enshi's Poem-Picture Contest" *(Eishō Gonen Shigatsu Nijūrokunichi Saki no Reikeiden no Nyōgo Enshi no Uta-e Awase)* of 1050. The passage that concerns us reads as follows:

> On the evening of the eleventh of the Third Month, as the moonlight was striking the bamboo blinds, several ladies-in-waiting were in attendance, and while talking about things, everyone said: "Rather than passing the spring

days in idleness, if only we could present some unusual contest to Her Ladyship! . . . Now, not to mention Okura's—what do they say it is called?—*The Forest of Verse,*[24] we are not even interested in the old *Man'yō Shu.*[25] But the *Kokinshū* and *Gosenshū!* Even if we read them repeatedly *(kuri-kaesu),* like the spinning *(kuri)* of the threads of the willows, we never tire of them and they deeply color our affections, dyed like a brocade of autumn leaves." So saying, they divided into two teams, Left and Right. "Since the painting of poem-pictures is commonplace, we should [instead] paint the topic *(dai)* and poet *(yomi-bito).* If one takes the headnote, the poem is difficult to paint, and in choosing the poem, the headnote is not expressed.[26]

In other words, rather than attempting to pictorialize the poem itself—as was usually the case with *uta-e* and as we see in the *Kanfugen-kyō Sasshi-e*—Lady Reikeiden's ladies are proposing to pictorialize the headnote and poet, that is, the purported circumstances of the poem's composition: its occasion. We can understand such a difference in method when we look at the *Kanfugen-kyō Sasshi-e.* The headnote to this poem in the *Kokinshū* reads: "Composed on snow that had fallen on trees. Tsurayuki" *(yuki no ki ni furi-kakarerikeru wo yomeru).* Were one to paint this topic and its poet, one might imagine a male courtier, Tsurayuki, gazing at snow on trees. What we have instead is a female speaker for the poem, the pictorialization of the metaphor of the poem (it is the flowers that are depicted on the tree, not snow), and verbal motivation through the inclusion of the visual pivot word *ko,* that is, the child, even though *ko* does not function as a pivot word in this poem. In contrast to this pictorialization of the poem itself, the other mode—the one that Lady Reikeiden's ladies are proposing—would pictorialize the occasion when the poem was composed: its circumstance of composition. An example of this mode is the *Ashi-de Kokin Waka Shūgire,* traditionally attributed to Murasaki Shikibu's contemporary, Fujiwara no Kintō (966–1041) (Figure 7).[27] The poem, by Archbishop Henjō (816–890), which begins with the third line from the right, reads:[28]

*a*sa midori	It twists together
ito yori kakete	leafy threads of tender green
shira-tsuyu wo	and fashions jewels
*tama ni **nu**keru ha*	by piercing clear, white, dewdrops—
*haru **no ya**nagi ka*	the willow in springtime.[29]

Underneath the ornamental script we see a pagoda and temple. The *ashi-de,* or "reed-hand," birds seem to alight on a willow, and gazing at them from beneath the tree is a monk. The headnote to this poem in the *Kokinshū* reads: "Composed on the willows near the Great Western Temple. Archbishop Henjō *(Saidaiji no hotori no yanagi wo yomeru. Sōjō Henjō).*" What is depicted is clearly the same Henjō, composing his poem while looking at the willow in front of the temple. This, then, is a pictorialized headnote, an illustration of the moment of composition. This mode, therefore, would depict the poem's circumstances of composition—the who and the when—while *uta-e* represents an attempt at pictorialization of the poem itself.

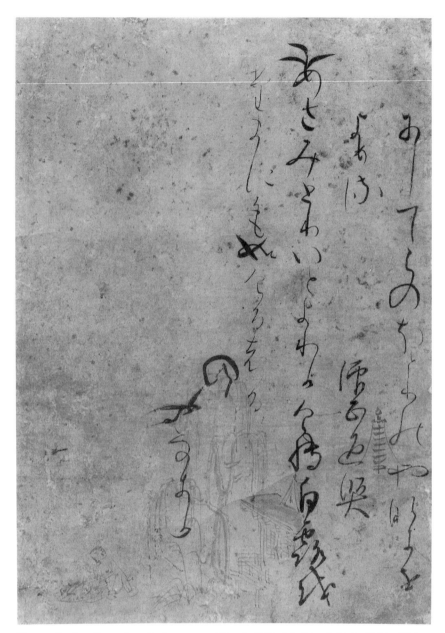

Figure 7. Attributed to Fujiwara no Kintō (966–1041), *Ashi-de Kokin Waka Shū-gire*. Ink on paper, mounted as a hanging scroll. 18.3 × 13 cm.

Teika and Poem-Pictures

The *One Hundred Poets,* as noted earlier, is believed to have been originally created to decorate the sliding doors of Teika's villa at Ogura. Teika inscribed the poems on cartouches, some of which survive to this day, and they were presumably affixed to the sliding doors. It seems highly likely that these doors were covered with pictures, but the question remains whether these pictures were portraits of the poets, pictorializations of their poems, or both. In his *Sui'a Ganmoku*, the Nijō disciple Ton'a (1289–1372) writes that "*nise-e* of one hundred immortal poets from ancient to modern times were painted on the sliding doors of [Teika's] villa at Saga; each was accompanied by one poem."[30] If this is true, then the original *One Hundred Poets* would have resembled Shigeyasu's portraits of contemporary poets with cartouches of their poems done on partitions.

But there is also the possibility that the cartouches of the *One Hundred Poets* were attached to pictorializations of the poems, rather than to portraits of the poets. We find one use of the term *uta-e* in Teika's diary, when he was called upon to find or compose poems on the topic of "snow on bamboo." These poems were to be attached to a picture of the same "to make it a poem-picture."[31] In other words, the picture was of a poetic "topic" *(dai)* or conception. Teika was also called upon to compose poems for other screens and sliding doors: poems for screens of famous places *(meisho-e)* that decorated the Saishō Shitennō-In temple commissioned by Retired Emperor GoToba in 1207; poems for a twelve-month screen made for the arrival of Shunshi, the future consort of Emperor GoHorikawa, at court in 1229; and poems on birds and flowers of the twelve months for screens in the private residence of Cloistered Prince Dōjo in 1214.[32]

Whether the pictures in Teika's villa represented pictorializations of the poems or not, the term *uta-e* seems to die out during the Kamakura period and there is no evidence for any transmission of *One Hundred Poets* poem-pictures through the Muromachi and Momoyama periods. Today the earliest extant examples of *One Hundred Poets* pictorializations, like portraits of the One Hundred Poets themselves, are from the Edo period.

Edo-Period Pictorializations of the *One Hundred Poets*

We should take a moment to consider some of the reasons for the new interest in the *One Hundred Poets* in the Edo period. We have seen that the Taga Taisha *hengaku kasen-e* can be attributed to a Kanō school artist, the school officially patronized by military leaders from the 1480s through the entire span of the Tokugawa period, and that production of images of the Thirty-Six Poetic Immortals was continuous throughout the medieval period. A fruitful way of approaching speculation about the new prominence of the One Hundred Poets, then, might be to compare them with the Thirty-Six Poetic Immortals.

Origins of *One Hundred Poets* Poem-Pictures

The salient differences between the two groups can be summarized as follows: the One Hundred Poets are almost three times as many as the Thirty-Six; the *One Hundred Poets* collection is a linear and chronological survey of the history of *waka*, while the *Thirty-Six* is not;[33] and the One Hundred Poets were selected by Teika whereas the Thirty-Six were chosen by Kintō. Each of these differences contributed to the new popularity of the *One Hundred Poets* collection in the seventeenth century. Let us deal with each in turn, starting with the last. We have seen how practically all poetry experts of the medieval period traced their lineage in some way or other back to Teika. In this sense, then, he was the progenitor of medieval poetry and it is hardly surprising that his works and selections should receive more interest than those of someone like Kintō. By the late fifteenth century, Teika's poetics, Teika's anthologies, Teika's poetry, even his arthritic calligraphy, became the model of aristocrats, *renga* masters, tea masters, and artists of all media.[34]

Pointing out that the *One Hundred Poets* collection has almost three times as many poets as the *Thirty-Six Poetic Immortals* collection may seem obvious, but it is significant—a representation of one hundred poets would take almost three times as much material resources as thirty-six. In other words, there is an element of conspicuous display in the choice of the *One Hundred Poets*, rather than the *Thirty-Six*. In this light, it is hardly surprising that the *Soan-bon* edition of the *Thirty-Six* seems to precede that of the *One Hundred* by at least a decade. Finally, the appearance of printed images of the One Hundred Poets and their poems suggests the reason for the biggest difference between the seventeenth century and earlier times: a much larger and more obviously commercial market. The *One Hundred Poets* became one of the first texts to be taught publically, rather than through private (and secret) transmission. Its historical organization made it a natural textbook. Hence it is perfectly natural that it should be the text chosen most frequently for publication and illustration.

Due to the close connections in Kyoto between aristocrats, merchants, and the warrior houses, these three factors mutually reinforced and influenced each other. Thus the popularity of the *One Hundred Poets* at all levels of society encouraged its appreciation by courtiers as well. This appreciation is apparent in the earliest extant seventeenth-century productions of the *One Hundred Poets*. The very earliest seems to be a printed version called the *Soan-bon*, named after its artist and calligrapher, Suminokura Soan (1571–1632), who, together with Hon'ami Kōetsu, produced a highly influential series of illustrated printed editions at their press in Saga, near Kyoto.[35] Soan was "heir to one of the greatest commercial fortunes of his day, a fortune built in the licensed silk and spice trade with Annam first under the patronage of Hideyoshi and, then, under Ieyasu's control."[36] Soan studied the Confucian classics with Fujiwara Seika (1561–1619), the tea ceremony with the flamboyant Furuta Oribe (1544–1615), and calligraphy with Kōetsu. For his editions of the classics he had the cooperation of learned courtiers such as Nakanoin Michikatsu (1558–1610), a student of Yūsai, who prepared the *Saga-bon* edition of the *Tales of Ise*. And while such printed texts eventually led to the much wider dissemination of these classical works, the early *Saga-bon* were costly productions in which printing was most likely used for its novelty and technological appeal rather than for its economic efficiency.

Following the long-established format for the *Thirty-Six Poets*, the *Soan-bon* edition of the *One Hundred Poets* limits itself to *kasen-e*, the imaginary portraits of the poets, with their respective poems inscribed above them. By the third quarter of the seventeenth century, however, the Kanō school in Edo was producing both *kasen-e* and *uta-e* of the *Hyakunin Isshu* for patrons in the warrior class.[37] Three albums (*gajō*) of the *One Hundred Poets* survive from the atelier of the official Tokugawa government painter, Kanō Tan'yū (1602–1674).[38] The most deluxe of these albums is a volume of *kasen-e* formerly owned by the Date family; it is also the only one that can be firmly dated.[39] It was a collaborative project by five painters, including Tan'yū and three other major artists in his workshop (Masunobu, Tsunenobu, and Yasunobu, all identified by signatures and seals; the fifth artist is unknown), who worked in a consistent, fastidious style in rich mineral pigments on silk. The calligraphy in the accompanying cartouches is by no less than nineteen members of the court aristocracy. Based on these names and their recorded ranks, the album can be dated to the period between 1662 and 1669.[40]

Mori concludes that the Date album is based on an earlier work of Tan'yū's individual design and believes that this earlier work is reflected in the album in his style in the Tokyo National Museum, a set of sketches in ink and light colors on paper.[41] It is in this version that we see, for the first time, landscape backgrounds that have an obvious relationship to the contents of the poems. For instance, the landscape behind Emperor Tenji (Figure 8) includes a hut, while the figure of Semimaru (Figure 9) includes the Ōsaka Barrier. Twenty of the one hundred pictures have no elements related to the meaning of the poem at all, however, and many of these have no background painting but simply blue wash. This suggests that the original album was something of

Figure 8. Kanō Tan'yū (attrib.), *Hyaku-nin Isshu Gazō, Tan'yū-hitsu, Kan,* "Tenji Tennō." Undated (17th century?). Ink and colors on paper, remounted as an album, 1 vol. 30 × 20 cm.

Figure 9. *Hyakunin Isshu Gazō, Tan'yū-hitsu, Kan,* "Semimaru."

an experiment for Tan'yū; perhaps there were no earlier pictorializations of the poems for him to rely on.[42]

Pictorializations of the *One Hundred Poets* poems do not seem to appear in printed editions until the 1670s: in 1671 we find in a catalog of published books the title *Hyakunin Isshu Kenzu,* or *One Hundred Poets, One Poem Each, with Explanatory Pictures,* which the catalog describes as "setting out the heart of the poems in pictures" *(uta no kokoro o e ni shirusu).*[43] The titles of several other such books are listed in catalogs from 1675 and 1691, but the oldest example extant today is the *Hyakunin Isshu Zōsan Shō,* or *Commentary on the One Hundred Poets, One Poem Each, with Portraits and Inscriptions* (Figure 10). First published in 1678, the text of this edition consists of several elements: an imaginary portrait of the poet with his or her name and poem inscribed directly above and about the poet in a clear hand of *kana* with some *kanji;* a pictorialization of the poem to the side of the *kasen-e;* a version of the Yūsai commentary above the *uta-e* and frequently continuing onto the next page; and a brief biography of the poet and abbreviated family tree.[44] The pictures are by the great early *ukiyo-e* artist Hishikawa Moronobu (ca. 1618–1694). Katagiri Yōichi, a literary scholar, is quite dismissive of Moronobu's efforts, arguing that in the *kasen-e* he does no more than to *areenji* (or rearrange) the elements found in the *Soan-bon;* we would see that Moronobu used the same imitative technique in the poem-pictorializations, Katagiri says, if any earlier examples were extant.[45] Katagiri's criticisms are worth examining, because they can and should be refuted.

Katagiri points out that if we compare Moronobu's rendering of the poet Yakamochi (Figure 11) with that of the *Soan-bon* (see page 158), the position of the feet, the direction of the gaze, and the patterns on the clothing are virtually identical. Much the same can be said of the representations of Semimaru (Figure 12 and page 171) or the Empress Jitō (Figure 13 and page 145, where the poses are in mirror image but the costume has been changed), or Sarumaru (Figure 14 and page 155, where the poses are different but the textile patterns the same). To Katagiri, the changes that Moronobu introduces are meaningless variations on a pattern without any significance in themselves. While Moronobu did avail himself of design motifs from the *Soan-bon,* in this activity he did so no more and no less than has been standard practice in Japanese pictorial design throughout history. What Katagiri overlooks is that the overall effect of Moronobu's imaginary portraits is quite different from that of either of his predecessors. Indeed, if we compare the *kasen-e* of the *Soan-bon* edition, the Tan'yū album, and Moronobu's *Zōsanshō,* using the image of Emperor Tenji (see Figures 8 and 10 and page 141), we can see that each of these images manifests signs of its intended audience. The Tan'yū image, to start, is sinitic and hieratic, emphasizing Tenji's position as emperor, and is clearly related to Confucian-inspired images of sage-kings. In fact, Tenji is shown sitting on his throne in his audience chamber. By contrast, the *Soan-bon* image is more obviously "Japanese." Yet compared to Moronobu's rendition, we can see how the *Soan-bon* Tenji, with its prominent "butterfly-style" eyebrows (the mark of an aristocrat), its more intricately decorated robe, and its greater volume and nearness to the picture plane, gives a more human yet powerful, authoritative yet courtly, impression than that

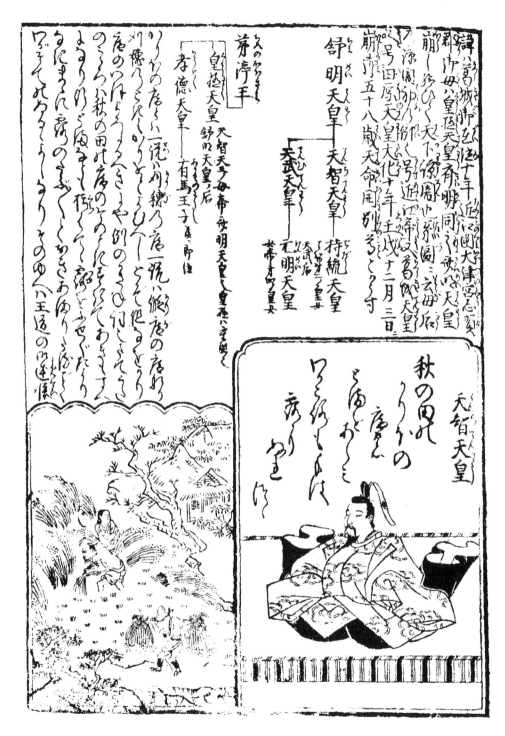

Figure 10. Hishikawa Moronobu, *(Kan'yō E-iri Uta to Kenzu) Hyakunin Isshu Zōsan Shō (Denki Keifu),* "Tenji Tennō." Edo: Urokogataya, 1678. 3 vols. 27 × 18.5 cm.

Figure 11. Moronobu, *Hyakunin Isshu Zōsan Shō,* "Chūnagon Yakamochi."

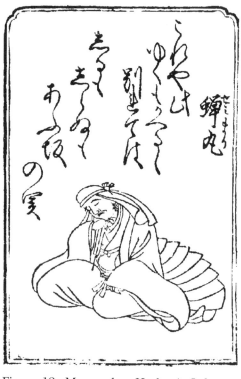

Figure 12. Moronobu, *Hyakunin Isshu Zōsan Shō,* "Semimaru."

Figure 13. Moronobu, *Hyakunin Isshu Zōsan Shō,* "Jitō Tennō."

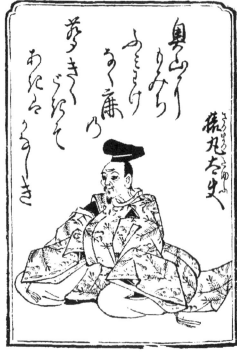

Figure 14. Moronobu, *Hyakunin Isshu Zōsan Shō,* "Sarumaru."

of the plebeian Moronobu, whose Tenji is somewhat overwhelmed by the tatami matting on which he sits, much more a sign than a person.

While one can trace the genealogies and influences of the various *kasen-e*, the case of the pictorializations of the "hearts" of the poems is harder to establish. As we have seen, the earliest extant images are by Kanō Tan'yū, completed sometime before 1662–1669. These are imaginary portraits with a minor landscape element behind them. In Moronobu, rather than serving as background, the pictorializations of the poems are given their own space, equivalent to the poet's "portrait" and parallel to the written commentary on the verse.

Little is known about Moronobu beyond what can be deduced from his products. He was born in Hoda in Awa province (modern Chiba prefecture) sometime around 1618. He was the son of an embroiderer, Yoshisa'eimon, one of whose few surviving works is an embroidered *kasen-e* of Hitomaro dated 1650.[46] From Moronobu's work it is apparent that he learned the fundamental techniques of both the Kanō and Tosa schools, but where or with whom he studied is unknown. Nonetheless, as Kobayashi Tadashi remarks, his use of the term *yamato eshi* for himself indicates that he considered himself the successor to the courtly painting tradition of *yamato-e*. Kobayashi also credits Moronobu as being the first Edo-period illustrator to include his own name in the books for which he provided pictures.[47]

To illustrate the kinds of meanings Moronobu was able to bring to his work, let us compare three versions of illustrations for a scene from Ihara Saikaku's *Life of an Amorous Man (Kōshoku Ichidai Otoko).* Saikaku originally published this work in Osaka in 1682, complete with illustrations drawn by Saikaku himself (Figure 15). Saikaku's work was reprinted in Edo in 1684, this time with illustrations by Moronobu (Figure 16).[48] Even in this most minimal of adaptations by Moronobu of Saikaku's design, we can see his differing interests. Rather than a figure of embarrassment cowering in a tub, in Moronobu's picture the maid offers herself to the viewer's gaze, no longer constrained and boxed in by the strong lines of the fence. The figure of the boy, as well, is perched less precariously on the roof and seems to take in the scene much more at his leisure, encouraging a closer identification between him and the male reader. Moronobu's reworking of this theme for another text, a "picture-book" *(e-hon)* entitled *Yamato-e no Kongen* (Figure 17),[49] is even more successful in employing the visual vocabulary of his day. The fence and robe have now been draped in the fashion of a *taga-sode* screen (Figure 18),[50] allowing for the display of the kimono pattern and suggesting, ironically, the conspicuous display of high-ranking samurai and wealthy merchants. Such humorous juxtaposition is also supplied by the now very Kanō-esque tree trunk, whose sharp, calligraphic lines contrast with the sinuous curves of the woman's body.[51] Most significantly, note the difference in the woman's gesture: the contemporary reader no doubt saw it as a visual joke in which, rather than attempting to fend off the boy and his prying eyes, it actually suggested a far different attitude on the woman's part. This we see most clearly in a circa 1708 print by Okumura Masanobu (Figure 19),[52] with its inscription about wanting a "strong man" *(tsuyohi otoko),* but also in a mid-1680s print by Sugimura Jihei (Figure 20)[53]—both derived from the image of the far more likely situation of a man entreating a

Figure 15. Ihara Saikaku, *Kōshoku Ichidai Otoko.* 8 vol. *Ōbon* format (11 × 7.5 in.).

Figure 16. Moronobu, *Kōshoku Ichidai Otoko.*

Figure 17. Moronobu, *Yamato-e no Kongen.*

woman for her favors, as in an anonymous painting dating from the 1660s.[54] Moronobu's image, then, delivers much different information from that of Saikaku's text: while the words say that the woman was resisting, the visual images (and Saikaku's punchline at the end of the episode) reinforce the male fantasy that she is actually inviting both the boy protagonist and the male viewer of the picture.

In much the same fashion, the *One Hundred Poets* could be appropriated and put to a variety of different uses. An example of one such use was created by Moronobu himself and entitled the *(Fūryū) Sugata-e Hyakunin Isshu*, or *(Elegant) Portraits of the* One Hundred Poets, One Poem Each *Collection*.[55] By examining both this work and his earlier *Zōsanshō*, not only will we see two distinct receptions of the *One Hundred Poets* but we will also be able to situate those receptions in the social and intellectual context of the period. In the process, too, we may get a clearer idea about artists like Moronobu's own familiarity with the classical tradition. The preface to the work notes that the *One Hundred Poets* has already seen many portraits and inscriptions by famous artists and calligraphers explicating a variety of lineages' secret interpretations. To make this work more accessible to the young, however, the creator has depicted the contents in a humorous form *(fūkyō shitaru katachi)*. He makes specific reference to Nonoguchi Ryūho (1595–1669), a *haikai* poet and disciple of Matsunaga Teitoku (1571–1653). He concludes by noting that the written commentary follows various previous interpretations.

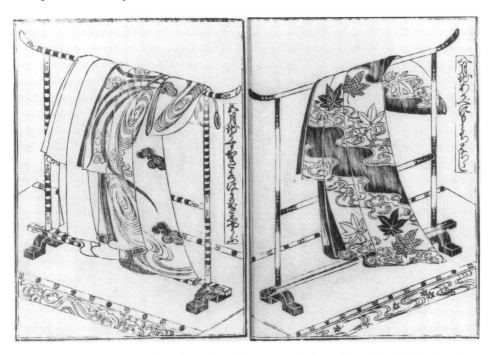

Figure 18. Anonymous. [Attributed to Moronobu.] *Onna Shorei Shū (Collection of Rules of Etiquette for Women)*, "Taga Sode." Vol. 1, *Dress and Table Manners*. Edo: Yamada Ichirobei, 1660.

Figure 19. Okumura Masanobu, Erotic Print. *Aiban* format (9 × 13 in.). Ca. 1708. Signed *"Buko gashi Okumra Masanobu."* Publisher: Nishimura Denzaemon.

Figure 20. Sugimura Jihei, Erotic Print. *Ōban* format (10 × 15 in.). Ca. 1708.

We might start with some examples of the use of robe patterns to carry meaning relevant to the poem. The clearest example is in regard to the poem by Ono no Komachi (Poem 9). As we have seen, the poem is about falling cherry blossoms and is found among the spring poems of the *Kokinshū*. Throughout the medieval period there was a debate about whether the poem was a simple nature poem or whether the cherry blossoms were meant to symbolize the poet's own beauty. While the *Zōsanshō* pictorialization of this poem (Figure 9-2) simply shows the poet gazing at a cherry tree, the *Sugata-e* version (Figure 9-3) has made the association between woman and flower explicit by decorating her robe with a cherry-blossom motif.

We see a similar use of robe pattern in the *Sugata-e* for the poem by Ki no Tomonori. The poem reads:

hisakata no	In these spring days
hikari nodokeki	with the tranquil light encompassing
haru no hi ni	the four directions,
shidzu-kokoro naku	why should the blossoms scatter
hana no chiruramu	with uneasy hearts?

The *Zōsanshō* of 1678 (Figure 33-1) prominently displays the shining sun, under which the poet gazes at the scattering cherry blossoms.[56] The *Sugata-e* version (Figure 33-3) has a man being entertained by a woman playing the shamisen. While one might think that the motif of the shining sun has disappeared, it has simply been transposed to the sunflowers (*hi-mawari*) on the woman's robe.

While Tomonori's poem is about spring, Moronobu, in his *Sugata-e*, has inserted it into the world of the pleasure quarter. This "eroticization," as I shall call it, of a verse that originally had nothing to do with sex or romance is not unusual in *ukiyo-e*. Interestingly, it is not unusual in the commodification of high culture, either. Another example of this tendency, this time in France, comes from an engraving by Pierre Filloeul (Figure 21) of Jean-Baptiste Chardin's *Soap Bubbles* (Figure 22). Of this print Philip Conisbee writes:

> It is common for eighteenth-century reproductive engravings to bear "explanatory" verses at the bottom of the image along with the title, credit, and publication lines. These verses are usually moralizing in tone and were supplied by the engraver. Their meaning was not necessarily endorsed by the original painter. Often they are mildly amorous in tone, but their intention was rarely anything more serious than an attempt to catch as wide a public as possible. The verses on Filloeul's *Soap Bubbles* read:

> [Contemple bien jeune Garçon,
> Ces petits globes de savon
> Leur mouvement si variable
> Et leur éclat si peu durable
> Te feront dire avec raison
> Qu'en cela mainte Iris leur est assez semblable.]

> *Consider well, young man,*
> *These little globes of soap.*

> *Their movements so variable,*
> *Their luster so fragile,*
> *Will prompt you to say with reason,*
> *That many an Iris in this is very like them.*[57]

While eighteenth-century French engravers provided the verses for the pic-
tures, Moronobu and his contemporaries provided the pictures for the verses.
Both, however, tailored their interpretation to appeal to their target market.[58]
This is not the place to compare the buyers of Filloeul's and Moronobu's works.
However, I would like to examine what Moronobu's *Sugata-e* version of the *One
Hundred Poets* tells us about his audience in the early Edo period and how that
audience determined his readings of specific poems.

Let us return for a moment to Saikaku. According to Paul Schalow,
Saikaku's

> earliest venture into prose in 1682 [*Kōshoku Ichidai Otoko*] was a great
> commercial success, and Saikaku quickly developed a sense of himself as a
> popular fiction writer. With that new-found identity came ambitions to
> reach beyond his native Osaka. When he undertook the writing of *Nanshoku
> ōkagami* [*The Great Mirror of Male Love*] in 1687, it was with the express pur-
> pose of extending his readership and satisfying his ambition to be published
> in the three major cities of his day, Osaka, Kyoto, and Edo. He chose the
> topic of male homosexual love because it had the broadest appeal to both
> the samurai men of Edo and the townsmen of Kyoto and Osaka, his regular
> audience.[59]

LES BOUTEILLES DE SAVON

Figure 22. Jean-Baptiste Chardin, *Soap
Bubbles,* (1733–1734?) *(above)*. Oil on can-
vas, 23⅝ × 28¾ in. (60 × 73 cm).

Figure 21. Pierre Filloeul, *Soap Bubbles,*
1739 *(left)*. Engraving, 10¾ × 8 in. (27.3 ×
20.3 cm).

In other words, Saikaku believed that a work about *nanshoku,* or male homosex-
ual love, would appeal to the samurai market in Edo. Moronobu, too, working
in Edo, was interested in this same audience. And in fact it is at this point that
we should remember that the first signed and dated work we have by Moronobu
is the *Buke Hyakunin Isshu* (Figure 23),[60] or *One Hundred Warrior Poets,* a work
from 1672 that predates his first treatment of the original *One Hundred Poets* in
1678. Note that the *One Hundred Warrior Poets* is not a version of Teika's collec-
tion but an independent work bringing together one hundred poems by one
hundred famous samurai. Although the *One Hundred Warrior Poets* represents an
effort to interest the samurai of Edo in the courtly *waka* tradition, it does not
seem to attempt this through eroticization. Such eroticization, both heterosex-
ual and homosexual, is what Moronobu's *Sugata-e Hyakunin Isshu* is all about.
Yet the erotic content of Moronobu's images is easy for the modern viewer to
overlook: the *Sugata-e* pictures are erotic, but they are not pornographic—
rather like the first picture from one of his *shunga* albums that starts tamely
(Figure 24) before proceeding to something more explicit (Figure 25).[61]

Now, many of the poems in the *One Hundred Poets* are in fact love poems—
indeed, love poems predominate in Teika's collection (forty-three out of the
hundred). Consequently, we are not surprised to see Moronobu foreground,
literally, the romantic interpretations of the poems. Let us look, for example, at
Poem 14 by Minamoto no Tōru:

michinoku no	Whose fault is it
shinobu mojhi-zuri	that my feelings have begun to tangle
tare yuwe ni	like the tangle-patterned prints
midare-somenishi	of Shinobu from the distant north?
ware naranaku ni	Since it is not mine, it must be . . .

The word *shinobu* is a pivot word that refers to a kind of plant used in making
patterned cloth; it is also the name of a village where that cloth was made; and
it is also a verb meaning "to long for" or "to love secretly." The *Zōsanshō* (Figure
14-2) has the poet examining *shinobu*-cloth, which highlights the major pivot
word of this poem in the manner of the visual pivot words we noted in Heian-
period works. In the *Sugata-e* (Figure 26), by contrast, *shinobu*-ferns have been
set off in the background, while in the foreground a samurai, stretched out
with his short sword loosened from his belt and lying beside him, looks mean-
ingfully at a young woman. Thus we can see, even in the love poems, how the
Sugata-e gives a more erotic presentation than the earlier *Zōsanshō.*

Nor are we surprised when, like Filloeul, Moronobu takes a poem, such as
Tomonori's, and adapts it erotically. We see a similar situation in Poem 11 (Fig-
ures 11-2 and 11-3), by Takamura, written when he was sent into exile, classified
in the *Kokinshū* under the category "Travel":

wata no hara	O, tell them that
yaso shima kakete	I have rowed out, towards
kogi-idenu to	the innumerable islands
hito ni ha tsugeyo	of the ocean's wide plain,
ama no tsuri-bune	you fishing boats of the sea-folk!

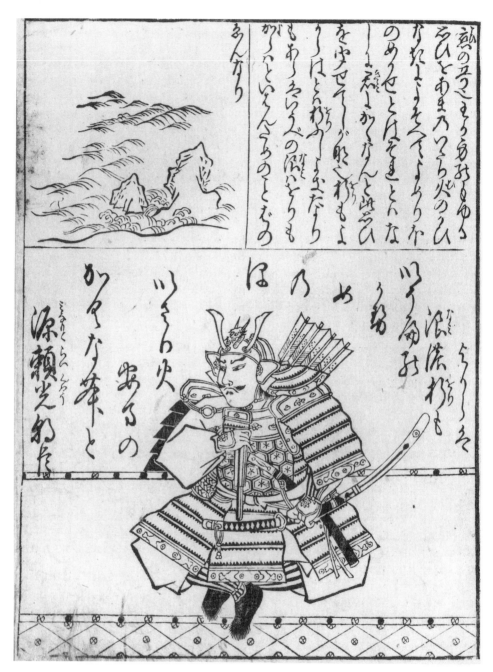

Figure 23. Hishikawa Moronobu (artist), *Chū-iri Kashira-zu Buke Hyakunin Isshu (One Hundred Poets of Military Families with Commentaries and Illustrations)*. Vol. II-2. Edo: Tsuruya Kiyemon, 1672.

Figure 24. Hishikawa Moronobu (Japanese, ca. 1618–1694), "Behind the Screen,"
1680s. Ōban format. Woodblock print from a *shunga* set.

Figure 25. Hishikawa Moronobu (Japanese, ca. 1618–1694), "Couple," 1680s. Ōban
format. Woodblock print from a *shunga* set.

Figure 26. Moronobu, *Sugata-e Hyakunin Isshu,* "Kawara Sadaijin."

As early as the *Chōkyō Shō* of 1487 we find the suggestion, generally ignored by other commentaries, that Takamura was exiled due to a secret affair with a woman in the palace, presumably the *hito* of the poem, which might then be translated as "O, tell her that. . . ." Generally it is such romantic interpretations that Moronobu offers in his *Sugata-e.*[62]

But not all the erotic innuendo in Moronobu's works is heterosexual, and Moronobu appears to interpret many of the poems in homoerotic terms. In this he was working along the same lines as the great scholar and poet Kitamura Kigin (1624–1705),[63] who in 1676 completed a work entitled *Iwatsutsuji,* or *Wild Azaleas,* a collection of "thirty-four homoerotic love poems and prose passages from sixteen classical works of literature . . . [that showed] how men of the past —primarily monks and priests—expressed their love for youths."[64] While Kigin's focus in *Wild Azaleas* was solely on *nanshoku,* or men's love for men, Schalow claims that in the *renga*, or linked poetry of this period, " 'love verses' *(koi no ku)* modulated between male love and female love in the haikai code," that is, between men's love for men and men's love for women: "An important surviving example of a haikai love sequence revealing this modulating tendency is Sōin['s] *'Hana de Sōrō'* ('My Name Is Blossom') from *Rakkashū* ('A Collection of Scattered Blossoms'), 1671. It opens with the words of a youthful kabuki actor [i.e., a male prostitute], proceeds through various moods and modes of love—marital, extra-marital, male and female—returning at the end to the lingering image of an actor of female roles *(onnagata)* on the kabuki stage."[65]

This is the same variety of love that Moronobu portrays in his *Sugata-e*, transforming Teika's *hyakushu* into a kind of *haikai hyakuin*, or humorous hundred-link *renga* sequence, exploring a variety of erotic situations: a man interrupting his reading to stare at the woman seated next to him (Figure 27); a man comparing the beauty of a young man to the plum blossoms (Figure 28); a woman preparing a man's hair as he gets ready to spend the night with another woman (Figure 29); another lord gazing down on a young male retainer (Figure 30). Perhaps equally important is the fact that many of the verses in Sōin's piece are parodies of classical poems, a technique that obviously requires the reader to have a fair familiarity with the poetic canon, including poems contained in the *One Hundred Poets*. In fact, it is quite clear that some of the *Sugata-e* pictorializations are parodies of the Tan'yū album. This is particularly evident in the picture of Tsurayuki (Figure 28), which quite obviously derives from the Tan'yū album (Figure 31).

In any event, what is important here is how Moronobu chose, or invented, different interpretations of the *One Hundred Poets* verses for his *Sugata-e* in contrast to the *Zōsanshō* version. In fact, the *Zōsanshō* pictures on occasion contradict something explicitly stated in the accompanying commentary.[66] An example of this is Poem 73:

takasago no	Above the lower slopes
wonohe no sakura	of the high mountains, the cherries
sakinikeri	have blossomed!
toyama no kasumi	O, mist of the near mountains,
tatazu mo aranamu	how I wish you would not rise!

The Yūsai commentary that appears on the same page as the *Zōsanshō* picture explicitly states that the word *takasago* is a common noun that means "high mountains" and is not a proper noun for the mountain named Takasago in Harima province.[67] Nonetheless, the *Zōsanshō* picture (Figure 73-1) of a steep cliff or mountain beside the ocean is the standard representation of Takasago (see Poem 34). This rendering has been "corrected" in the *Sugata-e* (Figure 73-3) to being a generic mountain, while Moronobu has also added a pun of his own: the verb *tatsu* can also mean "to leave," which is what it appears the man is asking the woman not to do.

We can compare Moronobu's understanding of the verses and their original headnotes with that of other artists. One particularly confusing headnote appears in connection with Poem 75. The headnote to this poem in the *Senzaishū* reads literally:

When Bishop Kōkaku requested to be made a lecturer for the Vimalakīrti Ceremony, he was repeatedly overlooked, so he complained to the former chancellor, the Buddhist Novice of Hosshōji. Although he said, "The fields of Shimejhi . . . [i.e., rely on me]," when he was again passed over the next year, he sent [the following].

What all this means is that when Fujiwara no Mototoshi's son, the Bishop Kōkaku, was overlooked for a certain position, Mototoshi appealed on his son's

Figure 27. Moronobu, *Sugata-e Hyakunin Isshu,* "Fujiwara no Okikaze."

Figure 28. Moronobu, *Sugata-e Hyakunin Isshu,* "Ki no Tsurayuki."

Figure 29. Moronobu, *Sugata-e Hyakunin Isshu,* "Kiyohara no Fukayabu."

Figure 30. Moronobu, *Sugata-e Hyakunin Isshu,* "Fun'ya no Tomoyasu [Asayasu]."

Figure 31. Kanō Tan'yū (attrib.), *Hyakunin Isshu Gazō, Tany'ū-hitsu, Kan,* "Ki no Tsurayuki" *(left)* and "Fujiwara no Okikaze" *(right).*

behalf to Tadamichi, the former chancellor who had taken Buddhist vows but was still highly influential. Tadamichi promised to help, but the following year Mototoshi's son still did not get the position, whereupon Mototoshi sent the following poem to Tadamichi in complaint:

chigiri-okishi	Depending with my life
sasemo ga tsuyu wo	on promises that fell thick
inochi nite	as dew on *sasemo* plants—
ahare kotoshi no	alas! the autumn of this year too
aki to inumeri	seems to be passing.

In the *Zōsanshō* picture (Figure 75-2) it is hard to tell if the poet is meant to be the monk or the courtier, and which of the two is of the higher rank, despite the fact that Tadamichi far outranked Mototoshi. An anonymous Kyoto artist (whom we will encounter again) in 1746 attempted to improve the *Zōsanshō* design (Figure 75-3):[68] he adds the scene of a religious ceremony, for instance. He seems to have had no understanding of the relationship between Tadamichi and Mototoshi, however, moving the priestly figure farther out onto the veranda. In fact, the clearest pictorialization of the correct relationship between these two men is to be found in Moronobu's *Sugata-e* (and not seen in the Tan'yū album), where we see the lay figure kneeling on the ground in the background scene (Figure 75-4). This clarity would seem to allow a sharper contrast between the original context of the poem and Moronobu's contemporary resetting of it, where the higher-ranking samurai or merchant is gazing wistfully at a young woman who seems, at best, distracted: manifesting another kind of "plea in vain."

Sometimes Moronobu's reason for choosing the "more correct" interpretation is related to concerns far removed from the original poem. An excellent example of the relationship between interpretation, commentary, pictorialization, and market is provided by Poem 20, by Prince Motoyoshi:

wabinureba	Miserable,
ima hata onaji	now, it is all the same.
naniha naru	Channel-markers at Naniwa—
miwotsukushite mo	even if it costs my life,
ahamu to zo omofu	I will see you again.

This poem's headnote in the *Gosenshū* reads: "Sent to the Kyōgoku Lady of the Wardrobe, after their affair had come out." The lady in question was Fujiwara no Hōshi, daughter of Tokihira. Her father had planned to have her enter the reigning emperor's service, but Retired Emperor Uda insisted that she serve at his residence—she bore him three princes. This, however, did not prevent an affair with Motoyoshi, which eventually became public knowledge.

The poem centers on a pivot word: *miwotsukushi* was a kind of channel-marker used to guide boats through the waterway—it can also be read *mi wo tsukushite mo,* literally, "even if it consumes [my] body." Interpretations split into two equally represented camps, even among modern commentators, depending on what one understands to be "the same now." One interpretation is that "even if it costs my life" *(mi wo tsukushite mo),* it is "now the same"; in other words, the poet is so miserable that it doesn't matter whether he lives or dies. The second interpretation understands the topic to be *na,* that is, "name" or reputation (understanding the place-name "*Na*niwa" as a pivot word). This reputation can be either the poet's or the couple's reputation. While the first interpretation implies that it is other people who are keeping the lovers apart and that the man will risk his life to see his lady again; the second interpretation can be understood to mean that the lady, worrying about further damage to her reputation, is reluctant to see the man. The latter interpretation is closer to the anecdotes told about Prince Motoyoshi in *Tales of Yamato,* and it also encourages identifying this scenario with the one in *The Tale of Genji* involving Genji and the retired emperor's lady Fujitsubo. It is this second interpretation that was most often followed and may well have been how Teika himself read the poem.

A late Edo-period version (Figure 20-1), one of the few to pictorialize the *Gosenshū* headnote (that is, the circumstances of composition), shows the poet alone in his room writing the poem to be sent to the lady.[69] The standard presentation is shown in Moronobu's *Zōsanshō* (Figure 20-2), where the poet is pleading at the lady's blind, following the more *monogatari*-like interpretation. The anonymous Kyoto illustrator (Figure 20-4) adopts the *Zōsanshō* design wholesale, but he adds in the upper corner a *miwotsukushi* to suggest the pivot word of the poem. Now, in fact, picturing the channel-marker was not a new idea, and we see it in Tan'yū's album (Figure 32). More interestingly, we also see it in Moronobu's *Sugata-e* (Figure 20-3), but there its function seems to be to provide a shape to be mirrored by the figures of the male adolescents. The collocation of the two young men, together with an older master-figure, and the phrase *mi wo tsukushite mo,* no doubt brought to mind stories about young samurai sacrificing their lives for their male lovers, as found in the first half of Saikaku's *Great Mirror of Male Love.*

Space will not allow further examples of such changes between the *Zōsan-shō* and *Sugata-e.* It is important to note, however, that the changes in the *Suga-ta-e* do not always conform to a more "correct" reading of the original poem but are sometimes dictated by the needs of Moronobu's resettings. In any event, the designs of the *Sugata-e* are sufficiently different from those of the *Zōsanshō* and frequently close enough to variant, exegetical traditions to prove that Moronobu was being highly inventive in an informed way, and not simply copying "traditional images," when he pictorialized the *One Hundred Poets.*

The *One Hundred Poets* and Kimono Design

By at least the mid-eleventh century, the practice of poem-pictures extended into costume design. We read the following description by the somewhat breathless narrator of the second part of *A Tale of Flowering Fortunes* (*Eiga Monogatari,* ca. 1092–1107) of some robes worn at the Palace Poetry Contest of 1049:

> The ladies-in-waiting were wearing robes with light purple lining showing through the gossamer, beaten robes of lustrous light green, double-layered

Figure 32. Kanō Tan'yū (attrib.), *Hyakunin Isshu Gazō, Tan'yū-hitsu, Kan,* "Motoyoshi Shinnō" *(left)* and "Ise" *(right).*

mantles of yellow figured silk, jackets of purple, and their light green trains had pictures drawn on them, done in embroidery, mother-of-pearl and edging and so forth, and on one the poem "My Heart Goes Out" was written in small silver fragments in a dazzling way, and the figure of a cherry tree in bloom with its petals falling was painted as a poem-picture.[70]

The poem alluded to is by Mitsune and found in the *Kokinshū* 7 (Felicitations): 358:

yama takami	So high the mountains that
kumowi ni miyuru	the cherry blossoms
sakura-bana	seem to be among the clouds:
kokoro no yukite	yet there is never not a day
oranu hi zo naki	that *my heart goes out* to pluck them!

The robe presumably showed a cherry tree with scattering blossoms and had the one phrase from Mitsune's poem written in silver. Some idea of how this might have been done can be seen in the *Gonnō-hon* cover of the *Heike Nōkyō* of 1164 (Figures 33 and 34), where we see the *kana so, no, ho,* and *to* and, among the rocks at the foot of the tree, the characters *jhōya*. Julia Meech has suggested that this phrase, *sono hodo jhōya,* comes from the following *imayō,* or song "in the modern style," found in the *Ryōjin Hishō,* compiled about 1169:

shiyaka no tsuki ha	Shakamuni's moon
kakureniki	has become hidden,
jiji no asahi ha	and Maitreya's morning sun
mada haruka	is distant still—
sono hodo jhiyauya no	in the darkness
kuraki wo ba	of so long a night
hoke-keu nomi koso	only the Lotus Sutra
terai-tamehe[71]	shines for us!

We also read descriptions of poem-picture-like robes near the end of the Kamakura period in *The Confessions of Lady Nijō* (*Towazu-gatari,* ca. 1307):

> The costume I wore was intended to represent the poem, "I heard the waterfall." . . . On my left sleeve I fastened balls of fragrant aloe wood carved to look like rocks, and over them sewed a tiny waterfall of white silk thread. I attached a twig of cherry blossoms and scattered petals on my right sleeve. The motif of blossoms, rocks, and waterfalls was carried out in the designs on my trousers as well."[72]

However, like the term "poem-picture" *(uta-e)* itself, we lose the thread of these robes through the late medieval period, only to have them reappear in the early Edo period, both in extant robes and in kimono pattern books, or *hinagata-bon*. *Hinagata-bon* were woodblock-printed books designed by largely anonymous artisans for the use of their mostly female customers and other drapers, attesting once again to the high level of literacy in Edo society.[73] While the earliest printed pattern book is dated 1666, it seems to derive from two earlier forms. The first is hand-drawn ink designs from the *kosode* merchant house of

Figure 33. Anonymous, *Heike Nōkyō. Gonnō-hon* cover. 1164.

Figure 34. *Gonnō-hon Ashide.*

Karigane-ya, called *OnE-chō* ("Customer Picture-Order Books"), and dating from 1661 and 1663. Karigane-ya was patronized by aristocratic women and those from the highest samurai families for many generations. Its founder, Ogata Dōhaku (d. 1604), was married to a sister of Kōetsu (1558–1637) and was the great-grandfather of Ogata Kōrin (1658–1716) and Kenzan (1663–1743).[74] Drawn during the tenure of Dōhaku's calligrapher grandson, Sōken (1621?–1687), many of the robes depicted in the *OnE-chō* make use of calligraphic designs (Figure 35). The earliest printed reproductions of robe designs are found in a text entitled the *Onna Shorei Shū,* or *Collection of Rules of Etiquette for Women,* dated 1660 (Figure 18). This was one of the etiquette books published for brides and young matrons. Although a designer could follow the textile designs depicted on the robes, the main purpose of the images was to show the proper way of displaying robes for a decorative effect, a practice again attested to as early as *The Confessions of Lady Nijō.*[75]

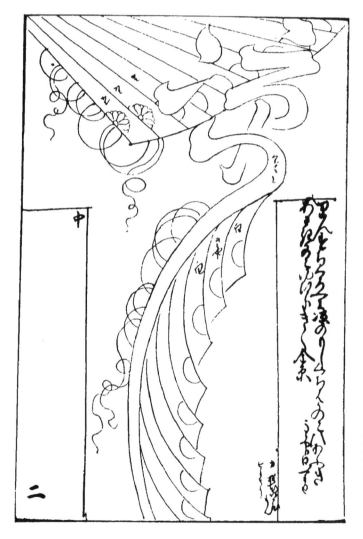

Figure 35. Ogata Family, *OnE-chō.* Manuscript. 1661.

The earliest extant robe displaying calligraphic design dates from between the Kan'ei and Meireki eras, or 1624–1658 (Plate 1). Interestingly it is a poem-picture of Poem 42 of the *One Hundred Poets:*

chigiriki na	But we promised!
katami ni sode wo	while wringing out the tears from
shibori-tsutsu	each other's sleeves,
suwe no matsu yama	that never would the waves cross over
nami kosaji to ha	Sue-no-Matsu Mountain.

It is remarkably appropriate that this poem should appear on the oldest extant robe of this type, for not only does the poem speak of the sleeves of a robe, but this robe is dyed with a *shibori* technique, usually translated as "tie-dyed" but literally meaning "wrung." On the right shoulder is the character for "mountain," while the large patch surrounding the left underarm contains a stylized rendering of the character for "to cross over." At the top, near the collar, is a wave pattern done in the tie-dyed *shibori* technique, which is also used for the pine at the bottom hem (*matsu* means "pines").

As noted earlier, the first printed pattern book, the *OnHiinakata,* dates from 1666. The move from handwritten texts, such as Karigane-ya's *OnE-chō,* to printed books can be taken as evidence of a market expanding from beyond its original aristocratic and samurai circles to wealthy townsmen. And while many calligraphic designs appear in the *OnE-chō,* fully forty-four of the two hundred designs in the *OnHiinakata* employ characters.[76] It is tempting to see this predominance of characters as a conspicuous display of literacy on the part of *chōnin* women, perhaps not unlike the ubiquitous use of English (of a sort) on the sports clothing of modern Japanese.

Moronobu, of course, came from a house of garment designers, and although the *Onna Shorei Shū* of 1660 has been attributed to him, the only pattern book that can be securely assigned to him is the *Ishō Hiinagata.*[77] His *Hyakunin Isshu Zōsan Shō* is from 1678, and by 1688 we see pattern books based entirely on the *One Hundred Poets.* Kirihata Ken gives much of the credit for this revival of literary motifs in clothing to Miyazaki Yūzen, a fan painter active from the late 1600s to early 1700s, after whom a widely employed technique of paste-resist dyeing was named. Kirihata conjectures that Yūzen transferred designs from his fans to robe patterns.[78] An example of his fan design is contained in a pattern book produced by Yūzen's student Yūjinsai Kiyochika: the *Yūzen Hiinakata* (1688) (Figure 36). The design alludes to Poem 5 of the *One Hundred Poets:*

oku-yama ni	When I hear the voice
momijhi fumi-wake	of the stag crying for his mate
naku shika no	stepping through the fallen leaves
kowe kiku toki zo	deep in the mountains—then is the time
aki ha kanashiki	that autumn is saddest.

The fan shows a branch of maple leaves with a letter *(fumi)* tied to it, lying under a tread-pestle *(fumi-usu)*. Beside it is a stag horn. The pestle and letter suggest the sound /fumi/ of the poem, while the horn refers to the deer.

We are fortunate to have an actual robe surviving that is based on designs

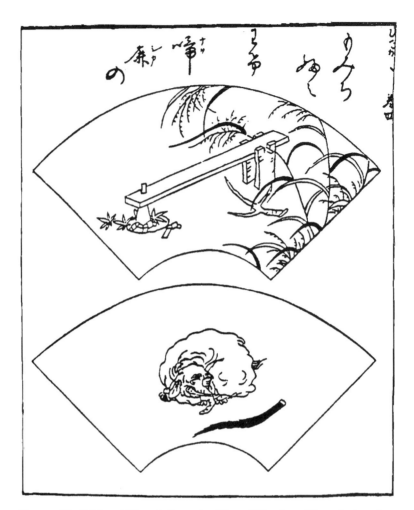

Figure 36. Yūjinsai Kiyochika, ed., *Yūzen Hiinakata* [Fan designs].
Kyoto: 1688.

from the earliest *One Hundred Poets* pattern book, the *Ogura Yama Hyakushu Hinagata,* published in 1688.[79] The robe (Plate 2) dates from the late seventeenth to early eighteenth centuries, and is clearly modeled on the design for Poem 35 by Tsurayuki (Figure 37):

hito ha isa	With people, well,
kokoro mo shirazu	you can never know their hearts;
furusato ha	but in my old village
hana zo mukashi no	the flowers brightly bloom with
ka ni nihohikeru	the scent of the days of old.

While the pattern book has the characters for "old village" and "the past," these have been omitted from the robe itself. This perhaps reflects a tendency that we see in the *Ogura Yama Shikishi Moyō* (also called the *Shikishi OnHinagata*) of

1689, which uses considerably fewer Chinese characters in its designs.[80] The artist of this later volume, Take Heiji, signs himself as a "Yamato Jō-Eshi." A *yamato-eshi* was an artist of the "Japanese" style exemplified by the Tosa school, Kōetsu and the so-called Rimpa style, and Moronobu. The term *jō-eshi*, however, seems to refer specifically to a pattern designer, in contradistinction to a book illustrator. Whereas earlier printed pattern books seem to have been designed by the same artists who illustrated books and the other visual work produced by such publishers as the Yezōshiya (whose name, after all, means "The House of Picturebooks," or *e-zōshi*), with Take we find kimono designers establishing a distinct identity as a profession.[81] Certainly the quality of Take's design seems a significant step from that of the *Hyakushu Hinagata* artist.

With increasing commercialization, the names of certain artists became identified as a kind of trade name, or brand, and we can then see how the *One*

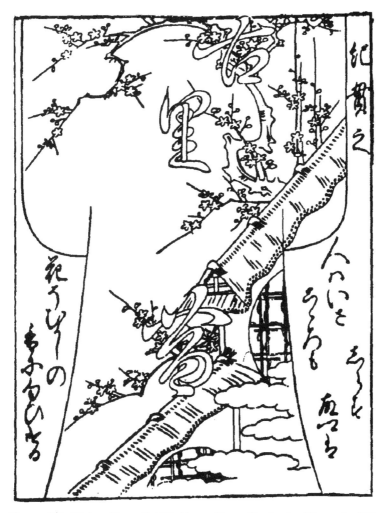

Figure 37. Hakuyōken Gyōjō, *Ogura Yama Hyakushu Hinagata*, "Ki no Tsurayuki." Kyoto: Yezōshiya, Jōkyō 6 (1688).

Hundred Poets was adapted to fit the style of those particular "brand names." This is most apparent in a work entitled *Tōsei Hinagata Enpitsu Yaemugura,* published in 1721. This pattern book offers designs in the distinctive styles of both Yūzen and Kōrin.[82] The production of pattern books gradually diminished, however, with the last being produced in 1820.[83]

We can see, then, that Edo-period pictures connected with the *One Hundred Poets* were not meaningless visual decorations but were understood as pictorializations that put "the heart of the poem" into visual form. We have seen that the same artist might create more than one pictorialization of a particular poem, adapting his interpretation to fit both the genre and the context of his visual work. In the next chapter, I want to explore the implications of taking these pictorializations as interpretations of the poems—that is, I want to limn the use of these images in a reception history of *waka* in general and the *One Hundred Poets* in particular.

CHAPTER 5

Pictorialization as Reception

The *One Hundred Poets, One Poem Each* collection has been, since at least the fourteenth century, Japanese literature's preeminent collection of exemplary poems. Yet, as we have seen, its role and function in the urban culture of the early modern Edo period (1600–1868) are in some ways the most compelling part of its history. A charming example of the wide diffusion of these poems to all levels of society is found in a late Edo-period *rakugo* story centered on the well-known Poem 5, by Sarumaru-Dayū:

An impoverished wagon-driver took a samurai on board, going toward Shinagawa.

"Master, you're in luck! The autumn foliage at Kai'anji is at its height—won't you stop for a moment of sightseeing?"

"I guess that would be alright," the samurai said, and off they went.

"I can't say how kind it was of you to notice this and bring me here," said the samurai. "Shall I compose a poem about it?"

"That would be most good of you."

"Hmm, maybe something like this?

> When I hear the voice
> of the stag crying for his mate
>   stepping through the fallen leaves
> deep in the mountains—then is the time
> that autumn is saddest."

"How splendid! This is surely one of the finest poems of recent times!"

"Have a drink, as a reward for bringing me here," the samurai said, and they went to a tavern. The wagon-driver drank heavily, and when he was flushed scarlet, another wagon-driver came in.

"Gonbei, drinking during the day, huh? You sure must have a lot of money."

"What? Don't be an idiot—I'm not paying!"

"Who is?"

"Sarumaru here!"[1]

If we look at Moronobu's pictorializations we can say that, on the one hand, he was reviving a practice of poem pictorialization, called *uta-e,* that dated back to the tenth century. On the other hand, Moronobu's illustrations—that is, the interpretations of the poems they pictorialize—often disagree with explicit statements in Yūsai's accompanying commentary. This is apparent in the very first poem, attributed to Emperor Tenji (626–671) (Figure 10). The poem reads:

aki no ta no	In the autumn fields
kari-ho no iho no	the hut, the temporary hut
toma wo arami	its thatch is rough
wa ga koromo-de ha	and so the sleeves of my robe
tsuyu ni nuretsutsu	are dampened night by night with dew.

As we have seen, Yūsai's commentary notes that some interpret the word *kari-ho,* in the phrase *kari-ho no iho,* to mean "reaped ears [of grain]," rather than as a contraction of *kari-iho.* Yet Yūsai rejects this interpretation not once but three times in the course of his commentary.[2] Nonetheless, we see just such an interpretation suggested by Moronobu's reapers. How are we to explain this?

Different pictorializations can, of course, simply reflect different interpretations of the same poem. As we noted in Chapter 2, Poem 4, by Yamabe no Akahito, has traditionally been interpreted in two very different ways. The original situation described by the poet seems to be the occasion of seeing Mount Fuji from a boat in the bay. This moment of composition is illustrated by an anonymous Kyoto artist (1746) (Figure 4-3). Yet the wording of the poem had undergone considerable change by the time Teika included it in the *One Hundred Poets,* and his version was most often understood to be describing a scene of seeing the mountain from the beach. It was this interpretation that seems to have been followed by early Edo artists, such as Moronobu in the *Zōsanshō* (Figure 4-2), though the "boat," rather than "beach," interpretation is found in some medieval commentaries (such as the *Minazuki Shō*). With the freer circulation of knowledge that characterized the Edo period, these alternative interpretations became known; in fact, the written commentary in Moronobu's *Sugata-e* offers the "boat" interpretation, though it seems to have had no influence on his pictorialization. By the mid-eighteenth century, this interpretation was confirmed by the National Learning scholars. Thus we can see the Kyoto artist reflecting the new philological research of such scholars as Kamo no Mabuchi (whose *Hyakunin Isshu Kosetsu* dates from 1743).

Yet sometimes the visual artist's ingenuity in creating associations between the visual and verbal text led to confused interpretations in the popular mind. An example of this is the second poem in the collection, attributed to Empress Jitō:

haru sugite	Spring has passed, and
natsu kinikerashi	summer seems to have arrived.
shiro-tahe no	Heavenly Mount Kagu
koromo hosu tefu	where, it is said, they dry robes
ama no kagu-yama	of the whitest mulberry!

This poem, too, as we have seen, has been radically altered from its original form in the *Man'yō Shū*. What concerns us here is the various attempts later artists made to represent what they understood to be the metaphorical meaning of the phrase "dry robes of the whitest mulberry." This was generally understood by commentators to be a metaphor for spring mist, as seen in the late Edo picture reproduced in William Porter's translation of the *One Hundred Poets* (Figure 2-2).[3] Yet Moronobu and many others after him apparently felt obliged to visualize the vehicle as well as the tenor (Figure 2-4). Perhaps influenced by such pictorializations, readers came to see an association between this poem and the *Hagoromo* legend, as seen in William Porter's translation (emphasis added):

> The spring has gone, the summer's come,
>   And I can just descry
> The peak of Ama-no-Kagu,
>   *Where angels of the sky*
>   Spread their white robes to dry.

Porter in his commentary notes:

> The poem refers to a snow-capped mountain just visible on the horizon. One of the Nō dramas relates, that an angel once came to a pine forest on the coast near Okitsu, and, hanging her feather mantle on a pine tree, climbed a neighbouring mountain to view Mount Fuji; a fisherman, however, found the robe and was about to carry it off with him, when the angel re-appeared and begged him to give it her, as without it she could not return to the moon where she lived. He only consented to do so, however, on condition that she would dance for him; and this she accordingly did, draped in her feathery robe on the sandy beach under the shade of the pine trees; after which she floated heavenward, and was lost to view.[4]

Yet there were other commentaries which insisted that no metaphor was involved and that the poem referred to the actual washing and drying of clothes, even though the grammar of the poem disallowed such an interpretation. One can imagine how such a situation might lead to something like the set of illustrations by Katsushika Hokusai (1760–1849) entitled "Pictures of the *One Hundred Poets, One Poem Each* Collection as Explained by the Wet Nurse"[5] *(Hyakunin Isshu Uba ga Etoki)* (Figure 38), where villagers are shown drying linen cloth. In fact, just such a case of folk etymology is evidenced in Hokusai's print for Poem 8, by Priest Kisen (Figure 39), where not only do we see travelers and farmers but also hunters with matchlocks aiming at deer on a distant hill—not typical imagery for an example of court poetry.[6] The poem reads:

wa ga iho ha	My hut is to
miyako no tatsu-mi	the capital's southeast,
shika zo sumu	and thus I live. But
yo wo ujhi-yama to	people call it "Uji, hill
hito ha ifu nari	of one weary of the world," I hear.

By as early as the mid-Muromachi period there seems to have been the "popular interpretation" *(zokkai)* that the word "thus," or *shika,* was a pun that also

Figure 38. Hokusai, *Hyakunin Isshu Uba ga Etoki,* "Jitō Tennō." Color woodblock print. Edo: Nishimuraya.

meant "deer."[7] Since the poem reads *miyako no tatsu-mi shika,* there was the further explanation that the inclusion of the word *shika* was meant to suggest the order of the zodiac, *tatsu–mi–uma,* ("dragon–serpent–horse"), since a deer was considered the same kind of animal as a horse.[8] Such a popular interpretation explains the inclusion of deer in Hokusai's print. Such popular interpretations were also frequently used as the basis of *kyōka,* or comic *tanka,* with whose practitioners Hokusai was closely associated. For instance, there is the following verse by Hanamichi no Tsurane, the pen name for the famous kabuki actor Ichikawa Danjūrō V (1741–1806):

Retiring to Ox Island

wa ga iho ha	My hut is to
shibai no tatsu-mi	the theatre's southeast,
shika zo sumu	and thus I live. But
yo wo ushi-shima to	people call it "*Ushi,* Ox Island,
hito ha ifu nari[9]	of one weary of the world," I hear.

We can, then, use Edo-period pictorializations as data for a reception history of the poems. But we must also bear in mind another important factor in the production of these images: the *market* for which a pictorialization was intended. This issue of market has both what I would call "formal" and "ideological" repercussions, and these in turn influenced the visual artist's choice of

PLATE 1. *Kosode with Abstract Wave Pattern (Seigaiha), Pine Trees, Clouds, Flowers, and Characters.* Tie-dyeing *(kanoko* and *nui-shime shibori)* on blue, brown, and white particolored *(some-wake)* figured silk satin *(rinzu).* 53 1/8 X 49 1/4 in. (135 X 125 cm). 1624–1658.

PLATE 2. *Kosode with Plum Tree and Architectural Motif.* Late 17th–early 18th century.

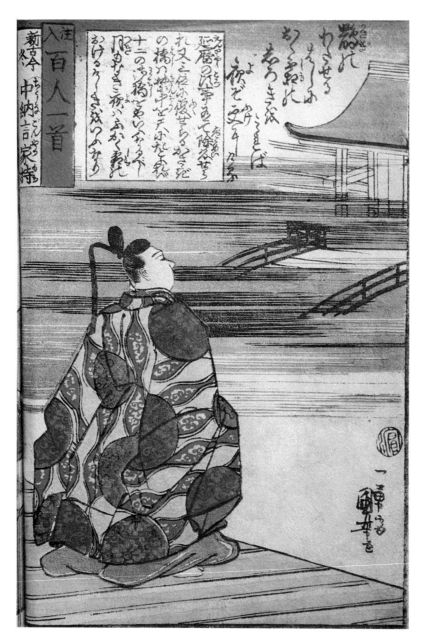

PLATE 3. Utagawa Kunisada and Utagwa Kuniyoshi, *Nishiki-e Chū-iri Hyakunin Isshu*, "Ōtomo no Yakamochi." Polychrome printed book, 18.5 X 12.5 cm. Edo: Tōto Shorin (Izumiya Ichibei), 1849.

PLATE 4. Utagawa Kunisada, *Sakae-gusa Tōsei Musume. Ōban* triptych. Edo: Izumiya Ichibei, Tempō era (1830–1843).

PLATE 5. Hokusai, *Hyakunin Isshu Uba ga Etoki*, "Abe no Nakamaro." Color woodblock print. Edo: Iseya, 1835–1838.

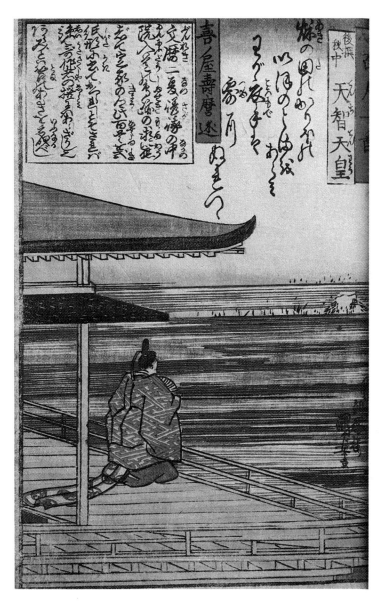

PLATE 6. Kunisada and Kuniyoshi, *Nishiki-e Chū-iri Hyakunin Isshu*, "Tenji Tennō." 1849.

PLATE 7. Kuniyoshi, *Hyakunin Isshu no Uchi*, "Suō no Naishi." 1861.

most appropriate for a game of concentration. The same logic, then, would explain the kimono design, where an element of recognition is also entailed.

In fact, the original poem has nothing to do with the Tanabata legend, and in the Heian period the "magpie bridge" was an elegant way to refer to bridges and staircases that led to the imperial palace—as illustrated by Toyokuni III (Kunisada, 1786–1864) and Kuniyoshi (1797–1861) in an 1849 edition (Plate 3). Nonetheless, as we have seen, this scholarly interpretive advance was generally ignored—most readers *wanted* this poem to refer to the Tanabata legend. In fact, from the very beginning of the eighteenth century the *One Hundred Poets* was used specifically as a textbook for young women.[12] Its literal centrality to female education can be seen in a woodblock print from the Tenpō era (1830–1843), *Sakae-gusa Tōsei Musume* ("Prosperous Grasses, Contemporary Daughters") by Kunisada (Plate 4): with daughters on either side engaged in activities related to the silk industry, the middle daughter diligently practices her calligraphy while reading the *One Hundred Poets,* with female educational texts such as the *Onna Ima-gawa* on the floor in front of her. Besides providing models for calligraphy, as we see a young girl practicing in yet another late Edo edition (Figure 43),[13] such editions became general handbooks of etiquette and classical literature, providing references for famous literary stories (such as the title poems for the chapters of *The Tale of Genji;* Figure 44) and practical information (such as the proper way to fold a letter; Figure 46). Accordingly, the more references to commonly known stories in the poems themselves, the better: the Tanabata legend was always included (Figure 45). In fact, the Tanabata legend gave rise to the Tanabata Festival, part of which was the writing of Japanese poems, and editions of the *One Hundred Poets* are a regular feature in artists' depictions of the festival.[14] Connected in this way to the feminine arts of sewing and to the image of connubial fidelity, deluxe copies of the *One Hundred Poets,* often combined with ethical texts such as the *Onna Ima-gawa,* were standard elements of the bridal trousseau well into the twentieth century.

Thus an artist's pictorialization was the result of a complex interaction between exegetical traditions, ideologies, and markets. Besides the issue of education for women, another obvious example can be seen in the pictorializations of Poem 7 by Abe no Nakamaro:

ama no hara	As I gaze out, far
furi-sake-mireba	across the plain of heaven,
kasuga naru	ah, at Kasuga,
mikasa no yama ni	from behind Mount Mikasa,
ideshi tsuki kamo	it's the same moon that came out then!

This poem was purportedly composed at a farewell banquet in China just before Nakamaro's attempted voyage back to Japan. Although the poem's basic meaning is not in dispute, notice how the balance between Japanese and Chinese elements varies, first, in Moronobu's picture of 1678 (Figure 7-2), then in the Kyoto illustrator's of 1746 (Figure 7-3), then the Porter illustrator from the early nineteenth century (Figure 7-1), and finally in Hokusai's print of 1835–1838 (Plate 5),[15] which seems to presage popular Meiji prints from the Sino-Japanese War.

Figure 42. Kanō Tan'yū (attrib.), *Hyaku-nin Isshu Gazō, Tan'yū-hitsu, Kan*, "Ōtomo no Yakamochi."

Figure 43. Anonymous, *Ogura Hyakunin Isshu*, "Fun'ya no Asayasu." Printed book, 25.7 × 18 cm. Edo: Kinkadō, Suwaraya Sasuke, n.d.

Figure 44. Anonymous, *Ogura Hyakunin Isshu*, "Ōe no Chisato."

Figure 45. Anonymous, *Ogura Hyakunin Isshu*, "Sangi Hitoshi."

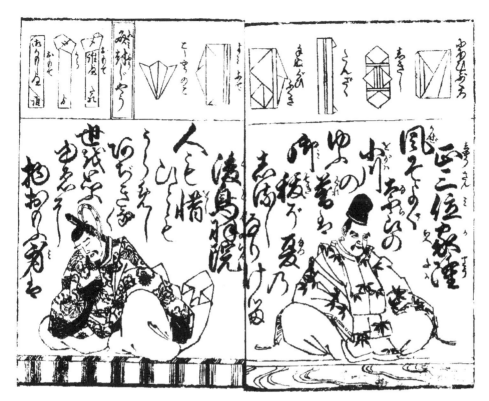

Figure 46. Anonymous, *Hyakunin Isshu*, "GoToba In" *(L)* and "Shō Sanmi Ietaka" *(R)*.

Clearly there was a variety of markets for a variety of interpretive images, and Hokusai's rendition was probably not meant to appeal to the same audience who preferred their *One Hundred Poets* in sinophilic *man'yō-gana* (Figure 47).[16]

Let us return now to the most overdetermined, if atypical, example: the various pictorializations of the very first poem in the anthology, by the Emperor Tenji—the same poem we used earlier to examine the commentary tradition. Let us look again at Moronobu's first picture, the 1678 version (Figure 10): he shows us a thatched hut in which the emperor is presumably staying; the bare, autumnal tree beside it, and the almost equally bare old man in the center, suggesting the emperor's empathy for his toiling subjects. Compare these elements to the 1746 Kyoto version (Figure 1-1): the poor hut has been turned into a residence worthy of an aristocrat; the sere tree has been replaced by an auspicious pine. The Porter version (Figure 1-2) greatly reduces the attention paid to peasant labor, relegating it to landscape elements, and introduces instead the three hills in the background, allusions to the poem on the three hills of Yamato for which Tenji is most famous as a poet. Contrarily, the Keisai Eisen's *Shūgyoku Hyakunin Isshu Ogura Shiori* of 1836 emphasizes the fruits of agricultural labor, relegating the huts (plural) to the far background (thus entirely eliminating the presumed presence of the emperor) and creating a genre scene (Figure 48).[17]

Figure 47. Nakagawa Tsuneki, ed., *Man'yō Hyakunin Isshu,* "Abe no Nakamaro." N.p., 1700. 1 vol. 25.8 × 18.3 cm.

When a figure is depicted in the hut, it is not necessarily that of the emperor but may be a peasant, as in the *Kangyoku* version of 1804 (Figure 49).[18] These pictorializations reflect the insistence of such commentators as Keichū and Mabuchi that the speaker of the poem (as contrasted with the author) is a peasant and not the emperor. Adapted to kimono design (Figure 1-3), the poem becomes a celebration of the harvest, emblazoned with the *kanji minori,* that is, "ripening." In Moronobu's *Sugata-e,* even though the accompanying written commentary interprets the ruined hut as a metaphor for the decline of imperial authority, Tenji's position at the beginning of the collection becomes an opportunity for a self-referential gesture of offering the collection itself to the emperor (Figure 50). It is easy to see how some might read a political statement into the compelling image (Plate 6) from 1849 by Kunisada and Kuni-yoshi—with its echoes of *kuni-mi,* or the imperial surveying of the domain, and its bare landscape in contrast to the usual depictions of autumnal harvest,

Figure 48. Keisai Eisen, *(Nichiyō Zatsu-roku Fujin Shu-Bunko) Shūgyoku Hyakunin Isshu Ogura Shiori,* "Tenji Tennō." Edo, n.p.

echoing the *Ōei Shō*'s interpretation of the poem as a lament over the passing of imperial authority.[19]

With the Meiji period, the need to depict the sovereign arose, as we see in Toyohara Kunichika's 1885 *Portrait of Nobility* (Figure 51),[20] and the "one hundred poets, one poem each" format was taken over in such works as the *Meiji Eimei Hyakuninshu,* or *A Collection of Poems by One Hundred Poets Famous in the Meiji Era* (1881), with the Meiji emperor himself in Tenji's position. Even today we can see that contemporary functions of the emperor and the court literary tradition within the market economy determine the reading of the poem. In the *Manga Hyakunin Isshu,* the creators combine most of the possible interpretations into one grand narrative synthesis. Yet in contrast to most earlier interpretations, they read Tenji's poem as essentially a love poem written while on a journey (Figure 52):

> "Master, your eyes are red!"
>
> "No, it's—the evening dew is drizzling down, and my eyes are tearing"—
>
> "And that's why I complain about your using things like your sleeve to wipe your nose—changes of clothing are already scarce when we're traveling, and who do you think is going to do the laundry? Here, use these!"
>
> "Alright, alright!" . . .
>
> But is it true? Is it really only because of the evening dew that these sleeves are wet?
>
> In the morning, in the waves of the reaped ears of grain,
>
> the wind rises—hearts clamor—
>
> "Perhaps I *was* crying, like a man who sheds tears of lingering affection, mourning the days since she left—"
>
> *Hooonk!* "If only it were *just* tears . . ."[21]

And so a poem traditionally read as an expression of an emperor's concern for the hard life of his subjects is emptied of any overt political import—a move that itself is of no little political significance.

Figure 49. Sōisekishi, *Kangyoku Hyakunin Isshu Suishōsō,* "Tenji Tennō." Edo, 1804.

Figure 50. Moronobu, *Sugata-e Hyakunin Isshu,* "Tenji Tennō."

Figure 51. Toyohara Kunichika, *Portrait of Nobility.* Polychrome woodblock print. 1885.

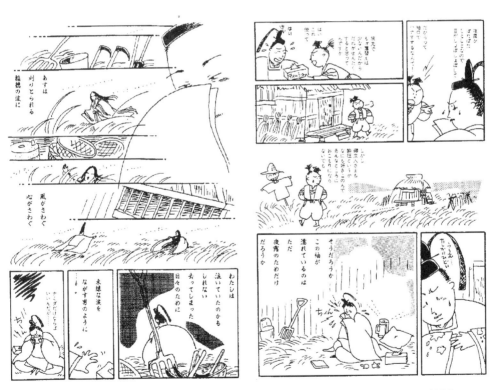

Figure 52. Yoshihara Sachiko and Nakada Yumiko, *Manga Hyakunin Isshu.* 1986.

In many cases the political import—in terms of ideological and historical tensions—can be put back into our "reading" of these poems' reception. And an analysis of this cultural semiosis will not only aid our understanding of how these poems were read in the Edo period but also improve our understanding of our own reception of the classical canon. The translations and commentaries, both verbal and visual, presented in Part Two should provide some of the data and impetus for such future analysis.

PART TWO

TRANSLATION, COMMENTARY, AND PICTURES

A NOTE ON TEXTS
AND SOURCES

This part of the book presents a complete translation of the *Hyakunin Isshu*. The translations represent modern scholars' best estimate of how Fujiwara no Teika, the compiler of the collection, interpreted the poems. To each translation is appended the name of the imperial anthology from which the poem was chosen and a list of other exemplary collections in which it was included. A brief biography of the poet is given, too, emphasizing his or her representation in imperial anthologies through the ages and his or her relationship to other poets in the collection.

The Commentary is meant to help the reader understand the rhetoric of the poem that may be obscured by translation and discusses the major interpretive debates surrounding each verse. I have relied primarily on Ariyoshi Tamotsu's *Hyakunin Isshu ZenYakuchū* (1983); on Shimazu Tadao's *Hyakunin Isshu* (1969), which gives a modern Japanese paraphrase representing Teika's interpretations; and to a lesser extent on Kubota Jun's *Hyakunin Isshu Hikkei* (1982) and Shimazu and Kamijō Shōji's *Hyakunin Isshu Kochū Shō* (1982). For general reference I have used *The Princeton Companion to Classical Japanese Literature* (1985), by Earl Miner, Hiroko Odagiri, and Robert E. Morrell, and Ariyoshi's *Waka Bungaku Jiten* (1982). All other sources have been documented in the notes.

The pictures chosen are meant to illustrate the variety of visual interpretations of the poems throughout the Edo period, but especially in the seventeenth century. The chief sources for these pictures are as follows:

1. Pictures of the poets *(kasen-e)* are the so-called *Soan-bon* images reproduced in Shimazu's *Hyakunin Isshu* (1969). I have used a virtually identical edition, mistitled *Hyakunin Isshu Kōetsu-hitsu*, in the Atomi Gakuen Tanki Daigaku Toshokan.

2. *Hyakunin Isshu Zōsan Shō (Commentary on the* One Hundred Poets, One Poem Each *Collection with Portraits and Inscriptions)* (Edo: Urokogataya, 1678); signed by Hishikawa Moronobu.

3. *(Fūryū) Sugata-e Hyakunin Isshu ([Elegant] Portraits of the* One Hundred Poets, One Poem Each *Collection)* (Edo: Kinoshita Jin'emon, 1695); the poets in a Genroku-period setting; designs by Moronobu; published a year after his death by his son.

4. *Ogura Yama Hyakushu Hinagata (Pattern Book of the Ogura Mountain One Hundred Poems [Hyakushu Hinagata]*). (Edo: Yezōshiya Hachiyemon; Kyoto: Yezōshiya Kisaemon, 1688); designs by Hakuyōken Gyōjō.

5. *Ogura Yama Shikishi Moyō (Pattern Book of Ogura Mountain Cartouche Designs [Shikishi Moyō]*). (Edo: Hon'ya Seibei, 1689); designs by Take Heiji.

6. *(Ko-gata) Hyakunin Isshu Zōsan Shō* (Kyoto: Kōto Shorin, 1746); a small-format anonymous edition based largely on the earlier *Zōsanshō* designs but with significant changes.

7. *Dansen Hyakunin Isshu Taisei (The Great Compendium of the* One Hundred Poets, One Poem Each *Collection on Round Fans)* (Osaka: Ōsaka Shorin, 1755); signed by Hasegawa Mitsunobu.

8. *Kangyoku Hyakunin Isshu Suishōsō (The Jeweled Crown* One Hundred Poets, One Poem Each *Collection Crystal Box)* (1804); pictures by Sōsekishi.

9. *A Hundred Verses from Old Japan,* by William N. Porter (Oxford, 1909).

10. *(Nichiyō Zatsuroku Fujin Shubunko) Shūgyoku Hyakunin Isshu-kan ([The Housewife's Everyday Miscellany Jewel Box Library] Surpassing Gem One Hundred Poets, One Poem Each Guidebook)* (Edo: Hakkō Shorin, 1836); pictures by Keisai Eisen (1790–1848).

11. *Eiga Hyakunin Isshu* Monjū *Shō (The Flowering Fortunes One Hundred Poets, One Poem Each Literary Selections Commentary)* (Edo, 1817); pictures by Utagawa Sadahide.

POEM 1

aki no ta no
kari-ho no iho no
toma wo arami
wa ga koromo-de ha
tsuyu ni nuretsutsu[1]

In the autumn fields
the hut, the temporary hut,
   its thatch is rough
and so the sleeves of my robe
are dampened night by night with dew.

Emperor Tenji

Tenji Tennō (626–671) ruled 668–671; he is numbered as the thirty-eighth emperor. Son of Emperor Jōmei and Empress Kōgyoku (also known as Empress Saimei), he was also called "Prince Katsuragi" and "Prince Naka no Ōe." Together with Nakatomi no Kamatari (614–669) he destroyed the power of the Soga clan in 644–645 by assassinating Soga no Iruka. As crown prince he took part in the Taika Reform; as emperor he published a legal code called the *Ōmi-ryō*. Since the time of Emperor Kōnin (r. 770–781), Tenji has been revered as the progenitor of the imperial line. He gave Kamatari the surname Fujiwara in 669. Tenji has four poems in the first book of the *Man'yō Shū*, including a "long poem" *(chōka)* on the Three Mountains of Yamato (see Poem 2). He is credited with two more poems in later imperial anthologies, including the poem collected in the *One Hundred Poets*, but the attributions are considered dubious.

Commentary

This poem appears in the *Gosenshū* (Autumn 2): 302. However, Mabuchi argued that this poem was no more than a reworking of *Man'yō Shū* 10: 2174 (anon.), which must have originally been some sort of folk song:

aki-ta karu	I build a temporary hut
kari-ho wo tsukuri	to reap the autumn fields
ware woreba	and as I keep watch
koromo-de samuku	at night, my sleeves are so cold
tsuyu zo okinikeru	that the dew settles on them.

This same poem appears as *ShinKokinshū* (Autumn 2): 454, but with the first line *aki-ta moru*, "to guard the autumn fields." Its inclusion in the *ShinKokinshū* suggests that Teika viewed it and the *One Hundred Poets* verse as two separate poems.

   Kari-ho is a contraction of *kari-iho* ("temporary hut"). However, some commentators see it as a pivot word *(kake-kotoba)* also meaning "reaped ears [of grain]" *(kari-ho)*. While there is no evidence that the word had this second meaning in the *Man'yō* period, Teika's father, Shunzei (Poem 83), composed the following poem on the accession of Emperor Rokujō (1165):

kazu shirazu	It is because it gathers
aki no kari-ho wo	the reaped ears of autumns
tsumite koso	beyond all number
ohokura-yama no	that it bears the name
na ni ha ohikere[2]	"Great Storehouse Mountain."

Here *kari-ho* clearly means "reaped ears," so Teika may well have considered it a pivot word in Tenji's poem.

   A poem of similar grammatical structure to the one in the *Man'yō Shū* is also credited to Tenji and included in the *ShinKokinshū* (Misc. 1): 1687:

asakura ya	Asakura!
ki no maru-dono ni	when I am here
wa ga woreba	in the hall of unbarked logs,
na-nori wo shitsutsu	whose child is that,
iku ha taga ko zo	who passes by, announcing his name?

Fujiwara no Kiyosuke (1104–1177) attributed this poem to Tenji in his *Ōgi Shō*. Asakura was where Tenji's mother, Empress Saimei, died while she and Tenji were leading an army to Korea to aid the kingdoms of Koma and Kudara. Some commentators *(Yoritaka-bon)* argued that the *One Hundred Poets* poem too was composed while Tenji was at Asakura or, more particularly, that it was a song of mourning over his mother's death there *(Yūsai Shō)*. The *Yoritaka-bon* identifies the poem as a *jukkai no mi-uta*, or poem "expressing personal grievances."[3] While the *Yoritaka-bon* interprets the poem as a complaint about being away from the capital, that is, a complaint about homesickness, most commentaries that see the poem as a *jukkai* (such as *Ōei Shō*) believe that Tenji is lamenting the decline of imperial authority. However, the generally accepted interpretation is that Teika saw this as a poem expressing an emperor's compassion for the lot of the peasants and that he regarded Tenji as a model emperor. This, of course, makes the poem eminently well suited to begin the anthology. Moreover, it was Tenji who bestowed the surname "Fujiwara" on Teika's anscestors, marking in a sense their own beginning as well.

The Pictures

The Tan'yū album shows in its upper register a simple hut and autumn fields. The *Zōsanshō* [Figure 10] shows peasants reaping, clearly representing the pivot word *kari-ho,* even though the accompanying commentary by Yūsai rejects this interpretation not once but three times.[4] In the Kyoto version [**1–1**], the *Zōsanshō*'s ill-thatched hut has been transformed into a residence worthy of sheltering the emperor, who is presumably looking out on the scene below him. Moreover, the earlier scrawny and withered tree has been replaced by an auspicious pine, symbol of longevity.

The picture reproduced in Porter [**1–2**] is a markedly different composition, far more elegiac than pastoral. The low mountains in the background might be taken to suggest the poem on the Three Mountains of Yamato for which Tenji was best known as a poet (see Poem 2). Finally, the *Shikishi Moyō* kimono design [**1–3**] converts the poem into a celebration of the harvest with the Chinese character for "ripening" *(minori)* superimposed on sheaves of grain, based on the earlier *Hyakushu Hinagata* pattern book.

1-1

1-2

1-3

POEM 2

haru sugite
natsu kinikerashi
shiro-tahe no
koromo hosu tefu
ama no kagu-yama[5]

Spring has passed, and
summer has arrived, it seems.
Heavenly Mount Kagu
where, it is said, they dry robes
of the whitest mulberry!

Empress Jitō
Jitō Tennō (645–702), ruled 687–696 and
is counted as the forty-first sovereign. She
was the second daughter of Emperor
Tenji (Poem 1); her mother was the
daughter of Soga no Ochi and empress
to Emperor Tenmu. She marched with
Tenmu during the Jinshin Disturbance
(672) and succeeded him at the age of
forty-two, moving the court to Fujiwara
no Miya. After eleven years she abdicated
in favor of her nephew Monmu. The
Man'yō Shū includes two *chōka* (one on
the death of Tenmu) and five *tanka* by
her, including this one. She made many
tours, or "imperial progresses," which
provided Hitomaro (Poem 3) an oppor-
tunity for some of his finest *chōka*. She
has one poem each in the *ShinKokinshū*
and *ShinChokusenshū*, but the latter is not
considered authentic.

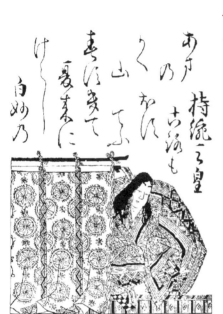

Commentary
This poem originally appears as *Man'yō Shū* 1:28, attributed to Jitō:

haru sugite
natsu kitarurashi
shiro-tahe no
koromo hoshitari
ame no kagu-yama

Spring has passed
and summer has come, it appears,
for they are drying robes
of the whitest mulberry
on heavenly Mount Kagu.

The original *man'yō-gana* transcription gave rise to many different readings in
the Heian period, such as *koromo hoshitaru* and *koromo kawakasu,* so that the
ShinKokinshū editors had to choose one from several possible readings. It is
generally agreed that the version they chose is not as forceful as the original,
kinikerashi contrasting with the more definite *kitarurashi*. Yet the biggest prob-
lem is in the fourth line: *koromo hosu tefu,* "they dry robes, it is said," contrasting
with the original's simple "they dry robes." The original poem is presumed to

have been written from Jitō's palace, the Fujiwara no Miya, which is only about one mile to the northwest of Mount Kagu—in other words, the empress is writing about a scene before her eyes. The *tefu* of the *ShinKokinshū* version makes it a matter of hearsay, not direct observation. The confusion this change entailed is seen clearly in the commentary to this poem in the *Hyakunin Isshu Hitoyo-gatari* of 1833:

> In the *ShinKokinshū* version it is hard to know whether the words were corrected to conform to the writing of the period [the *ShinKokin* era], or whether there was an error made during the transmission and they were written this way. . . . While there are many complicated explanations found in the many commentaries to the *Hyakunin Isshu,* one finds none that can clearly explain the matter.

(See Chapter 2.) Far more time, however, has been spent disputing the meaning of *shiro-tahe.* While it is clear that in the original poem this meant white clothes made out of *tahe,* a kind of paper mulberry, with the exception of the *Keikō Shō* all commentators have taken this expression to be a metaphor. The question then becomes just what it is meant to be a metaphor for.

The interpretation of the *Ōei Shō,* Yūsai, and others is reflected in Kitamura Kigin's mid-Edo-period commentary in the *Hachidaishū Shō:*

> Ama no Kaguyama during spring is completely hidden by mist *(kasumi)* and cannot be seen; but when summer comes the mist rises and is dispelled and in the early summer weather, this mountain can be clearly seen—this is called "drying the white robes" *(shiro-tahe no koromo hosu).* "To dry" is a word association *(engo)* with "robe." Summer comes and strips off the garment of mist, and the mountain becomes clearly visible, so the poet sings of this by the phrase *shiro-tahe no koromo hosu.*[6]

Contrarily, the *Yoritaka-bon* argues that the phrase means *covering* by mist. Shimazu, following the *Kamijō-hon* (mid-Muromachi), argues that *shiro-tahe* was understood by Teika as a metaphor for *unohana,* or deutzia. As evidence he cites the following poem from Teika's own collected poems, the *Shūi Gusō:*

shiro-tahe no	They dry the robes
koromo hosu tefu	of white mulberry, it is said,
natsu no kite	when summer comes,
kaki-ne mo tawa ni	and even the fence bends under their
	weight—
sakeru unohana	the deutzia in bloom.

Yet Katagiri cites a poem by GoToba, *ShinKokinshū* (Spring 1): 2, as evidence that Mount Kagu was also associated with mist in Teika's day. In any event, the *One Hundred Poets* poem is placed at the beginning of the summer section of the *ShinKokinshū* and was no doubt taken to refer to the seasonal changing of clothes. Finally, as Katagiri notes, Mount Kagu was used in poems celebrating the sovereign's longevity, as in this poem from the imperial anthology that preceded the *ShinKokinshū,* the *Senzaishū* (Felicitations): 608 (presented 1188):

kimi ga yo ha	During my lord's reign
ama no kago-yama	I pray there be no limit
idzuru hi no	to the shining of the sun
teramu kagiri ha	that emerges from
tsukiji to zo omofu	Heavenly Mount Kago!

The reason for this association is that Mount Kagu was the location of the stone door that Amaterasu, the Sun Goddess and ancestor of the imperial line, closed behind her when she withheld her light from the world; thus these poems make a specific link between the light of the Sun Goddess and the rays of beneficent rule of her earthly descendant, the mikado. Likewise, Teika's placement of this poem in the *One Hundred Poets* may well have been meant to suggest such celebratory poems. Moreover, Emperor Tenji was best-known as a poet for his *chōka* on the Three Mountains of Yamato, of which Kagu-yama was one.[7] Finally, by choosing the daughter of the first poet in the collection, Teika is asserting the hereditary nature of poetry, something he mirrors in the relationship of the last two poems in this anthology, by GoToba and his son Juntoku.

The Pictures

Artists made various attempts to represent what they understood to be the metaphorical meaning of the phrase "dry robes of the whitest mulberry." This was generally understood by commentators to be a metaphor for spring mist, as seen in the Porter pictorialization [2–2], though we are unable to tell whether the mist is coming or going. That it is rising to reveal Mount Kagu is clearer in the *Shūgyoku Hyakunin Isshu-kan* of 1836 [2–3], where the clouds are completely above the mountain. Yet Moronobu and others after him included the metaphoric image as well, the robe floating in the sky [2–4]. Such pictorializations seem to have been suggested by the popular association between this poem and the *Hagoromo* legend (mentioned explicitly in the *Sugata-e* commentary). The floating robe motif is marvelously transformed in the *Hyakushu Hinagata* [2–5], where we see the trailing skirts of the rising heavenly maiden disappearing over the right shoulder. (The butterflies, or *chō*, are meant to represent the words *tefu*, pronounced /chō/.) Other illustrators, such as Hasegawa [2–1], emphasize the seasonal airing of robes, despite the illogical nature of this interpretation as pointed out in the *Hyakunin Isshu Hitoyo-gatari*.

2-1

2-2

2-3

2-4

2-5

POEM 3

ashi-biki no
yama-dori no wo no
shidari-wo no
naga-nagashi yo wo
hitori kamo nemu[8]

Must I sleep alone
through the long autumn nights,
    long like the dragging tail
of the mountain pheasant
separated from his dove?

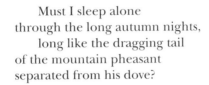

Kakinomoto no Hitomaro

Hitomaro (dates unknown) was a court poet under Empress Jitō (Poem 2) and Emperor Monmu (r. 697–707). He served as a low-ranking official and is said to have died (ca. 707–708) while posted to Iwami province (modern Shimane prefecture). The representative *Man'yō Shū* poet, with eighteen *chōka* and sixty-seven *tanka*, he was venerated and worshiped as the saint of poetry since the middle ages. *The Collected Poems of Kakinomoto (Kakinomoto Shū)* is a posthumous collection. Some 248 poems attributed to him appear in the *Kokinshū* and later imperial anthologies, but as these are all drawn from the *Kakinomoto Shū*, their authenticity is dubious. Hitomaro is one of the Thirty-Six Poetic Immortals *(sanjūrokkasen).*

Commentary

Teika drew this poem from the *Shūishū* (13 [Love 3]:778). Its original appearance in the *Man'yō Shū* (anon. 2802), however, is a good example of how much two poems could differ and still be thought of as "the same" poem by early Japanese editors. The *Man'yō Shū* text reads:

omohedomo
omohi no kanetsu
ashi-hiki no
yama-dori no wo no
nagaki kono yo wo

Even though I vow not to think of her
I cannot help but think of her
    all through this night, long
like the tail of the mountain-pheasant
in the foot-wearying mountains.

We, however, shall concern ourselves only with the version found in the *Shūishū*.

The first problem for the Western translator is the first line: *ashi-hiki no.* This is a *makura-kotoba,* or "pillow word," a conventional epithet that modifies the first word of the following line, in this case "mountain" *(yama).* Pillow words are characteristic of *Man'yō Shū* period poetry and many, such as the one under consideration, are of unknown meaning. In the *Man'yō Shū* this phrase is also written with the Chinese characters that mean, literally, "foot-cypress-'s." Dickins argued that the "least unacceptable explanation seems to be *ikashi-hi-ki,* flourishing or abundant *hi (chamaecyparis)* trees."[9] Medieval poets, however, seem to have taken *ashi* to mean "reed."[10] In any event, the most commonly used characters were those that signified "foot-pull," and since the nineteenth century it has been the practice of English scholars to translate the phrase as "foot-dragging," "foot-wearying," or some such. Modern Japanese paraphrases either omit the phrase or leave it untranslated.

Not only does this poem give an example of an unambiguous pillow word (unlike *shiro-tahe no* in Poem 2), it also gives a fine example of a *jo,* or "preface." This is "a section of unspecified length that precedes the main statement in the poem and is joined to it by wordplay, similarity of sound, or an implied rhetorical relationship."[11] In this poem the entire first three lines serve only as a preface for the adjective *naga-nagashi* ("long"). If this preface is seen as connected only to the immediately succeeding word, then the preface would be considered *mushin,* or minimally motivated. The *ushin,* or fully motivated, interpretation notes that the long-tailed mountain pheasant was believed to part from its mate at night to sleep in separate ravines, a belief attested to in *Toshiyori's Poetic Essentials (Toshiyori Zuinō,* ca. 1111) and suggested as early as *The Pillow Book of Sei Shōnagon (Makura no Sōshi)* (and thus leading to the translation with "separated from his dove" given above).[12] The poem comes from a group of poems in the *Man'yō Shū* called *kibutsu-chinshi-ka,* or "pathetic fallacy poems," while in the *Shūishū* it was grouped with a set of poems all starting with the pillow word *ashi-hiki no.* In Teika's day, technical appreciation focused on the repetition of the syllable *no* to suggest the long night.[13]

The Pictures

While the figure of Hitomaro in the Tan'yū album clearly follows the standard iconography, seen also in the Satake-bon, the face has a decidedly Chinese cast, for the poet's beard is longer and wispier.[14] This beard style is kept in the *Zōsanshō kasen-e* where, however, the poet is portrayed as much older—a characterization that is then utilized in Moronobu's *Sugata-e,* where the poet, being led to bed by both a young woman and young man, is most clearly not sleeping alone. In terms of the poem's pictorialization, the *Zōsanshō* figure is fairly straightforward [**3–1**]. Both it and the Kyoto artist [**3–2**] seem to disregard the sense of the poem by having both a male and female pheasant—no doubt influenced by the convention of bird-and-flower paintings *(kachōga)* popular at the time (though the *Hyakushu Hinagata* uses only the male pheasant). The Kyoto artist adds autumn leaves to indicate the season with the longest nights of the year, as well as grasses or reeds with dewdrops on them—whether the flora is meant to suggest *ashi*, or the dew "beads" *(tama)*, an *engo* for *hiku*, is unclear. Both the Porter artist and the *Eiga* [**3–3**] give only one bird, but the setting is not a ravine as in the other pictures and the latter has added a river. The *Kangyoku* [**3–4**] shows the lonely poet in bed.

3-1

3-2

3-3

3-4

POEM 4

tago no ura ni
uchi-idete mireba
shiro-tahe no
fuji no taka-ne ni
yuki ha furitsutsu[15]

As I set out on
the beach of Tago, and look,
I see the snow constantly falling
on the high peak of Fuji,
white as mulberry cloth.

Yamabe no Akahito

Akahito (dates unknown) was an early
Nara-period (646–794) court poet and a
contemporary of Hitomaro (Poem 3),
with whom he is ranked in the *Kokinshū*
preface. One of the Thirty-Six Poetic
Immortals, he has thirteen *chōka* and
thirty-seven *tanka* included in the *Man'yō
Shū*, all composed during the reign of
Emperor Shōmu (r. 724–749), including
poems composed for Shōmu's visits to
Yoshino, Naniwa, and Kii. He has about
forty-six poems in the imperial antholo-
gies, starting with the *Gosenshū*, though
all are of doubtful authenticity. *The Col-
lected Poems of Akahito (Akahito Shū)* is a
later compilation.

Commentary

The original poem appears as an envoi
(hanka) to a *chōka, Man'yō Shū* 3:317, with
a headnote *(kotoba-gaki):*

Poem on viewing Mount Fuji by Yamabe Akahito, with tanka:

tago no ura yu
uchi-idete mireba
mashiro ni zo
fuji no taka-ne ni
yuki ha furikeru

Coming out
from Tago's nestled cove,
I gaze:
white, pure white
the snow has fallen
on Fuji's lofty peak.[16]

Like Poem 2 by Empress Jitō, there appear to have been many different read-
ings of the *Man'yō* script of this poem in the Heian period. Of the three differ-
ences between the *Man'yō Shū* source poem and the *One Hundred Poets* version,
two have received attention. The *One Hundred Poets* version has the first line

reading *tago no ura ni,* that is, "at/on Tago no Ura," which in turn forces the *uchi-idete* to mean "setting out on," while the original clearly has "coming out of/from *(yu)* Tago no Ura," with *uchi-idete* then meaning "coming out (from the shadow)." Thus Tago no Ura itself was at the time some spot in mountain shadow where Fuji could not be seen, probably somewhere around present-day Yubi, Nishi Kurazawa, or Mount Satsuta.[17] Under the influence of the *One Hundred Poets* reading of this poem, the location of Tago no Ura was relocated to a place where Fuji could in fact be seen, with *ura* being translated as "beach" rather than "bay." Despite its changed wording, both the "bay" and the "beach" interpretations were followed in the early Edo period.

The second problem is the last line, where *One Hundred Poets* has *furi-tsutsu* for the original's *furikeru.* The latter simply means "the snow is falling (and has been falling, but I just became able to see it)," while the former's *-tsutsu* indicates the repetition of an action (as in Poem 1's "my sleeve keeps getting wetted *repeatedly* by the dew"). Yet if Akahito is speeding through Tago Bay and seeing Fuji for the first time, he is not present long enough to be able to assert that the snow "keeps" falling.[18]

The Pictures

The *Zōsanshō* picture [**4–2**] clearly follows the "beach" interpretation, while the 1746 Kyoto illustrator [**4–3**] has adapted the "bay" interpretation. Hasegawa's fan [**4–1**] is distinctive in its emphasis of the coldness, with Akahito's hands in his sleeves and snow on the bamboo grass beside him, suggesting a plaint about the cold (perhaps suggested by the poem's similarity to Poem 1, both with the suffix *-tsutsu*) rather than a celebration of natural beauty. Contrarily, in Moronobu's *Sugata-e* [**4–4**], the poet looks very comfortable indeed (and on the beach, despite the accompanying commentary's specific explanation of the poet going out in a boat). The *Hyakushu Hinagata* has a bay full of boat sails, as well as snowflakes bearing words of the poem falling onto an outline of Mount Fuji.

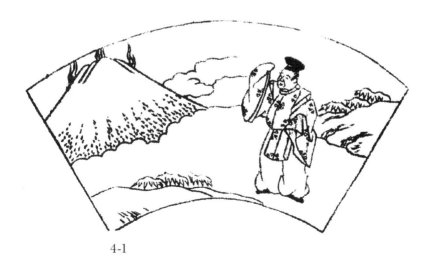

4-1

4-2

田子乃
浦ゆ
うち出て
みれは
白きえの
ぬしのうへに
雪はふりける

4-3

4-4

POEM 5

oku-yama ni
momijhi fumi-wake
naku shika no
kowe kiku toki zo
aki ha kanashiki[19]

When I hear the voice
of the stag crying for his mate
   stepping through the fallen leaves
deep in the mountains—then is the time
that autumn is saddest.

Senior Assistant Minister Sarumaru
Absolutely nothing is known about Saru-maru-Dayū (also read "Sarumaru Taifu"). In the Chinese preface *(manajo)* to the *Kokinshū*, Ōtomo no Kuronushi (830?–923?) is described as the stylistic inheritor of the "Illustrious Sarumaru,"[20] on the basis of which Sarumaru is assumed to be a real person who lived sometime prior to the latter half of the eighth century. *The Collected Poems of Senior Assistant Minister Sarumaru (Sarumaru-Dayū Shū)* is a later compilation, and the poems in it are of dubious authenticity. Besides this poem none of his poems are included in any imperial anthologies. In fact, this poem is listed as anonymous in the *Kokin-shū* (Autumn 4:215), and simply labeled as composed for a poetry contest spon-sored by Prince Koresada in 893. It is also included in the personal (Japanese) poetry collection of Michizane, casting further doubt on the authorship of this poem. Mention of Sarumaru's grave is found in Kamo no Chōmei's *Account of a Ten-Foot-Square Hut (Hōjō Ki)* and his *Untitled Treatise (Mu'myō Shō)*. Given that so little is known of him, and that *saru* means "monkey," many portraits portray the poet as monkey-faced. He is included among Kintō's Thirty-Six Poetic Immortals.

Commentary

For such a beautifully simple poem, the problems of interpretation it has engendered are legion. The first question is: *who* is stepping on the leaves—the poet or the deer? Although it appears in the *Sarumaru Shū* as *shika no naku wo kikite* ("when I listen to the crying of the deer"), Mabuchi in his *Kokin Waka Shū Uchi-giki* of 1789 claimed that it is the poet who is walking though the leaves—an interpretation seconded by modern editors of the *Kokinshū*.[21] Historically, however, this has been a minority view. Rather, the poet has been understood to be in or near the hills of a village (*toyama* or *hayama* in contrast to *okuyama*) where he hears the stag's cry coming from deep within the mountains. This interpretation is further reinforced by the poem's position in the *Kokinshū,* where it is the second in a group of five poems on deer. In fact, the placement of the poem in both the *Kokinshū* and in Teika's *Nishidai Shū* (compiled in 1234–1235) tells us a great deal about how the reading of this poem changed over three hundred years.

As Ariyoshi has pointed out, in the *Kokinshū* this poem appears just after the midpoint of Autumn Book 1, the second poem in a group of five on deer. The next three poems are on deer and bush clover (*hagi*). Clearly the poem is set in midautumn and the word *momijhi* ("autumn leaves") refers to the yellowing leaves of the bush clover that the deer or poet is passing through. (In the version of this poem that appears in the *Shinsen Man'yō Shū, momijhi* is written with characters that mean "yellow leaves," rather than the "scarlet leaves" used for the maple, or *kaede.*) Yet in his *Nishidai Shū* collection Teika placed the poem in a group of late autumn poems. In the *Ōei Commentary* we learn that it was believed that the leaves changed in the villages before they changed in the fastness of the mountains, and several commentaries point to the following poem by Priest Shun'e (Poem 85) (*SKKS* Autumn 2:451):

tatsuta-yama	Mount Tatsuta:
kozuwe mabara ni	as the treetops
naru mama ni	become thinner,
fukaku mo shika no	deeper still the deer go
soyogu naru kana	into the mountain, crying!

Accordingly, the *One Hundred Poets* poem was believed in the medieval and early modern periods to be set in late autumn and the *momijhi* to refer to fallen maple leaves.

The Pictures

The Tan'yū album depicts an aged Sarumaru, with a single stag in low hills covered with autumn leaves of yellow and red. The *Zōsanshō* [**5–1**] has two deer, male and female, deep within a mountain ravine, accompanied by maple leaves. The *Sugata-e* [**5–2**] suggests a combination of the Tan'yū album and *Zōsanshō,* while in front the relaxed poet seems to be receiving a massage from a young woman.[22] In all of these the leaves, whether maple or not, are clearly on the trees rather than fallen to the ground, a feature preserved by the Porter artist as well [**5–3**]. Nonetheless, the *Sugata-e* commentary clearly indicates that the poem was read as set in late autumn, with fallen leaves. The *Shūgyoku* of 1836 [**5–4**] is clearly related to the Porter version, but the artist has added fallen leaves for the deer to track through, perhaps showing the influence of Shun'e's poem with its *soyogu*. Both these latter two versions also seem to suggest that the deer are *entering* the mountain.

5-1

5-2

5-3

5-4

POEM 6

kasasagi no
wataseru hashi ni
oku shimo no
shiroki wo mireba
yo zo fukenikeru[23]

When I see the whiteness
of the frost that lies
on the bridge the magpies spread,
then do I know, indeed,
that the night has deepened.

Middle Counselor Yakamochi

Chūnagon Ōtomo no Yakamochi (718–785), best known as the final editor of the *Man'yō Shū* (ca. 759), which includes many of his poems: over forty *chōka* and close to four hundred *tanka*. He is one of the Thirty-Six Poetic Immortals. *The Collected Poems of Yakamochi (Yakamochi Shū)* is by a later compiler. With poems first included in the *Shūishū* (ca. 1005–1011), Yakamochi has sixty-two poems included in imperial anthologies.[24]

Commentary

This poem is taken from the *Yakamochi Shū* but does not appear in the *Man'yō Shū;* in fact, the expression "magpie bridge" appears nowhere in the entire collection, suggesting that this poem is a creation of the early Heian period, rather than the late Nara period when Yakamochi lived. The understanding of the phrase *kasasagi no wataseru hashi* has divided interpretations into two camps. One camp understands the poem as having been composed when the poet was looking at the stars sparkling coldly in the winter sky and, seeing the whiteness of the heavens filled with frost, was reminded of the autumn night of Tanabata, when frost lays on the bridge of magpies spread across the River of Heaven, allowing the Ox Herd (the constellation Aquila) to make his yearly visit to the Weaver Maid (Vega). However, the evidence from the *Tales of Yamato (Yamato Monogatari)* makes it quite clear that in the Heian period "the magpie's bridge" referred to bridges or stairs that led up to the palace.[25] In such a case, the poet is keeping nightwatch in the palace and sees actual frost on an actual bridge.

Poems by Teika's contemporaries, however, indicate that poets of the thirteenth century onward understood this poem to be alluding to the Tanabata legend.[26]

The Pictures

While the Tan'yū album shows a frosty streak in the sky (see Figure 42), the Tanabata interpretation is used in the *Zōsanshō* [**6-2**]. This is made the upper-register inset in the *Sugata-e,* (see Figure 40) where the foreground presents the thoroughly contemporary image of a playboy being led back from an evening in the Yoshiwara brothel district. The *Sugata-e* commentary glosses *kasasagi* as "crows" *(karasu),* suggesting that the meaning of the former term was not commonly known; it is taken for a kind of heron *(sagi)* by both the *Hyakushu Hinagata* kimono design [**6–3**] and the *Shikishi Moyō* [**6–4**], which allows the transformation of black birds into auspicious white ones. In the former pattern book the characters for *oku shimo* are drawn in archaic Chinese script (this poem was long believed by many commentators to be based on a famous Chinese verse), while Tanabata is indicated by the bamboo-stalks from which Tanabata poems were typically hung. The *Shikishi Moyō* [**6–4**] frees the cranes from the bridge format and dispenses with the character for *oku* ("to fall" in relation to dew but meaning more literally "to place") with the character for "frost" *(shimo)* set on a bridge. As noted above, however, the original poem has nothing to do with the Tanabata legend, and in the Heian period the "magpie bridge" referred to bridges leading up to the imperial palace, as illustrated by Kuniyoshi and Kunisada in their 1849 edition (see Plate 3). Nonetheless, this scholarly interpretive advance was generally ignored—most readers *wanted* this poem to refer to the Tanabata legend, as seen most clearly in the Porter illustration [**6–1**].

6-1

6-2

6-3

6-4

POEM 7

ama no hara
furi-sake-mireba
kasuga naru
mikasa no yama ni
ideshi tsuki kamo[27]

As I gaze out, far
across the plain of heaven,
ah, at Kasuga,
from behind Mount Mikasa,
it's the same moon that came out then!

Abe no Nakamaro

At the age of sixteen, Nakamaro (701–770) went with the priest Genbō and Kibi no Makibi to study in China.[28] He rose to high position in the service of the T'ang emperor Hsüan-tsung and became friends with such famous poets as Li Po and Wang Wei. In 753 he set out to return to Japan with Fujiwara no Kiyokawa, but they were shipwrecked off the coast of Annam in Southeast Asia. He returned to China, where he died at the age of seventy. He has one poem in the *Kokinshū* and one in the *ShokuKokinshū*.

Commentary

This poem is Nakamaro's sole inclusion in the *Kokinshū*, but it is set as the first poem in the "Travel" section, a place of honor. To it is appended the following story:

Long ago, Nakamaro was sent to study in China. After he had had to stay for many years, there was an opportunity for him to take passage home with a returning Japanese embassy. He set out, and a group of Chinese held a farewell party for him on the beach at a place called Mingzhou. This poem is said to have been composed after nightfall, when Nakamaro noticed that an extraordinarily beautiful moon had risen.[29]

A longer and more romanticized account is found in Tsurayuki's *Tosa Diary* (ca. 935):

The Twentieth-night moon appeared. With no mountain rim from which to emerge, it seemed to rise out of the sea. Just such a sight must have greeted the eyes of Abe no Nakamaro when he prepared to return home from China long ago. At the place where he was to board ship, the Chinese gave him a farewell party, lamenting the separation and composing poems in their language. As they lingered there, seemingly reluctant to let him go, the Twenti-

eth-night moon rose from the sea. Nakamaro recited a composition in
Japanese, remarking, "Such poems have been composed by the gods in our
country ever since the divine age. Nowadays people of all classes compose
them when they regret the necessity of parting, as we are doing, or when they
feel joy or sorrow:"

aounabara	When I gaze far out
furi-sake-mireba	across the blue-green sea plain,
kasuga naru	I see the same moon
mikasa no yama ni	that came up over the hill
ideshi tsuki kamo	of Mikasa at Kasuga.

Although Nakamaro had feared that the poem would be unintelligible to the
Chinese, he wrote down the gist in characters and explained it to someone
who understood our language, and then it received unexpectedly warm
praise. They must have been able to appreciate his emotions, after all.
Although China and this country use different languages, moonlight must
look the same in both places, evoking the same human feelings.[30]

Commentaries on this poem concerned themselves with chiefly two
points: whether this poem was in fact composed on the occasion described
in the *Kokinshū* (though debate on this point only starts with the *Iken* in
1815); and the interpretation of the second line, *furi-sake-mireba*. Only the
latter point need concern us here. *Sake* means "to remove," "to release," or
"distant." The whole phrase *ama no hara furi-sake-mireba* is in fact found in
three other *Man'yō Shū* poems, including 3:317 by Akahito, to which Poem 4
originally served as an envoi.[31] The *Ōei Commentary* and the *Minō Commentary*,
however, read the main verb as *sage* ("to carry in one's hand"); the latter text
paraphrases the whole line as "seeing it as if one had taken it in one's
hands."

The point of the poem has frequently been missed by English translators.
As Ogawa Masao has pointed out in his edition of the *Kokinshū*, Kasuga Shrine
was where envoys such as Nakamaro prayed for safe return before setting out to
China. Thus Nakamaro is not comparing the moon he sees in China to the
moon that rises over Kasuga (to the detriment of the former, as the chauvinistic
Kamijō-bon would have it), but to the moon that rose *(ideshi)* the night he
prayed there.

The poem was included in the *Wakan Rōei Shū* and universally admired as
take-takashi, yosei kagiri nashi (as it says in the *Ōei Shō*), or "vast in scale and limit-
less in resonance." The resonance, of course, was due more to the story sur-
rounding the poem than anything inherent in the verse itself.

Like the phrase *ama no hara furi-sake-mireba*, the lines *kasuga naru mikasa
yama ni* also appear in other *Man'yō Shū* poems (7:1295; 10:1887). Modern
commentators also point out that the expletive *kamo* marks this as a Nara-
period poem. This poem is, in fact, the oldest datable poem in the *Kokinshū*,
and thus the image of Nakamaro gazing wistfully toward Japan serves as a fine
bridge to the next section of poems, drawn from the *Kokinshū* era itself, with its
distinctively different poetic style.

The Pictures

The *Zōsanshō* [**7–2**] has Nakamaro sitting with a figure that calls to mind such images as the Chinese poet depicted in the twelfth century *Tōji Landscape Screen (Tōji Senzui Byōbu)*—most likely we are to take the figure specifically as a poet, perhaps Li Po or Wang Wei. The 1749 Kyoto artist [**7–3**] may be depicting the *sage* reading, with the poet's hand outstretched; Moronobu uses a somewhat similar gesture in his *Sugata-e* (see Figure 41). The Kyoto drawing presents the poem as a soliloquy, following just the headnote of the *Kokinshū*, or, rather, not incorporating the appended story into the pictorialization. By contrast the Porter artist [**7–1**] alludes clearly to the banquet occasion, and his fantastic rocks and creeper-hung tree present a distinctly "Chinese" setting. The possibility for a chauvinistic interpretation of this poem, as seen in the *Kamijō-bon* commentary, is fully realized in Hokusai's rendition (see Plate 5), where the Chinese are kowtowing to an elevated Nakamaro.

7-1

7-2   7-3

POEM 8

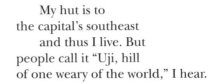

wa ga iho ha
miyako no tatsu-mi
shika zo sumu
yo wo ujhi-yama to
hito ha ifu nari[32]

My hut is to
the capital's southeast
    and thus I live. But
people call it "Uji, hill
of one weary of the world," I hear.

Master of the Law Kisen

Kisen Hōshi (mid-ninth century) is a legendary figure. He is mentioned in the Japanese preface of the *Kokinshū* (and hence counted among the Six Poetic Immortals), but otherwise he is unknown. The preface states:

> The poetry of Priest Kisen of Mount Uji is vague, and the logic does not run smoothly from beginning to end. Reading his poems is like looking at the autumn moon only to have it obscured by the clouds of dawn. Since few of his poems are known, we cannot make comparisons and come to understand them.[33]

In fact, this is the only poem of his in the *Kokinshū* and the only one that can be firmly attributed to him.

Commentary

As discussed in Chapter 1, this poem is based on a pivot word place-name *(uta-makura)*: the lines *yo wo ujhi-yama to / hito ha ifu nari* contain two sentences: *yo wo u* ("the world is bitter") and *ujhi-yama to hito ha ifu nari* ("I hear people call it Uji Mountain"), which are joined only by the "pivoting" syllable *u,* which is part of both sentences. Both Uji Mountain and Uji River became associated with gloom.

The third line of this poem reads literally: "Thus [or "like this"], indeed, I live." The question then becomes to what "thus" or "like this" refers—like *what?* One interpretation has it referring to the second hemistich, yielding a meaning such as: "people say the world is full of grief and call this place 'Grief Mountain,' and I, too, thinking that way, live here." The other interpretation (which includes all of the old commentaries) sees the *ha* of *hito ha* as contrastive ("people say . . . but *I* say . . ."), yielding: "although [other] people call it Grief Mountain, *I* live here thus [contentedly]." The *Kokin Roku-jō* has the last line as *ifu ramu* ("they say, it seems"), which would support this latter interpretation. *Nari* also serves here to indicate hearsay.[34]

The Pictures

As noted in Part One (pp. 125–126), premodern commentaries made much of the potential wordplay on *shika*, meaning both "thus" and "deer," but standard pictorializations, such as the *Zōsanshō* [8–1], have no deer. The Kyoto artist [8–2] emphasizes the natural feature for which Uji had become most famous since *The Tale of Genji*—its river—to which the *Kangyoku* [8–3] adds its equally famous bridge. The *Shikishi Moyō* kimono design [8–4] includes characters for the place-name "Uji"; but rather than using any images associated with that place, it links the "u" of "Uji" with the *unohana* (an unconventional association), or deutzia, a flower associated with early summer, thus avoiding any suggestion of *ushi,* or "weariness."

8-1   8-2

8-3

8-4

POEM 9

hana no iro ha
utsurinikeri na
itadzura ni
wa ga mi yo ni furu
nagame seshi ma ni[35]

The color of the flowers
has faded indeed
   in vain
have I passed through the world
while gazing at the falling rains.

Ono no Komachi
Active during the reign of Emperor Nin-myō (r. 833–850), Komachi is the only woman among the Six Poetic Immortals discussed by Tsurayuki in the Japanese preface to the *Kokinshū*. *The Collected Poems of Komachi (Komachi Shū)* is a much later collection, and only the twenty-one poems attributed to her in the *Kokinshū* and *Gosenshū* (ca. 951) can be viewed as authentic. In the medieval period, a variety of legends grew up around her, her beauty, her cruelty to men, and her unhappy old age, which in turn provided material for *nō* plays and visual art, most notably the *Nana Komachi* ("The Seven Komachi").

Commentary
Debate in interpretation revolves around whether to view the first and second lines as simply referring to flowers (specifically, cherry blossoms), as the poem's placement in the Spring section of the *Kokinshū* might suggest, or to see these lines as also alluding to Komachi's own charms, which are in decline as well. Even in the seasonal books the metaphorical meaning of the fallen blossoms is an issue. In fact, the poem immediately preceding Komachi's in the *Kokinshū* reads:

chiru hana wo
nani ka uramimu
yo no naka ni
wa ga mi mo tomo ni
aramu mono ka ha

Why begrudge
the scattering blossoms?
   in this world
do you think that, together with them,
you could live forever?

Clearly, then, the flowers are to be taken as symbolic of various aspects of decay, including the poet's decline.

Komachi's poem is a technical tour-de-force. The third-line adverb "in vain/uselessly *(itadzura ni)*" can be seen to modify either the lines above, or below, or both. The second half of the poem is built around the pivot words *furu* and *nagame*. The latter means both "to gaze pensively, lost in thought," and "long rains *(naga-ame)*." *Furu* can mean (1) "to fall (as in rain)," (2) "to pass (time), elapse, experience," and (3) "to grow old." In the age of the *Kokinshū* apparently the pun was understoood to entail meanings 1 and 3 (thus yielding a translation of the fourth line something like "have I grown old in this world"), while Teika probably understood the pun to entail meanings 1 and 2.

The Pictures
The Tan'yū album has the poet sitting under a weeping cherry with just the fewest of blossoms remaining among its new leaves. The *Zōsanshō*'s standard iconography [**9–2**] presents us with the poet leaning on an armrest, gazing out at the cherry blossoms just past full bloom and starting to put forth leaves. The blossoms are shown still on the tree, although the poem is drawn from a section of the *Kokinshū* on "fallen blossoms." Moronobu makes the association between the woman and the flowers explicit in his *Sugata-e* [**9–3**] by decorating her robe with a cherry-blossom motif (an interpretation made explicit in the accompanying commentary). She is also rearranging her collar, a conventional gesture used to indicate primping or concern over one's appearance. The *Shikishi Moyō* kimono design [**9–4**] includes a rope that binds the cherry trees as if to hold them back and forms a dam across a stream (seen in many versions, and perhaps meant to suggest *nagareru,* "to flow," and the passage of time), as if to block the drifting blossoms. The character for *yomu,* or "to compose a poem" is inscribed above. Curiously, many artists change the type of flower depicted: the Porter artist uses what appears to be azaleas, while Hasegawa [**9–1**] shows the poet in a maple-leaf patterned robe, gazing at *ayame* (translated as "sweet-flag" or "iris"), perhaps meant to suggest the phrase *aya nashi,* or "in vain."

9-1

9-2

9-3

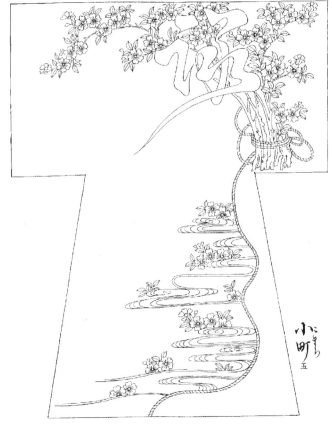

9-4

POEM 10

kore ya kono
yuku mo kaheru mo
wakaretsutsu
shiru mo shiranu mo
afusaka no seki[36]

This it is! That
going, too, and coming, too,
    continually separating,
those known and those unknown,
meet at the Barrier of Ōsaka.

Semimaru

Absolutely nothing is known of Semimaru, if in fact he ever existed. Mid-Tokugawa-period documents in Satsuma claim he was the fourth leader of a *mōsō* ("blind priest") tradition based in Ōmi province. *Mōsō,* or *biwa hōshi,* accompanied the chanting of sutras with the lute-like instrument called *biwa* to placate local dieties. The *Tales of Times Now Past Collection (Konjaku Monogatari Shū,* ca. 1100) records Semimaru as a former servant of Prince Atsumi, a son of Emperor Uda, who, blinded, built a hut near Ōsaka Barrier and became a famous *biwa* player. Kamo no Chōmei claims in his *Mu'myō Shō* that Semimaru became the tutelary diety of Ōsaka Pass. By at least 1242, as recorded in the *Tōkan Kikō,* he was identified as a son of Emperor Daigo, abandoned because of his blindness. As such he became the subject of various plays, including Zeami's nō, *Semimaru.* Four poems are attributed to him in the *Gosenshū* and later imperial anthologies.

Commentary
In most editions of the *One Hundred Poets*, the third line is given as *wakarete ha*. In the *Gosenshū*, however, it appears as *wakaretsutsu* (compare Poem 1 and Poem 4). It also appears this way in Teika's other anthologies, such as the *Kindai Shūka*. The change appears to have taken place through the process of transmission since the time of the *Ōei Shō*.[37]

The headnote to this poem reads: "On seeing people coming to and fro, when living in a hut he had built at the Barrier of Ōsaka." The Barrier of Ōsaka, or *afusaka no seki*, has long served as an *uta-makura* ("poem-pillow") and famous place-name because *afu* (modern *au*) can also mean "to meet." (This is not the modern Osaka, which was known in earlier days as Naniwa.) The name is frequently translated as "Barrier at Meeting Hill." The folklorist Origuchi Shinobu has drawn attention to two other poems that start with the words *kore ya kono*, one in the *Tales of Ise* (*Ise Monogatari*, episode 62) and one in the *Tales of Times Now Past*. Both these poems come from the area of Ōmi province, and Origuchi "conjectures that this line may have been a phrase of invocation to summon Sakagami, the god of Ausaka [Ōsaka] Pass, to hear supplicant travelers' pleas for safe passage." Susan Matisoff, in her study on Semimaru, notes that:

> These poems share with the Semimaru poem more than just the opening invocatory line and the puns on "meeting." Each has for its third line a verb in the continuative *-tsutsu* form . . . it may be that the common features of these three poems are remnants of a regional song style associated with the Ausaka-Omi area. If so, the Semimaru poem in the *Gosenshū* would, in its day, have been immediately identifiable from the opening line as a song from the Ausaka area.[38]

Like Poem 9 by Ono no Komachi, differences of interpretation surrounding this poem center on how symbolically it is to be read. Katagiri suggests that in the era of the *Gosenshū*, the poem was seen as simply a poem about the Ōsaka Barrier. But by the middle ages, this poem had taken on a profoundly Buddhist cast and was read as a comment on the transitory nature of life, along the lines of the expression "all who meet must part *(esha jōri)*."[39] Clearly this is the way Teika read this poem, perhaps influenced by the kind of story about Semimaru that appears in the *Tales of Times Now Past:* "The Story of How Lord Minamoto no Hiromasa Went to the Blind Man's Place at Ōsaka."[40] One of the poems in that tale also appears in a set of three anonymous poems in the *Kokinshū*. In the *ShinKokinshū*, Teika and the other editors attributed all three to Semimaru.

The only other interpretive debate surrounds the lines *yuku mo kaheru mo*. Some suggest that this should be understood to mean not "those that go [to the East] and those who return [from the East]," but rather "those who go [to the East] and those who [see them off and then] return [to the capital]." They point to the fact that this poem appears in the *Collected Poems of Sosei (Sosei Shū)*, but with the second and third lines reading *yuku mo tomaru mo wakarete ha*, "those who go and those who *stay*." Historically, however, such an interpretation has not been followed.

The Pictures

The *Zōsanshō* [**10–1**] has the travelers in Edo-period costume, with Semimaru's presence indicated only by the hut (compare Poem 1). This poem is alluded to by Saikaku in his *Eternal Storehouse of Japan* when describing an enterprising peddler:

> He crossed the Osaka Barrier, where people leaving the capital pass those who return, and thrust his wares "on people who knew each other and those who were strangers." Even sharp needle pedlars and men who sold writing brushes, accustomed though they were to the wiles of itinerant salesmen, were tricked by Shinroku's deception.[41]

Moronobu's *Sugata-e* [**10–2**] is much the same, except that the travelers now seem of a higher class and include women. Semimaru himself is included this time, though without any musical instrument. The lute is a prominent feature of the *Hyakushu Hinagata* design [**10–3**], however, and is added to the Kyoto composition as well. The Tan'yū album gives us both the actual figure of Semimaru and his lute in the same composition, also seen in the *Eiga* [**10–4**].

10-2

10-1

10-3

10-4

POEM 11

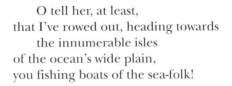

wata no hara
yaso shima kakete
kogi-idenu to
hito ni ha tsugeyo
ama no tsuri-bune[42]

O tell her, at least,
that I've rowed out, heading towards
    the innumerable isles
of the ocean's wide plain,
you fishing boats of the sea-folk!

Consultant Takamura

Sangi Ono no Takamura (802–852), though little of his poetry is extant, was considered the leading Chinese poet of his day, thought to rival Po Chü-i himself. He is best known for being exiled to Oki Island for refusing to join the A.D. 837 embassy to T'ang China; he was granted clemency after only a year. He was also known in his youth for his love of archery and horsemanship, which may explain his military image in the accompanying *kasen-e*. He has six poems in the *Kokinshū* and six more in later imperial anthologies. His Chinese verse is included in the *Wakan Rōei Shū* and other collections. He became a frequent figure in popular tales, and a short romance about his love life is still extant.[43]

Commentary

In the *Kokinshū* the headnote to this poem reads: "Sent to the home of someone in the capital, as [Takamura's] boat was setting out, when he was going into exile on Oki Island." The poem follows directly after Nakamaro's poem (see Poem 7), which opens the "Travel" section.

The phrase *yaso shima kakete* has caused some confusion. Modern commentators parse it either as "aiming or heading toward the innumerable islands" *(kazu-ōku no shima-jima no hō o me-zashite)* or "passing or threading through innumerable islands" *(kazu-ōku no shima no aida o nuu yō ni shite).* Shimazu is the only critic to offer evidence for his reading along the lines of the former *(Man'yō Shū* 998):

mayu no goto
kumowi ni miyuru
aha no yama
kakete kogu fune
tomari-shirazu mo

The Mountain of Awa,
seen among the clouds
    that look like its eyebrows—
the boats that row out, heading there,
have no idea where they will rest.

Another issue is the identity of the "person in the capital." The *ha* is contrastive: "if not everyone, at least tell the one for whom I long." Some suggest that this person might be an aged mother, but as early as the *Chōkyō Shō* (dated 1487) we find the suggestion that Takamura was exiled when he was discovered to be having an affair with a woman at court. Otherwise, the main point of contention is whether the poet personifies the boats in an ironic fashion, knowing that his plea will fall on the deaf ears of inanimate objects, or whether the poet is comparing his messenger to these small craft returning to their harbor, a return denied the poet himself.

The Pictures

The Tan'yū album has a very sinified (and not at all martial-looking) Takamura raising his hand to his hat as if setting off; in the background is a ship under full sail and a smaller skiff beside it. The *Zōsanshō* [11–2] has Takamura being rowed out from between large rocks, well illustrating the phrase *yaso shima kakete;* the other boat seems to hold Edo-period samurai out on a fishing trip. In fact, Moronobu's *Sugata-e* [11–3] is less historically anachronistic in its rendering of the boats and focuses on the poet's address to the fishing boats—leaving out the rocks entirely. The two main figures show that the "person in the capital" is a young lady. The accompanying commentary explains that it is the fishermen who are "insensitive" (rather than the boats)—a thought commonly found in *nō* plays as well. The Kyoto illustrator [11–4] has a messenger waiting on the shore—following interpretations found in the *Kaikan Shō* and *Uimanabi*. (Interestingly, the posture of the figure on the shore duplicates that of Nakamaro [7–3].) Finally, Hasegawa's fan format [11–1] has Takamura already on the shore, addressing himself to an oblivious fisherman and utilizing many of the motifs also seen in the *Hyakushu Hinagata* design.

11-1

11-2

11-3

11-4

POEM 12

amatsu kaze
kumo no kayohi-jhi
fuki-tojhiyo
wotome no sugata
shibashi todomemu[44]

O heavenly breeze,
blow so as to block
    their path back through the clouds!
For I would, if but for a moment,
detain these maidens' forms.

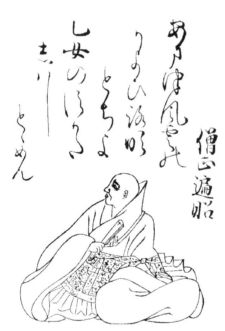

Archbishop Henjō
Sōjō Henjō (816–890), born Yoshimine no Munesada, served Emperor Ninmyō, taking vows upon the latter's death in 849. He is counted among both the Six and the Thirty-Six Poetic Immortals. He has thirty-five poems in the *Kokinshū* and later anthologies. A *Collected Poems of Henjō (Henjō Shū)* is extant.

Commentary
In the *Kokinshū*, the headnote to this poem reads: "Composed on seeing Gose-chi dancers"; the author is also listed as "Yoshimine no Munesada," indicating that this poem was composed sometime between 844, when the poet entered into Emperor Ninmyō's service, and Ninmyō's death five years later. The Gosechi dance celebrated the harvest in the Eleventh Month and was performed by four or five young unmarried women chosen from aristocratic households. The dance was believed to have originated when Emperor Tenmu (r. 673–686, brother of Tenji, Poem 1) was on an excursion to Mount Yoshino. As night fell and the emperor played the koto, heavenly maidens were seen to be dancing in the sky above. Henjō likens the real dancing maidens before his eyes to their heavenly predecessors and, by extension, Emperor Ninmyō's reign to that of the famous Tenmu. Teika most certainly read the poem through its legendary subtext.

The Pictures

The *Zōsanshō* [**12–1**] seems to be representing the actual circumstances of the poem's composition, as Henjō and another courtier observe the Gosechi dance in the emperor's presence. (The latter is presumed to be inside the blinds looking out.) For historical accuracy the poet should be presented in secular dress, however, as the poem was composed before he became a monk (a fact noted in the *Yūsai Shō* and other commentaries). Only Porter's artist seems to make this historical correction [**12–2**], presenting the poet as a courtier. This picture, too, is the only one to give a sense of the dancer's departure and a suggestion of the clouds that might block her way. The Kyoto illustrator [**12–3**] presents both the actual dancer and her heavenly counterpart, while Hasegawa [**12–4**] and the *Eiga* eliminate the real dancer altogether. Note that in this last rendition the heavenly maiden is no longer holding a musical instrument, but rather a lotus, and Henjō is actually fingering a rosary, giving the poem a more religious feeling—purple clouds and heavenly beings were thought to appear just before a believer entered the western paradise of the Buddha Amida. In fact, the *Kangyoku* (1804) closely resembles a *raigo-zu*, or picture of Amida descending to take up the faithful. The Hasegawa image can be traced in connection with the poem as far back as the *One Hundred Warrior Poets*, where a poem by Minamoto no Yoshi'uji that alludes to Henjō's is illustrated by the same lotus-bearing angel. The angel's appearance in Moronobu's *Sugata-e* with its comparison to a young man, is presumably humorous.

12-1

12-2

あしひきの
天津風
雲乃
かよひぢ
ふ(き)とぢ
よ
そとめろ
ちうゝん

12-3

12-4

POEM 13

tsukuba-ne no
mine yori otsuru
mina no kaha
kohi zo tsumorite
fuchi to narinuru[45]

Like the Mina River
that falls from the peak
of Mount Tsukuba,
so my longing has collected
and turned into deep pools.

Retired Emperor Yōzei

Yōzei In (868–949) reigned from 876 to 884, as the fifty-seventh sovereign. He ascended the throne at the age of nine but showed signs of mental instability, and was forced to abdicate after eight years by Regent Fujiwara no Mototsune (836–891). He was replaced by Emperor Kōkō (Poem 15), a son of Emperor Ninmyō (r. 833–850). After his abdication, Yōzei sponsored a number of poetry contests. He is represented in the imperial anthologies by this sole poem.

Commentary

In the *Gosenshū,* the headnote to this poem reads: "Sent to the princess of the Tsuridono." The Tsuridono was Kōkō's palace and the princess was his daughter Suishi (Yasuko), who did at some point enter Yōzei's household. Mount Tsukuba was often mentioned in love poems because *tsuku* means "to stick to," suggesting something like the English idiom "I'm stuck on you." The peak itself is divided into two parts, Nantai ("The Man") on the West and Jotai ("The Woman") on the East. Mina-no-gawa, curiously, is usually written with Chinese characters that mean "Waterless River," but the characters meaning "Man-Woman River" are also used. Many versions of this poem (as, for instance, in the *Kokin Roku-jō*) have the last line as *fuchi to narikeru* (*-keru* suggesting some surprise on the speaker's part), but the *One Hundred Poets* version, with the perfective *-nuru,* gives a stronger feeling and a greater sense of time having passed.

Perhaps simply because the author was an emperor, medieval commentators (such as the *Komezawa-bon*) tended to dismiss the obvious interpretation of this as a love poem and read it instead politically: the emperor's concern for his people flowed down to them, forming deep, tranquil pools of blessings. A similar conception can be found in the Japanese preface to the *Kokinshū* in praise of Emperor Daigo: "The boundless waves of his benevolence flow beyond the boundaries of the Eight Islands [Japan]; his broad compassion provides a deeper shade than Mount Tsukuba."[46]

Given Yōzei's meager reputation as both a poet and an emperor, we must ask why Teika chose to include him in his *One Hundred Poets*. The most likely answer seems to be that Yōzei was included because he was the father of Prince Motoyoshi, a famous poet represented by Poem 20. Here again, as in the selection of the father-daughter team Tenji and Jitō (Poems 1 and 2), Teika is underscoring the hereditary nature of the poetic tradition.

The Pictures

This poem is most typically represented by a pure landscape design. The *Zōsan-shō* [13–1] depicts Mount Tsukuba with the Mina River flowing down between Nantai and Jotai; the foregrounded trees also suggest autumn as the season. This rendition is then placed in the background of Moronobu's *Sugata-e* [13–3], where we see two lovers mirroring the shapes of the two peaks.

As early as the *Ōei Shō*, commentators paraphrase this poem by speaking of a love that starts like weak trickles dripping down from on high, gradually joining together into several streams, and finally all flowing down into a deep pool. Such an interpretation is certainly suggested by the Kyoto illustrator [13–2] with his many streams and mighty flow at the bottom. Rather than a slow accumulation, both Hasegawa and the *Shikishi Moyō* kimono artist [13–4] use the image of a plunging waterfall to suggest the poet's passion.

13-1   13-2

13-3

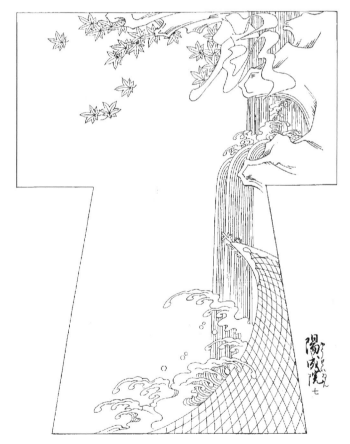

13-4

POEM 14

michinoku no
shinobu mojhi-zuri
tare yuwe ni
midare-somenishi
ware naranaku ni[47]

Whose fault is it
that my feelings have begun to tangle
    like the tangle-patterned prints
of Shinobu from the distant north?
Since it is not mine, it must be . . .

The Riverbank Minister of the Left

Kawara Sadaijin—Minamoto no Tōru (822–895)—was the son of Emperor Saga (r. 809–823). His sobriquet comes from the grand mansion he built on the west bank *(kawara)* of the Kamo River, where he hosted gatherings of the most famous poets of his day, such as Tsurayuki (Poem 35), Mitsune (Poem 29), Egyō (Poem 47), and Motosuke (Poem 42). He is considered the very epitome of courtly elegance *(fūryū)* and may have served as a partial model for the hero of Murasaki Shikibu's *Tale of Genji*. He is one of the Thirty-Six Poetic Immortals and has two poems in both the *Kokinshū* and *Gosenshū*.

Commentary

No information about the circumstances of the poem's composition is provided in the *Kokinshū*, where this poem appears as "occasion unknown" *(dai shirazu)*. *Michinoku* refers to the northeastern area of the principal Japanese island. *Shinobu mojhi-zuri* originally referred to cloth that had been imprinted *(zuri)* with the design of the moss fern *(shinobu; Davallia bullata)*. *Shinobu* is a pivot word: it is both the name of the fern and a verb meaning "to love secretly." Based on the *Toshiyori Zuinō*, or *Toshiyori's Poetic Essentials* (?1115), however, we know that by the mid-Heian period it was thought that *shinobu* also referred to the village of Shinobu in Iwashiro (present-day Fukushima). In any case, the phrase *michinoku no / shinobu mojhi-zuri* serves as a preface *(jo)* for the word *midare*, or "disordered."

In the *Kokinshū*, the fourth line reads *midaremu to omofu*, and the last two lines could then be translated as "since I am not one who thinks to have his feelings disordered by anyone else." The four books of love poems in the *Kokinshū* are often read in order so as to suggest the progress of a love affair. Placed in the fourth book, this poem suggests that the man, suspected of being unfaithful, is earnestly protesting his fidelity. In the *One Hundred Poets,* however, this fourth line reads *midare-somenishi,* the same form that appears in the first episode of the *Tales of Ise.* Here *some* serves as another pivot word, meaning both "to dye" and "to begin," the former providing word association *(engo)* back to *shinobu* and hence alluding to "hidden love" *(shinobu kohi).* In this reading, the poem changes from the defense of a rebuked lover to a complaint of secret love—that is, the poet is saying that it is not his fault that he has fallen into a forbidden love, but the fault of the lovely lady herself. In contrast, then, to Teika's *One Hundred Poets* reading, the *Kokinshū* interpretation of this poem would read:

> Please believe: I am not one
> who thinks to have his feelings stirred,
>   like cloth imprinted with moss fern
> from the deep north of Michinoku,
> by anyone but you.

The Pictures
Like the interpretations of the poem itself, pictorializations of it fall essentially into two groups, though within these groups there is an unusual degree of diversity. One rendition, as in the *Zōsanshō* [**14–2**], shows the poet examining cloth dyed with what is to be taken as a *shinobu mojhi-zuri* pattern. The other tradition shows the speaker of the poem with a sleeve to his or her face, a standard posture used to indicate crying and thus suggesting the topic of "hidden love." Tōru is often shown with a sleeve to his face as depicted in *kasen-e,* and Hasegawa simply transfers that figure to his fan [**14–1**], though writing utensils are added. Writing brushes and folded love letters are the major motifs, along with *shinobu* ferns, in the *Hyakushu Hinagata.* The Porter illustrator, curiously, depicts a woman [**14–3**]. Although this might be thought to suggest that the speaker of the poem was understood as a woman, another contemporaneous version, closely resembling the Porter edition, presents the same woman but this time with a male courtier showing her a roll of *shinobu* cloth.[48] The *Shūgyoku* [**14–4**] actually shows two lovers, suggesting a dispute, though this may be a composition that derives from Moronobu's *Sugata-e.* The Tan'yū album shows *shinobu* fern hidden by grasses and mist, also emphasizing the "hidden love" interpretation.

14-1

14-2

14-3

14-4

POEM 15

kimi ga tame
haru no no ni idete
waka-na tsumu
wa ga koromo-de ni
yuki ha furitsutsu[49]

For my lord's sake
I went out into the fields of spring
　　to pick young greens
while on my robe-sleeves
the snow kept falling and falling.

Emperor Kōkō

Kōkō Tennō (830–887, r. 884–887), counted as the fifty-eighth sovereign, was the third son of Emperor Ninmyō (r. 833–850); he was placed on the throne by Regent Fujiwara no Mototsune at the age of fifty-five, replacing the deranged Emperor Yōzei (Poem 13). A collection of his poems, the *Ninna GyoShū*, is extant, and he has fourteen poems in imperial anthologies.

Commentary

The headnote to this poem in the *Kokinshū* reads: "A poem sent together with young greens to someone when the Ninna Emperor [Kōkō] was still a prince." Young greens *(waka-na)* were gathered and eaten as part of the new year festivities. This poem was written to accompany a gift of such greens, as a kind of new year's greeting. Since the poem was written by an emperor, medieval commentators read it metaphorically—that is, as a poem in which the emperor sympathizes with the hardships of his subjects. The *Komezawa-bon*, for instance, says: "the same topic as at the beginning," that is, Emperor Tenji's poem (Poem 1). This is not how the poem was originally interpreted, nor is it likely how Teika read it. Nonetheless, the verbal similarities between this poem and Poems 1 and 4 are conspicuous.

The Pictures

The political interpretations of this poem seem to have had little impact on its visualizations. The two approaches either show an aristocrat (presumably "my lord") receiving the greens that are being cut by a courtier, as in the *Zōsanshō* [**15–1**], or they show a high-ranking courtier (presumably the prince) directing the gathering of the greens, as in Hasegawa [**15–3**] and the *Kangyoku* [**15–2**]—

the latter interpretation is somewhat closer to the poem's original context. The Tan'yū album has Kōkō as emperor with young greens on a presentation stand before him, making it seem as if the greens were offered to Kōkō rather than by him. The *Shikishi Moyō* kimono design [15–4] shows the edible greens and pine saplings and has the repeated character for "snow" *(yuki)* drifting across to the sleeve and written in a gradually more cursive style, as if to represent the melting of the snowflake.

15-1

15-2

15-3

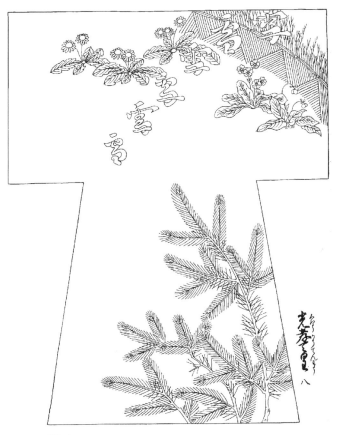

15-4

POEM 16

tachi-wakare
inaba no yama no
mine ni ofuru
matsu to shi kikaba
ima kaheri-komu[50]

Even if I depart
and go to Inaba Mountain,
    on whose peak grow
pines, if I hear you pine for me,
I will return straightway to you.

Middle Counselor Yukihira

Chūnagon Yukihira—Ariwara no Yukihira (818–893)—is the older brother of Narihira (Poem 17). He is mentioned in the Chinese preface to the *Kokinshū* for his skill in Chinese verse, and four of his Japanese poems are included in the same anthology. While altogether he has eleven poems in imperial anthologies, only the four in the *Kokinshū* and four in the *Gosenshū* can be considered authentic.

Commentary

Inaba no yama is a specific mountain in Inaba province, north of Kyoto on the Sea of Japan, where Yukihira went to serve as governor in 855. (Commentators such as Mabuchi mistakenly believed that the term was not a proper noun but simply meant "mountains of Inaba.") The name also serves as a pivot word, since *inaba* can mean "(even) if I leave." The entire first three lines serve as a preface (*jo*) for the word *matsu*. This word too is a pivot word, meaning both "to wait" and "pine tree," much like the English word "pine."

Yukihira is best known for his exile to Suma, mentioned in *Kokinshū* 18 (Misc. 2): 962, and providing precedent for Genji's exile there in *The Tale of Genji*. Stories around this incident in turn led to the *nō* play *Matsukaze,* or "Pining Wind," in which we are told of the love affair between Yukihira and two fisher girls of Suma, Matsukaze and her sister Murasame ("Autumn Rain"), who wait in vain for Yukihira to visit them after he returns to the capital.[51] This legend and play seem to have in turn influenced the interpretation of the *One Hundred Poets* poem (owing perhaps to the prominence of the word *matsu*); thus although the poem's grammar makes it clear that the poet is leaving *for* Inaba, both the *Keikō Shō* and *Kamijō-bon* interpret the poet as leaving *from* Inaba.

The Pictures

The Tan'yū album has a background of several hills with pine trees on them. By contrast the *Zōsanshō* [**16–1**] shows only one pine on a peak, with a figure of the poet making his way down a path. The Kyoto illustrator repeats this picture but removes the poet and the path. The lone pine tree on a crag also appears in the *Sugata-e* [**16–2**], to which Moronobu adds an obvious reference to the *nō* play *Matsukaze*, showing two sisters in tears over a departing young aristocrat.[52] Hasegawa's fan [**16–3**] is the most accurate interpretation, showing Yukihira on someone's veranda, making his farewells, and looking at a pine tree. Commentators spent much time imagining to whom this poem was addressed: his mother, his wife, his mistress? The Porter illustrator seems to reject all of these possibilities and shows the poet leaving from a pair of men [**16–4**], reflecting the same commentary contained (but ignored) in the *Sugata-e*—that this poem was composed during a farewell party hosted by Yukihira's friends *("tomodachi uma no hanamuke ni idashi toshi")*.

16-1

16-2

16-3

16-4

POEM 17

chihayaburu
kami-yo mo kikazu
tatsuta-gaha
kara-kurenawi ni
midzu kuguru to ha[53]

Unheard of
even in the legendary age
of the awesome gods:
Tatsuta River in scarlet
and the water flowing under it.

Lord Ariwara no Narihira
Ariwara no Narihira Ason (825–880), younger brother to Yukihira (Poem 16), is one of the Six and one of the Thirty-Six Poetic Immortals. He was generally understood to be the protagonist of the mid-tenth-century *Tales of Ise* (in which this poem also appears), which seems to have formed itself around a collection of his poems. He has almost ninety poems in the various imperial anthologies.

Commentary
The headnote to this poem in the *Kokin-shū* reads: "Composed on the topic of autumn leaves flowing down Tatsuta River, as painted on a screen belonging to the Second Ward Empress [Fujiwara no Kōshi] when she was still called the Lady of the Wardrobe of the Spring Palace [that is, mother of the crown prince]." The original poem could be translated as:

> Unheard of
> even in the legendary age
> of the awesome gods:
> Tatsuta River, tie-dyed
> the deepest Chinese scarlet!

The original point of the poem was to compare the surface of the Tatsuta River, with red autumn leaves floating here and there on it, to a band of blue cloth tie-dyed with scarlet. Teika, however, followed the interpretation of this poem promoted by Kenshō (1130–1209), who read the last verb not as *kukuru* ("to tie-dye") but as *kuguru*, meaning "to pass under" and yielding the translation seen above—that is, an image of blue water flowing under the river's surface, which has been completely covered by scarlet leaves.

The Pictures

Starting with the Tan'yū album, most artists show the poet in front of a screen—for example, Porter [**17–1**]—reflecting the circumstance of the poem's composition as described in the *Kokinshū*. The Kyoto illustrator also adds a river outside [**17–4**]. A woman is shown, as well, and perhaps she is meant to be identified as Kōshi, with whom Narihira was reputed to have had a love affair. In fact, the *Shisetsu Shō* (1658) claims that the hidden meaning of the poem is that Narihira is praising Kōshi's good fortune by likening it to the unchanging nature of the screen picture. In Hasegawa [**17–2**] we see the poet looking at the river itself, rather than a painting of it, which follows the setting of the poem found in the *Tales of Ise* (Episode 106). The usually reliable Kunisada/Kuniyoshi booklet also follows this reading. The *Shikishi Moyō* kimono designer [**17–3**] gives in the top half a lovely image of the river and leaves flowing in and out, off and onto, the screens; in the lower half the artist adds bird-clappers to reinforce the autumnal season of this poem.

17-1

17-2

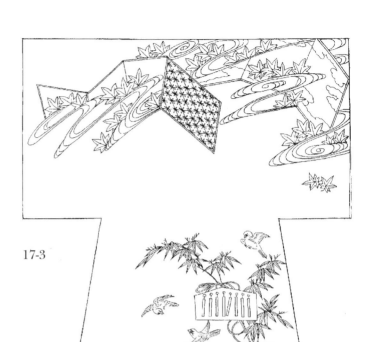

17-3

17-4

POEM 18

suminoe no
kishi ni yoru nami
yoru sahe ya
yume no kayohi-jhi
hitome yokuramu[54]

Must you so avoid others' eyes
that not even at night,
    along the road of dreams,
will you draw nigh like the waves
to the shore of Sumi-no-e Bay?

Lord Fujiwara no Toshiyuki

Fujiwara no Toshiyuki Ason (d. 901) par-
ticipated in many poetry contests during
the reigns of the four emperors he served,
from Seiwa (r. 858–876) through Uda (r.
887–897). He is one of the Thirty-Six
Poetic Immortals and was also famous as a
calligrapher. He has twenty-eight poems in
the various imperial anthologies, and a
collection of his poems, the *Toshiyuki Shū*,
is extant.

Commentary

This poem's headnote in the *Kokinshū* indi-
cates that this poem was used in what is
known as "the Empress' Poetry Contest
[held] during the Kanpyō Era (953)" (Kan-
pyō no ŌnToki Kisai no Miya no Uta-
awase). Sumi-no-e is another name for
Sumiyoshi Bay (Sumiyoshi no Ura), site of a famous shrine originally built to the
god of the sea. Even today it is a popular spot known for its distinctive bridge.

Rather than pivot words (one word used in two different meanings),
Toshiyuki's poem uses a kind of sound repetition and association: *kishi ni yoru
nami* means "the waves that approach *(yoru)* the shore," while *yoru sahe* means
"even at night *(yoru)*." Thus, the first two lines serve as a "preface" *(jo-kotoba)*—
essentially an ornament—to the word *yoru* in the third line.

It was widely believed that those truly in love would visit their lover in their
dreams. Interpretive controversy centers on the subject of the final verb: is it
the poet's lover who does not visit the poet, or is it the poet himself who does
not go to her in his dreams? The latter interpretation suggests that the poet is
examining his own feelings, but it is the former interpretation that is generally
followed.

The Pictures

The *Zōsanshō* rendition [**18–1**] shows the poet watching the waves roll in at Sumiyoshi, indicated by its bridge and pine-trees on the shore. The same motifs are used in the *Shikishi Moyō* kimono design [**18–2**], linked by the trailing stoke of the character for "dream" *(yume)*, perhaps suggesting a road or path along the shore. Moronobu's *Sugata-e* [**18–3**] actually shows the poet bedding down for the night under the kind of heavy robe that served as bedcovers; the poet's reproach may be addressed to the woman sitting nearby, but this is unclear. The Kyoto illustrator [**18–4**] shows the poet in his house with wild waves crashing on the shore nearby. Although the waves may be meant to suggest the poet's passion, they may also be meant to conform to the accompanying interpretation by Yūsai—that the poet cannot see his love in his dreams because the noise of the waves keeps him awake.

18-1

18-2

18-3

18-4

POEM 19

naniha-gata
mijikaki ashi no
fushi no ma mo
ahade kono yo wo
sugushiteyo to ya[55]

To go through this life, not meeting
for even as short a time as the space
between two nodes of a reed
in Naniwa Inlet—
is that what you are telling me?

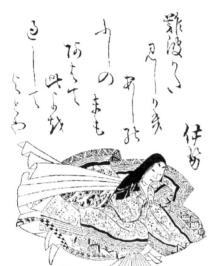

Ise
Also called Ise no Go or Ise no Miyasu-dokoro (ca. 875–ca. 938), she was the daughter of Fujiwara no Tsugukage (sometimes read "Tsugikage"), governor of Ise (whence her sobriquet). The storylike beginning section of her collected poems, the *Ise Shū*, relates her love affairs with the brothers Fujiwara no Nakahira and Toki-hira, as well as her pregnancy by Emperor Uda. She is one of the Thirty-Six Poetic Immortals and has 22 poems in the *Kokin-shū* alone, with more than 170 poems in all the imperial anthologies combined.

Commentary
In the *Ise Shū* this poem is given with three others under the heading: "Around Autumn, when he had spoken cruelly" *(aki-goro, utate hito no mono-ihikeru ni)*. In the *ShinKokinshū* it is given as "topic unknown" *(dai shirazu)* and placed among poems on "hidden love" *(shinobi-kohi)*, which changes its interpretation considerably—from a poem sent to an unfeeling lover to a private complaint about being unable to reveal one's love.

Naniwa has long been associated with reeds. A *-gata* (or *kata*)is the beach revealed at low tide (see Poem 92). *Yo*, as in *kono yo*, "this life," is also the word for a segment of a reed and thus is synonymous with the expression "space between the nodes of a reed" *(ashi no fushi no ma)*, but commentators consider this a case of word association *(engo)* rather than punning *(kake-kotoba)*.

The Pictures
Although practically all the commentators state that this poem was written to be sent to a cruel lover and was not composed as a soliloquy *(doku'ei)*, Ise is shown in all pictorializations as addressing herself to reeds, as seen in the *Zōsanshō* [**19–1**]. Howard Link notes that the figure of Ise in the *Sugata-e* [**19–2**] "comes close to the famous *Mikaeri Bijin* painting signed Moronobu in the

Tokyo National Museum."[56] The *Shikishi Moyō* kimono designer [**19–4**] has added fishing nets, appropriate to Naniwa Bay, but also perhaps reinforcing the interpretation of withheld or constrained love. Finally, Kubota suggests that the word *fushi* may also serve as a pivot word—meaning both "nodes" of the reeds and "to fall over [easily]" as reeds do—thus creating some association between the reeds and the supine woman. No artist shows Ise as actually prostrate, however, and the reeds, as in Moronobu, usually stand quite straight and tall—the Kyoto illustrator [**19–3**] represents something of an exception.

19-1

19-2

19-3

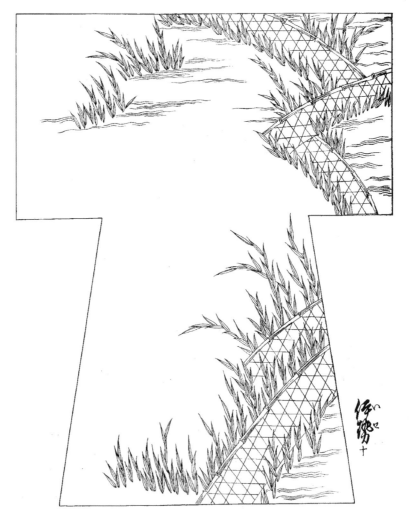

19-4

POEM 20

wabinureba
ima hata onaji
naniha naru
miwotsukushite mo
ahamu to zo omofu[57]

Miserable,
now, it is all the same.
　　Channel-markers at Naniwa—
even if it costs my life,
I will see you again!

Prince Motoyoshi

Motoyoshi Shinnō (890–943), eldest son of Emperor Yōzei (Poem 13), was famous as a lover. He appears several times in the mid-tenth-century collection of poetic anecdotes, the *Tales of Yamato (Yamato Monogatari)*. His poetry first appears in the *Gosenshū* (compiled 951), and he has twenty poems in it and later imperial anthologies.

Commentary

This poem's headnote in the *Gosenshū* reads: "Sent to the Kyōgoku Lady of the Wardrobe after their affair had come out." The lady in question was Fujiwara no Hōshi, daughter of Tokihira. Her father had planned to have her enter the reigning emperor's service, but Retired Emperor Uda insisted that she serve at his residence—she bore him three princes. This, however, did not prevent an affair with Motoyoshi, which eventually became public knowledge. The poem centers on a pivot word: *miwotsukushi* was a kind of channel-marker used to indicate the waterway for boats—the phrase can also be read *mi wo tsukushite mo*, literally, "even if it consumes [my] body."

Interpretations split into two equally represented camps, even among modern commentators, depending on what is understood to be "the same now." One interpretation is that "even if it costs my life" (*mi wo tsukushite mo*), it is "now the same"—in other words, the poet is so miserable that it does not matter whether he lives or dies. The second interpretation understands the topic to be *na*, that is, "name" or reputation (understanding the place-name "Naniwa" as a pivot word). This can refer to either the poet's or the couple's reputation. While the first of these readings implies that it is other people who are keeping the lovers apart, and that the man will risk his life to see his lady again, the second can be understood to mean that the lady, worrying about further damage to her reputation, is reluctant to see the man. This interpretation is closer to the anecdotes told about Prince Motoyoshi in the *Tales of Yamato,* and it also encourages identifying this scenario with the one in *The Tale of Genji* involving Genji and the emperor's lady, Fujitsubo. As noted here in the discussion of the pictures, it is the second interpretation that was most often followed and may well have been how Teika himself read the poem.

The Pictures
The Tan'yū album shows the prince with paper and brush in hand, writing his poem to the lady he is unable to see, while in the background we see a marsh with channel-markers (Channel-markers are also a motif in the *Hyakushu Hinagata,* to which, curiously, cranes are added.) The depiction of the circumstances of the poem's composition (that is, as a letter), however, was not favored; it reappears only in the relatively late *Kangyoku* [**20–1**]. The standard presentation is shown in the *Zōsanshō* [**20–2**], where the poet pleads at the lady's blind. The Kyoto illustrator [**20–4**] adopts all of the *Zōsanshō* design but adds a channel-marker to the river to represent the pivot word. In the *Sugata-e* [**20–3**], Moronobu also includes a channel-marker, but the interest is clearly focused on the two adolescent samurai whose forms echo that of the marker. Practically all of the homoerotic stories in Saikaku's *Great Mirror of Male Love (Nanshoku Ōkagami)* end in one partner giving his life for the other, which may have encouraged Moronobu to illustrate this poem (with its phrase "even if it costs my life") with males.

20-1

20-2

20-3

20-4

POEM 21

ima komu to
ihishi bakari ni
naga-tsuki no
ariake no tsuki wo
machi-idetsuru kana⁵⁸

> It was only because you said
> you would come right away
> that I have waited
> these long months, till even
> the wan morning moon has come out.

Master of the Law Sosei

Sosei Hōshi, born Yoshimine no Haru-toshi, was a son of Henjō (Poem 12). He is the fourth-best-represented poet in the *Kokinshū* and has over sixty poems in the various imperial anthologies. He is one of the Thirty-Six Poetic Immortals. His collected poems, the *Sosei Hōshi Shū*, are extant.

Commentary

Although given as "occasion unknown" *(dai shirazu),* this poem appears in the *Kokinshū* in a group of poems on the subject of "waiting love," where it would be assumed that the speaker of the poem is a woman (since it was the men who visited the women's houses rather than vice versa). The main difference in interpretation concerns *how long* the woman has been waiting. *Kokinshū* scholars agree for the most part that the woman has waited one night, albeit a long autumn one. From the *Kenchū Mikkan,* a collection of commentaries on the *Kokinshū* edited by Teika in 1221, we know, however, that Teika probably read this poem more narratively, imagining that the woman had waited several months, as translated above. The *Kokinshū* interpretation would read:

> It was only because you said
> "I'll come right away"
> that I have ended up waiting
> for nothing more than the wan moon
> in the morning sky of this long, Ninth Month.

The Pictures

Although the speaker of Sosei's poem is meant to be a woman, all pictures show the priestly Sosei himself as the speaker—as in the Porter version [**21–1**]—

watching the moon. Further, an *ariake no tsuki,* or "morning moon," is a moon that rises late and can still be seen in the morning sky—something that occurs only after the twentieth day of the lunar month when the moon is waning. Yet all the illustrators, following the Tan'yū album and the *Zōsanshō* [**21–2**], show a full moon. Moronobu attempts to rationalize Sosei's presence in his *Sugata-e* [**21–3**], where he shows the famous poet grading the poetic efforts of the anxious and waiting young man in front of him. Finally, the *Shikishi Moyō* kimono design [**21–4**], following that of the *Hyakushu Hinagata,* superimposes the characters *ariake* over the branches of a willow (the willow does not appear in the earlier design and has probably been added to suggest the length of time passed), while autumn flowers, such as maiden-flowers *(ominaeshi)* and Chinese bellflowers *(kikyō),* bloom near a veranda.

21-1

21-2

21-3

21-4

POEM 22

fuku kara ni
aki no kusaki no
shiworureba
mube yama-kaze wo
arashi to ifuramu[59]

As soon as it blows,
the autumn trees and grasses
    droop, and this must be why,
quite rightly, the mountain wind
is called "the ravager."

Fun'ya no Yasuhide
Yasuhide's dates are unknown, but he was active around the same time as Narihira (Poem 17) and Sosei (Poem 21). One of the Six Poetic Immortals, he is mentioned in both the Japanese and Chinese prefaces to the *Kokinshū*. He is also counted among the Thirty-Six Poetic Immortals, though he has only five poems in the *Kokinshū* and one in the *Gosenshū*.

Commentary
This poem is a good example of the kind of witty verse written in the early Heian period under the influence of Chinese Six Dynasties "court-style" poetry. It is a kind of *ri'aishi*, or "reasoning poem," that works in an oblique manner. The original point of the poem is that since the Chinese ideograph for the word "storm" *(arashi)* is made up of the elements for "wind" and "mountain," it is logical that mountain winds should be called "storms." In other words, this poem relies on the elements of a word's ideographs, in the fashion of a rebus. Such wittiness was not to the taste of later Japanese poets and readers, however, who expected a deeper seriousness from their writers. Accordingly, the earliest commentaries (and, presumably, Teika as well) vehemently reject the "ideograph-play" interpretation. Rather, they read the poem as one that evoked the forlorn feeling of windswept fields. Hence they understood the word *arashi* as no more than the nominalized form of the the verb *arasu,* "to ravage."

The Pictures
One gets some idea whether the ideographic play was considered legitimate by the way the poem is inscribed on the picture: most artists, excepting Tan'yū

207

and the Kyoto illustrator [**22–1**], write the word *arashi* in *kana*, rather than with the Chinese ideograph. The *Shikishi Moyō* kimono design [**22–3**] is ambiguous (intentionally, no doubt): the characters can be read either as *yama-kaze* or as *arashi*. The *Zōsanshō* interpretation [**22–4**] shows nothing more than a landscape of blasted foliage, while the *Kangyoku* artist [**22–2**] more successfully evokes, with the inclusion of a human figure, the poignant interpretation of this poem favored by Teika.

22-1

22-2

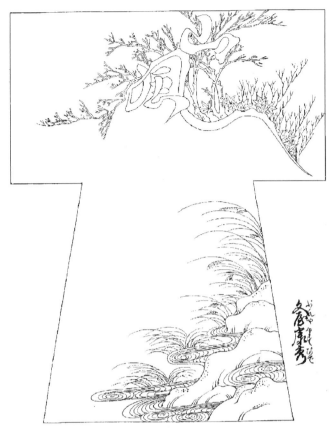

22-3

22-4

POEM 23

tsuki mireba
chi-jhi ni mono koso
kanashikere
wa ga mi hitotsu no
aki ni ha aranedo [60]

When I look at the moon
I am overcome by the sadness
   of a thousand, thousand things—
even though it is not Fall
for me alone.

Ōe no Chisato

Chisato's dates are unknown; he flourished ca. 889–923. A nephew of Yukihira (Poem 16) and Narihira (Poem 17), he is best known for his collection of poetry *Kudai Waka*, ordered by Emperor Uda in 894, where the poet composed 110 poems, each based on a line of Chinese poetry.[61]

Commentary

Historically this poem can be seen in relation to the previous poem by Yasuhide. Yasuhide's was a typical product of Six Dynasties wit, more Chinese in conception than Japanese. Chisato's poetry, by contrast, marks an important point in the assimilation and adaptation of Chinese poetry to native verse. The poem by Chisato chosen for the *One Hundred Poets* is not drawn from his *Kudai Waka*, yet commentators early on linked it to lines by the Chinese poet Po Chü-i that are included in the *Wakan Rōei Shū* (no. 235):

> Within the Swallow Tower, the night's frosty moonlight:
> Autumn has come—is it long for her alone?

This is from one of three poems written about the courtesan Men-men after her patron died. The line is also alluded to in the *Sagoromo Monogatari*.[62] Presumably it was in such a narrative context that Teika interpreted the poem.

The Pictures

Since according to the *Kokinshū* the poem was originally composed for a poetry contest—and given its relation to the poem by Po Chü-i—it is likely that the poet intended the speaker of the poem to be a woman. Nonetheless, all illustrators show Chisato himself as the speaker, as we see in the *Zōsanshō* [**23–1**]. The *Sugata-e* [**23–2**] has the poet's legs being massaged by a *kaburo*, or young servant, who presumably has her own sorrows as well. Hasegawa [**23–3**] differs from all other artists by showing a crescent, rather than full, moon. There was, in fact, a fair amount of debate among commentators about the meaning of the expression *chi-jhi ni*. While it is now understood as "a thousand, thousand [things]," or "various and countless," the *Keikō Shō* (1530) paraphrases it as *shidai ni*, or "gradually, little by little," which might be suggested by a waxing moon (though Hasegawa's is actually waning). The *Shikishi Moyō* kimono design [**23–4**] gives a sense of the limitless nature of the poet's thoughts with the addition of spirals to the characters *chi-jhi* and the many leaves of the bush clover, a plant closely associated with longing.

23-1

23-2

23-3

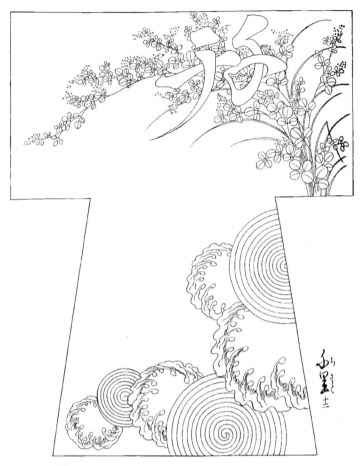

23-4

POEM 24

kono tabi ha
nusa mo tori-ahezu
tamuke-yama
momijhi no nishiki
kami no mani-mani[63]

This time around
I couldn't even bring sacred streamers
    —Offering Hill—
but if this brocade of autumn leaves
is to the gods' liking . . .

Kanke

"Kanke" means literally "the Sugawara family" but refers here to Sugawara no Michizane (845–903). The term derives from the titles of the two collections containing Michizane's Chinese works: the *Kanke Bunsō (The Sugawara Family Literary Drafts)* and the *Kanke Kōshū (The Later Sugawara Collection)*, the former of which contains pieces not only by Michizane but also by his father and grandfather.

Michizane was a famous statesman and scholar. He was greatly promoted by Emperor Uda to act as a foil to the Fujiwara clan's hegemony under Tokihira. In this both Michizane and Uda were ultimately unsuccessful, and Michizane died in exile. It was believed that his vengeful spirit was responsible for a variety of calamities, and he was posthumously pardoned, promoted, and finally deified as Kitano Tenjin, still worshiped today as the god of learning. In addition to his two collections of Chinese poetry and prose, he edited two histories of Japan (again in Chinese), and is traditionally credited with editing an anthology of Japanese poetry, the *Shinsen Man'yō Shū*.[64]

Commentary

This poem's headnote in the *Kokinshū* reads: "Composed at Tamuke Yama ("Offering Hill") when the Suzaku Retired Emperor [Uda] went to Nara." This poem was composed during an elaborate twelve-day excursion Uda made to Nara and Sumiyoshi in 898.[65]

Tabi functions as a pivot word meaning both "journey" and "occasion." The location of Tamuke Yama is unclear, but it was somewhere on the road between the capital and Nara. It does not refer to the present Tamuke Yama in Nara near Tōdaiji. There is also a theory that *tamuke-yama* was actually a common noun referring to mountains where travelers made offerings to the gods for a safe journey; nonetheless, the *tamuke yama* in Nara between Yamashiro and Yamato provinces was particularly well known, and most commentators take the term's use here as a proper noun.

The major division in interpretations comes with the expression *tori-ahezu,* "to be unable to take properly."[66] While there is no debate that the poet is saying that he was unable to bring, as he should, sacred streamers to the mountain, commentators have been divided in their explanations as to *why* the poet was unable. Most medieval readers, including Teika, believed that the suddenness of Uda's excursion had caught Michizane unprepared. Given the elaborateness of this procession, however, this is hardly likely. The other explanation was that since the journey was a public one, centering on the retired emperor, Michizane was not able to take the occasion to make a private offering to the deities. In fact, Michizane's poem is just a typical *Kokinshū* witticism based on the punning potential of a place-name and the conceit of autumn leaves as brocade.

The Pictures

Most artists show Michizane directly addressing the shrine, though there is a difference in the formality of his dress: the *Zōsanshō* shows a relatively casual Michizane [**24–2**], while the *Kangyoku* has the poet in full formal robes [**24–1**]. A work called *Sugawara Jikki* (Edo period) has a depiction of Uda's journey, with Michizane's poem inscribed above the poet [**24–3**]; the only *One Hundred Poets* artist to use a similar conception is the Kyoto illustrator [**24–4**]. Yet the Kyoto illustration represents a very different reading: we are meant to imagine that it is Michizane, rather than the emperor, who is in the cart. The prominence of the ox calls to mind the episode in the *Kitano Tenjin Engi* that tells how the ox pulling the cart with Michizane's remains refused to move just outside of Dazaifu.[67] (To this day bulls are a frequent symbol at Tenjin shrines.) We next notice that the man behind the cart is an armed guard—the picture thus alludes to Michizane's exile. Whether the poem itself was interpreted to conform with this context is unclear.

24-1

24-2

24-3

やまびこを
　とり
　あへど
　たかき山
　ぐらの
　神のき
　まつく

24-4

POEM 25

na ni shi ohaba
afusaka-yama no
sanekadzura
hito ni shirarede
kuru yoshi mogana[68]

If they bear such names:
the "come-sleep vine" of
  "Meeting-Slope Hill"—
how I wish there was a way to come to you,
as if pulling in a vine, unknown to others.

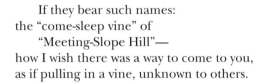

The Third Ward Minister of the Right

Sanjō no Udaijin was born Fujiwara no Sadakata (873–932). His sobriquet comes from his residence in the capital's Third Ward. He has one poem in the *Kokinshū*, nine in the *Gosenshū*, and nine in later imperial anthologies. He is the father of Asatada (Poem 44).

Commentary

This poem is a tour de force of pivot words: the place-name *afusaka* (pronounced "Ōsaka" but a different place from the modern city of that name), taken to mean "Meeting-Slope"; *sanekadzura,* a kind of vine whose name includes the phrase *sa ne,* or "Come, sleep!"; and the verb *kuru,* which means both "to come" and "to draw or reel in" (something ropelike, such as a vine). The headnote to this poem says: "Sent to a woman's house." Most likely Sadakata attached his poem to an actual piece of vine. In the Heian period, men and women of the aristocracy tended to keep separate residences, and it was the man who would come to visit the woman rather than vice versa. Nonetheless, most medieval commentators took the last line in this poem to mean "how I wish there was a way to have you come to me, like drawing a vine in."

The Pictures

Following the interpretation prevalent at the time, the *Zōsanshō* and the Kyoto illustrator [25–1] show the poet on his veranda beckoning for the woman to approach; the Kyoto illustrator simply adds *kadzura* vines to the earlier design.

Vine-covered hills are also shown in the *Sugata-e* [**25–2**], perhaps derived from the Tan'yū album. Moronobu shows the poet sitting dejectedly while a servant prepares to leave, perhaps to take his poem to his lover. The Porter illustrator [**25–3**] uses the same basic situation but places the two on a mountain path, perhaps to suggest the place-name "Meeting-Slope Hill." Only the *Kangyoku* [**25–4**] shows the poet going to the woman, representing what has become the standard interpretation of this poem.

25-1

25-2

25-3

25-4

POEM 26

wogura-yama
mine no momijhi-ba
kokoro araba
ima hito-tabi no
mi-yuki matanamu[1]

O autumn leaves
on the peak of Ogura Hill,
if you have a heart,
I would that you would wait
for one more royal progress.

Lord Teishin
Teishinkō is Fujiwara no Tadahira (880–949). "Teishinkō" is his posthumous name; his sobriquet while alive was "the KoIchijō Chancellor."[2] He was the fourth son of Mototsune and took control of both the Fujiwara clan and the country after the death of his eldest brother, Tokihira. It was his descendants who continued to monopolize political power: he was father to Morosuke, who was in turn the grandfather of Michinaga. Tadahira's diary, the *Teishinkō Ki*, is extant. His poety was first selected for the *Gosenshū*, in which he has seven poems; six more are included in later anthologies.

Commentary
In the *Shūishū*, the headnote to this poem reads:

Teiji In [Retired Emperor Uda] went on an excursion to the Ōi River, and when he said, "This is a place where the Emperor [Daigo, his son] should also make a royal outing," [Tadahira] composed the following to convey the retired emperor's will.

This occasion is also described in the *Tales of Yamato* (Episode 99), where it says that "this is how the traditional imperial visits to the Ōi River began."[3] It is also mentioned in the *Great Mirror (Ōkagami)*, where it is praised as "an elegant gesture."[4]

Most medieval commentators followed the *Shūishū* headnote, and there was little disagreement over the basic interpretation of the poem. In the early modern period, attention turned to the question of during *which* of Uda's trips to the Ōi River this poem was composed: in 898, 899, 907, or 926? Modern scholars, such as Ishida Yoshisada, have asked why Teika included this poem, suggesting that it was because the villas of both Teika and his father-in-law, Utsunomiya no Yoritsuna, were on Ogura. Shimazu points out that Tadahira's poem follows the same conception as one by his grandfather, Yoshifusa, collected in the *Kokin Roku-jō*:

yoshino-yama	O autumn leaves
kishi no momijhi shi	on the cliffs of the Yoshino mountains,
kokoro araba	if you have a heart,
mare no mi-yuki wo	please wait, without changing your color,
iro kahede mate	for a rare royal outing.

Moreover, the basic situation of Tadahira's poem is identical to that of Michizane's (Poem 24). Given that *mi-yuki*, or "royal outing," is also a chapter title from *The Tale of Genji*, Teika seems to be insisting on the regular, almost seasonal nature of royal outings accompanied by (hereditary) poets. Following Edward Kamens' work on Teika's involvement in the screen paintings and poems for Emperor GoToba's Saishō Shitennō In,[5] a more political interpretation, emphasizing Teika's loyalty to the disenfranchised imperial family, might also be possible.

The Pictures

As noted above, the setting for Tadahira's poem is very similar to that of Michizane's (Poem 24); indeed, in the Kyoto illustration [**26–1**] only the addition of a river distinguishes the landscape from that for Michizane's poem [**24–4**]. The Kyoto artist closely follows the *Zōsanshō* here but has emphasized both the autumn leaves and the river. The *Hyakushu Hinagata* [**26–2**] has a mountain, inscribed "Ogura Yama," and a rushing stream that forces the fallen maple leaves through the weirs that would hold them back. Moronobu's *Sugata-e* [**26–4**] is a lyrical reinterpretation that depicts the poet as an old man with a cane asking for yet one more year in which to see the fall foliage. This more lyrical reading leads in turn to versions such as that in the *Kangyoku* [**26–3**].

26-1

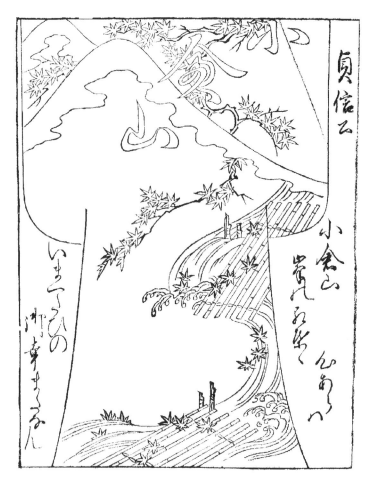

小倉山 みねのもみちは

いまひとたひの みゆきまたなん

貞信公

26-2

26-3

26-4

POEM 27

mika no hara
wakite nagaruru
idzumi-kaha
itsu miki tote ka
kohishikaruramu[6]

Like Izumi River
that wells up and flows,
 dividing the Moor of Urns—
when did I see her, I wonder,
that I should yearn for her so?

Middle Counselor Kanesuke
Chūnagon Fujiwara no Kanesuke (877–933), brother of Sadakata (Poem 25), was known as "the Counselor of the Levée" (Tsutsumi Chūnagon) after his mansion beside the dam of the Kamo River. His residence was a meeting place for literati such as Tsurayuki (Poem 35) and Mitsune (Poem 29), for whom he acted as patron. Not surprisingly, then, his poetry first appears in the *Kokinshū*. He is one of the Thirty-Six Poetic Immortals and has some fifty-seven poems in the various imperial anthologies. A personal poetry collection is extant as well.

Commentary
This poem is also collected in the *Kokin Roku-jō*, where it is listed as anonymous; thus its attribution to Kanesuke in the *ShinKokinshū* is suspect. Medieval debate centered on whether the poem exemplified the topic *ahite ahazaru kohi*—that is, where the lovers have met and pledged their love once, only to be unable to meet again—or *ahazaru kohi*, when the lovers have not yet actually met. Since the poem appears in the first book of love poems in the *ShinKokinshū*, it would appear that Teika followed the second interpretation.

The poem is a skillful example of the use of a "preface" *(jo)*, poetic place-name *(uta-makura)*, and pivot words *(kake-kotoba)*. *Mika-no-Hara* is a place-name from the Kyoto area; *mika* literally means "jars" or "urns." The verb *wakite* means both "to bubble up, spring, gush forth" and "to divide." The poem is centered, however, on the pivot word *idzumi*. As a common noun, *idzumi* is a "spring," thus connecting with the verb *wakite*. The Izumi River is an actual river, today called Kizu-gawa. The whole first three lines serve as a "preface" to *itsu miki*, "when did I see," where "when see *(itsu mi)*" echoes "Izumi River."

The Pictures

The fact that *mika* means "urn" is pointed out in the early *Keikō Shō* (1530). The *Zōsanshō* [**27–1**] and the Kyoto illustrator [**27–2**] place an urn in the middle of the river. The *Zōsanshō*, in particular, gives a wonderful sense of a plain or moor *(hara)* being intersected *(wakite)* by the river, barring the poet from seeing his lady. The Kyoto illustrator, by contrast, interprets *hara* to mean "wilderness," placing the poet in a mountain setting. Both have the poet with hand to brow, miming "to see." The Porter artist and the *Kangyoku* naturalize the scene by removing the urn or returning to the Tan'yū album's more naturalistic interpretation. The *Shikishi Moyō* kimono designer [**27–4**] takes advantage of the nonseasonal nature of the poem to embellish his design with blossoms, emblazoning the back with the ideograph for *idzumi*. The *Hyakushu Hinagata* [**27–3**] ignores conventional spelling of the place-name Mika-no-Hara and writes it with the ideographs for "Plain of Beautiful Fragrance," not attested in any other source.

27-1

27-2

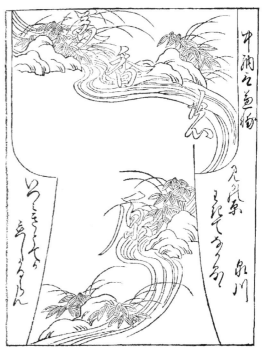

27-3

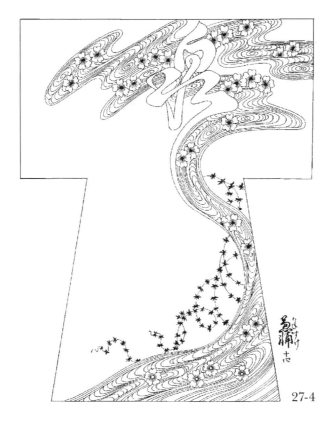

27-4

POEM 28

yama-zato ha　　　　In the mountain village,
fuyu zo sabishisa　　it is in winter that my loneliness
masarikeru　　　　　increases most,
hito-me mo kusa mo　when I think how both have dried up,
karenu to omoheba[7]　the grasses and people's visits.

Lord Minamoto no Muneyuki

Minamoto no Muneyuki Ason (d. 939) was a grandson of Emperor Kōkō (Poem 15). He participated in famous poetry contests and appears in the *Tales of Yamato*. His personal poetry collection contains many exchanges with Tsurayuki (Poem 35). He has six poems in the *Kokinshū*, three in the *Gosenshū*, and six in the remaining imperial anthologies.

Commentary

This poem appears in the *Kokinshū* with the headnote: "Composed as a winter poem." In conception it is very similar to a poem in the "Prince Koresada Poetry Contest" (Koresada Shinnō no Ie no Uta-awase; 893), which involves an elegant debate on the issue of which season is sadder, autumn or winter. In other words, Muneyuki's poem is written in response to the assumption that autumn is saddest. Ariyoshi notes that while poets during Muneyuki's time thought that mountain villages, removed from life at the capital, were sad and neglected during all four seasons,[8] by Teika's day aesthetic reclusion was viewed in a positive light and "mountain villages" became places to appreciate nature. The word *hito-me* ("people's eyes') is often used in the sense of "prying eyes" in secret love affairs; its use here to mean "people's visits" is unusual. It allows the verb *kare*, however, to act as a pivot word meaning both "to wither" and "to avoid, keep away."

The Pictures

Despite virtual unanimity among medieval commentators, the pictorializations of this poem show a surprising degree of diversity. The *Zōsanshō* [**28–1**] shows a snowbound mountain hut (similar to the *Hyakushu Hinagata* design), with Muneyuki seeming to gaze pensively at it from across his *kasen-e* frame. A similar landscape serves as the background for Moronobu's clearly homosexual interpretation in the *Sugata-e* [**28–2**], with the man looking out from under his bedclothes at the young man. The Kyoto artist [**28–3**] puts a courtier into the picture, but in a way which suggests that the poet is not the resident of the hut (Hasegawa, by contrast, has the poet on the veranda looking out at his gate)— his raised hand suggests "looking" and thus the "eyes" of the phrase *hito-me* ("people's eyes," meaning "people's visits"). Most interestingly, the *Shikishi Moyō* kimono design [**28–4**] has placed *ayame*, or sweetflag, at the bottom of the trailing character for "mountain" (*yama*, of "mountain village"), also picking up on the *me* of *hito-me*, though this gesture then transposes the poem from winter to the Fifth Month, that is, in Spring.

28-1

28-2

やぎじは
めぐそ
びさ
まほり
ろろ
人めを
まも
うれぬと
せんら

28-3

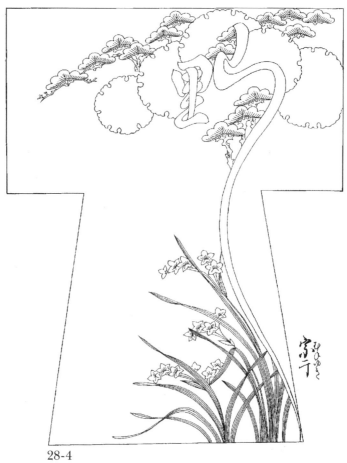

28-4

POEM 29

kokoro-ate ni
woraba ya woramu
hatsu-shimo no
oki-madohaseru
shira-giku no hana[9]

Must it be by chance,
if I am to pluck one, that I pluck it?—
   white chrysanthemums
on which the first frost
lies bewilderingly.

Ōshikōchi no Mitsune

Mitsune (died ca. 925) was one of the compilers of the *Kokinshū* and a friend of Tsurayuki (Poem 35), with whom he frequented the mansion of Kanesuke (Poem 27). One of the Thirty-Six Poetic Immortals, he has almost two hundred poems in post-*Kokinshū* imperial anthologies. His personal poetry collection contains a large number of poems from screens *(byōbu-uta)* and poetry contests *(uta-awase)*.

Commentary

At least five distinct interpretations of this poem can be found, all centering on the second line, *woraba ya woramu*. The *Yoritaka-bon*, *Kamijō-bon*, and *Shūe Shō* believe this is simple word repetition *(kasane-kotoba)*, meaning no more than "must I pluck one (by hazard)?" Other interpretations focus on the *-baya* construction. The *Ōei Shō* and *Komezawa-bon* say that this indicates a wish on the speaker's part ("O, if I could pluck one!"). The *Yoritaka-bon* says that it represents the speaker's internal dialogue ("Shall I pluck one or shall I not?"). Kageki argues that the phrase simply represents an exclamation *(eitan)* ("Shall I pluck one!"). Ariyoshi, following the preponderance of remaining commentaries, sees the phrase as a rhetorical question ("Is it only by chance that I shall be able to pluck one?—Yes, I am unable to pluck one other than by chance"). Typical of this period of poetry, the poet has personified *(gijinka)* the frost, which camouflages the chrysanthemums. The poem's attraction to Teika, however, no doubt lay in its white-on-white imagery.

The Pictures

Clearly the kinds of interpretive debate that occupied commentators could not be represented pictorially, and so, despite a wide variety of interpretations, the pictorializations show little difference. The *Zōsanshō* [**29–1**] remains the basic

model in all later illustrations. The *Sugata-e* [**29–2**] again gives an erotic inter-
pretation: the older poetry master seems to be confused as to which to
"pluck"—the boy or the girl—though the girl, with the chrysanthemum-pat-
terned robe, is adjusting her collar in a self-conscious manner. Above them, the
choice seems to be between chrysanthemums and maple leaves.[10] Hasegawa
[**29–3**] maintains the *Soan-bon* posture of the poet and places him on a veranda
looking out to his garden in a somewhat awkward *contrapposto*. The *Shikishi
Moyō* kimono designer [**29–4**] superimposes the characters for "first frost"
(hatsu-shimo) on clusters of chrysanthemums.

29-1

29-2

29-3

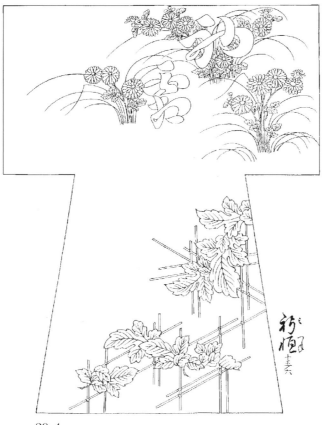

29-4

POEM 30

ariake no
tsurenaku mieshi
wakare yori
akatsuki bakari
uki mono ha nashi[11]

There is nothing so depressing
as the break of day and
　　leaving you after
having seen the heartless
morning moon.

Mibu no Tadamine

Mibu no Tadamine (b. ca. 850), another of the *Kokinshū*'s compilers, is the father of Tadami (Poem 41). One of the Thirty-Six Poetic Immortals, he has thirty-five poems in the *Kokinshū* and almost fifty in the remaining imperial anthologies. A personal poetry collection, the *Tadamine Shū,* and a poetic treatise, the *Tadamine Jittei,* are extant, though the latter is of dubious authenticity.

Commentary

Interpretations of this poem divide into two camps. The context originally imagined for this poem seems to have been a disappointed lover returning home after trying unsuccessfully all night to have his chosen lady receive him. Hence the poem makes a metaphorical comparison between the cold lady and the cold moon. (*Ariake* refers to the late-rising moon in the latter half of the lunar month that is still visible in the sky at morning.) A translation following this interpretation might read:

> Ever since that parting,
> with its coldhearted-looking
> 　　morning moon,
> there is nothing so depressing
> as the hours before dawn.

Kenshō's and Teika's interpretation, however, is far happier: they read the poem as a morning-after poem *(kinu-ginu no uta)* sent by a still-unsated lover after dawn has forced him from his lady's side. Almost all medieval commentators follow the first interpretation, however.

The Pictures

While the *Shūgyoku* pictorialization has a man leaving a still-closed gate, early Edo-period artists, as seen in the *Zōsanshō* [**30–1**], by and large seem to have followed Teika's interpretation of this poem—showing the two lovers parting at dawn—perhaps because the context is then visually recognizable as romantic. Hasegawa's rendition [**30–3**] probably does not represent a different interpretation; most likely it is simply the result of his placing the *Soan-bon* figure in his usual veranda-plus-landscape format. The *Kangyoku* [**30–2**], on the other hand, seems to show some influence from the *Saga-bon* illustration for Episode 14 of *The Tales of Ise,* a well-known poem in which the woman curses the rooster for making her lover leave (see Poem 62), and a rooster and hen are also seen in the *Hyakushu Hinagata.* The Porter illustrator [**30–4**] seems to hedge his bets— there could be a woman sitting out of view behind the lattice. Yet other late-Edo illustrators also use this basic, poet-alone format (such as Kunisada and Kuni-yoshi in the 1849 *Nishiki-e* edition), suggesting that the poem was read as the poet's reverie or recollection of an event in the distant past.

30-1

30-2

30-3

30-4

POEM 31

asaborake
ariake no tsuki to
miru made ni
yoshino no sato ni
fureru shira-yuki[12]

So that I thought it
the light of the lingering moon
    at dawn—
the white snow that has fallen
on the village of Yoshino.

Sakanoue no Korenori

Korenori (dates uncertain) is a representative poet of the *Kokinshū* period and one of the Thirty-Six Poetic Immortals. He has eight poems in the *Kokinshū* and over thirty in later imperial anthologies. A personal poetry anthology is extant.

Commentary

This poem seems to treat a topic very similar to that of the immediately preceding poem by Tadamine. But whereas Tadamine's is clearly a love poem, Korenori's is seasonal: unlike *akatsuki,* which can be used to refer to "dawn" in any season, *asaborake* refers specifically to dawn in either autumn or winter. Commentaries such as the *Ōei Shō* thought of Korenori's poem as one of pure scenic description. But in fact the poem is in the conventional "elegant confusion" mode that harks back to Chinese poetry.

There has been little explicit disagreement over the meaning of the poem. Nevertheless, while most other commentators believed the scene to be one of light snow, Keichū argued that the position of the poem in the *Kokinshū* suggested deep snow instead. This poem has marked similarities with Poem 29 by Mitsune: both are "elegant confusion" poems based on conceits that derive from Chinese poetry, and both present the images of whiteness so treasured by Teika.

The Pictures

Here the Tan'yū album delivers one of its most sensitive renderings: an unhappy-looking Korenori gazing at a finely rendered mountain village, with bright white snow reflecting the moonlight off the thatched rooftops and surrounding hills. Korenori's expression is such to suggest that the artist has interpreted this poem as a lover's lament, along the same lines as the previous Poem

30. The standard interpretation shows the poet leaning on an armrest, gazing out from under his bedding, as in the *Zōsanshō* [**31–1**]. The Kyoto artist follows this design closely but removes the poet's hat and makes the snowfall heavier, perhaps following Keichū. The *Hyakushu Hinagata* [**31–4**] also presents heavily covered plants, but together with flowering cherries, indicating that it is a late snow. It is the "first snow" interpretation that is recorded in the *Sugata-e* [**31–3**] *(hatsu-yuki no usuku mo furitaru)* and thus rendered in the background. The way the old poet is gazing at the shaved pate of the young man suggests some kind of association between the first snow and the young man's first head-shaving. The *Hyakushu Hinagata*'s snow-encrusted bamboo reappears in Hasegawa [**31–2**], though in both cases the treatment is in fact anachronistic: Teika was once asked to find a poem to pair with a picture depicting the topic "snow on bamboo." While looking through his library, however, Teika discovered that the topic was actually a relatively new one and there were no examples of it before the *Horikawa Hyakushu* of 1105–1106. Hence it might be argued that it is inaccurate to show Korenori composing his poem while gazing at snow-clad bamboo.[13]

31-2

31-1

31-3

31-4

POEM 32

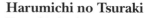

yama-gaha ni
kaze no kaketaru
shigarami ha
nagare mo ahenu
momijhi narikeri [14]

Ah, the weir
that the wind has flung
across the mountain stream
is the autumn foliage that
cannot flow on, even though it would.

Harumichi no Tsuraki
Tsuraki died in 920; little else is known of him. He graduated from the imperial university in 910 and died ten years later just as he was about to take up his post as governor of Iki province. Only five of his poems are extant: three in the *Kokinshū* and two in the *Gosenshū*.

Commentary
The expression "the weir that the wind has flung" is widely praised by the medieval commentators. Both this personification *(gijinka)* and the basic pattern of the poem ("as for *x*, it is *y*") are typical of the *Kokinshū* period. Given the relative obscurity of the poet, it must have been Teika's high regard for this particular poem that led him to include it in the *One Hundred Poets*.

While there is little major disagreement over the interpretation of this poem, commentators have debated about the situation that gave rise to Tsuraki's conceit. The majority of commentators, following the *Ōei Shō*, suggest that the autumn leaves are falling continuously and their quantity has covered the stream and blocked it up. But Keichū, following the *Keikō Shō*, insists that it is not that the leaves have blanketed the stream, but simply that some of them have become stuck in a shallow section of the water's course.

The Pictures
Keichū's interpretation seems to have had little effect on the pictorializations of this poem; in the *Zōsanshō* [**32–1**] and the Kyoto version [**32–2**], the profusion of trees above the stream suggests that it is their quantity that has caused the blockage. Hasegawa [**32–3**] pictorializes the metaphorical weir. Moronobu's *Sugata-e* [**32–4**] seems to represent a distinctively different interpretation, closer to that of Keichū: there are fewer trees and the stream takes a sharper bend, emphasized by a large rock. The scene below shows a man hav-

ing his hair dressed while a young woman stands before him. Just as in other pictures from this set, the young woman's outline vaguely echoes the shape of the rock in the landscape above. Presumably the man would "flow on" and away, but he finds himself held back by the young woman (or the two women, who seem to be exchanging glances), as if by a weir.

32-1

32-2

32-3

32-4

POEM 33

hisakata no
hikari nodokeki
haru no hi ni
shidzu-kokoro naku
hana no chiruramu[15]

In these spring days
with the tranquil light encompassing
   the four directions
why should the blossoms scatter
with uneasy hearts?

Ki no Tomonori

An older cousin of Tsurayuki (Poem 35), Tomonori was also one of the compilers of the *Kokinshū* but died before its completion (died ca. 905 or 907). He is one of the Thirty-Six Poetic Immortals and a collection of his poetry is extant. He has forty-six poems in the *Kokinshū*, and over twenty in the remaining imperial anthologies.

Commentary

In the *Kokinshū* the headnote to this poem reads: "Composed on the falling of the cherry blossoms." One line of interpretation argues that it is not the flowers whose hearts are unquiet, but the hearts of those who watch them fall. The *Komezawa-bon,* however, gives an explicitly political reading: "When the august reign is tranquil like this, why are the flowers uneasy?"

The Pictures

Every illustrator includes a human figure, making it impossible to tell whether it is the flowers whose hearts are unquiet, or the man who watches them fall. The prominence of the shining sun in the *Zōsanshō* [**33–1**], the Kyoto illustrator, and others, may suggest the political interpretation of the *Komezawa-bon.* No sun appears in the Porter illustration [**33–2**]. Nor does it appear in Moronobu's *Sugata-e* [**33–3**]: here it seems to have been transformed into the sunflowers (*hi-mawari*) on the woman's robe.[16] Finally, the *Shikishi Moyō* kimono designer [**33–4**] gives a weeping cherry (*shidare-zakura*) over which are superimposed the two ideographs for *hisakata.* The fallen petals seem to be held in place or restrained by the wickerwork below. The weeping cherry itself seems to be meant to function in a manner similar to the motif of cherry blossoms and willows, seen at least as early as the *Illustrated Scroll of Lord Takafusa's Love Song* (*Takafusa-kyō Tsuya-kotoba Emaki,* late thirteenth to early fourteenth century, National Museum of Japanese History, Chiba prefecture), and seeming to indicate, as does Tomonori's poem, the beauty of spring and the tranquility of a peaceful reign.[17]

33-1

33-2

33-3

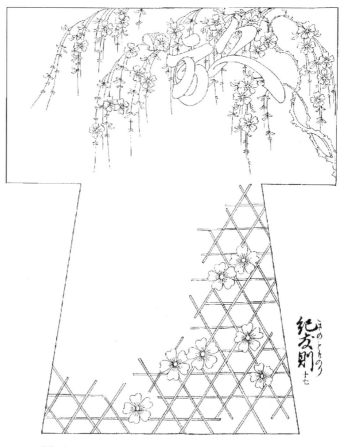

紀友則
十七

33-4

POEM 34

tare wo ka mo
shiru hito ni semu
takasago no
matsu mo mukashi no
tomo naranaku ni[18]

Whom, then, shall I have
as someone who knows me—
    since even the ancient pines
of Takasago
are not friends from my past?

Fujiwara no Okikaze

Okikaze (dates uncertain) was an active participant in the poetry world around the time of the *Kokinshū*. One of the Thirty-Six Poetic Immortals, he has seventeen poems in the *Kokinshū* and twenty-one in later imperial collections. A collection of his poems is also extant.

Commentary

This poem is specifically alluded to in Tsurayuki's Japanese preface to the *Kokinshū,* where he is enumerating occasions for poetry and says "the poet might . . . think of the pine trees of Takasago and Suminoe as having grown up with him [*ai'oi*]."[19] Takasago is in Harima province (modern Hyōgo prefecture) on the west bank of the Kakogawa River and was long famous for its pine trees. However, *takasago* was also a common noun meaning a high dune or hill. Although the land around Takasago was quite flat, it was typically collocated with the word *wonohe* ("peak," from *KKS* 908) and depicted as a high bluff or hill. Moreover, by the medieval period the expression *ai'oi* was no longer understood to mean that the poet and pines had grown up together, but was taken to refer to a specific pine in Takasago and another in Sumi-no-e, which were understood as "paired," as husband and wife, and it is this understanding that is reflected in Zeami's highly influential *nō* play, *Takasago.*[20] Finally, *ai'oi* came to mean two tree trunks growing out of a single base and, in reference to Takasago, a black pine and red pine so joined within the Takasago Shrine precincts.

The basic sense of Okikaze's poem is clear: the speaker is an old man whose friends have all died. Even though the pines of Takasago are also long-lived, there is no way they can provide companionship to the man. Despite the clearness of the sentiment, commentators have exercised their imaginations in debate over why the pines cannot be the poet's friend. The *Tenri-bon Kiki-gaki* (1564) claims that the pines are too virtuous to befriend a human being. The

Shisetsu Shō (1658) claims that the pine is too long-lived to be able to commiserate with a human being, no matter how aged. Contrarily, the *ShinShō* (1804) claims that it is the pine which is too young to be the man's friend from the past. The other point of dispute was whether *takasago* was a place-name (as claimed at least as early as Keichū's commentary on the *Kokinshū*) or simply a common noun (as argued by Yūsai, Mabuchi, and others).

The Pictures

Tan'yū depicts two pines trees, joined at the base, growing on a bluff overlooking the ocean, reflecting the early modern understanding of the term *ai'oi*. Contrarily, the *Zōsanshō* [**34–1**] shows only one pine tree, which would seem to follow the *Kokinshū*-period understanding of the term. Yet again, both the *Kangyoku* [**34–2**] and the *Eiga* depict the pines (twinned in the former text) on a beach, reflecting the shrine's seaside location. The *Shikishi Moyō* kimono designer [**34–3**] insists on the specificity of Takasago by including the word *wonohe,* which can also be understood as a place-name and appears in the poem that immediately precedes Okikaze's in the *Kokinshū*:

kakushitsutsu	Hiding myself away
yo wo ya tsukasamu	here I shall exhaust my days—
takasago no	even though I am not
wonohe ni tateru	a pine that stands on O-no-e
matsu naranaku ni	in Takasago.

Moronobu's *Sugata-e* (see Figure 27) suggests a kind of *mitate* that would reappear in the work of such artists as Utamaro, where the Old Man and Old Woman of Zeami's play are transformed into contemporary lovers; the books may be meant to allude to the idea of "friends from the past."

34-1

34-2

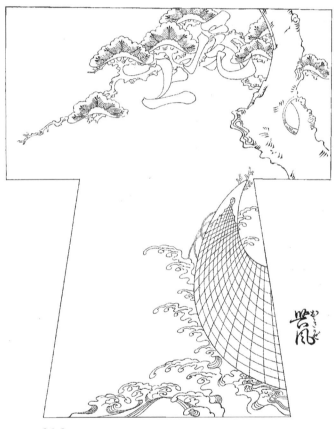

34-3

POEM 35

hito ha isa
kokoro mo shirazu
furu-sato ha
hana zo mukashi no
ka ni nihohikeru[21]

With people, well,
you can never know their hearts;
　　but in my old village
the flowers brightly bloom with
the scent of the days of old.

Ki no Tsurayuki

Tsurayuki (ca. 868–945) was the chief editor of the *Kokinshū* and the author of its polemical Japanese preface. He led the battle to have Japanese verse accepted as the equal of Chinese. Besides the *Kokinshū*, his best-known work is the *Tosa Diary* (*Tosa Nikki*, ca. 935), a fictional travel account based on his own journey back from serving as governor of Tosa province in Shikoku. He has 202 poems in the *Kokinshū*, and more than 450 in all the imperial collections combined. A large personal poetry collection also survives.

Commentary

This poem is preceded by a lengthy head-note in the *Kokinshū:*

There was a house of someone with whom the poet stayed whenever he made a pilgrimage to Hatsuse. However, for a long time he did not have occasion to stay there. Time passed, and later, when he did finally visit again, the owner of the house sent out the following upon his arrival: "As you can see, there is always lodging for you!" Whereupon the poet broke off a branch of a plum that had been planted there and composed [the following].

In this context, the poem can be paraphrased as: "People's hearts change easily, and I don't know whether you feel about me the same way you did in the past. However, in this long-familiar village, the flowers at least are blooming with the same scent as always." While one modern scholar has suggested that the owner was probably a woman, bitter at the man's neglect of her, the poem has been traditionally understood to be addressed to another man. The idea that the poet can both know and rely on the plum is of course in marked contrast to the idea presented in the previous poem by Okikaze (Poem 34).

The Pictures

Although the headnote says that the owner "sent out word" *(ihi-idashi)*, most illustrations show the poet and the host face to face, as in the *Zōsanshō* [**35–1**]. The *Kangyoku* [**35–2**] seems closest to the actual situation—interestingly, the host or his servant is depicted as a monk or recluse. Moronobu's *Sugata-e* (see Figure 28) shows the poet perhaps critically comparing a young boy to the reliable plum; as discussed in Part One, this picture in particular seems to be a parody of the Tan'yū album. The comparison of boys to the plum is made explicit in the following passage of Saikaku's *Great Mirror of Male Love (Nanshoku Ōkagami)* describing a lord's first view of a young retainer: "When he appeared before the lord, his lordship was smitten immediately with the boy's unadorned beauty... One by one his other qualities became apparent, from his nightingale voice to his gentle disposition, as obedient and true as a plum blossom."[22]

The *Shikishi Moyō* kimono design [**35–3**] has the plum depicted with the ideographs for both "scent" *(ka)* and "to bloom brightly" *(nihofu,* which can also mean "scent" or "perfume"); the roofed walls of the villa depicted in the earlier *Hyakushu Shikishi* (Part One, Figure 37) have been reduced to a brushwood fence.

35-1

35-2

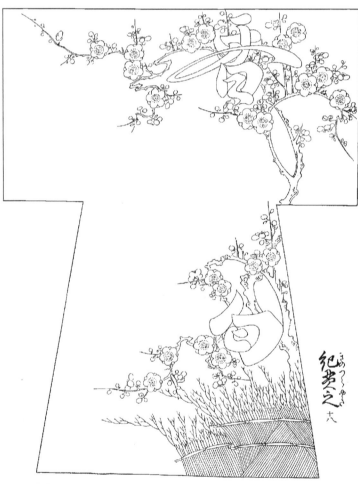

35-3

POEM 36

natsu no yo ha
mada yohi nagara
akenuru wo
kumo no idzuko ni
tsuki yadoruramu[23]

The short summer nights:
while it seems yet early evening,
    it has already dawned, but
where in the clouds, then,
does the moon lodge, I wonder?

Kiyohara no Fukayabu

Fukayabu (dates uncertain) has seventeen poems in the *Kokinshū,* and his personal poetry collection seems to have been used in compiling this first imperial anthology. He is the grandfather of Motosuke (Poem 42) and the great-grandfather of Sei Shōnagon (Poem 62).

Commentary

This poem presupposes a great deal of knowledge on the part of the reader—knowledge that was part of every poet's cultural assumptions. The poem starts with the phrase "summer nights" *(natsu no yo ha).* One of the chief characteristics of summer nights, according to the poetic conventions of the time, was their brevity. Hence the first line of Fukayabu's poem says that summer nights are so brief that day has already dawned while

he thought that night had barely begun. The moon rises in the east and sets in the west. Yet the night has been so short that the poet does not see how the moon could have possibly already arrived at the edge of the western hills where it usually sets. Moreover, the poet cannot see the moon because of the clouds. Thus he asks himself where in the clouds the moon must be lodging, since the night was too short for it to have made its way across the sky to the western hills.

This poem was highly regarded during the *Kokinshū* era and was included in Tsurayuki's *Shinsen Waka* and the *Kokin Roku-jō.* Fukayabu was not included by Kintō among the Thirty-Six Poetic Immortals, however, and his reputation suffered accordingly until Shunzei included this poem in his *Korai Fūtei Shō.* Thereafter this poem was used allusively by many *ShinKokinshū* period poets. This poem may have been linked to the previous poem in Teika's mind by the use of the verb *yadoru* ("to lodge"), which also appears in the headnote to Tsurayuki's verse (Poem 35).

The Pictures

It is not until the *Iken* (1823) that we find an interpretation suggesting that the poet is actually looking at the moon which remains in the morning sky. Rather, in the standard interpretation the moon is not visible to the poet. Nonetheless, only the *Kangyoku* [**36–3**] demonstrates such a reading—all other artists clearly show the moon, as in the *Zōsanshō* [**36–1**]. Moronobu's *Sugata-e* (see Figure 29) shows a man having his hair dressed by a woman, which could be read as the man leaving after a very short night with his lover.[24] The commentary cited above specifically talks of the poet's "bitterness" *(urami)* at no longer being able to see the moon (see also the next poem). Such a reading would help explain the inclusion of a bird, which could then be identified as a *hototogisu,* often used as a metaphor for a fickle male lover. The *Shikishi Moyō* kimono design [**36–2**] has added the summer flora of irises (also seen in **36–3**) and wisteria, over which the ideographs for "cloud" *(kumo)* and "moon" *(tsuki)* have been superimposed.

36-1

36-2

36-3

POEM 37

shira-tsuyu ni
kaze no fuki-shiku
aki no ta ha
tsuranuki-tomenu
tama zo chirikeru[25]

In the autumn fields
where the wind blows repeatedly
    on the white dewdrops,
the gems, not strung together,
do scatter about indeed.

Fun'ya no Asayasu
Almost nothing is known of this poet (read in some Edo texts as "Tomoyasu," dates unknown) except that he was a son of Yasuhide (Poem 22), one of the Six Poetic Immortals. Moreover, only three of his poems are extant: one in the *Kokinshū* and this and one other in the *Gosenshū*.

Commentary
Although the headnote in the *Gosenshū* states that this poem was written during the reign of Emperor Daigo (r. 897–930), it is found in *The Empress' Poetry Contest of the Kanpyō Era* and in the *Shinsen Man'yō Shū* (both circa 893) and hence is clearly a product of Emperor Uda's reign (887–897).

The conceit of dew as gems was a common one in the period—with any number of poems written on it. Add to this the extremely minor reputation of Asayasu and one might be tempted to believe that Teika included this poem simply because of the parent-child relationship between Asayasu and Yasuhide (Poem 22). As the poem's frequent inclusion in his exemplary anthologies shows, however, Teika apparently thought this poem truly something remarkable. Its worth is perhaps less apparent today. Ariyoshi notes that while other poems of this type are concerned only with comparing the dewdrops to gems, Asayasu's poem concentrates on the sight of the dewdrops being scattered. He also suggests that this image of scattering dew may call to mind the transcience of existence. Moreover, one notes that Asayasu describes the jewels as "not strung," rather than suggesting that they have become somehow unstrung.

The Pictures
The dominant interpretation has this poem describing the beauty of an autumn scene with the dew falling. However, three commentaries, the *Yoritaka-bon* (Muromachi period), the *Minō Shō* (late Muromachi), and the *Komezawa-*

bon (1452), interpret the poet as complaining that even though the dewdrops are strung together (by the autumn grasses), still the wind scatters them. Only the Porter artist [**37–2**] manages to convey the sense of the standard interpretation: presenting the dewdrops as loose and unstrung. Other artists, such as the Kyoto artist [**37–1**] (as always, following the *Zōsanshō*), by picturing the dew aligned on the grasses, seem to suggest that the dewdrops have, in fact, been strung together. This idea of regret at the scattering dew—rather than the sense of celebratory description found in the standard interpretation—may be the basis for Moronobu's *Sugata-e,* (see Figure 30) where the older man may be wishing that the boy's forelocks will never be shaved off—a coming of age ritual that will make him a man and thus no longer a suitable object of the older man's sexual attentions.[26] As in the previous poem, the accompanying commentary speaks of the poet's feelings of "fondness and regret" *(mede-aharemu).* The *Shikishi Moyō* kimono design [**37–3**] has the usual autumnal flora—bush clover *(hagi),* aster *(kikyō),* field chrysanthemum *(no-giku),* and maiden-flowers *(ominaeshi)*—with the ideographs for "white dew" *(shira-tsuyu)* on top.

37-1

37-2

37-3

POEM 38

wasuraruru
mi woba omohazu
chikahiteshi
hito no inochi no
woshiku mo aru kana[27]

Forgotten by him,
I do not think of myself.
    But I can't help worry
about the life of the man who
swore so fervently before the gods!

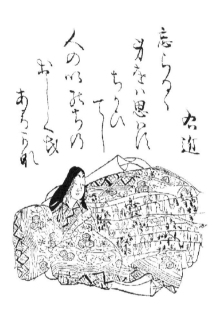

Ukon

Ukon (dates uncertain) was the daughter of Lesser Captain of the Left Bodyguards *(ukon'e no shōshō)* Fujiwara no Suenawa (the infamous lover called "the Lesser Captain of Katano"). Her sobriquet comes from her father's position. She was a lady-in-waiting to Emperor Daigo's empress Onshi and is known to have had liaisons with Fujiwara no Atsutada, Morosuke, Asatada, and Minamoto no Shitagō. There is a set of five anecdotes about her (Episodes 81–85) in the mid-tenth-century *Tales of Yamato (Yamato Monogatari)*. She was an active participant in poetry contests. She has five poems in the *Gosenshū*, three in the *Shūishū*, and one in the *Shin-Chokusenshū*.

Commentary

This poem first appears in the *Tales of Yamato* with the following introduction: "A certain gentleman promised Ukon time and again that he would never forget her. Nonetheless, he did forget her in time, and so Ukon wrote. . . . I do not know what his response was."[28] From this it is clear that the poem was sent to the man. In such a case the most natural reading sees the poem as highly sarcastic. When this poem was anthologized in the *Shūishū*, however, the headnote listed it simply as "topic unknown." In this context the poem was read, not as a letter, but as a private expression of grief *(doku'ei)*. This approach in turn seems to neutralize the sarcastic reading: now the situation is one in which the woman truly gives no thought to herself and is concerned only for the man's safety from the wrath of the gods. It is presumably this reading that Teika followed. While accepting this interpretation, the early modern nativist scholar Mabuchi criticized the idea of worrying about the life of someone who had betrayed one: this was simply a Confucian-inspired hypocrisy, he said, that is antithetical to the true Japanese spirit.

The Pictures

Both the *Zōsanshō* and the Kyoto artist [**38–1**] show a woman at home, sleeve held to tearful eyes, gazing at a shrine. In the *Sugata-e* upper register [**38–2**] we see a private house, with a figure of the poet, who has presumably been waiting all through the night, until the moon is about to sink behind the western hills. In the foreground we see another woman, sleeve to face, her robe decorated with *kemari* footballs (a sport exclusive to the court) and willow branches that suggest the length of her wait. The Porter illustrator [**38–3**] uses yet another building, this one resembling the famous Hase Temple, which is known for its peonies *(botan)*, a traditional symbol of fidelity. These are included in the *Shikishi Moyō* kimono design [**38–4**] in conjunction with folded paper, which could represent both love letters and written vows left at temples.

38-1

38-2

38-3

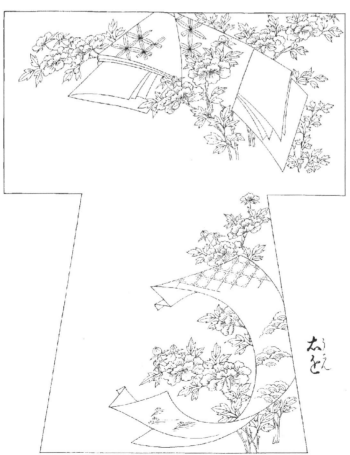

38-4

POEM 39

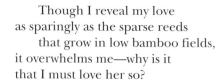

asajhifu no
ono no shinohara
shinoburedo
amarite nado ka
hito no kohishiki[29]

Though I reveal my love
as sparingly as the sparse reeds
　　that grow in low bamboo fields,
it overwhelms me—why is it
that I must love her so?

Consultant Hitoshi
Sangi Minamoto no Hitoshi (880–951)
held many provincial posts, but his career
as a poet is not clear. He has only four
anthologized poems, all collected in the
Gosenshū.

Commentary
The first two lines are a common preface
(*jo*) to the verb *shinobu* ("to love se-
cretly"), due to the sound repetition *shi-
nohara shinobu*. The idea of scarcity in
"sparse reeds" and "low bamboo" is nicely
reversed in the fourth line with *amarite*
("it overwhelms me"—literally, "it is too
much"). The last line can be translated as
"why is it / that I must love her so?" or
"why is it / that I must love *you* so?" The
headnote in the *Gosenshū* states that the
poem was sent to the woman, which

would suggest "you." However, most medieval commentators since the *Ōei Shō*
read the poem as a soliloquy.

The Pictures
If we compare the *Zōsanshō* [**39–1**] and the Kyoto edition [**39–2**], we can see
that the latter has added bamboo with dew (representing tears) and a few reeds
and has Hitoshi's sleeve to his face, indicating that he is crying. In other words,
there seems to be almost nothing in the earlier rendition that is specifically
connected to the poem. But the composition in both scenes—a figure seated in
an interior—is often used to indicate that the poet has sent the poem as a letter
(though the same composition is also used in the upper register of **40–4**).
Moronobu changes the conception entirely in his *Sugata-e* [**39–3**]—both in the
foreground, where the object of the poet's as yet unrevealed affections has

been changed into a young man, and in the upper register, where the original poem is set in the clouds and Hitoshi is shown on a sparse field. The model of the poet in a field is used by later artists, such as the *Kangyoku* and the Porter artists [**39–4**], though here the sense of "sparse reeds" seems to have been lost: the poet stands amidst a wild profusion, perhaps now meant to suggest the verb *amarite* ("to be profuse").

39-1

39-2

39-3

39-4

POEM 40

shinoburedo
iro ni idenikeri
wa ga kohi ha
mono ya omofu to
hito no tofu made[30]

Even though I hide it,
it shows all over my face,
        such is my longing,
so that people ask me
"What *are* you thinking about?"

Taira no Kanemori

Kanemori (d. 990) was a descendant of Emperor Kōkō (Poem 15). He is a representative poet of the *Gosenshū* period, the second imperial anthology, ordered in 950. Three of his poems, although labeled "anonymous," are in the *Gosenshū;* he is credited with thirty-eight in the *Shūishū* and forty-six in the remaining imperial anthologies. He is counted as one of the Thirty-Six Poetic Immortals, and a collection of his poetry survives.

Commentary

This poem and the next, by Mibu no Tadami (Poem 41) are presented together at the very beginning of the first book of love poems in the *Shūishū* with a headnote: "From a Poetry Contest of the Tenryaku Era." This refers to the Palace Poetry Contest of 960 *(Tentoku Yonen Dairi Uta-awase)* in twenty rounds. As related in a collection of anecdotes, the *Fukuro-Zōshi,* compiled by Fujiwara no Kiyosuke (1104–1177), Kanemori's and Tadami's poems were pitted against each other in the last round, but the judge, Fujiwara no Saneyori, was unable to decide which was superior. He asked for the aid of Minamoto no Taka'akira, but he too was unable to decide. The case was brought to Emperor Murakami, who let his opinion be known by humming Kanemori's verse under his breath. It was probably this story that appealed to Teika, as much as the poem itself, but the poem has also been highly prized for the conversational quality of its lower half. Thus although this poem repeats a line identical to the previous poem (*shinoburedo* in Poem 39), its conversational nature would have seemed a contrast to the internal monologue of the former.

The Pictures

The Tan'yū album has Kanemori and Tadami facing each other in poses reminiscent of pictured poetry competitions, such as the *Jidai Fudō Uta-awase-e*.[31] Often, however, as we see in the *Zōsanshō* [**40–1**], the poet is presented with his interlocutor while he attempts to cover his face. This idea of hiding his blushing face is even more explicit in the *Sugata-e* [**40–4**], where a shy samurai seems to be having some difficulty expressing himself to the prostitute in front of him. "Color" then leads to the *Shikishi Moyō* kimono design [**40–3**] with its crimson leaves and ideograph for "hidden love" *(shinobi)*. The maple leaves appear on the poet's robe in the imaginary portrait *(kasen-e)* in the *Zōsanshō*, as well as in Hasegawa's fan [**40–2**]. The *Sugata-e* written commentary mentions an interpretation, attributed to the *renga* poet Sōchō, emphasizing the months and years that the poet has endured his secret love. This may explain the willowlike tree in the upper register of the *Sugata-e*, as well as the use of late wisteria, rather than autumn foliage, in the *Hyakushu Hinagata*.

40-2

40-1

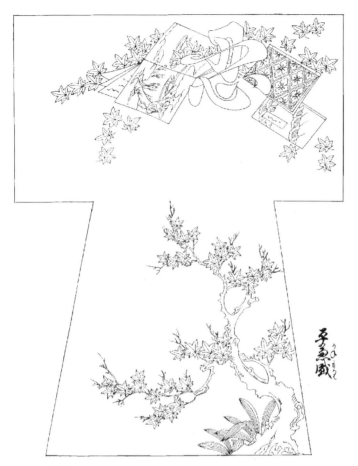

40-3

40-4

POEM 41

kohi su tefu
wa ga na ha madaki
tachinikeri
hito shirezu koso
omohi-someshika[32]

My name already
is bandied about with
    rumors I'm in love—
though, unknown to anyone, I thought,
I had only just begun to love her!

Mibu no Tadami

Tadami (dates uncertain) was a son of Mibu no Tadamine (Poem 30) and is one of the Thirty-Six Poetic Immortals. A personal poetry collection survives, and he has one poem in the *Gosenshū*, fourteen in the *Shūishū*, and twenty-two in later imperial anthologies.

Commentary

This poem was matched against that by Kanemori (Poem 40) in the Palace Poetry Contest of 960 and lost. As recorded in *The Collection of Sand and Pebbles* (*Shaseki Shū*, composed 1279–1283) by priest Mujū, legend had it that Tadami was so distraught that he stopped eating, sickened, and died as a result. His personal poetry collection makes it clear that in fact he lived on many years longer, practicing poetry all the while. Indeed, although the "losing" poem, this verse was also highly regarded, as its placement in the *Shūishū* shows. While Muromachi-period commentators generally agreed in their reading of this poem, in the Edo period the last line became a point of disagreement. Rather than *omohi-someshika*, Yūsai and others insisted that the line should read *omohi-someshiga*, meaning "how I wish I could start to love with no one knowing!"

The Pictures

Both the *Zōsanshō* and the Kyoto illustrator [**41–2**] show the poet with the lady concerned. In conjunction with the Yūsai commentary that accompanies it, this would suggest that the poem was read to mean: "How I wish there was some way I could start loving you with no one knowing." The plants in the gardens of both are meant to represent *shinobu-gusa* (see Poem 100). Moronobu gives the original setting as a soliloquy in the upper register of his *Sugata-e* [**41–1**], and the vine on the man's robe again suggests hidden love (see Poem 25), while his interlocutor has changed to a young man (see **43–1**). The poem has no seasonal designation, but the *Shikishi Moyō* kimono designer [**41–4**] places it in early spring by presenting young greens *(wakana),* with patches of snow on them, placed on the bottom of the robe to correspond to the phrase "my name" *(wa ga na)* written above. On the other hand, the *Hyakushu Hinagata* [**41–3**] shows folded letters with *shinobu* ferns on them and the words *omohi-someshika* written above; the character for *kohi* (love) is written three times with butterflies nearby—the butterflies, called *chō,* are meant to represent the words *tefu* of the poem, which are also pronounced /chō/ (see Poem 2).

41-1

41-2

41-3

41-4

POEM 42

chigiriki na　　　　　But we promised!
katami ni sode wo　　while wringing out the tears from
shiboritsutsu　　　　　each other's sleeves,
suwe no matsu-yama　that never would the waves wash over
nami kosaji to ha[33]　Sue-no-Matsu Mountain.

Kiyohara no Motosuke

Motosuke (908–990) was the grandson of Fukayabu (Poem 36) and the father of Sei Shōnagon (Poem 62). One of the Thirty-Six Poetic Immortals, he was also one of the editors of the second imperial anthology, the *Gosenshū* (ca. 951). A collection of his poetry is extant. He has forty-eight poems in the *Shūishū* and fifty-eight in later imperial anthologies.

Commentary

This poem alludes to another famous verse recorded in the *Kokinshū* 20 (Court Poetry): 1093:

kimi wo okite	if ever I should
adashi-gokoro wo	change my mind
	and banish you
	from my heart
wa ga motaba	then would
	great ocean waves
	rise and cross
suwe no matsu yama	Suenomatsu
nami mo koenan	Mountain[34]

The headnote to Motosuke's poem in the *GoShūishū* reads: "To a woman whose feelings had changed, on behalf of someone else." In other words, Motosuke wrote this poem for a male friend whose lover's feelings had grown cold. The poem actually includes a direct quote of words exchanged by the lovers ("Never will the waves cross / Sue-no-matsu Mountain"), continuing the conversational aspect that runs through Poems 40 and 41, as well as the topos of broken pledges, seen also in Ukon's Poem 38.

The Pictures

Surprisingly, both the *Zōsanshō* [42–1] and the Kyoto illustrator depict the circumstances of the poem's composition and show two men, presumably the poet and the man for whom he writes the poem. The exact meaning of *suwe no matsu-yama* has long been debated.[35] The background landscape in the *Zōsan-*

shō is essentially identical to that in the *Shikishi Moyō* kimono design [**42–4**], whereas Moronobu uses a much different conception in the *Sugata-e* [**42–2**], where we also see in the foreground the poet in the midst of writing his poem, obviously on his own behalf rather than for someone else. Later artists use yet another model, showing the poet on a seashore, as in the *Kangyoku* [**42–3**]. All, however, reflect the fact the *matsu-yama* can be understood to mean "pine-clad mountains."

42-1

42-2

42-3

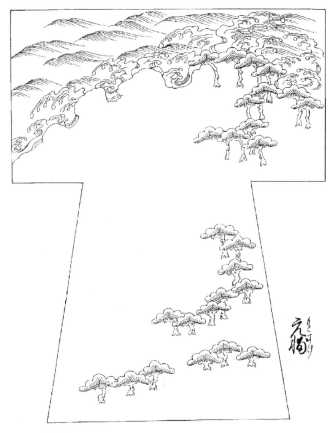

42-4

POEM 43

ahi-mite no
nochi no kokoro ni
kurabureba
mukashi ha mono wo
omohazarikeri[36]

When compared to
the feelings in my heart
    after we'd met and loved,
I realize that in the past
I had no cares at all.

Supernumerary Middle Counselor Atsutada

GonChūnagon Fujiwara no Atsutada (906–943) was the third son of the powerful minister Tokihira. He was renowned for his poetic ability and appears in episodes of the *Tales of Yamato* with other poets such as Ukon (Poem 38). He is one of the Thirty-Six Poetic Immortals and has an extant personal poetry collection. He has ten poems in the *Gosenshū* and twenty in later imperial anthologies.

Commentary

This poem appears in the *Shūishū* as "topic unknown." In the earlier draft of this anthology, the *Shūishō*, however, the headnote reads: "Sent the next morning, after he had started visiting the woman." The poem is also included in the *Kokin Roku-jō* in the "miscellaneous, morning" section. Accordingly, this was a "morning after" poem: the man has at last been able to meet the woman he has been wooing. Under such an interpretation, the last two lines of the poem could be translated as "I realize that in the past / I never loved at all." In other words, since actually being with the woman, the poet's love seems to have changed not only quantitatively but qualitatively. This conception is related to another *ahi-mite ha* poem, found in the *Man'yō Shū* (11: 2567):

ahi-mite ha
kohi-nagusamu to
hito ihedo
mite nochi ni somo
kohi-masarikeru

"Having met
your longing will be eased,"
    people say, but
it is precisely after meeting
that my longing increases!

The explanatory headnote was removed in the *Shūishū*, however, and of course does not appear in the *One Hundred Poets* either. Accordingly, some medieval commentators argued that this was not a poem of "love after first meeting" but rather one of "love unable to meet again" *(ahite ahazaru kohi)*. This interpretation, offered by such commentaries as the *Chōkyō Shō* (1487), would yield a translation such as the one given here. Other commentaries, such as the *Ōei Shō* and the *Yoritaka-bon,* suggested that it was not that the lovers could not meet again, but that, having now pledged his love, the poet found himself assailed with worries about rumors starting or the woman's affections changing. While it is not possible to firmly establish how Teika read the verse, his placement of it in the third book of love poems in his *Nishidai Shū* would suggest that he followed the second or third interpretation, and not that suggested by the *Shūishō.*

Finally, in the *Shūishū* and *Nishidai Shū* the fourth line appears as *mukashi ha mono mo,* but this somehow changed to the now-standard *One Hundred Poets* version during the course of the Muromachi period. The difference is minimal and need not be reflected in translation.

The Pictures
The *Zōsanshō* [**43–2**] shows the couple meeting, a situation that does not accord with any of the standard interpretations but is probably meant to emphasize the words "met and loved" of the poem. In the garden we see a cherry tree in bud next to some kind of evergreen—the implication is that the poet is concerned about the fleeting nature of human relationships. In the *Sugata-e* [**43–1**] we see a young retainer bringing his lord not cherry but plum, which symbolizes loyalty. It is plum that then replaces the cherry in the Kyoto artist's redrawing of the *Zōsanshō* [**43–3**], emphasizing the man's concerns over the woman's fidelity. The motif becomes almost elegaic in the *Shikishi Moyō* kimono design [**43–4**], where the ideograph for "the past" *(mukashi)* is surrounded by flowering plum.

43-1

43-2

43-3

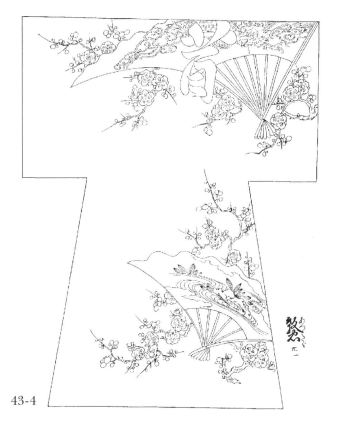

43-4

POEM 44

afu koto no
taete shi naku ha
naka-naka ni
hito wo mo mi wo mo
uramizaramashi[37]

If there were no such thing
as ever having met her, then,
    contrary to all expectations,
neither her coldness nor my pain
would I have to resent!

Middle Counselor Asatada
Chūnagon Fujiwara no Asatada (910–
966); (read "Tomotada" in many of the
Edo-period editions) was the fifth son of
Sadakata (Poem 25). One of the Thirty-
Six Poetic Immortals, he has four poems
in the *Gosenshū* and seventeen more in
the remaining imperial anthologies.

Commentary
This poem comes from the same poetry
competition of A.D. 960 as Poems 40 and
41. It is included in the first book of love
poems in the *Shūishū*, grouped among
poems about "love before the first meet-
ing" *(imada ahazaru kohi)*. In this context
the poem might be translated: "If there
were no such thing as a tryst at all, then,
in fact, I'd have no cause to reproach
either her or myself." In other words, the
poet is complaining that the woman has not yet consented to let him come to
her at night. Were there no such thing as "meeting" (that is, love), the poet
declares, then he would, contrary to expectation, be happy and would neither
resent her nor feel so sad. This poem is fashioned after a famous verse by Nari-
hira (Poem 17), *Kokinshū* (Love 1): 53:

yo no naka ni
taete sakura no
nakariseba
haru no kokoro ha
nodokekaramashi

If a world where
there were no such thing as cherry blossoms
    we were to imagine,
then how tranquil would be
our hearts in spring!

However, Teika placed Asatada's poem in the third book of love poems in his
Nishidai Shū, among poems on the topic of "love unable to meet again" *(ahite
ahazaru kohi;* see Poem 43). This placement transforms the poem's meaning:

now the poet is complaining about a cold lady who will not see him again, no doubt due to the dangers and complications it would entail. It is the interpretation based on this more involved narrative that the first translation follows.

The Pictures

The *Zōsanshō* illustration [**44–1**] shows a man pleading his love to a woman hidden behind a curtain. Presumably they have already met, but the woman is refusing further (or renewed) intimacy (see Poem 20). Moronobu's *Sugata-e* [**44–4**] transposes the scene to a contemporary setting: the poet is forlornly holding a pillow, implying that while he can see the woman, literally, he is not "seeing" her. The *Shikishi Moyō* kimono design [**44–3**] has the ideograph for *afu,* "to meet," but has made the cherry blossoms from Narihira's famous poem (also seen on the *Sugata-e* poet's robe) the main motif, hindered by fences. Later illustrators, such as the *Kangyoku* [**44–2**] and the Porter artist, show the poet looking backwards, activating a potential pun in *urami,* which means "to be resentful of" but can also be read as *ura-mi,* "to look behind." The *Hyakushu Hinagata* shows a veritable gauntlet of barriers: blinds, balustrade, and both brushwood and wooden fence, with the words *afu koto* emblazoned above, which no doubt served as a teasing enticement to admirers of the young woman who wore such a robe.

44-1

44-2

44-3

44-4

POEM 45

ahare to mo
ifu-beki hito ha
omohoede
mi no itadzura ni
narinu-beki kana[38]

　　　Not one person who would
call my plight pathetic
　　　comes at all to mind,
and so, uselessly
I must surely die!

Lord Kentoku

Kentokukō—Fujiwara no Koremasa (also read "Koretada", 924–972)—was the eldest son of Morosuke and regent *(sesshō)* from 970. He was involved in the planning of the second imperial anthology, the *Gosenshū*. He edited a collection of his own poetry into a poem-tale about a fictional character named Toyokage; it is now found in his larger personal poetry collection, *The Collected Poems of the First Ward Regent (Ichijō Sesshō GyoShū)*. He has thirty-seven poems in imperial anthologies.

Commentary

This poem appears in the *Shūishū* with the headnote: "When a woman he had been seeing later became cold and would not see him again." The poem appears originally as the first in the "Collected Poems of Toyokage" *(Toyokage Shū)* with the following introduction:

> Among the women he sent letters to, there was one who, although no different from him in rank, made no reply to his repeated letters, even after months and years. Thinking, "I will not be defeated!" he wrote the following.

Regardless of the difference between the two headnotes, the main point is that this poem was sent to a woman (who sent a reply). Medieval commentaries differed over how to interpret the *hito* of the poem: did it mean people in general or specifically the woman to whom the poem was addressed? In fact, it means both: the poet's words are indirect; *hito* literally refers to people in general, but in the context of a letter to a woman *hito* obviously means her in particular.

The Pictures

Yūsai's commentary states that *hito* refers to people of the world at large, but the *Zōsanshō* picture [**45–1**] and most other pictorializations show the poet addressing the back of a retreating woman. The Yūsai commentary could lead to a reading of the poem as a soliloquy (as seen in Hasegawa's fan [**45–3**]), and that is what Moronobu seems to suggest in the upper register of his *Sugata-e* [**45–2**]. Nonetheless, the foreground shows a more complicated drama: a presumably gravely ill man is having his pulse taken while looking at an impassive young man. The *Shikishi Moyō* kimono design [**45–4**] gives us the most "pathetic" *(ahare)* flower, the morning glory *(asa-gao)*, together with what would appear to be the ideograph for *ahare* itself.

45-1

45-2

45-3

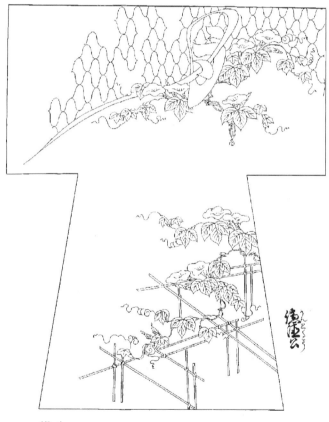

45-4

POEM 46

yura no to wo
wataru funa-bito
kajhi-wo tae
yukuhe mo shiranu
kohi no michi kana[39]

Like a boatman, crossing
the Strait of Yura,
    whose oar-cord has snapped,
I'm lost and know not my way
on the road of love!

Sone no Yoshitada

Virtually nothing is known about this poet. He was active in the latter half of the eleventh century and was a secretary (*jō*) in Tango province, from which came his sobriquets "Sotango" or "Sotan." He has a personal poetry collection, the *Sotan Shū*, but his verse was considered eccentric and was little valued until Teika's day. Thus the majority of his eighty-nine poems in imperial anthologies appear in the *Shikashū* (compiled 1151–1154) and the *ShinKokinshū* (compiled 1205). The *Yoshitada Hyakushu* is one of the earliest examples of a hundred-poem sequence.

Commentary

There are a number of points of contention in this poem. Since locations named Yura existed in both Ki and Tango provinces, it is unclear to which the poet is referring. The biggest debate, however, concerns the phrase *kajhi-wo tae*. The dominant interpretation among *One Hundred Poets* commentaries is that *wo* is an object marker and hence the line means "he loses his oar" *(kajhi wo tae)*. However, some commentators argued that *wo* means "cord" and thus *kajhi-wo tae* means "the oar-cord snaps." That this latter was also Teika's interpretation is supported by two poems contained in the *Fuboku Waka Shō* (ca. 1310), compiled by Fujiwara no Nagakiyo, a follower of Reizei Tamesuke. One poem is attributed to Ono no Komachi; the other is by Teika's own son, Tame'ie, and is clearly an allusive variation *(honka-dori)* on Yoshitada's poem:

chigiri koso
yukuhe mo shirane
yura no to ya
wataru kajhi-wo no
mata mo musubade

Not just our vows, but
my future, too, I am unsure of!
    Without binding once again
the oar-cord, shall I cross
the Strait of Yura?

This poems suggests that *musubi* and *tae* are antonyms, the latter then meaning "to break" rather than "to lose." Given Teika's authority, we may presume that his son's usage reflects his father's interpretation of this classic poem.

The Pictures

The Tan'yū album shows a boat tossed in the waves with neither boatman nor oar. The Hasegawa version [**46–3**] shows a boatman at his oar with the oar-rope still affixed. The Kyoto artist [**46–2**] shows a man in a rowboat with the oar already sinking beneath the waves. This conception is clearly modeled on the *Zōsanshō* pictorialization [**46–1**], though the latter includes a sail on the boat: by the Edo period, the word *kajhi* was used to refer not only to "oars" but also to the "rudder" of a sailboat. While the *Zōsanshō* pictorialization is ambiguous, the *Sugata-e* [**46–4**] clearly invites us to read the poem's third line as "who has lost his rudder." (It seems unlikely that the *kamuro* sitting in front of the poet, despite her wave-patterned robe, is meant to represent the "ocean"—that is, love object, in which the poet is lost.) By the late Edo period, the "rudder" interpretation becomes visually dominant, as seen in the Porter artist [**46–5**], who shows a large rudder falling off a galleon-like vessel.

46-1   46-2

46-3

46-4

46-5

POEM 47

yahe mugura
shigereru yado no
sabishiki ni
hito koso miene
aki ha kinikeri[40]

To the lonely house
where the weeds, eight layers deep,
   have grown rank,
not a soul can be seen—
but autumn, at least, has come.

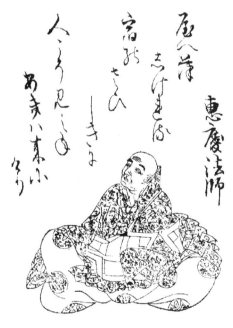

Master of the Law Egyō

Egyō Hōshi (also sometimes read "Ekei"; dates unknown) was active in the latter half of the tenth century and is a representative poet of the *Shūishū* period. He associated closely with such other poets as Shigeyuki (Poem 48), Yoshinobu (Poem 49), and Motosuke (Poem 42), who frequently congregated at the Kawara mansion of Priest Anpō. Anpō was a descendant of Minamoto no Tōru (Poem 14), who built the famous Kawara In on the western bank of the Kamo River. Egyō is one of the Late Classical Thirty-Six Poetic Immortals *(chūko san-jūrokkasen),* and a collection of his poetry is extant. He has fifty-six poems in the *Shūishū* and later imperial anthologies.

Commentary

The headnote to this poem in the *Shūishū* reads: "When people were composing poems on the subject of 'autumn comes to the dilapidated house' at the Kawara In." Accordingly, some commentators (for example, the *Minazuki Shō*) see the poem as simply about the arrival of autumn. Most, however, take the "house" of the poem to refer to the Kawara In itself. In this context the poem is contrasting the constancy of the seasons with the ephemerality of human elegance or, as Yūsai's commentary states, "only the autumn, which never forgets the past, returns" *(mukashi wasurenu aki nomi kaheru).* Teika no doubt also read this poem with Tōru in mind.

The Pictures

The *Zōsanshō* [**47–1**] has Egyō looking at a dilapidated house; the addition of a river by the Kyoto artist [**47–2**] makes it clear that the house is in fact the Kawara In. The Porter artist [**47–4**] ignores the original headnote and reads the poem as if the house were the residence of the poet himself (similar to Poem 28). In Moronobu's *Sugata-e* [**47–3**], although the poem says there are no visitors but the autumn, we see an obviously pleased Egyō receiving an attentive young man.

47-1   47-2

47-3

47-4

POEM 48

kaze wo itami
iha utsu nami no
onore nomi
kudakete mono wo
omofu koro kana[41]

Waves that beat against the rocks,
fanned by a fierce wind—
it is I alone
who breaks, those times
when I think of her!

Minamoto no Shigeyuki

Shigeyuki's dates are uncertain; he seems to have died in 1001. An associate of Kanemori (Poem 40) and Sanekata (Poem 51), he is one of the Thirty-Six Poetic Immortals. A collection of his poetry survives, and he has sixty-seven poems in the *Shūishū* and later imperial anthologies.

Commentary

This poem is described as "one composed when [Shigeyuki] submitted a hundred-poem sequence, during the time the Retired Emperor Reizei was still called the crown prince." Reizei was crown prince from 950 to 967. Hundred-poem sequences *(hyakushu)* did not become popular until the late Heian period, a trend marked by the "Horikawa Hyakushu" of 1105–1106 (see Chapter 2). Accordingly, this sequence by Shigeyuki is one of the earliest examples of a poetic genre that was to become of major importance and lead to such anthologies as Teika's *One Hundred Poets* itself. Commentaries on the poem are largely in agreement. The poem compares a heartless lover to a rock that remains unmoved by the waves that beat against it.

The Pictures

The *Zōsanshō* shows the poet contemplating a rough and rocky surf [**48–1**], as does the *Kangyoku*. Curiously, the Kyoto artist changes the setting to what appears to be a riverbank [**48–2**], a setting perhaps more natural to Kyoto. In his *Sugata-e* [**48–3**] Moronobu shows the hard-hearted woman unmoved by the man's entreaties; the *uchiwa* fan in her hand may be meant to suggest the word *utsu* ("beat"). Finally, the *Shikishi Moyō* kimono design [**48–4**] contents itself with a depiction of wild waves crashing against craggy rocks.

48-1

48-2

48-3

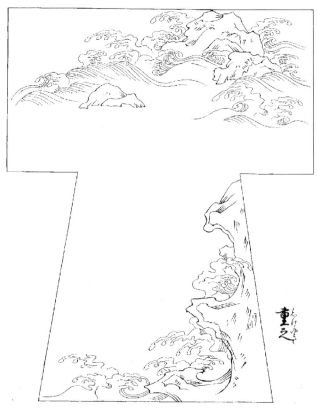

48-4

POEM 49

mi-kaki-mori
weji no taku hi no
yoru ha moe
hiru ha kietsutsu
mono wo koso omohe[42]

Like the fire the guardsman kindles,
guarding the imperial gates:
   at night, burning,
in the day, exhausted,
over and over, so I long for her.

Ōnakatomi no Yoshinobu

Yoshinobu (921–991) was one of the "Five Gentlemen of the Pear Chamber" *(nashi-tsubo no gonin)* who edited the *Go-senshū*. He was grandfather to Ise no Tayū (Poem 61). He is also one of the Thirty-Six Poetic Immortals and a self-edited collection of his poetry is extant. He has 125 poems in the *Shūishū* and later imperial anthologies. Since this poem does not appear in Yoshinobu's own collection of poetry and appears in the *Kokin Roku-jō* as anonymous, it is unlikely that the poem is in fact by Yoshinobu.

Commentary

Disagreement centers on the line *hiru ha kie*—what does it mean that in the day-time the fires "go out"? The *Keikō Shō* and other commentators take *kie* to mean *kie-iru*, "to be overcome with grief." Yūsai, on the other hand, claims that it means that the poet hides his love from people's eyes during the day; the *Minō Shō* suggests that the poet is in fact able to divert himself during the day. The first interpretation is followed by most scholars today.

The Pictures

The kind of interpretive debates discussed above are not likely to appear in pictorializations. In these, however, we find a new set of issues. While the Tan'yū album shows a small bonfire in front of a fence of woven-reed matting (meant to suggest the *kaki*, or "fence," of *mi-kaki-mori*), the *Zōsanshō* [**49–4**] shows the fire as a *kagari-bi*, or a hanging "basket light." This is probably an influence from illustrations to the *Kagari-bi* ("The Flares") chapter in *The Tale of Genji*, as seen, for instance, in Yamamoto Shunshō's widely distributed version [**49–2**]. The Kyoto artist [**49–3**] corrects the earlier design, making the light a simple bonfire. Yet the setting does not seem to be the imperial palace but rather some suburban estate. Moronobu's *Sugata-e* [**49–1**] again uses the basket light, this time in conjunction with a stream (which also derives from the *Genji* chapter). The foreground image here is explicitly homoerotic, suggesting the kind of story about the illicit relationship between a lower-ranking guard and the lord's page found in Saikaku's *Great Mirror of Male Love*. Finally, the *Kangyoku* artist seems to make the poet himself the guardsman, tending a fire outside a gate.

49-1

49-2

河花鏡

49-3

49-4

POEM 50

kimi ga tame
woshikarazarishi
inochi sahe
nagaku mogana to
omohinuru kana[43]

Even the life that
I'd not have been sorry to lose
  just to meet you once,
now, having met, I think:
"I want it to last forever!"

Fujiwara no Yoshitaka

Yoshitaka (954–974) died at the age of twenty-one of smallpox. He was the third son of Koremasa (Poem 45) and father of the great calligrapher Yukinari. He is one of the Late Classical Thirty-Six Poetic Immortals, and a collection of his poetry is extant. There are twelve of his poems in the *GoShūishū* and later imperial anthologies.

Commentary

The headnote to the poem states that it was sent after returning home from a woman's house. In other words, this is a "morning after" poem, sent after the man had spent the night with the woman for the first time. The poet says literally "the life I would not have been sorry to lose for your sake," but it was not exactly clear to commentators why he valued his life so little. Some of the reasons suggested were:

1. He would have given his life to meet her once *(Ōei Shō)*.
2. He would have not been sorry to give his life for her sake *(Yoritaka-bon)*.
3. Unable to meet her, he wanted his life to end *(Chōkyō Shō)*.
4. His lover would not see him, so he wished he were dead *(Kamijō-bon)*.

It is the first interpretation that is generally followed today.

The Pictures

Many of the woodblock prints show the poet writing a letter, as is also depicted in the Tan'yū album. The *Zōsanshō* [**50–1**] shows a very forlorn-looking man writing a letter and gazing out into space. The Kyoto artist does much the same [**50–2**] but has the figure echoing Yoshitaka's *kasen-e* posture. In addition, he has added a bridge and another wing with some sturdy-looking blinds, inviting us to imagine that the woman is perhaps behind them (see Poem 20). This in turn might suggest an interpretation along the lines of that given in the *Kamijō-bon*. Only the *Kangyoku* artist [**50–4**] makes the flora in the garden a meaningful element, placing there autumn flowers that suggest the shortness of life. Moronobu's *Sugata-e* [**50–3**], with its two-tier composition, suggests a parallel in the relationships between the four figures.

50-1   50-2

50-3

50-4

POEM 51

kaku to dani
e ya ha ibuki no
sashimo-gusa
sa shimo shiraji na

moyuru omohi wo[1]

Can I even say
"I love you this much"?—No, and so
    you do not know of it
anymore than of the *sashimo* grasses of
    Ibuki,
my burning love for you!

Lord Fujiwara no Sanekata

Fujiwara no Sanekata Ason died in 994 at around the age of forty. He was a great-grandchild of Tadahira (Poem 26). He has sixty-seven poems in the *Shūishū* and later imperial anthologies, and a personal poetry collection survives. He is counted among the Late Classical Thirty-Six Poetic Immortals.

Commentary

In the *GoShūishū* the headnote states that this poem was the first sent to the woman when the poet was starting to woo her. Hence we must read it as a first declaration of love, in essence saying: "I love you deeply, but you probably don't even know I exist." This poem is a complicated web of pivot words and word associations *(engo).* "Ibuki" is the name of a mountain famous for *sashimo* grass or *mogusa*. *Mogusa* was, in turn, used for moxabustion—that is, incense-like cones of *mogusa* were burned on the skin in a kind of thermal acupuncture. Thus there is an association between *mogusa* and burning. This association is furthered in connection with *omohi,* or "desire," which contains the syllable *hi,* the word for "fire." The *sashimo* of *sashimo-gusa* can also be read *sa shimo,* "that much," just as the *ibu* of *ibuki* can be read as *ifu,* "to say." Despite the complexity of this poem, or perhaps because of it, disagreement about its meaning has been generally limited to the identity of Mount Ibuki: is it the one in Shimotsuke or the one on the Ōmi-Minō border (the modern interpretation)?

The Pictures

The Tan'yū album clearly depicts the distinctive shape of the Ōmi Mount Ibuki and *sashimo* grass. The shape of the mountain is recognizable in the *Zōsanshō* [**51–1**] and *Sugata-e* [**51–2**] as well. In the latter we see a man undergoing a rather therapeutic-looking massage at the hands of a young man. Hasegawa [**51–3**] shows the poet on a veranda looking at the plant. (It is mentioned for its attractiveness by Sei Shōnagon in her *Pillow Book,* together with *yae-mugura* [see Poem 47].) The *Kangyoku* [**51–4**] is one of the few versions to include the poet in the landscape; indeed, it depicts him as hidden and removed, like his secret love (see Poem 39).

51-1

51-2

51-3

51-4

POEM 52

akenureba
kururu mono to ha
shiri-nagara
naho urameshiki
asaborake kana²

Because it has dawned,
it will become night again—
this I know, and yet,
ah, how hateful it is—
the first cold light of morning!

Lord Fujiwara no Michinobu

Fujiwara no Michinobu Ason (972–994) was adopted by Fujiwara no Kane'ie, husband of Michitsuna no Haha (Poem 53). He died at the age of twenty-three. A collection of his poetry is extant, and he has forty-eight poems in the *Shūishū* and later imperial anthologies. He is one of the Late Classical Thirty-Six Poetic Immortals.

Commentary

The *GoShūishū* headnote identifies this as a "morning after" poem *(kinu-ginu no uta)*. Most commentaries are in agreement as to its basic meaning, but the *Minazuki Shō* (late Muromachi period) interprets the poem as written from the woman's point of view. Ariyoshi speaks of the poem "making one imagine a scene in a literary romance *(monogatari)*," and the *Yūsai Shō* specifically associates it with the "Evening Faces" *(Yūgao)* chapter of *The Tale of Genji*.

The Pictures

Both the *Zōsanshō* [52–1] and the Kyoto artist show the woman on the veranda and the man in the middle of the room, which might suggest that it is the woman who is leaving, rather than the man. Yet the man is holding out to her a letter (on which this poem is presumably written). Thus the picture does not seem to represent the *Minazuki Shō* interpretation mentioned above. The positioning of the figures might suggest that the man is of a higher rank than the woman; perhaps he is meant to be seen as Genji from *The Tale of Genji*, but the reference made to this work in the *Yūsai Shō* is deleted from the commentary accompanying Moronobu's picture. The *Kangyoku* [52–3] brings the pictorialization a little more in line with the headnote, showing the man leaving through the woman's gate, but only the Porter illustrator [52–4] manages to depict the man leaving the woman while also suggesting the morning light.

Due to its frequent pairing with the next poem, a wall or gate motif is often added to pictorializations, evident as early as the Tan'yū album. The *Zōsanshō* and Kyoto pictures too seem designed to provide a contrast with the next poem, where the man is clearly on the outside and the woman inside; Moronobu's *Sugata-e* [**52–2**] serves as a clear pendant to his rendering of Poem 51 [**51–2**], with a woman now replacing the figure of the boy, urging her customer on his way.

52-1

52-2

52-3

52-4

POEM 53

nagekitsutsu
hitori nuru yo no
akuru ma ha
ika ni hisashiki
mono to ka ha shiru³

The span of time
that I sleep alone, sighing,
    until night lightens—
can you at all know
how long *that* is?

The Mother of Major Captain of the Right Michitsuna
Udaishō Michitsuna no Haha (ca. 937–995) was a secondary wife of Fujiwara no Kane'ie, by whom she had her son Michitsuna. A skilled poet, she was also reputed to be one of the three most beautiful women of her day. She is best known for her autobiographical *Kagerō Nikki, The Gossamer Journal,* which describes her marriage with Kane'ie. She is one of the Late Classical Thirty-Six Poetic Immortals and has thirty-six poems in the *Shūishū* and later imperial anthologies.

Commentary
In the *Shūishū,* the headnote to this poem reads: "Once when the Buddhist Novice Regent (Nyūdō Sesshō) [Kane'ie] had come [to her house], since they were slow in opening the gate, he said "I grow tired of standing," [and she replied]. . . ." In this context, the poet is understood to be comparing the very short time the man has had to stand outside while the gate is opened with her own long waiting for him to come home at night. This interpretation is followed by all early commentators.

It was not until the early nineteenth century that Kagawa Kageki pointed out that the *Shūishū* headnote differs considerably from the diary passage describing this episode. In the diary, Kane'ie has begun seeing another woman and has not come to Michitsuna's Mother's house for nights on end:

> Two or three days later, there was a rapping on my gate toward dawn. I thought it must be he, but was too miserable to have my people open the gate, and he went off in what seemed to be the direction of the [new woman's] house on Machijiri Street. The next morning, unwilling to let the incident pass, I composed a poem, wrote it out with special care, and attached it to a faded chysanthemum.⁴

In such a context, specific words of the poem would be interpreted differently: *nagekitsutsu* now means "sighing night after night," rather than simply "while sighing"; *yo* means not just the one night in question but several nights on end. In this context we might translate the first half of the poem: "The span of time / those nights I sleep alone till dawn / sighing continuously." It is unclear how Teika read this poem, since he may well have known the diary context, but the uniformity of the early commentaries persuades me to render the poem to conform with the *Shūishū* headnote.

The Pictures

As noted above, all commentators, including Yūsai, followed the *Shūishū* headnote until the early nineteenth century. Consequently, in the pictorializations, such as the *Zōsanshō* [**53–1**] and the Kyoto artist, we see Kane'ie at the gate and a serving lady rushing to open it while Michitsuna's mother looks on. Through the generally simplifying process that we see in the *Kangyoku* [**53–2**], the serving woman is eventually replaced by Michitsuna's mother herself. Yet Moronobu's *Sugata-e* rendition [**53–4**] presents the poem as either sent to the absent man or as a soliloquy. However, a sense of contrast, between the fleeting and the enduring, is suggested by the woman's robe pattern of cherry blossoms and pine branches. The *Shikishi Moyō* kimono design [**53–3**] shows a rustic gate with two plants known for the length of their leaves or branches: the willow and the banana plant. No illustration includes the chrysanthemum mentioned in the diary, but the *Kangyoku* artist also adopts the banana plant. The *Hyakushu Hinagata* design incorporates willows and a rooster.

53-1

53-2

53-3

53-4

POEM 54

wasureji no
yuku-suwe made ha
katakereba
kefu wo kagiri no
inochi to mogana[5]

Because that future, until which,
you say, you will "never forget,"
     is hard to rely on,
oh, if only today could be
the last day of my life!

The Mother of the Supernumerary Grand Minister

Gidōsanshi no Haha, Takako (or Kishi) (d. 996), was a daughter of Takashina no Naritada. She was married to Fujiwara no Michitaka and was the mother of Sadako (or Teishi), the first empress of Emperor Ichijō and patron of Sei Shōnagon (Poem 62). Her title comes from her son Korechika, who in 1005 was given the privileges "equivalent to the Three Ministers" (Chancellor, Minister of the Left, and Minister of the Right), or *gidōsanshi*. *The Great Mirror (Ōkagami)* gives a succinct biography of her:

> Even the women in Naritada's family are learned. Kishi, the mother of Michitaka's daughters, is the lady everyone knows as Kō no naishi.... She is a serious Chinese poet. She participated in Emperor Ichijō's Chinese poetry parties, and her compositions outshone the perfunctory efforts of certain gentlemen.[6]

She took vows upon Michitaka's death. She left no personal poetry collection and has only five poems in the *Shūishū* and later imperial anthologies.

Commentary

The headnote in the *ShinKokinshū* indicates that this poem was composed when Michitaka (the "Middle Regent," or Naka no Kanpaku) had started visiting the poet, that is, just after they were married. There are no disagreements of note over the interpretation of this poem.

The Pictures

There is a great range of visual interpretations for this poem. The Tan'yū album shows the poet with an open fan, perhaps to suggest that she is actually addressing the man. Fans are a major motif in the *Hyakushu Hinagata* design as

well. The Kangyoku shows the man standing outside the lady's gate, while the
Eiga depicts her standing alone in a field of bamboo. The motifs of bamboo
and plum—symbols, especially in Chinese verse, of fidelity—predominate, as
seen in the *Shikishi Moyō* kimono pattern [**54–2**] (with the words *yuku-suwe*) and
the *Sugata-e* [**54–3**]. The *Zōsanshō* [**54–1**] and Kyoto renditions are something
of a mystery, as they show two women. There seems to be nothing in any com-
mentary to suggest what this might mean. The only possibility seems to be that
commentators as early as Keichū (1640–1701) frequently discussed this poem
in comparison with two poems by Izumi Shikibu and Akazome Emon (*GSIS* 711
and 712). Otherwise, there is nothing to explain why this poem would suggest a
female interlocutor. Finally, both the Porter artist [**54–4**] and the *Shūgyoku* add
a long bridge, which is perhaps meant to suggest the idea of "the future" (*yuku-
suwe* means literally "end of the road").

54-1

54-2

54-3

54-4

POEM 55

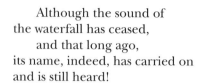

taki no oto ha
taete hisashiku
narinuredo
na koso nagarete
naho kikoekere[7]

Although the sound of
the waterfall has ceased,
    and that long ago,
its name, indeed, has carried on
and is still heard!

Major Counselor Kintō
Dainagon Fujiwara no Kintō (966–1041)
was the poetic arbiter elegantiarum of
his day. He edited the *Wakan Rōei Shū*
(ca. 1013) and authored such poetic
treatises as the *Waka Kuhon* and *Shinsen
Zuinō (The Essentials of Poetry, Newly Com-
piled)*. His *Sanjūrokunin Sen* established
the Thirty-Six Poetic Immortals, and his
Kingyoku Shū (Collection of Gold and Jewels)
is also an anthology of exemplary poems.
His *Shūi Shō* became the basis for the
third imperial anthology. He was the
grandson of Tadahira (Poem 26) and the
father of Sadayori (Poem 64). He has his
own collection of poems and eighty-nine
poems in the *Shūishū* and later imperial
anthologies.

Commentary
The headnote in the *Shūishū* states that
this poem was composed on the subject
of an old waterfall, when a number of people went to Daikakuji Temple. All
extant copies of the *Shūishū* have the first line as "the threads of the waterfall"
(taki no ito ha), but it appears in Kintō's own collected poems and elsewhere
with *oto*, or "sound." There is no great disagreement among commentators,
though many suggest that the poem is an allegory on the transcience of human
fame. This poem appears in none of Teika's other exemplary collections, and it
has been suggested that it was included in the *One Hundred Poets* either because
of Kintō's undeniable historical importance (which still would not explain the
choice of this particular poem) or because Daikakuji is in the same area as
Teika's and his father-in-law's villas on Mount Ogura.

The Pictures
The Tan'yū album shows what appears to be a lake with islands and a pavilion
of some sort. This would appear to be similar to the design of the *Kangyoku*

[55–4], which represents the scenery around Daikakuji, especially the Ōsawa ("big marsh") Pond. The *Zōsanshō* [55–1] shows the poet contemplating the now-defunct waterfall and has added to the sense of decay by showing the foundations of a ruined building behind, though Daikakuji was not in disrepair at this time, having been refurbished under Emperor GoMizuno'o (r. 1611–1629). In fact, as early as the medieval period the waterfall was repaired and called "Nakoso no Taki." The Kyoto artist [55–2] reintroduces this functioning waterfall even though the poem says the "sound has ended." The *Shikishi Moyō* kimono design [55–3] effectively uses the character for "waterfall" *(taki)* to suggest the flow of water and includes pines (a symbol of longevity) and cherry blossoms (a symbol of transcience), suggesting a seasonal progression from the plum blossoms in the design for Poem 54.

55-1

55-2

55-3

55-4

POEM 56

arazaramu
kono yo no hoka no
omohide ni
ima hito-tabi no
afu koto mogana[8]

Among my memories
of this world, from whence
I will soon be gone,
oh, how I wish there was
one more meeting, now, with you!

Izumi Shikibu

Shikibu's dates are uncertain, but she appears to have been born sometime between 976 and 979. She was a daughter of Ōe no Masamune. Her mother was a daughter of Taira no Yasuhira. She married Tachibana no Michisada, a governor of Izumi province (from which comes the "Izumi" of her sobriquet) and had a daughter by him called KoShikibu (Poem 60), herself a respected poet. Later she had relationships with Prince Tametaka (d. 1002) and his half-brother Atsumichi (d. 1007). Her courtship with the latter is depicted in *The Diary of Izumi Shikibu (Izumi Shikibu Nikki)*.[9] Later still, she served in the salon of Empress Shōshi along with Murasaki Shikibu (Poem 57) and Akazome Emon (Poem 59). A number of different versions of her collected poems survive, and she has 242 poems in the *Shūishū* and later imperial anthologies. She is one of the Late Classical Thirty-Six Poetic Immortals.

Commentary

The headnotes to this poem in both the *GoShūishū* and the *Izumi Shikibu Shū* state that the poem was sent to the house of someone when the poet was ill. Commentaries can be divided into those that follow the headnote and those that do not. Those that do are in general agreement, though the *Minō Shō* says (perhaps under the influence of the next poem by Murasaki Shikibu) that it was sent to a group of friends *(tomodachi-domo);* all others believe the recipient to be a husband or lover. Other commentaries, such as the *Kamijō-bon* and the *Minazuki Shō,* read the poem simply as a love poem: the lovers have met once but are unable to meet again. The poem is clearly a kind of inverse to Poem 54 by Takako.

The Pictures

The Tan'yū album shows the poet leaning on an armrest, perhaps to indicate she is ill. The *Zōsanshō* [**56–1**] shows the poet lying on her sickbed, and the lady-in-waiting is presumably gesturing to send the young attendant off with the message, as is clearly seen in the *Kangyoku* [**56–2**]. The state of the health of the portly court lady in the *Sugata-e* [**56–4**] is not clear, but the young attendant is presumably being entrusted with a message. Hasegawa [**56–3**] presents the poet healthy and alone, suggesting a simple love-poem reading.

56-1

56-2

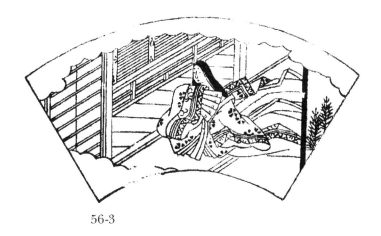

56-3

56-4

POEM 57

meguri-ahite
mishi ya sore tomo
wakanu ma ni
kumo-gakurenishi
yoha no tsuki-kage[10]

As I was wondering
whether or not I had seen it
   by chance,
it became cloud-hidden,
the face of the midnight moon!

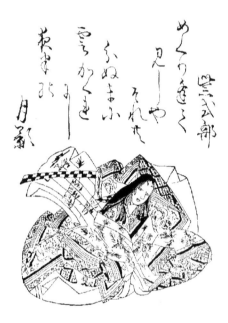

Murasaki Shikibu

Murasaki Shikibu's dates are uncertain.
The daughter of Fujiwara no Tametoki, a
governor of Echigo, she was married to
Fujiwara no Nobutaka in 998 and gave
birth to a daughter, Daini no Sanmi
(Poem 58). They had not been married
three years when Nobutaka died. In 1005
Murasaki Shikibu became a lady-in-wait-
ing to Empress Shōshi. She is the author
of *The Tale of Genji,* as well as a diary
(Murasaki Shikibu Nikki) and a collection
of poems *(Murasaki Shikibu Shū).* She has
sixty poems in the *GoShūishū* and later
imperial anthologies and is one of the
Late Classical Thirty-Six Poetic Immortals.

Commentary

This is the first poem of *The Collected
Poems of Murasaki Shikibu,* where the
headnote reads:

> I met someone I had known long ago as a child, but the moment was brief
> and I hardly recognized them. It was the tenth of the Tenth Month. They left
> hurriedly as if racing the moon.[11]

In the *ShinKokinshū* the month is identified as the Seventh Month, and this is
generally accepted as the correct date—a time when the moon rises early and
has set by midnight. Both the *ShinKokinshū* and the *Murasaki Shikibu Shū* have
the last line as *yoha no tsuki-kage,* but most Edo-period texts have *yoha no tsuki
kana,* "the moon at midnight!" In any case, the first word *meguri* associates with
the last word "moon" *(tsuki): meguri-ahi* means "to meet by chance," but *meguri*
alone means "to go around," like the moon.

    There is a fair variety of interpretations of this poem. Most follow the
headnote and take the friend to be a woman, with whom the poet is comparing
the moon. The *Minazuki Shō,* however, takes the person to be a male lover. The
modern critic Komashaku Kimi associates this poem with what she sees as

Murasaki Shikibu's homosociality.[12] The *Komezawa-bon* claimed that the friend is leaving hurriedly in order to go see the early autumn moon!

The Pictures

The *Zōsanshō* [**57–1**] and the Kyoto artist show the poet looking out from her room as her friend leaves, with a full moon peeking out from behind the clouds. In the *Sugata-e* [**57–2**] Moronobu shows a woman with a letter, perhaps meant to suggest the Seventh Month, also called "the Letter Month" *(fumi-dzuki)*, but clearly also suggesting the poem be read as addressed to a lover who has recently left. Hasegawa [**57–3**], in a design inspired by the Tan'yū album, has the poet near a veranda with a barely visible moon overhead. In all these cases, the moon is actually a full moon and not the still-waxing moon of the tenth day. The only exception to this is the *Shikishi Moyō* kimono design [**57–4**], which depicts a crescent moon embroidered with clouds and the characters for "midnight" *(yoha)* superimposed over it. All texts read *tsuki kana*.

57-1

57-2

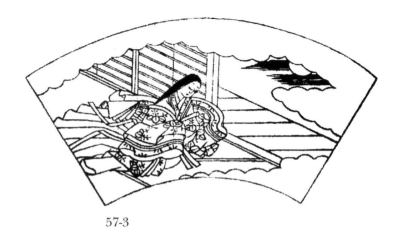

57-3

57-4

POEM 58

arima-yama
wina no sasahara
kaze fukeba
ide soyo hito wo
wasure ya ha suru[13]

When the wind blows
through the bamboo-grass field of Ina
near Arima Mountain
soyo—so it is:
how could I forget you?

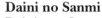

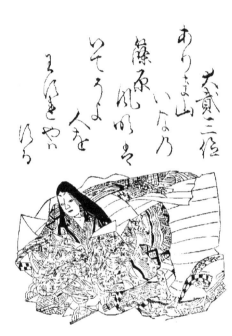

Daini no Sanmi

Daini no Sanmi (dates uncertain) was the daughter of Murasaki Shikibu (Poem 57). She served Empress Shōshi, and in 1037 she married Takashina no Nari'akira, the Senior Assistant Governor-General of Dazaifu *(Daini)*. She was the wet nurse of Emperor GoReizei (r. 1045–1068), and was promoted to the Third Rank *(sanmi)*. A collection of her poems is extant and she has thirty-seven poems in the *GoShūishū* and later imperial anthologies.

Commentary

The headnote to this poem reads: "Composed when a man who had grown distant said, 'I am uneasy [that your feelings for me have changed].' " The whole first half of the poem is a preface *(jo)* to introduce the wordplay *soyo*. *Soyo-soyo* is onomatopoiea for wind rustling. *So yo* by itself can also mean "That's so!", "So it is!", or "That's it!"; in other words, the woman is referring to his statement "[I am] uncertain" and saying "Indeed, it is I who am uncertain."

Prefaces are thought of as being either "with heart" *(ushin)* or "without heart" *(mushin)*—that is, either having some semantically meaningful relationship to the words they introduced or being used simply for their sound value. In the present poem, the question becomes whether there is any metaphorical relationship between the first half of the poem and the second half. Taking the preface as *ushin* would yield a translation such as that by Steven Carter:

> Near Arima Hill
>   the wind through Ina's bamboos
>   blows constantly—
>   and just as constant am I
>   in my resolve not to forget.[14]

The translation offered earlier, following the *Ōei Shō* and Yūsai, takes the preface as being "without heart." In other words, there are two relatively independent statements—"when the wind blows through the bamboo-grass field of Ina near Arima Mountain [it sounds] *soyo-soyo*" and "It is *so:* how could I ever forget you?"—that are joined simply by the wordplay of *soyo.*

The Pictures

Despite the accompanying commentaries by such authorities as Yūsai, visual artists virtually ignore the poem's original context. Only the Tan'yū album—where the poet looks coyly over her fan—suggests the original interview. None of the others shows a couple conversing; practically all of them show the poet alone, gazing at the bamboo grass near a hill, as does the *Zōsanshō* [**58–1**]. This treatment perforce makes the preface metaphorically relevant *(ushin)*—the pictures invite us to see some similarity between the wind through the bamboo grass and the woman. This relationship is suggested even more strongly in later versions such as Porter [**58–2**] and the *Kangyoku*, where the woman is placed in the midst of the field itself. Finally, the kimono pattern books provide a clear example of their differing concerns: the *Hyakushu Hinagata* [**58–3**] gives mountains with bamboo grass and the characters for the names of both "Arima Yama" and "Ina no Hara," making recognition of the poem virtually certain, while the *Shikishi Moyō* pattern book [**58–4**] has only the character for "wind" *(kaze)* literally running through the bamboo grass at the top of the robe (and some rather insect-eaten specimens down below).

58-1

58-2

58-3

58-4

POEM 59

yasurahade
nenamashi mono wo
sayo fukete
katabuku made no
tsuki wo mishi kana[15]

Though I'd have preferred
to have gone off to bed
    without hesitating,
the night deepened and
I watched the moon till it set!

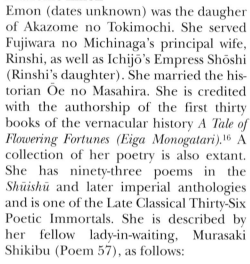

Akazome Emon

Emon (dates unknown) was the daugher of Akazome no Tokimochi. She served Fujiwara no Michinaga's principal wife, Rinshi, as well as Ichijō's Empress Shōshi (Rinshi's daughter). She married the historian Ōe no Masahira. She is credited with the authorship of the first thirty books of the vernacular history *A Tale of Flowering Fortunes (Eiga Monogatari)*.[16] A collection of her poetry is also extant. She has ninety-three poems in the *Shūishū* and later imperial anthologies and is one of the Late Classical Thirty-Six Poetic Immortals. She is described by her fellow lady-in-waiting, Murasaki Shikibu (Poem 57), as follows:

> The wife of the Governor of Tanba is known to everyone in the service of Her Majesty and His Excellency as Masahira Emon. She may not be a genius but she has great poise and does not feel that she has to compose a poem on everything she sees merely because she is a poet. From what I have seen, her work is most accomplished, even her occasional verse.[17]

Commentary

In the *GoShūishū* the headnote to this poem reads:

> When the Middle Regent [Michitaka] was still a lesser captain, he used to visit [Emon's] sister. Composed in her stead on a morning when he had made her expect him and then he didn't come.

Most early commentaries follow the headnote. There is some doubt as to whether this poem is in fact by Akazome Emon, as it also appears in another woman's collected poems, the *Uma no Naishi Shū,* and Shunzei attributes it to her in his *Korai Fūtai Shō.* Critics such as Keichū assumed that this woman must have been the sister mentioned in the headnote, but this is not the case. Michitaka was a Lesser Captain from 974 to 977, during which time he was married to Takashina no Takako, whose poem written after their wedding we have already seen (Poem 54). Later commentaries call the poem one of "regret" *(kōkai)*, suggesting it was read as a soliloquy.

The Pictures

The most interesting difference in the pictorializations is in their treatment of the moon. Kageki in his *Iken* (1823) is apparently the first to explicitly gloss *yasurafu* as *izayofu*, which means "to hesitate" but also is used in *izayohi-dzuki* to refer to the waning moon of the sixteenth lunar day. The Tan'yū album shows the poet inscribing her poem while behind her what appears to be a full moon sinks behind a hill. The *Zōsanshō* [**59–1**] is much the same, but the Kyoto artist has added clouds [**59–2**], which make it impossible to determine the shape of the moon. The *Hyakushu Hinagata* pattern book [**59–3**] gives the crescent moon of the second day of the month. (The characters are *sayo fukete*, and both the *hagi* plant and pillows suggest waiting for a lover.) By the time of the Porter artist [**59–4**], however, the intention is evident.[18] All pictorializations interpret the poem as expressing the poet's inner thoughts.

59-1

59-2

59-3

59-4

POEM 60

ohoe-yama
ikuno no michi no
tohokereba
mada fumi mo mizu
ama no hashidate[19]

Ōe Mountain and
the road that goes to Ikuno
    are far away, and so
not yet have I trod there, nor letter seen,
from Ama-no-Hashidate.

Handmaid KoShikibu

KoShikibu no Naishi, the only child of Izumi Shikibu (Poem 56), died in 1025 while still in her late twenties. Like her mother, she too served Empress Shōshi. She has no personal poetry collection and has only four poems in the *GoShū-ishū* and later imperial anthologies.

Commentary

This poem is preceded in the *Kin'yōshū* by a rather lengthy headnote:

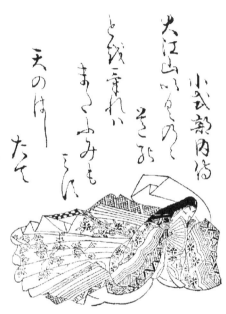

> When Izumi Shikibu was in the province of Tango, having accompanied [her husband] Yasumasa, there was a poetry contest in the capital and Handmaid KoShikibu was chosen as one of the poets. Middle Counselor Sadayori came to her room in the palace and teased her, saying: "What will you do about the poems? Have you sent someone off to Tango? Hasn't the messenger come back? My, you must be worried." Whereupon she held him back and recited [the following].

Sadayori (Poem 64) taunts KoShikibu that she will have to ask for her mother's help to write her poems for the competition. In response, KoShikibu delivers a devastating impromptu poem that includes the names of three places in Tango (in geographical order, no less), two puns (the *iku* of Ikuno means "to go," while *fumi* means both "to step" and "letter"), and word association between *fumi* "to step" and the "bridge" *(hashi)* of Ama-no-Hashidate. This was a popular story in Teika's day and was recounted in both the *Toshiyori Zuinō* and the *Fukuro-Zōshi,* both of which claim that KoShikibu literally pulled at the sleeve of Sadayori's robe to stop him and that, unable to think of a response, he fled.

The Pictures

With such an explicit and well-known story behind it, there was little room for disagreement among commentators. Visual artists, however, still managed a fair degree of variation. The Tan'yū album has KoShikibu with a fan in front of her face (the album's usual sign that the poem was actually said to someone) with the sand-spit of Ama-no-Hashidate, pine trees, and mountains in the background. The *Zōsanshō* [**60–1**] shows KoShikibu standing and taking hold of Sadayori's sleeve—women of the period, however, usually remained seated or on their knees. Moronobu modernizes the setting in his *Sugata-e* [**60–3**], and his two-register format allows him this time to depict Ōe Mountain as well; the poet's interlocutor would appear to be a procuress. The *Kangyoku* artist [**60–2**] avoids the problem of KoShikibu's posture by showing us only the man from outside the blinds. Finally, the Porter artist [**60–4**] shows a seated KoShikibu; rather than physically holding the man back, she seems to be detaining him by handing him her poem. The *Hyakushu Hinagata* pattern book approaches a rebus: it includes a bridge, the characters of "Ikuno," the outline of a mountain, and a road with tied love letters on it.

60-1

60-2

60-3

60-4

POEM 61

inishihe no
nara no miyako no
yahe-zakura
kefu kokonohe ni
nihohinuru kana[20]

The eight-petalled cherries
from the Nara capital
of the ancient past
today nine layers thick
have bloomed within your court!

Ise no Tayū

Ise no Tayū (also pronounced "Ise-dayū" and "Ise no Ōsuke"), dates uncertain, was a daughter of Ōnakatomi no Sukechika and granddaughter of Yoshinobu (Poem 49). She married Takashina no Narinobu and became the mother of many well-known poets. She served Empress Shōshi along with Izumi Shikibu (Poem 56) and Murasaki Shikibu (Poem 57). A collection of her poems is extant and she is one of the Late Classical Thirty-Six Poetic Immortals. She has fifty-one poems in the *GoShūishū* and later imperial anthologies.

Commentary

In the *Shikashū* this poem's headnote reads:

> During the time of Emperor Ichijō, someone presented eight-petalled cherry blossoms from Nara. On that occasion, since she was in attendance, she was commanded to compose a poem with those flowers as the topic.

However, the description in Ise no Tayū's own *Collected Poems* is more interesting:

> When the Imperial Lady (Shōshi) was still empress, I was at court when the eight-petalled cherry blossoms were presented by the bishop from Nara. "Let the new lady-in-waiting [Ise no Tayū] be the person to [go out and] accept them this year," Murasaki Shikibu deferred, and when His Lordship the Buddhist Novice [Michinaga] heard this, he said "It is not something that you can simply accept [without composing a poem]," and so [I composed the following].

It is this situation that must have so appealed to Teika and the poets of his period: new to court service, Ise no Tayū is called upon for an impromptu poem in front of so formidable a poet as Murasaki Shikibu and so powerful a figure as Michinaga. Her poem is technically very accomplished, balancing "the ancient past" with "today" and "eight-petalled" with "nine layers." Since this "nine layers" is also a word for the imperial court, her poem is not simply in praise of the blossoms (as the *Keikō Shō* maintained) but also a clever compliment to Michinaga and his daughter the empress (as commentaries as early as the *Ōei Shō* recognized).

The Pictures
All portraits of the poet have her shyly raising her sleeve to her face. The Tan'yū album places a presentation stand in front of her with a branch of cherry blossoms on it. The *Zōsanshō* [**61–1**] chooses the more narratively interesting description from the *Ise no Tayū Shū*, showing the poet and another woman and a male courtier (presumably Murasaki Shikibu and Michinaga) although Yūsai's accompanying commentary refers only to the *Shikashū* headnote. The Kyoto artist [**61–2**] follows the earlier design, but the accompanying figures are simply nameless courtiers. In his *Sugata-e* [**61–3**], Moronobu ignores the pun in *kokonohe* that also refers to the imperial court and simply shows a woman gazing at flowers, stripping the poem of its court reference and turning it into a simple paean to the woman's beauty. The Porter artist [**61–4**] follows the *Shikashū* headnote and shows the poet by herself in front of the emperor; however, following a number of commentaries (the *Chōkyō Shō, Yoritsune-bon*, and *Minō Shō*) which claimed that the cherries had actually been transplanted to the palace, the artist shows the thriving tree from which the poet has apparently pulled her branch. This may also explain the cherry tree in the *Zōsanshō* version.

61-1   61-2

61-3

61-4

POEM 62

yo wo komete
tori no sora-ne ha
hakaru tomo
yo ni afusaka no
seki ha yurusaji[21]

Although, still wrapped in night,
the cock's false cry
   some may deceive,
never will the Barrier
of Meeting Hill let you pass.

Sei Shōnagon

Sei Shōnagon (dates uncertain), a daughter of Kiyohara no Motosuke (Poem 42), served Empress Teishi until the latter's death in the year 1000. She recorded the splendors of Teishi's court, and the riches of her own wit, in her *Pillow Book (Makura no Sōshi)*, for which she is best remembered. Although she is one of the Late Classical Thirty-Six Poetic Immortals, she has only four poems in the *GoShūishū* and later imperial anthologies.

Commentary

This poem and its accompanying anecdote appear originally in *The Pillow Book:*

> One evening Yukinari, the Controller First Secretary, came to the Empress's Office and stayed there until late at night.

"Tomorrow is a day of Imperial Abstinence," he said as he left, "and I have to remain in the Palace. I must certainly go home before the Hour of the Ox."

On the following morning a messenger brought me several sheets of Kōya paper of the type the Chamberlains use in the Emperor's Private Office. "Today," I read, "my heart is full of memories of our meeting. I had hoped that I might stay until the morning to tell you of bygone tales, but the cock's crow forced me to take my leave. . . ." It was a long letter, very elegantly written and *contrived to give an impression that was quite contrary to the truth*. I was much impressed and replied,

"Can the cock's crow that we heard so late at night be that which saved the Lord of Meng-ch'ang?" Yukunari answered, "It is said that the cock's crow opened the barrier of Han Ku and allowed the Lord of Meng-ch'ang to escape in the nick of time with his three thousand followers. But we are concerned with a far less distant barrier—the Barrier of Ōsaka." I then sent him this poem. . . . And as a postscript: "I am told that the gate-keeper is a very shrewd man."

Yukinari promptly replied:

afusaka ha	I have heard it said
ito koe-yasuku	That Ōsaka Barrier can be freely crossed.
seki nareba	No need here for the cock to crow:
tori nakanu ni mo	This gate is ever opened wide,
akete matsu to ka	And waits each wanderer who comes.[22]

The headnote in the *GoShūishū* gives essentially the same information, though more briefly and without Yukinari's responding verse. Practically all commentaries interpret the poem through its accompanying story. This poem is the third in a series (starting with Poem 60) intended to show the quick wit of court women, and it is presumably for this reason that Teika chose it.

The Pictures

Despite the detail of the original context and the near-unanimity of the commentators, the visual artists appear to have been much more influenced by forms in their visual repertoire. The *Zōsanshō* picture [**62–2**] is reminiscent of the Saga-bon illustration to Episode 14 of the *Tales of Ise* [**62–3**], which has a rooster and hen in the tree. This rendering suggests that the man is using the rooster's crowing as an excuse to leave while the woman wishes he would stay— a point made explicit by the Kyoto artist [**62–4**], where the woman pulls at the man's sleeve to hold him back. This, of course, is completely contrary to the sense of the poem, in which the woman declares that she will never let the man spend the night with her. It is tempting to read Moronobu's *Sugata-e* [**62–1**] as a

pictorialization of Yukunari's verse—certainly the gate is wide open. Other artists, such as the *Kangyoku* artist and Hokusai, illustrate the Chinese story directly.

62-1

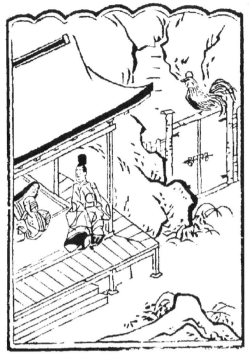

62-2

62-3

62-4

POEM 63

ima ha tada
omohi-taenamu
to bakari wo
hito-dzute narade
ifu yoshi mogana[23]

Now, the only thing
I wish for is a way to say
to you directly
—not through another—
"I will think of you no longer!"

Master of the Western Capital Michimasa

Sakyō no Daibu was Fujiwara no Michimasa (992–1054). The capital of Heiankyō (modern Kyoto) was divided into eastern and western sectors (literally, Right and Left), each of which was under the control of an administrative office headed by a "master," or *daibu*.[24] Michimasa was a son of Korechika (see also Poem 54); he spent the latter half of his life in elegant retirement after his family was supplanted by Michinaga. He has only six poems in the *GoShūishū* and later imperial anthologies.

Commentary

The occasion for this poem is recounted in the *GoShūishū:*

> He was secretly seeing somone who had returned from being the High Priestess of Ise. Composed when the court heard of this and posted guards so that he could no longer visit her even in secret.

This story of Michimasa's relationship with the former Ise Priestess Tōshi—and the anger of her father, Retired Emperor Sanjō (Poem 68), over it—is related in the *Midō Kanpaku Ki,*[25] the *Tale of Flowering Fortunes (Eiga Monogatari),* and the *Fukuro-Zōshi.* Both the author of *Flowering Fortunes* and Teika saw a parallel between this affair and the famous affair purported to have occurred between Narihira and the Ise Virgin as described in the *Tales of Ise.*[26] Apparently the Michimasa anecdote was sufficiently well known to stifle much debate over the poem's meaning, and there is virtual agreement in all Japanese commentaries.

The Pictures

The *Soan-bon* edition shows Michimasa in a hunting outfit of the same sort worn in most depictions of Narihira (Poem 17). The Tan'yū album has Michimasa, in court robes with a cherry-blossom design, gazing out into the distance with a sheaf of papers clutched to his breast and a writing box beside him. This design has clearly influenced the *Sugata-e* [**63–4**], where we see a man also wearing a robe with cherry blossoms, looking forlornly at his writing paper with a brothel go-between, or procuress, in front of him, emphasizing what is actually the point of the poem: the poet wants to be able to speak to his love directly, even if only to tell her that he has given up. The *Zōsanshō* [**63–1**] and the Kyoto artist show the poet turning away from a guarded gate—the basic composition repeated by many artists, including Hokusai. Hasegawa [**63–3**] pairs the poet with a river (also visible in the *Sugata-e*), which may be meant to suggest the verb *tae* ("to cease"). The *Hyakushu Hinagata* pattern book [**63–2**] provides a fascinating concatenation of images: the fence would suggest the posted guard, the evergreen the unending nature of the man's love, and the vines the idea of secret visits (as in Poem 25). The calligraphy gives the first full line of the poem: *ima ha tada*. Unlike the previous poem (Poem 62) we see no interference from *Ise* illustrations in any pictorializations of the poem itself, despite Michimasa's association with Narihira in the *kasen-e*.

63-1   63-2

63-3

63-4

POEM 64

asaborake　　　　　　As the winter dawn
ujhi no kaha-giri　　breaks, the Uji River mist
tae-dae ni　　　　　　thins in patches and
arahare-wataru　　　revealed, here and there, are
se-ze no ajiro-gi[27]　all the shallows' fishing-stakes.

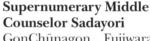

Supernumerary Middle Counselor Sadayori

GonChūnagon Fujiwara no Sadayori (995–1045), son of Kintō (Poem 55), is the antagonist in KoShikibu no Naishi's poem (Poem 60).[28] He has forty-five poems in the *GoShūishū* and later imperial anthologies and is counted one of the Late Classical Thirty-Six Poetic Immortals. A collection of his poems survives.

Commentary

Most commentators, medieval and modern, follow the headnote to this poem—which declares that it was written when the poet was at Uji River—and take the poem as a description of an actual landscape before the poet's eyes. However, as early as the *Ōei Shō* we see an insistence that the poem has a hidden meaning. This meaning is based on seeing the poem as an "allusive variation" *(honka-dori)* on a poem by Hitomaro found in both the *Man'yō Shū* (3: 264) and the *ShinKokinshū* (Misc. 2): 1648:

mononofu no　　　　　Like the waves that wander
yaso ujhi-gaha no　　among the fishing stakes
ajiro-gi ni　　　　　　in Uji River,
isayofu nami no　　　　of the eighty warrior clans,
yukuhe shirazu mo　　I do not know which way to turn.[29]

With this intertext, Sadayori's poem is understood to refer to the circle of death and rebirth, to which the shifting mist is compared. The *Yoritaka-bon*, however, believes that the poem is a metaphor for hidden love. None of these readings is currently accepted.

The Pictures
The Tan'yū album depicts the Uji Bridge, fishing weirs, and fishing stakes, emphasizing the "famous place" *(meisho)* quality of the poem. The *Zōsanshō*'s [**64–1**] rendition is ambiguous—clearly the fishing stakes are oversized and there is an insistence on the many streams of the river, though one cannot say whether this is meant to correspond to the *se-ze* (literally, "rapids-rapids") of Sadayori's poem or perhaps the *yaso* ("eighty") of the base poem. It may instead be meant to suggest the romantic interpretation of the poem (compare Poems 13, 27, 48). In the *Sugata-e* [**64–2**] Moronobu also depicts the famous Uji Bridge, associating the poem more closely with *The Tale of Genji*, just as Teika may have, and clearly agreeing with the *Yoritaka-bon*'s romantic interpretation. Hasegawa [**64–3**] shows neither fishing weirs nor the bridge but instead includes a tree—as if the *gi (ki)* of *ajiro-gi* referred to an actual tree. The *Shikishi Moyō* kimono design [**64–4**] is a successful combination of fishing stakes in a fairly tranquil river, hung with fabrics as well as nets, with the character for "dawn" *(asa)* superimposed. The wild waves of the river are confined to the bottom of the robe.

64-1

64-2

64-3

64-4

POEM 65

urami-wabi
hosanu sode dani
aru mono wo
kohi ni kuchinan
na koso oshikere [30]

Although there are
my sleeves that never dry,
    bitter and sad,
what I really regret is
my name, made rotten by love!

Sagami

Sagami's dates are uncertain; she was probably born sometime between 995 and 1003. She is thought to be a daughter of Minamoto no Yorimitsu. Her mother was a daughter of Yoshishige no Yasuaki. Her sobriquet comes from her husband, Ōe no Kin'yori, a governor of Sagami province. After separating from him she entered the service of the imperial princess Shūshi. She has a personal poetry collection, forty poems in the *GoShūishū*, and sixty-nine in the remaining imperial anthologies. She is one of the Late Classical Thirty-Six Poetic Immortals.

Commentary

While the basic sense of this poem is clear, commentators have long divided over the meaning of the third and fourth lines: have the poet's sleeves rotted or not? The older school holds that the meaning is: "even though they never have a chance to dry because of my constant tears, it is not my sleeves that will become rotten (ruined), but rather my name (reputation)." The other reading, followed by most modern commentators, is: "even though my sleeves will probably rot right through, what I am really upset about is my rotten reputation." Ariyoshi claims that the evidence points to Teika's reading the poem according to this latter interpretation. The translation offered here allows for both readings. The poem was composed for a poetry contest that took place in the palace in 1051 (described in some detail in *A Tale of Flowering Fortunes,* or *Eiga Monogatari*) and is so identified in the *GoShūishū*.

The Pictures

Even though the Yūsai commentary follows the "sleeves not rotted" interpretation, it is unlikely that artists would have depicted literally rotted sleeves in any event. Most illustrators show a woman with her sleeve to her face. The *Zōsanshō* pictorialization [**65–1**] shows the poet looking out from her room at a tree, reminiscent of the composition used for Komachi [**9–2**], and the *Sugata-e* commentary specifically states that the woman has had a number of affairs, reinforcing the similarity to Komachi. Note how a change of perspective in the *Shūgyoku* version [**65–2**] accents the woman's isolation. Moronobu's *Sugata-e* [**65–4**] repeats the *Zōsanshō* composition in the upper register while showing a prostitute and her young servant reading below. The books may be meant to indicate the idea of leaving behind one to posterity nothing but scandalous stories. The *Hyakushu Hinagata* kimono design [**65–3**] has buckets in which salt-makers carry brine, indicating tears. The written phrase reads *hosanu . . . dani aru mono wo,* with the actual image of a sleeve inserted to represent the word "sleeves."

65-1

65-2

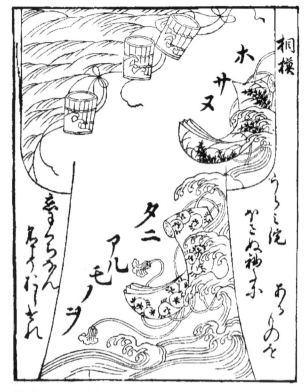

65-3

65-4

POEM 66

morotomo ni
aware to omohe
yama-zakura
hana yori hoka ni
shiru hito mo nashi[31]

Let us think of each
other fondly,
O mountain cherries!
for, outside of your blossoms,
there's no one who knows my feelings.

Major Archbishop Gyōson

DaiSōjō Gyōson (1055–1135) was a son of Minamoto no Motohira. He entered the priesthood at the age of twelve and became renowned as a *yamabushi*, or mountain ascetic. He was also a prolific poet, and a collection of his poetry is extant. He has forty-eight poems in the *Kin'yōshū* and later imperial collections.

Commentary

Scholars are still divided today over the correct interpretation of this poem. It is not the poem itself that is problematic, however, but its headnote, which in the *Kin'yōshū* reads: "Composed when he saw cherry blossoms unexpectedly at Ōmine." The debate is over the meaning of "unexpectedly" *(omohi-kakezu)* here. Commentators had long argued that the setting of the poem was early summer and the poet was surprised to see cherries (an early spring flower) still blooming deep in the mountains. But the *Kaikan Shō* (1688) argued that what surprises the poet is to see cherry blossoms amidst the evergreens of Ōmine, and modern scholars such as Shimazu follow this interpretation. The differences in interpretation are not as picayune as they might appear: the evergreens represent unchanging longevity, while the cherries are associated with the transitory nature of human life.

The Pictures

Depictions of Gyōson are of two very different types. The *Soan-bon* edition shows him as a high-ranking prelate, while the Tan'yū album shows him in the dress characteristic of the *yamabushi* mountain ascetics. The inscription of the poem in the *Soan-bon* is also distinctive, as it is written almost entirely using Chinese characters with virtually no *kana*. The *Zōsanshō* [**66–1**] predates the *Kaikan Shō* and, accordingly, shows the poet confronted simply by cherry trees. Contrast this version with the *Kangyoku* [**66–2**], which shows cherries amidst ever-greens and thus reflects the *Kaikan Shō* interpretation. Moronobu's *Sugata-e* [**66–3**] shows the poet as a rough mountain ascetic confronted, seemingly unexpectedly, by a young samurai. This image seems to be playing with a com-plex of subtexts: the figure of the poet is reminiscent of the famous warrior Benkei, and the way the samurai is holding the paper calls to mind the famous *Nō* play *Kanjinchō (The Subscription List)*, where Benkei attempts to bluff his way through a barrier post. Moreover, a number of *nō* plays entailed the theme of young boys being abducted by goblins *(tengu)* or *yamabushi*—again, the *Sugata-e* image seems to present an amusing role-reversal. The *Shikishi Moyō* kimono design [**66–4**] shows two horses, perhaps meant to suggest the idea of "together," heartlessly eating the cherry blossoms that fall from a tree trunk formed in the shape of the ideograph for "mountain" *(yama)*.

66-2

66-1

66-3

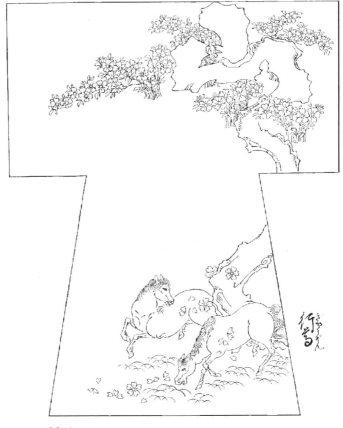

66-4

POEM 67

haru no yo no
yume bakari naru
ta-makura ni
kahi naku tatamu
na koso woshikere[32]

With your arm as my pillow
for no more than a brief
   spring night's dream,
how I would regret my name
coming, pointlessly, to 'arm!

The Suō Handmaid
Suō no Naishi's personal name was
Nakako (dates uncertain). Her sobriquet
comes from her father, Taira no
Munenaka, the governor of Suō prov-
ince. She served emperors GoReizei,
Shirakawa and Horikawa, and partici-
pated in various poetry contests. A collec-
tion of her poetry survives. She has
thirty-five poems in the *GoShūishū* and
later imperial anthologies.

Commentary
The headnote to this poem reads:

> Around the Second Month, on a
> night when the moon was bright, sev-
> eral people were passing the night at
> the Nijō In, talking about this and
> that, when the Suō Handmaid, half-

reclining, said softly, "Ah, I wish I had a pillow!" Hearing this, Middle Counse-
lor Tada'ie said, "Here, make this your pillow," and pushed his arm *(kahina)* in
from under the blinds. Whereupon she composed [the following].

The poem puns on the word "arm" *(kahina)* by relating it to the phrase "point-
less" *(kahi naku)*, though some commentaries, such as the *Ōei Shō,* dispute this.
(The foregoing translation attempts to convey the spirit of the pun through
"arm" and "[h]arm.") Otherwise, the specificity of the event has restrained
commentators. While some see this poem as another example of the quick wit
of court women (see Poems 60, 61, and 62), Ariyoshi claims that Teika's inclu-
sion and placement of this poem in the *Nishidai Shū* shows that he appreciated
the poem as simply a romantic lyric—embodying the flavor of *yōen* with its
vocabulary of "night of spring," "dream," and "pillowing arm"—removed from
the clever specifics of its genesis.

The Pictures
The potential visual awkwardness in the situation described by the headnote can be seen in the *Kangyoku* [**67–1**], where a disembodied arm appears from under the blinds. It is curious that this composition should be a problem as it is very similar to a scene, often illustrated, in the *Fuji-bakama* chapter of *The Tale of Genji*. The *Zōsanshō* seems to solve the problem by removing the blinds [**67–2**]—a solution that the Kyoto artist follows—and adding a cherry tree to emphasize the season, as well as a full moon. But Moronobu's *Sugata-e* [**67–3**] shows that he could devise a more successful method. This version is somewhat similar to the composition used by the Porter artist [**67–4**]. Perhaps the most charming version is Kuniyoshi's *Hyakunin Isshu no Uchi* of 1861 (see Plate 7). Interestingly, it is only the *Sugata-e* that, in its foreground drawing, gives the more lyrical interpretation thought to be favored by Teika, suggesting a stronger identification between the woman and the easily ruined cherry blossoms. The Tan'yū album, by contrast, has the poet looking out of the picture frame, from behind her fan, at the viewer, emphasizing the playful nature of the poem.

67-1

67-2

67-3

67-4

POEM 68

kokoro ni mo
arade uki yo ni
nagaraheba
kohishikarubeki
yoha no tsuki kana[33]

Though it is not what's in my heart,
if in this world of pain
    I should linger, then
no doubt I shall remember fondly
the bright moon of this dark night!

Retired Emperor Sanjō

Sanjō In (976–1017) reigned from 1011 to 1016. Prone to illness, he was forced to abdicate to make room for Michinaga's grandson GoIchijō. He has no personal poetry collection and only eight poems in the *GoShūishū* and later imperial anthologies.

Commentary

The headnote to this poem reads: "When he was not feeling well, and considering abdicating, he looked at the brightness of the moon [and composed the following]." The account in *A Tale of Flowering Fortunes (Eiga Monogatari)* is more detailed:

> Emperor Sanjō's illness persisted. . . . Meanwhile, the end of the year approached. Most people were busy and excited, but for Emperor Sanjō, plagued by constant suffering, it was a time of painful indecision. What should he do? On a brilliant moonlit night not long after the Tenth of the Twelfth Month, he composed a poem in the Imperial Apartment for Empress Kenshi. . . . On the Nineteenth of the First Month in the fifth year of Chōwa [1016], Emperor Sanjō relinquished the throne.[34]

However, most commentaries refer only to the *GoShūishū* headnote. Debate centers on why the poet will think of the moon fondly—that is, the reason for his present unhappiness. Early commentaries such as the *Ōei Shō* understand the reason to be the emperor's reluctance to abdicate. The *Keikō Shō* (1530) and the many commentaries that follow it argue instead that the issue is simply whether or not the emperor will continue to live—if he does, then the moon from the night that his life seemed uncertain will be a fond memory.

The Pictures

Although the *Flowering Fortunes* says that Sanjō In composed this poem for Ken-shi and that she replied with one of her own, no artist portrays the empress. The *Zōsanshō* [**68–1**] and the Kyoto artists, by showing the emperor standing (rather than sitting as if he were sick), in ceremonial robes, and with a gentle-man-in-waiting, suggest that it is the issue of abdication, rather than illness, that troubles the emperor. The *Kangyoku* [**68–3**] and the Porter artists instead show the emperor alone, though neither of them portrays a tenth-night moon. Moronobu's placement of the moon above mountains, in his *Sugata-e* [**68–2**], calls to mind the belief that emperors did not die but hid themselves in the mountains (in tumuli).[35] It may also be meant to allude to Nakamaro's poem (Poem 7), and there is a similarity between the *Zōsanshō*'s compositions for these two poems [**7–2** and **68–1**]. Finally, the *Shikishi Moyō* kimono design [**68–4**] makes clear that its artist was aware of the season of the poem (the Twelfth Month) by combining the moon and characters for "night" (*yoha*) with the chrysanthemums of winter.

68-1

68-2

68-3

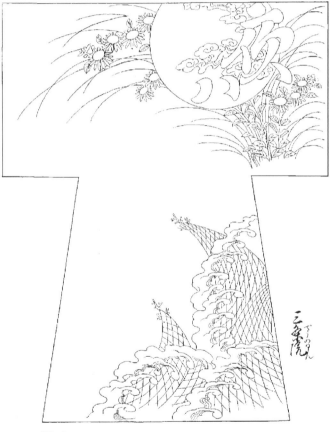

68-4

POEM 69

arashi fuku
mimuro no yama no
momijhi-ba ha
tatsuta no kaha no
nishiki narikeri[36]

It's the autumn leaves
of the hills of Mimuro,
    where the tempests blow,
that are the woven brocade floating
on the waters of Tatsuta River!

Master of the Law Nōin

Nōin Hōshi was born in 988 as Tachibana
no Nagayasu. Originally he studied at the
imperial university, but he took vows
at the age of twenty-six and traveled
through many provinces composing
poetry. He studied poetry under Fujiwara
no Nagatō (also read "Nagayoshi"),
which became a precedent for "learning
from a master" *(shishō)* in the "way of
poetry" *(kadō).* A collection of his poetry
is extant, as well as a collection of poetry
edited by him, the *Gengen Shū*, and a
poetic treatise, the *Nōin Uta-makura.* He
has sixty-five poems in the *GoShūishū* and
later imperial anthologies, and he is one
of the Late Classical Thirty-Six Poetic
Immortals.

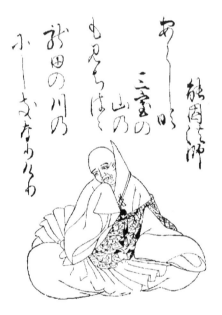

Commentary

As the *Ōei Shō* puts it, "there is nothing
hidden" in this poem, and it has accord-
ingly been valued for its direct and straightforward style. It was composed for a
palace poetry contest held in 1049. Both Mimuro and Tatsuta were famous for
their autumn foliage. While there has been no debate on the meaning of the
poem, commentators have argued about its value and even its geographical
accuracy.

The Pictures

The Tan'yū album effectively shows autumn leaves in a river and trees in fall
foliage on mountains in the far background—a two-tiered composition that
reappears in the *Eiga.* The *Zōsanshō* [**69–1**] shows the poet on a riverbank with
trees in autumn foliage, a format basically followed by most later artists. For his
Sugata-e [**69–2**] Moronobu puts the poet in simpler garb befitting a recluse or
wandering monk—in fact, the image of Nōin is a self-quotation from Moro-
nobu's first and most popular *kyōka e-hon,* the clearly homoerotic *Bokuyō Kyōka*

Shū of 1678 [**69–5**], where we see Master Bokuyō admiring a bevy of young men. The *Hyakushu Hinagata* kimono book shows two mountain peaks with autumn maples and the characters "Mimuro" blazoned over them; an S-shaped river rushes diagonally across the lower half of the robe, carrying the foliage with it. The *Shikishi Moyō* kimono design [**69–3**] takes the characters for "Tatsuta" (literally "Dragon Field") and divides the robe with them, showing autumn leaves in agitated water on one side and suggesting the more tranquil brocade near the hem on the other. This poem was clearly seen as paired with the next, also by a priest, and Hasegawa's design [**69–4**] makes it clear that the two were seen to provide both comparisons and contrasts: one made to look more like a monk while the other was depicted as ecclesiastical; one in black and one in white; and so forth.

69-1

69-2

69-3

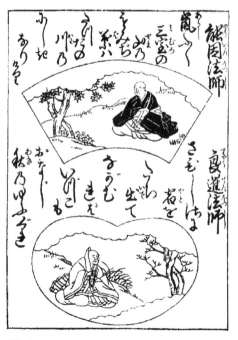

能因法師

嵐ふく
三室の山の
もみぢ葉は
たつたの川の
にしきなりけり

良選法師

さびしさに
宿を立ち出て
ながむれば
いづくもおなじ
秋の夕ぐれ

69-4

69-5

POEM 70

sabishisa ni
yado wo tachi-idete
nagamureba
idzuku mo onaji
aki no yufugure[37]

When, from loneliness,
I stand up and leave my hut
    and look distractedly about:
everywhere it is the same
evening in autumn.

Master of the Law Ryōzen

Ryōzen Hōshi (dates uncertain) was active during the reigns of GoSuzaku (r. 1036–1045) and GoReizei (r. 1045–1068) and participated in several poetry contests. He has thirty-one poems in the *Go-Shūishū* and later imperial anthologies.

Commentary

This poem is preceded by no explanation *(dai shirazu)* in the *GoShūishū*. The commentaries are in general agreement. It is the last two lines that have elicited the most comment, and even today there is disagreement whether the fourth line is a full stop *(shi ku-gire)* or whether "the same" modifies "evening" *(rentaikei)*. The translation offered here preserves this ambiguity. The *Kaikan Shō* (1688) is unique in suggesting that the poet is not simply getting up for a walk but is in fact abandoning the world. Most commentaries assume that the poet, as a monk, has already done this. There also seems to be some disagreement over whether the poet is grieved and unhappy (as explicitly argued by Mabuchi in *Uimanabi*) or is simply moved by the poignance of the scene.

The Pictures

Although the *Kaikan Shō* postdates the *Zōsanshō* pictorialization [**70–1**], the artist's rendering seems to imply that the poet is leaving home rather than just taking a stroll. This is suggested by the staff and by the dwelling the priest is leaving, which does not look like the simple hut one would expect, as well as by the fields and other signs of habitation—in other words, we are presented with not just the hut of the poem but an entire village. The Kyoto artist [**70–2**] follows the *Zōsanshō* closely, but his figure looks much less unhappy. In the *Sugata-e* [**70–3**], Moronobu depicts the poet as a Bodhidharma look-alike and in the upper register shows the poet looking across at a small hamlet, a composition suggested by the Tan'yū album. Here the implication seems to be that the poet has left his hut and is looking out on the mundane, secular world, where he sees that autumn twilight has also come. The *Kangyoku* [**70–4**] shows a very unhappy-looking priest (with no staff). The figure in the Porter picture is positively beaming, and the signs of habitation have been almost completely obscured.

70-1   70-2

70-3   70-4

POEM 71

yufu sareba
kado-ta no inaba
otodzurete
ashi no maro-ya ni
aki-kaze zo fuku[38]

As evening falls,
through the rice-plants before the gate,
    it comes visiting, and rustling
on the reeds of the simple hut—
the autumn wind does blow!

Major Counselor Tsunenobu

Dainagon Minamoto no Tsunenobu (1016–1097) was the father of Toshiyori (Poem 74) and grandfather of Shun'e (Poem 85). His poetry is first seen in the "Poetry Contest on Famous Place-Names at Princess Yūshi's Residence" (*Yūshi Naishinnō-ke Meisho Uta-awase;* see Poem 72). He was a poetic rival of Fujiwara no Michitoshi and compiled a countercollection to the latter's *GoShūishū* imperial anthology. A collection of his poetry survives, and he has eighty-six poems in the *GoShūishū* and later imperial anthologies. He is one of the Late Classical Thirty-Six Poetic Immortals.

Commentary

The headnote to this poem states that it was composed on the set topic "Country House and Autumn Wind" when the poet had joined Minamoto no Morokata and others at the latter's mountain villa at Umezu. Thus the poem is understood to have been composed on an actual scene before the poet's eyes. It is also appreciated as an early example of the kind of descriptive landscape poetry (*jokeika*) that emerged around this time. Nonetheless, there are several differences of interpretation concerning this poem—disputes about its wording and about its meaning as a whole. As early as the *Ōei Shō* and throughout the Edo period, the first line was read *yufusare ha* or *yufuzare ha*, with *yufuzare* understood as a noun (meaning "evening"), rather than the whole line as a phrase meaning "when evening comes." Commentators also seem unclear on just what an *ashi no maro-ya* was. Literally it is a "round hut of reed," and early commentators such as the *Ōei Shō* claimed that this was a hut made entirely of reed. There were yet other explanations, but the standard interpretation takes it to be a simple hut with a reed-thatch roof. *Otodzurete* means "to make sound (*oto su*) and come to visit (*oto-dzure*)," but the *Ōei Shō* takes the *dzu* as a negative and the whole phrase to mean "not able to hear." Finally, the *Kaikan Shō* suggests that the speaker of the poem is waiting for someone to visit, as the sound of the wind was often thought to be mistaken for the sound of someone approaching.

The Pictures
The Tan'yū album shows cultivated fields, two thatched huts with fences, and a tree in autumn colors. The *Zōsanshō* [**71–1**] seems to miss the sense of the wind coming to visit, as the rice is leaning away from the house. In Moronobu's *Sugata-e* [**71–2**] the outline of the young boys is clearly meant to echo the shape of the huts (the double huts deriving from the Tan'yū design) and the sense of "visiting" is paramount. Curiously, the last line of the poem is moved to the beginning of the inscription above the picture. The *Hyakushu Hinagata* kimono design [**71–3**] presents thatched roofs within bamboo medallions to suggest the *maro-ya* (which can also be understood as "round roof"). The words *kado-ta no* are superimposed over ripe ears of grain protected by wooden clappers used to scare away birds—these clappers, which suggest the "make a sound" *(oto su)* pivot word of the poem, also appear in the Porter version [**71–4**].

71-1   71-2

大納言殿絵

71-3

71-4

POEM 72

oto ni kiku
takashi no hama no
ada-nami ha
kakeji ya sode no
nure mo koso sure[39]

Known far and wide,
the unpredictable waves
　　of Takashi's beach—
I will not let them catch me—
For I'd be sorry should my sleeves get wet!

Kii of Princess Yūshi's Household

Yūshi Naishinnō-ke no Kii (dates uncertain) was a daughter of Taira no Tsunekata and a Lady KoBen, who also served the Imperial Princess Yūshi (in whose salon the author of the *Sarashina Nikki* also participated). She took part in several poetry contests and has a collection of poetry extant, sometimes called the *Ichi-no-Miya no Kii Shū*, following another of her sobriquets. She has thirty-one poems in the *GoShūishū* and later imperial anthologies.

Commentary

This poem was presented at the "Love Letter Competition" *(kesō-bumi awase)* held during the time of Retired Emperor Horikawa in 1102. It was pitted as a response to the following poem by Fujiwara no Toshitada (Teika's grandfather):

hito shirenu
omohi ariso no
ura-kaze ni
nami no yoru koso
ihamahoshikere

Unknown to any
I long—and how I long to say
　　that I come to you in the night
like the waves blown by
the bay-wind of Ariso!

This poem contains two pivot words: *ariso* is a place-name, but *omohi ari* means "I have thoughts of longing"; and *yoru* means both "to approach" and "night." In her reply, Kii uses the same structure: *takashi* is a place-name but is also the adjective "high" or "loud," in connection with sound, here meaning "often heard of" or "loudly rumored." *Kakeji* means that neither her robe nor her heart shall be caught by the *ada-nami,* or "fickle waves." Medieval commentators have questioned just what kind of waves *ada-nami* are or in which province Takashi was to be found, but otherwise interpretations are uniform.

The Pictures

The *Zōsanshō* [**72–1**] has the poet looking out at the waves while standing on the shore. The Kyoto artist [**72–2**] places her in a house and adds a pair of waterfowl, suggesting a romantic motif. Most unusual for Hasegawa [**72–3**], he does not place the poet in a house and has her looking back as the waves approach her trailing robe, an effective conception used also in the *Kangyoku.* Not surprisingly, the waves are the dominant motif in the *Shikishi Moyō* kimono design [**72–4**] with its characters *oto kiku* (rather than the place-name Takashi as one might expect).

72-1

72-2

72-3

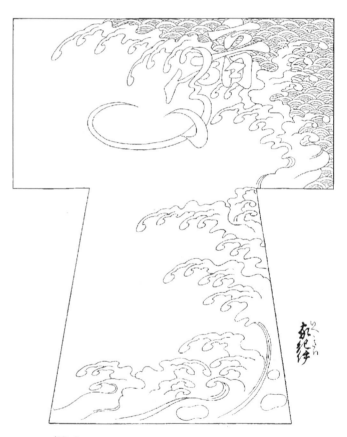

72-4

POEM 73

takasago no
wonohe no sakura
sakinikeri
toyama no kasumi
tatazu mo aranamu[40]

Above the lower slopes
of the high mountains, the cherries
  have blossomed!
O, mist of the near mountains,
how I wish you would not rise!

Supernumerary Middle Counselor Masafusa

GonChūnagon Ōe no Masafusa (some-times read "Tadafusa," 1041–1111) was a "confidant," or *kinshin*, of Retired Emperor Horikawa and participated in such poetry contests as the Horikawa Hyakushu. He was famous as a poet in Chinese as well. He was the source of several books, including a collection of anecdotes, *The Ōe Conversations (Gōdan Shō)*,[41] and a collection of his Japanese poetry, the *Gō no Sochi Shū*. He has 119 poems in the *GoShūishū* and later impe-rial anthologies.

Commentary

The headnote to this poem reads: "Com-posed on the sentiment *(kokoro)* of gazing at mountain cherries far away, when a group of people were drinking and composing poetry at the house of the Pal-ace Minister [Fujiwara no Moromichi]." This headnote makes the meaning of the poem clear: the poet asks the mist of the lower hills not to rise and obstruct his view of the cherries blooming on the high peaks. The only real debate was whether *takasago* referred to Takasago Mountain in Harima province or was simply a common noun for "high mountains" (see Poem 34).

The Pictures

The Tan'yū album makes a clear distinction between the Takasago of Poem 34 and the *takasago* of Masafusa's poem (shown as hills with cherry blossoms blooming on their slopes). Although the Yūsai commentary specifically states that *takasago* is not a place-name, the *Zōsanshō* [73–1] shows the same kind of mountain near the ocean as in [34–1], indicating the famous Takasago moun-tain in Harima province. The Kyoto artist shows a river instead [73–2], taking *takasago* as a common noun. In both cases, the cherries are placed on the slopes of the hills. *Wonohe* is usually paraphrased as "peak" *(mine)*, but *wo* itself literally means the lower slopes of a mountain. This understanding is what the first two pictures seem to be indicating, while Moronobu follows the more standard interpretation in his *Sugata-e* [**73–3**] by placing the cherries on the very peaks. Curiously, the Porter artist [**73–4**] has a very different conception with what look to be autumn leaves rather than cherry blossoms. His version is reminiscent of his rendition of Poem 16, suggesting (as does the *Sugata-e*) a pun on *tatazu,* which can mean "don't leave" as well as "don't rise."

73-1   73-2

73-3

73-4

POEM 74

ukarikeru
hito wo hatsuse no
yama-oroshi yo
hageshikare to ha
inoranu mono wo[42]

"Make that heartless
woman, O mountain storm
of Hatsuse Temple—
crueller still!"—this is not
what I prayed for, and yet . . .

Lord Minamoto no Toshiyori
Minamoto no Toshiyori Ason (1055–
1129)—his given name is also read
"Shunrai"—son of Tsunenobu (Poem
71) and father of Shun'e (Poem 85).
The leading poet of his day, he arranged
the Horikawa Hyakushu and edited the
fifth imperial anthology, the *Kin'yōshū*.
He also left a poetic treatise, the *Toshiyori
Zuinō*, and a collection of his own poetry
in ten books, the *Sanboku Kika Shū*. He
has over two hundred poems in the
Kin'yōshū and later imperial anthologies.

Commentary
The headnote to this poem reads:

> Composed on the sentiment *(kokoro)*
> of "love for a woman who will not
> meet one even though one has
> prayed to the gods," when composing ten love poems at the home of the
> Supernumerary Middle Counselor Toshitada.

As its inclusion in so many anthologies testifies, Teika valued this poem highly.
In the "sent version" of the *Superior Poems of Our Times (Kensō-bon Kindai Shūka)*,
Teika wrote of this poem:

> This poem is deep in feeling and the words give themselves up to the senti-
> ment, and even though one studies it, it is difficult to find fault with it—truly
> it is a configuration *(sugata)* that probably cannot be matched.

Hatsuse was the home of Hase Temple—a frequent object of pilgrimage for lov-
ers and presented as such in romances like *The Tale of Sumiyoshi (Sumiyoshi
Monogatari)*, as commentaries as early as the *Ōei Shō* pointed out. This and later
commentaries also claim that *hatsuse no yama-oroshi* is a pillow word *(makura-*

kotoba) for *hageshi,* or "cruel." (The *Iken* calls it a "preface," or *jo*). Many Edo-period printed versions of this poem have *yama-oroshi* instead of *yama-oroshi yo,* but the meaning is the same in both cases: the poet is calling out to the wind, to which he is implicitly comparing the heartless woman.

The Pictures

The *Zōsanshō* [**74–1**] shows Toshiyori looking across the picture frame at Hase Temple; the steep angle of the wall around the temple gives a sense of both the steepness of the mountain and the idea of the wind blowing down it (*oroshi* means literally "to drop down"). Many commentaries describe Hatsuse as "amidst mountains" (*yama-naka*), which is how the Kyoto artist portrays it [**74–2**]. This is also how Moronobu shows it in the *Sugata-e* [**74–4**], where presumably it is the woman who is complaining about the oblivious male (the poem simply says "person," or *hito*). (Note that the inscription here has *oroshi yo.*) The *Kangyoku* [**74–3**] gives a good sense of the wind blowing, but Hatsuse itself disappears entirely.

74-1

うらうらと人と
いやしげなせ乃を
いのりぬる

74-2

74-3

74-4

POEM 75

chigiri-okishi
sasemo ga tsuyu wo
inochi nite
ahare kotoshi no
aki no inumeri[43]

Depending with my life
on promises that fell thick
    as dew on *sasemo* plants—
alas! the autumn of this year too
seems to be passing.

Fujiwara no Mototoshi

Mototoshi (1060–1142), together with
Toshiyori (Poem 74), was a leading poet
of the Insei period (1086–1185).[44] A col-
lection of his poetry is extant, and he has
105 poems in the *Kin'yōshū* and later
imperial anthologies. He is one of the
Late Classical Six Poetic Immortals.

Commentary

The headnote to this poem reads:

> When [Mototoshi's son] Bishop
> Kōkaku requested to be made a Lec-
> turer for the Vimalakīrti Ceremony,
> he was repeatedly overlooked, so
> [Mototoshi] complained to Former
> Chancellor [Tadamichi], the Bud-
> dhist Novice of Hosshōji. Although
> Tadamichi said, " 'The fields of
> Shimeji . . .' [i.e., rely on me]," when his son was again passed over the next
> year, Mototoshi sent Tadamichi the following.

Tadamichi is alluding to a poem attributed to the Bodhisattva of Compassion,
Kannon, in the *ShinKokinshū* (Buddhism): 1917:

    naho tanome
    shimejhi ga hara no
    sasemo-gusa
    wa ga yo no naka ni
    aramu kagiri ha

    Still rely on me!
    for I will help those of
        this world for as long
    as there are *sasemo* plants
    in the fields of Shimeji.

Mototoshi in turn alludes to this poem in his complaint to Tadamichi by pick-
ing up on the image of the *sasemo* plants. Although Ariyoshi says there are no
differing opinions in the explanations of this verse, modern scholars disagree

as to whether or not *sasemo* is functioning as a pivot word. *Sasemo-gusa* is a variant of *sashimo-gusa*. As seen in Poem 51, *sa shimo* also means "to that extent," and it functions as a pivot word in Sanekata's poem. Most modern commentators, including Shimazu, claim that *sasemo* has the same function in this poem—in other words, the reader is meant to replace *sasemo* with *sashimo* and to understand the latter as a pun. This interpretation seems to start with Yūsai, but Ariyoshi does not mention it.

The Pictures

Given the complicated intertextuality and sequence of events surrounding this poem, it is not surprising that the artists seem somewhat confused as to who is petitioning whom. In the upper register of the *Sugata-e* [**75–4**], Moronobu shows the most clearly correct composition: the low-ranking Mototoshi is humbly petitioning the powerful Tadamichi from below the veranda. (The figures are even clearer in the *Eiga*.) But in the *Zōsanshō* version [**75–2**] it is hard to decide who is the figure of higher rank. A slight change in position by the Kyoto artist [**75–3**] makes it seem as if it is the monk who is petitioning the courtier, which is incorrect. Interestingly, the object of the petition—to be an officiant at the ceremony—is depicted in the middle register. Hasegawa [**75–1**] shows the poet (in a figure derived from the Tan'yū album) gazing out at what one must take as *mogusa*, much as he portrayed Sanekata [**51–3**], only in this case the plant is laden with dewdrops. The Tan'yū album also depicts *mogusa*, with yellow flowers, shrouded in mist.

75-1

75-2

ちぎるをさきと聞ゆるに
露とおかそ
裏もしの
のゝ袂を
しぼりつゝ
めつゝ

75-3

75-4

POEM 76

wata no hara
kogi-idete mireba
hisakata no
kumowi ni magafu
okitsu shiranami[1]

As I row out into
the wide sea-plain and look
all around me—
the white waves of the offing
could be mistaken for clouds!

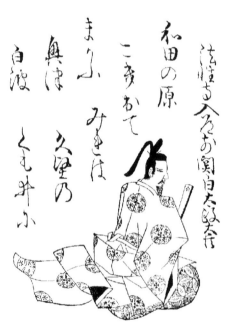

Former Prime Minister and Chancellor, the Hosshōji Buddhist Novice

Hosshōji Nyūdō Saki no Kanpaku Daijō-daijin was Fujiwara no Tadamichi (1097–1164). Son of Tadazane (1078–1162), he succeeded his father as Kanpaku in 1121, became regent *(sesshō)* on the accession of Sutoku in 1123, and then again on the accession of Konoe in 1141. After the death of Konoe in 1155, Tadamichi supported the selection of Toba's son Masahito (the future Emperor GoShirakawa) as emperor but was opposed by his own brother, Yorinaga (1120–1156), who supported Retired Emperor Sutoku's reaccession. This conflict led to the Hōgen Disturbance of 1156, during which Yorinaga was killed.

Tadamichi was the recipient of Poem 75 and the father of Jien (Poem 95). He was a great patron of poetry as well as an accomplished poet in both Japanese and Chinese. He has a collection of Chinese verse, the *Hosshōji Kanpaku Shū,* and one of Japanese verse, the *Tadamichi Shū.* He has fifty-eight poems in the *Kin'yōshū* and later imperial anthologies.

Commentary

The *Shikashū* states that this poem was composed during the reign of Emperor Sutoku (the poem can be dated to 1135) on the topic "gazing afar over the ocean" *(kaijō enbō).* There is a wide variety of disagreement about this poem. One argument is over what is being confused with what: clouds and waves (*Yoritaka-bon,* Mabuchi, and others); sky and waves (*Komezawa-bon,* Keichū, *Iken,* and others); or sky and sea (the *Kaikan Shō*). This question in turn influences the interpretation of the word *kumowi* and hence the import of the poem as a whole. The standard interpretation is that *kumowi* means "clouds," but other commentators take it to mean the sky or heavens. The *Komezawa-bon* (1452) relates a "secret interpretation" *(hisetsu),* which the *Shisetsu Shō* (1658) describes this way:

> The phrase *kumowi ni magafu* has a perilous significance: although, when looking at him from below, one would be envious of this regent, who has taken control of the government and conducts its affairs, in fact, if one thinks of his situation from his position, then one realizes that it is as perilous as a boat lost in the fog *(kumowi)* on the ocean.

As the *Zatsudan* (1692) points out, this reading relies on *kumowi* meaning "above the clouds"—that is, the court—and on understanding *magafu* ("to mistake one thing for another") as *mayofu* ("to be lost")—that is, "lost in the clouds" means "confused by affairs of state."[2] In contrast, the *ShinShō* (1804) categorically states that "there is nothing hidden" in this poem (echoing words of Yūsai).

The Pictures

The Tan'yū album has skiffs on the sea drawn in an ink-painting style. The phrasing of this poem of course invites comparison with that of Takamura (Poem 11).[3] If we compare the *Zōsanshō* picture for Takamura [**11–2**] with that for Tadamichi [**76–3**], we notice that the latter includes a building (not present in the Tan'yū painting for Tadamichi either). The only explanation for this element is that it represents the palace, along the lines of the *Komezawa-bon*'s political interpretation. This feature has been retained by the Kyoto artist [**76–4**], who also brings the cloud line down to emphasize the confusion between the clouds and the waves. These latter, in turn, are exaggerated by the *Kangyoku* artist [**76–1**], where the accompanying commentary explicitly states that the confusion is between the clouds and the waves (an issue Yūsai does not address). It is unclear whether there is also a political suggestion in the *Sugata-e* [**76–2**]: the male figure is obviously high-ranking, and the plum being brought to him is often used as a symbol of loyalty.

76-1

76-2

76-3

76-4

POEM 77

se wo hayami
iha ni sekaruru
taki-gaha no
warete mo suwe ni
*ahamu to zo omofu*⁴

Because the current is swift,
even though the rapids,
　　blocked by a boulder,
are divided, like them, in the end,
we will surely meet, I know.

Retired Emperor Sutoku
Sutoku In (often read "Shutoku" in early texts; 1119–1164) reigned 1123–1141 as the seventy-fifth sovereign. Eldest son of Emperor Toba, he succeeded his father at the age of five but was made to abdicate in favor of his younger brother, Konoe. When Konoe died, Toba placed another of his sons, GoShirakawa, on the throne rather than one of Sutoku's, and this led to an armed conflict known as the Hōgen Disturbance of 1156. Sutoku's side lost, and he was exiled to Sanuki province on the island of Shikoku, where he died in 1164. He sponsored many hundred-poem competitions and ordered the sixth imperial anthology, the *Shikashū*, from Akisuke (Poem 79). He has seventy-eight poems in the *Shikashū* and later imperial anthologies.

Commentary
Debate centers on whether the expression *warete mo* means simply "even though it is divided" or is also a pivot word meaning "by all means" *(warinaku)*. There are also those who believe the first three lines are simply a preface *(jo)* rather than a simile.

369

The Pictures
The biggest difference among the pictorializations seems to be how the artists understand the word *taki-gaha*. Literally the words indicate "waterfall-river," but the term means "rapids"—that is, a river rushing toward a waterfall. Visualizations of this notion range from shallows in the *Sugata-e* [**77–4**] (apparently following the Tan'yū album), to a series of small falls and rapids in the *Zōsanshō* [**77–1**] and the *Shikishi Moyō* kimono design [**77–3**], to a completely vertical falls in the Kyoto edition [**77–2**] and Hasegawa. These latter interpretations are perhaps suggested by the verb *tagiru*, "to seethe," which appears in commentary paraphrases. The conception of the boulder in the kimono design and the *Zōsanshō* is also similar. The *Sugata-e* shows the emperor shielding his face while two women approach, one with an incense burner, punning on the word *taki-mono*, which means "incense."

77-1   77-2

77-3

77-4

POEM 78

ahajhi shima
kayofu chidori no
naku kowe ni
iku yo ne-zamenu
suma no seki-mori[5]

The crying voices
of the plovers who visit
   from Awaji Island—
how many nights have they awakened him,
the barrier-keeper of Suma?

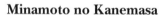

Minamoto no Kanemasa

Kanemasa (dates uncertain) participated in many poetry contests during the time of Retired Emperor Horikawa. There is no collection of his poems, and he has only seven poems in the *Kin'yōshū* and later imperial anthologies.

Commentary

Although this poem is grammatically irregular, there is surprisingly little debate over its basic meaning. While *nezamenu* would usually mean "do not wake," all commentators agree that the meaning is affirmative and perfective ("have they awakened him"), although their grammatical rationalizations vary.[6] Far more debate has gone into the question of whether the verb *kayofu* means that the plovers are coming from Awaji (Yūsai and most modern commentators) or going back and forth to Awaji, as suggested by the *Kamijō-bon* (mid-Muromachi) and others. The poem is understood to allude to the "Suma" chapter of *The Tale of Genji*, during which Genji was in exile. As such, it follows from the previous poem, though not one commentary suggests *ahajhi* as a pun for *ahaji*, "will not meet."[7]

The Pictures

Although the Yūsai commentary says that the birds are coming, the *Zōsanshō* [**78–1**] clearly has them going, as does the Tan'yū album. This poem is quoted in the famous *nō* play *Atsumori*, which may explain the prominent pine in the

Zōsanshō picture, which is rather reminiscent of the tree typically painted on the back wall of a *nō* stage. The birds' direction is reversed by the Kyoto artist [**78–2**], who adds boats and nets to the beach. Nets also appear in the *Shikishi Moyō* kimono design [**78–3**]. The *Hyakushu Hinagata* kimono pattern [**78–4**] demonstrates that a certain amount of deduction was needed to decipher the ideographs as well as the poetic allusion: the first character, in the upper right, is clearly *awa*, but the second character, *ji*, is written in a somewhat unorthodox form. This is even more true for the final character, *shima:* this ideograph for "island" is composed of the characters for "mountain" and "bird," and traditionally the "mountain" could be written under the bird (as in modern standardized orthography) or to its left. In the kimono pattern, however, "mountain" has been written *above* "bird." Only by reading all three ideographs—*awa-ji-shima*—together could a viewer be certain of the meaning of the last.

78-1 78-2

78-3

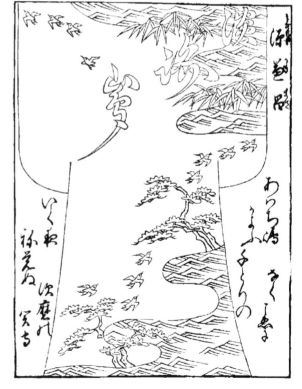

78-4

POEM 79

aki-kaze ni
tanabiku kumo no
tae-ma yori
more-idzuru tsuki no
kage no sayakesa[8]

From between the breaks
in the clouds that trail
on the autumn wind
leaks through the moon-
light's clear brightness!

Master of the Western Capital Akisuke

Akisuke is Sakyō no Daibu Fujiwara no Akisuke (1090–1155). The capital of Heian-kyō (modern Kyoto) was divided into eastern and western sectors (literally, Right and Left), each of which was under the control of an administrative office headed by a "master," or *daibu*.[9] Akisuke was the father of Kiyosuke (Poem 84) and Kenshō and founded the Rokujō school of poets who opposed the new styles championed by the Mikohidari, led by Teika's father, Shunzei (Poem 83). Akisuke was commissioned by Emperor Sutoku (Poem 77) to compile the sixth imperial anthology, the *Shikashū*. He has a personal collection of poems as well as eighty-four poems in the *Kin'yōshū* and later imperial anthologies.

Commentary

The headnote in the *ShinKokinshū* reads: "When he submitted a hundred-poem sequence to Retired Emperor Sutoku." There are no significant disagreements concerning this poem.

The Pictures

The *Zōsanshō* [**79–1**] has the poet on a veranda looking out at the moon breaking between the clouds; in the garden are maple leaves and autumn flowers. These are also the motifs used in the *Shikishi Moyō* kimono design [**79–4**]. The Kyoto artist [**79–2**], and most later artists, reduce the plant life to the maple leaves alone. The *Sugata-e* [**79–3**] has none of these but presents a customer with a professional musician beside him, suggesting a mood of contentment similar to that in Poem 33 [**33–3**]—this time using the moon, rather than the sun, as a topos.

79-1

79-2

79-3

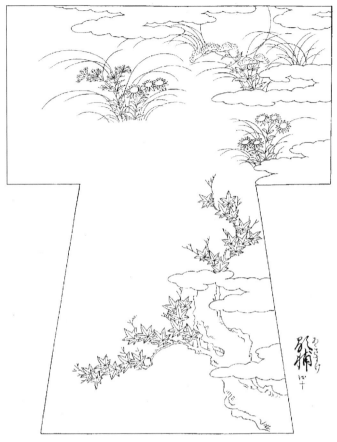

79-4

POEM 80

nagakaramu
kokoro mo shirazu
kuro-kami no
midarete kesa ha
mono wo koso omohe[10]

I do not even know
how long your feelings will last.
My long black hair
is all disheveled and, this morning,
my thoughts too are in a tangle!

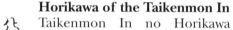

Horikawa of the Taikenmon In
Taikenmon In no Horikawa (dates uncertain) was a daughter of Minamoto no Akinaka. She served Taikenmon In, Emperor Toba's consort and the mother of Emperor Sutoku (Poem 77). One of the Late Classical Six Poetic Immortals, she has a personal poetry collection and has sixty-six poems in the *Kin'yōshū* and later imperial anthologies.

Commentary
The headnote to this poem in the *Senzaishū* reads: "When submitting a hundred-poem sequence, composed on the sentiment of love *(kohi no kokoro)*." Early commentaries (the *Yoritaka-bon, Chōkyō Shō, Komezawa-bon,* and *Minazuki Shō*) insisted that this was a "morning after" *(kinu-ginu)* poem written after the lovers had met for the very first time. Most commentators, however, do not specify whether the lovers had met before or not. There is continued debate on whether the poem comes to a grammatical halt after the second line *(shūshikei)* or continues *(ren'yōkei)*. All commentaries see the meaning as implying a "since" or "because," except for the *Kaikan Shō*, which sees the relationship as concessive: "although I do not know. . . ."

The Pictures
A bewildering variety of compositions are associated with this poem. The Tan'yū album has the poet hiding her face—or perhaps her hair—behind a fan. The *Zōsanshō* [**80–1**] shows a man leaving a woman, presumably after a night of love, and the Kyoto artist uses the same conception. In the *Sugata-e* [**80–4**] we have an insert of a court woman reclining and a stream running out-

378

side (most likely due to *nagakarumu* suggesting *nagaru*); in the foreground we see a woman in a robe decorated with pine branches observing a young woman preparing incense. The pine would seem to suggest longevity, and thus long fidelity, and we see it employed by Hasegawa [**80–2**] as well. Yet the *Shikishi Moyō* kimono design [**80–3**] abandons this motif and has instead the characters "this morning" *(kesa)* superimposed on a fan, along with two tigers sporting at either end of a clump of bamboo. The *Kangyoku* and Porter artists use different compositions yet.

80-1

80-2

80-3

80-4

POEM 81

hototogisu
nakitsuru kata wo
nagamureba
tada ariake no
tsuki zo nokoreru [11]

The *hototogisu:*
when I gaze out towards where
   he was singing,
all that remains is the moon,
pale in the morning sky.

The Later Tokudaiji Minister of the Left

GoTokudaiji Sadaijin Fujiwara no Sanesada (1139–1191) was a nephew of Shunzei (Poem 83) and first cousin to Teika (Poem 97). He was called "the Later" to distinguish him from his grandfather, Saneyoshi, who was known by the same sobriquet. A diary and a personal poetry collection, the *Rinka Shū*, survive, and he has seventy-eight poems in the *Senzaishū* and later imperial anthologies.

Commentary

This poem was composed on a set topic *(dai):* "Hearing the *hototogisu* at dawn" *(akatsuki ni hototogisu wo kiku).* According to Ariyoshi, the "essential character" *(hon'i)* of this topic is "waiting up all night, from midnight to dawn, for one cry" of the *hototogisu*. The *hototogisu* is considered a bird of early summer,[12] and some commentaries argue that the poet is waiting to hear the bird's first song of the season *(Ōei Shō* and *Keikō Shō).*

The Pictures

As early as the Tan'yū album this poem is paired with the preceding to form what appears to be an exchange of love poems, even though both were in fact written as set topics, not based on actual events: Horikawa is shown hiding behind a fan, a gesture usually reserved in the album for exchanged poems, and Sanesada is shown in the midst of writing, perhaps a "morning after" *(kinuginu)* letter. The association between the two poets is made explicit in the *Eiga,* where they smile across the binding at each other. Likewise, as if continuing from the "morning after" verse of Poem 80, the *Zōsanshō* [**81–1**] shows a courtier on his way home from a lady's house early in the morning, though there is no commentary that suggests such an interpretation.[13] The same idea is presented in the *Sugata-e* [**81–3**], where a young woman carrying an iris *(ayame)*—

to indicate the early summer—replaces the page carrying a sword, a replacement that can be seen as a parody of the samurai in the *Zōsanshō*. The *Kangyoku* [**81–4**] preserves the flower while following the standard interpretation seen also in the Kyoto version [**81–2**]: the *Keikō Shō*, the *Yoritaka-bon*, and the *ShinShō* all speak of the poet getting up and looking out when he hears the cry. In the *Kangyoku*, however, there is no bird to be seen.

81-1

81-2

81-3

81-4

POEM 82

omohi-wabi
sate mo inochi ha
aru monowo
uki ni tahenu ha
namida narikeri[14]

Miserable,
nonetheless, somehow
I cling to life, but
it is my tears
that cannot endure the pain!

Master of the Law Dōin
Dōin Hōshi (1090–?1179), whose secular name was Fujiwara no Atsuyori, was a son of Kiyotaka. He took the tonsure in 1172. From the Eiryaku era (1160) on he was a participant in the major poetic events of his day and a member of the "Garden in the Poetic Woods" (Karin'en), a circle of some three dozen poets that gathered about Shun'e (Poem 85). None of Dōin's poetic collections has survived, but he has forty-one poems in the *Senzaishū* and later imperial anthologies.

Commentary
This poem is based on a somewhat contrived contrast between the poet's "life" and his "tears": while the poet's life can endure the bitterness of unrequited love, his tears cannot and they fall in despair. This poem appears among the love poems of the *Senzaishū* as "topic unknown." Accordingly, we are unable to tell whether it was a love poem written for an actual person or simply composed on a set topic, as for a poetry contest. Nor do we know whether the poet wrote it before or after he had become a priest. Nonetheless, virtually all commentaries interpret this poem as a love poem bemoaning a lover's cruelty.

The Pictures
This poem provides the *Sugata-e* [82–1] with one of its most clearly homoerotic interpretations. A young samurai, coquettishly adjusting his collar, looks down on the scruffy monk in a composition derived from the Tan'yū album and in the manner of *mitate-e* parodies that typically paired a young prostitute with a religious figure such as Daruma (Bodhidharma, the Zen patriarch). As the upper register shows, however, the usual pictorialization shows the poet contemplating a natural scene, thereby deemphasizing, if not denying entirely, the romantic nature of the poem. Such pictorializations then had to deal with the

complete lack of natural imagery in the poem, characteristic of the Kyōgoku-Reizei poets.[15] The *Sugata-e* seizes upon the image of a river, which suggests both tears *(namida)* and endurance *(tafu)*.[16] The *Zōsanshō* [**82–2**] shows the poet contemplating autumn flowers, which may be meant to suggest dew (and tears) and evanescence. The Kyoto artist shows a barer, more forlorn scene; the Porter artist provides a landscape, again suggesting a more philosophical interpretation of the poem.[17] The two kimono designs provide a study in contrasts. The *Hyakushu Hinagata* [**82–3**] depicts a kind of crayfish: an *Ise ebi*. (The word *ebi* can be written with the characters "old man of the sea.") Strung across the robe are nets that cannot hold back the waves and buckets of tears, clearly indicated by the characters *omohi-wabi* ("miserable") superimposed on the design. The *Shikishi Moyō* [**82–4**], by contrast, seems to have emptied out any unhappiness and uses the poem only as a celebration of longevity, indicated by the phoenix and the chrysanthemums.

82-1

82-2

82-3

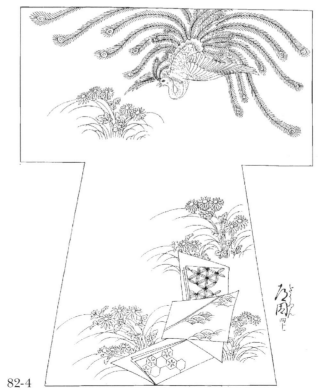

82-4

POEM 83

yo no naka yo	Within this world
michi koso nakere	there is, indeed, no path!
omohi-iru	Even deep in these mountains
yama no oku ni mo	I have entered, heart set,
shika zo naku naru[18]	I seem to hear the deer cry!

**Master of the Grand Empress'
Palace Shunzei**

Kōtaikō-gū no Daibu Shunzei, Fujiwara no Toshinari (1114–1204), was the poetic arbiter of his day and the father of Teika (Poem 97). He edited the seventh imperial anthology, the *Senzaishū*. His personal poetry collection is entitled the *Chōshū Eisō*. He has 452 poems in the *Shikashū* and later imperial anthologies.

Commentary

The headnote to this poem reads: "Composed on 'deer,' when composing a hundred-poem sequence on 'personal grievances' (*jukkai*)." *Omohi-iru* is a pivot word: *omohi-iru*, "to set one's heart on, be possessed with an idea"; *iru*, "to enter" (the mountains). Medieval commentaries concerned themselves chiefly with what the poet has his "heart set on" or what idea he was possessed with, for instance, the sorrow of "this world" or the transitoriness of life. Explanations were of three types:

1. The poet is possessed by the idea of the "melancholy" (*usa*) of the world (as in *Ōei Shō, Chōkyō Shō, Komezawa-bon, Minō Shō*, and others).
2. He is possessed by the idea of his own mortality (*wa ga mi no hakanasa*) (as in *Sōgi Shō*).
3. Bemoaning the political disorder of the world, he opts for reclusion.

The last interpretation is found as early as Keichū's *Kaikan Shō* and was repeated throughout the Edo period—especially in connection with the anecdote that Shunzei had originally withdrawn this poem from the *Senzaishū*, fearing that it would in fact be interpreted politically, and that it was included only after a special order from Retired Emperor GoShirakawa.[19]

The Pictures

This poem invites comparison with the other "deer" poem in this collection, by Sarumaru (Poem 5), a connection explicitly made by the *Keikō Shō*. Whereas in the earlier poem artists tended to depict only the deer [**5–1**], for Shunzei's poem most artists tend to show the poet looking at the deer, as in the *Zōsanshō* [**83–1**]. This depiction is curious, as the poem specifically indicates, with the word *naru*, that the speaker can hear but not see the deer. (*Naru* indicates conjecture based on auditory experience [MJ-*rashii, yō da*].) And in fact no deer is presented in the Tan'yū album. Nonetheless, the conception of the two poems in the *Sugata-e* [**5–2; 83–2**] is very similar, though the idea of seclusion is indicated in the latter by the motif of the brushwood fence on the man's robe. It is unclear whether the presence of both a woman and a young girl is supposed to represent some quandary for the man. Originally the cry of the deer was understood to mean the belling of a stag for a mate, as indicated visually (and paradoxically) by a pair of deer, both stag and doe [**5–1; 83–2**].[20] The *Kangyoku* [**83–3**] shows the poet actually "entering" the mountains and presents only one deer, a stag. The *Shikishi Moyō* kimono design [**83–4**] avoids the issue (if indeed it was one) by using the character for "deer" *(shika)*, which can be either singular or plural.

83-1

83-2

83-3

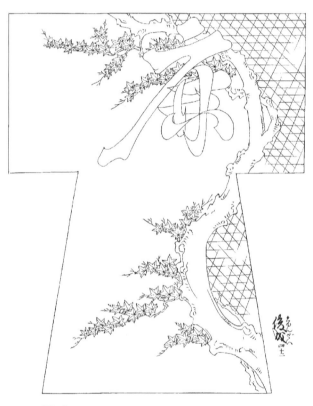

83-4

POEM 84

nagaraheba
mata kono goro ya
shinobaremu
ushi to mishi yo zo
ima ha kohishiki[21]

If I live on longer,
shall I again, I wonder,
    yearn for these days?
The world that I once saw as
bitter, now, is dear to me!

Lord Fujiwara no Kiyosuke

Fujiwara no Kiyosuke Ason (1104–1177) was the second son of Akisuke (Poem 79), with whom he frequently disagreed but from whom he eventually inherited the leadership of the Rokujō school of poetry. He compiled the *ShokuShikashū* for Emperor Nijō, but the emperor died before it was completed, preventing it from being officially made an imperial anthology. Kiyosuke is also known for his works on poetics, especially the *Ōgi Shō* and the *Fukuro-zōshi*. He has a personal poetry collection and is one of the Late Classical Thirty-Six Poetic Immortals. He has ninety-four poems in the *Senzaishū* and later imperial anthologies.

Commentary

While this poem is listed as "topic unknown" in the *ShinKokinshū,* in the *Kiyosuke Ason Shū* the headnote tells us that the poem was sent to the poet's cousin, Kinnori, sometime between 1130 and 1136. Medieval commentaries refer only to the *ShinKokinshū,* but all agree that the meaning of the poem is "clear" and spend little time asking what the poet's specific complaint might have been. Indeed, those that do ask this question see the poem as a lament over the general decline of the world (as in *Kamijō-bon, Tenri-bon, Shikishi Waka*) or, among early modern commentaries, a reference to the political disturbances of the Hōgen era (as in *Iken*). It is in early modern commentaries that we first see the suggestion that the poem is based on a verse by the Chinese poet Po Chü-i (as in *Zatsudan* and *San'oku Shō*).

The Pictures

Again, as in the previous poem, artists were confronted with a total lack of visual imagery in this poem, and no pictorialization appears in the Tan'yū album. The *Zōsanshō* [84–1] starts by showing the poet gazing at a pine tree, symbol of longevity. It is unclear whether the landscape is a beach, a river, or a field, though the first of these options seems most likely. The Kyoto artist [**84–2**] makes the scene clearly a river (perhaps from *nagarahe* suggesting *nagarahi*, "to keep on flowing"), changing the tree from a pine to something less distinct. The addition of some sort of cloth hanging over the railing is intriguing: it may be meant to suggest the *shinobu mojhi-zuri* cloth of Poem 14, making Kiyosuke's verse a lament for an unhappy love affair in the past. In the *Sugata-e* [**84–3**] the water motif has moved to the hem of the young woman's robe (see **82–3**), as have the blossoms that originally decorated Kiyosuke's robe in the *Zōsanshō*'s *kasen-e*. The poet's robe is now decorated with autumn leaves. The figure of the poet is clearly modeled on the rather Chinese-looking portrait in the Tan'yū album, both with identical beards, but in the *Sugata-e* a vague nostalgia has perhaps been sharpened into a lovers' spat. The *Shikishi Moyō* kimono design [**84–4**] keeps the winter pine tree, to which is added another symbol of longevity, the cranes. The character for "to yearn" *(shinobu)* is placed over the pine in a manner similar to the reed script *(ashi-de)* found in *maki-e* lacquerware. The *Kangyoku* has the poet contemplating what appears to be bush clover *(hagi)*.

84-1

84-2

84-3

84-4

POEM 85

yomosugara　　　　　　All through the night
mono-omofu koro ha　　recently, as I dwell on things,
akeyaranu　　　　　　　even the gap between the doors
neya no hima sahe　　　of my bedroom, which does not lighten,
*tsurenakarikeri*²²　　　　seems cruel and heartless to me.

Master of the Law Shun'e

Shun'e Hōshi (b. 1113) was the son of Minamoto no Toshiyori (Poem 74). He lived near Shirakawa in a residence called "The Garden in the Poetic Woods" (Karin'en), where he gathered a wide range of poets and held poetry meetings and contests. Among his students was Kamo no Chōmei, who recorded many of Shun'e's words in a work called the *Mumyō Shō*.²³ Shun'e's own personal poetry collection is called the *Rin'yō Shū*. He is one of the Late Classical Six Poetic Immortals and has eighty-three poems in the *Shikashū* and later imperial anthologies.

Commentary

The headnote of this poem says that it was "composed as a love poem"—in other words, that it was composed on a set topic. Accordingly, the speaker of the poem should be understood to be a woman complaining about her cruel lover whom she awaits through the night in vain: she keeps waiting for the first signs of light to peek through the gaps of her door, but even that does not come to end her watch. Some commentaries, such as the *Yoritaka-bon* and the *Kamijō-bon,* offer markedly different interpretations, based on reading the *ha* of *koro ha* as contrastive, but they are in a very small minority. *Akeyaranu* appears in all early copies of this poem, but many early modern editions, from the *GoYōzei Tennō Hyakunin Isshu Shō* (1606) on, have *akeyarade*—a significant change that would yield a translation such as "it does not dawn, / and even the gaps . . ."

The Pictures

The *Zōsanshō* [85–1], like all other artists, depicts the speaker as Shun'e himself, not a woman. The flowers in the foreground indicate that the season is autumn; the candle indicates that the night is still dark *(akeyarazu);* the roof is similar to that found in the Tan'yū album. The Kyoto artist [**85–2**] keeps the same conception but manages to depict the gap between the sliding doors through which the first signs of morning light would come. Like the earlier artist, he places the stairs so as to suggest that the speaker is waiting for someone, but he replaces the autumn flowers with maple leaves and reeds. The *Sugata-e* [**85–3**], unlike the previous two examples, has the poem transcribed as *akeyaranu*, rather than *akeyarade*, and written in two horizontal bands. Certainly the young acolyte suggests a homoerotic interpretation.[24] In contrast to the autumnal setting of the first two pictorializations, the *Shikishi Moyō* kimono design [**85–4**] identifies the poem with spring: plums coming out of a *bonseki* tray (*bon* could also mean "priest"), the suggestion of a moon on the left, and the phrase *yomosugara* written in the *katakana* syllabary associated chiefly with Buddhist scriptures, Chinese writing, and, by extension, men.

85-1   85-2

俊惠法師

父八後頼孙師

よもすから
もの思ふ比や
ふけの内の
やりど
のひまも
つれなから
りぬ

85-3

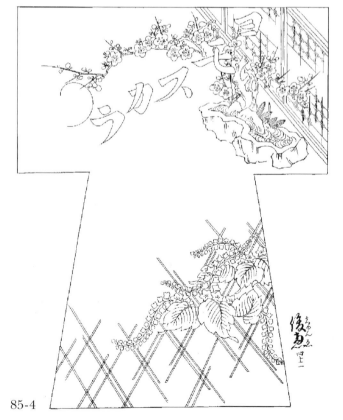

85-4

POEM 86

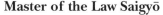

nageke tote
tsuki ya ha mono wo
omohasuru
kakochi-gaho naru
wa ga namida kana [25]

"Lament!" does it say?
Is it the moon that makes me
    dwell on things?—No, and yet,
look at the tears flowing down
my reproachful face!

Master of the Law Saigyō

Saigyō Hōshi (1118–1190), born Satō no Norikiyo, took vows at the age of twenty-three. He was a friend of Shunzei (Poem 83) and became famous for his poetic wanderings throughout Japan. He has several personal poetry anthologies; the best known is the *Sanka Shū*.[26] He has 266 poems in the *Senzaishū* and later imperial anthologies.

Commentary

In the *Senzaishū* the topic of this poem is given as "love before the moon." In Saigyō's *Sanka Shū* its topic is given as "the moon" in a section of thirty-seven love poems. Almost all commentaries agree that the poem is in the persona of a resentful lover: "Is it the moon that is causing me to be lost in thought, as if commanding me 'Lament!'?—no, that cannot be; I am brooding about love. And yet, as I gaze at the moon, my tears flow down just as if it were the moon's fault."

In contrast to this standard interpretation, both the *Keikō Shō* and the *Kamijō-bon* interpret Saigyō's poem as an allusive variation *(honka-dori)* of Poem 23 by Chisato. Such a reading changes the poem from one of love to a solitary and philosophical complaint. Finally, both the *Yūsai Shō* and the *Kaikan Shō* suggest that Saigyō's inspiration for this poem derived from verses by the Chinese poet Po Chü-i.

The Pictures

The *Zōsanshō* [**86–1**] shows the poet gazing out from his hut at the moon as a river flows underneath. Such a pictorialization is more in line with the minority *Kamijō-bon* interpretation of the poem as a philosophical, rather than romantic, lament. The Kyoto artist [**86–2**] gives much the same interpretation, though he removes the river and introduces a pine, perhaps to suggest the romantic idea of "pining" *(matsu)*. In keeping with the Kyoto artist's general tendency, the hut is better built and the poet is dressed in higher ecclesiastical garb than in the *Zōsanshō* version. In contrast to these depictions of the poet at home, the *Sugata-e* [**86–3**] presents the more popular image of Saigyō as traveler, though clearly it is based on the Tan'yū album. It was in this role that he was particularly important to the famous Edo-period poet Bashō, whose name means "banana plant." Thus it is perhaps not surprising that some artists, such as the *Kangyoku* and Hasegawa [**86–4**], show a banana plant beside Saigyō.

86-1   86-2

86-3

86-4

POEM 87

murasame no
tsuyu mo mada hinu
maki no ha ni
kiri tachi-noboru
aki no yufu-gure[27]

While the raindrops of
the passing shower have not yet dried from
near the leaves of the evergreens,
the mist is already rising, on
this evening in autumn.

Master of the Law Jakuren
Jakuren Hōshi (d. 1202) was born Fujiwara no Sadanaga. A nephew of Shunzei (Poem 83), he was one of the poets of the Mikohidari house, along with Teika (Poem 97) and Ietaka (Poem 98). He was one of the editors of the *ShinKokinshū*, as well, but died before its completion. He has a personal poetry collection and has 117 poems in the *Senzaishū* and later imperial anthologies.

Commentary
There is little basic disagreement about this descriptive poem, whose pictorial diction Ariyoshi suggests is based on monochrome ink-painting. Interpretations fall into two camps, however, over the issue of whether the poem's main interest is in the convergence of the various natural phenomena (as in *Ōei Shō, Keikō Shō,* Shimazu), as translated above, or in the transition from one to the other (as in *Yoritaka-bon, Kamijō-bon,* and others). Teika's appreciation of this poem seems to have come late in life: he did not vote for its inclusion in the *ShinKokinshū* or include it in many of his other anthologies. But by the time of the *Eiga no Ittei,* written by Teika's son Tame'ie (1198–1275), the phrase "the mist is already rising" *(kiri tachi-noboru)* was associated exclusively with Jakuren as a *nushi aru kotoba,* or "expression with an owner."

The Pictures
The Tan'yū album has a lovely mountain scene of mist rising through a grove of *maki (Sciadopitys verticillata).* The *Zōsanshō* pictorialization [**87–1**] presents scruffier, more pinelike trees, with some autumn grasses, and puts the primary emphasis on the shower, while introducing the posture of the poet raising his hand to his brow to gaze out at the scene. The Kyoto artist [**87–2**] takes the same basic composition but refines it considerably: the trees are more substantial; he has

added cloudlike mist; and raindrops lie among the grasses (they are said to be "near," not "on," the leaves). The *Kangyoku* artist [**87–4**] is perhaps even more successful: the rain is confined to one-half of the picture (suggesting transition rather than convergence), the mist is clearly rising from the ground, and the raindrops are on the grasses. Finally, the *Sugata-e* [**87–3**], following up on an erotic interpretation of this poem already suggested in the Tan'yū album through its pairing with the next poem, by Kōkamon In no Bettō, presents a monk gazing at a youth, as if marveling at the convergence of so much loveliness.

87-1

87-2

87-3

87-4

POEM 88

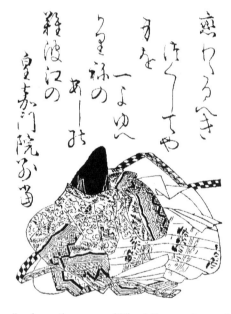

naniha-e no
ashi no kari-ne no

hito-yo yuwe
miwotskushite ya

kohi-wataru-beki[28]

Due to that single night
of fitful sleep, short as a reed's joint cut at
the root,
from Naniwa Bay,
am I to exhaust myself, like the channel-
markers,
passing my days in longing?

The Steward of Kōkamon In

Kōkamon In no Bettō (dates unknown)
was the daughter of Minamoto no Toshi-
taka and served Emperor Sutoku's
empress Seishi, who was later known as
Kōkamon In. Lady Bettō, as she is some-
times called, has only nine poems in the
Senzaishū and later imperial anthologies.

Commentary

The *Senzaishū* states that this poem was
composed for a poetry contest on the
topic of "love meeting at travel lodgings"
(tabi no yado ni afu kohi). As the length of
the translation suggests, this poem is a
tour de force of pivot words *(kake-kotoba)*.
Kari-ne means both "cut root" and "tem-
porary sleep," as on a journey. *Hito-yo*
means both "one segment (of a reed)"
and "one night." *Mi wo tsukushite* means
"exhausting myself," while a *miwotsukushi* is a channel-marker for boats. "From
Naniwa Bay" is a preface *(jo)* for "reeds." Both the *Komezawa-bon* and the *Yori-
tsune-bon* suggest that this poem is an allusive variation *(honka-dori)* on Poem 20
by Motoyoshi. While Ariyoshi states that it is not necessary to see the poem as
such, Lady Bettō's relative insignificance as a poet certainly suggests that Teika
included the poem to echo Motoyoshi's. A similarity to Lady Ise's verse (Poem
19) can also be noted.

The Pictures

The *Zōsanshō* pictorialization [**88–1**] contrasts with the same artist's composition for Lady Ise's poem [**19–1**]: the house is more rustic (perhaps to suggest a travel lodge), the reeds are less conspicuous, and unlike the picture for Motoyoshi's verse [**20–1**] it includes a channel-marker. The *Sugata-e* [**88–2**] gives greater emphasis to the reeds and shows a woman looking very forlorn in a wave-patterned underrobe. The same wave pattern appears in the *Shikishi Moyō* kimono design [**88–3**] embossed with the characters "one night" *(hito-yo)*. Finally, the Porter artist [**88–4**] dispenses with all suggestion of travel lodgings and places the poet in front of water and reeds outside, but in a palatial residence, perhaps influenced by the poet's title.

88-1

88-2

88-3

88-4

POEM 89

tama no wo yo
taenaba taene
nagaraheba
shinoburu koto no
yohari mo zo suru [29]

O, jeweled thread of life!
if you are to break, then break now!
For, if I live on,
my ability to hide my love
will most surely weaken!

Princess Shokushi

Shokushi Naishinnō (also read "Shiki-shi"; d. 1201) was a daughter of Emperor GoShirakawa. She served as Kamo Priestess from 1159 to 1169. She studied poetry under Shunzei (Poem 83), and it was for her instruction that he produced his *Korai Fūtei Shō*. She has a personal poetry collection and has 155 poems in the *Senzaishū* and later imperial anthologies.[30]

Commentary

This poem is given in the *ShinKokinshū* as composed on the topic "hidden love" (*shinobu kohi*) from a hundred-poem sequence. There is general agreement on the poem's meaning except for the interpretations found in the *Kamijō-bon* and the *Minazuki Shō,* both of which unwittingly provide exemplary lessons in classical Japanese grammar and orthography. The *Kamijō-bon* takes *taenaba* as *tahenaba*—that is, not "to cease" but "to endure, bear." Accordingly, the upper verse is taken to mean that since the poet fears the discovery of her secret love, she finds her life unbearable. The *Minazuki Shō,* apparently due to a faulty command of classical grammar, takes *nagaraheba* as "since I live long" rather than "if I live long"—yielding a meaning of "since I have come to live this long my feelings will surely be revealed."[31]

The Pictures

The Tan'yū album version (jacket illustration) is a powerful portrait far different from the cute depiction of the Date version. Although no background is rendered, the Tan'yū portrait vividly expresses the sense of the poet's anguished secret love. The *Zōsanshō* [**89–1**] takes the words *koto* and *wo* as pivot words: *koto* meaning "matter" as well as a musical instrument and *wo* meaning "string" as well as serving as an object marker. The Kyoto artist [**89–2**] follows the same format, but he removes the stream (which may have been used to represent either the verb *tae* or *nagarahe*) and introduces an autumnal maple (in lieu of the *Zōsanshō*'s cherry blossoms, which suggest a parallel to Komachi's poem [**9–2**]), which might reflect the *Minazuki Shō* interpretation—that is, because the poet has lived on, her love will become apparent, like the leaves taking on color. The *Sugata-e* [**89–3**] shows the priestess herself (indicated by her *hakama* pant-skirt and *kichō*, or "curtain of state") in the process of reading, perhaps her own poems of secret love, while a serving-girl looks on in commiseration. The Porter illustration [**89–4**] is distinctive in showing the poet with a male courtier; the motif of hidden love is suggested by the mist-covered grasses on the screen in the background.[32]

89-1   89-2

89-3

89-4

POEM 90

misebaya na
wojima no ama no
sode dani mo
nure ni zo nureshi
iro ha kaharazu[33]

How I'd like to show him!
The sleeves of the fishermen
   of Male Island,
when it comes to wet, are wet indeed,
but their color doesn't change!

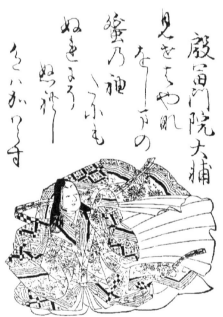

Inpumon In no Tayū
Dates uncertain, she lived sometime between 1131 and 1200. She was a daughter of Fujiwara no Nobunari and served Emperor GoShirakawa's daughter, Princess Ryōshi, called Inpumon In. She was a member of the poetic circle that centered on "the Garden in the Poetic Forest" (Karin'en) of Shun'e (Poem 85) and participated in many of its poetry contests. She has a personal poetry collection and has sixty-three poems in the *Senzaishū* and later imperial anthologies.

Commentary
The headnote to this poem indicates that it was composed on the topic of "love" for a poetry contest, probably one held at the Karin'en. The poem is an allusive variation *(honka-dori)* of a poem by Shigeyuki (Poem 48), contained in the *GoShūishū* (Love 4): 828:

matsushima ya
wojima no iso ni
asari seshi
ama no sode koso
kaku ha nureshika

Ah, Matsushima!
the sleeves of the fishermen
   who fish on the beach
of Male Island must be soaked
like these tear-soaked sleeves of mine!

Inpumon In no Tayū's poem rebuts Shigeyuki's over a distance of two hundred years: "How I would like to show that man [Shigeyuki] my sleeves! For, while the sleeves of the fishermen of Male Island [and his] may be very wet indeed, they do not change color like mine do, dyed by my blood-red tears!"[34] Male Island, or Ojima, is one of the larger islands in Matsushima.

The Pictures

While the *Soan-bon* figure seems to be lifting her sleeve to show it to her imaginary interlocutor, the Tan'yū figure [**90–1**] is startlingly bold with its sleeve high over the lady's head. Sleeves were typically thrown over one's head when caught in a sudden rainstorm, and sometimes too at moments of intense grief, though the expression on the poet's face belies this interpretation. In fact, the posture resembles nothing so much as dancing, such as we see in Yamamoto Shunshō's 1650 illustration to "The Maiden" *(Otome)* chapter of the *Tale of Genji*, his *E-iri Genji Monogatari* [**90–2**], a chapter that contains several love poems built on the image of sleeves and their color. The pictures of the *Zōsanshō* [**90–3**] and the Kyoto artist are virtually identical to each other in terms of composition. Matsushima has long been a famous scenic spot known for its seemingly countless little pine-clad islands. The *Zōsanshō* does not depict these islands, however, but indicates the place-name by showing a "salt cauldron" *(shiho-gama)*—another toponym associated with Matsushima.[35] "Salt" also suggests the pain associated with unrequited love or the death of a dear one. The composition contains three elements: men fishing with a net in a boat; a man bringing saltwater to another who is watching a cauldron; and the poet gazing at the scene from her veranda. Later pictorializations employ these same motifs. The *Shikishi Moyō* kimono design [**90–4**] uses the boat and nets, with the characters for "fishermen" *(ama)* embroidered on top. The fishing boat is also the main identifying element in the *Sugata-e*. The *Kangyoku* removes the figure of the poet, keeps the salt cauldron, and further suggests the place-name "Pine Island" (Matsushima) by the addition of pine trees.

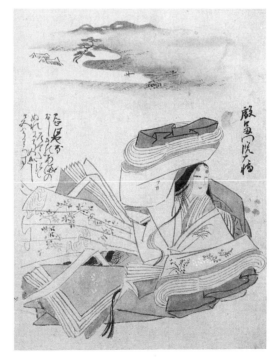

90-1

90-2

90-3

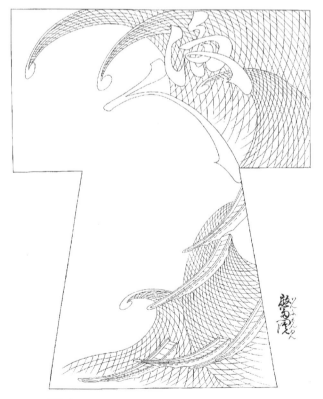

90-4

POEM 91

kirigirisu
naku ya shimo-yo no
sa-mushiro ni
koromo kata-shiki
hitori ka mo nemu[36]

When the crickets
cry in the frosty night,
    on the cold reed-mat,
spreading out my robe just for one,
must I sleep all alone?

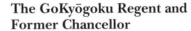

The GoKyōgoku Regent and Former Chancellor

GoKyōgoku Sesshō Saki no Daijō Daijin was Fujiwara no Yoshitsune (1169–1206). A son of Kanezane, his grandfather was Jien (Poem 95). He was a member of the Mikohidari poetic family, an editor of the *ShinKokinshū,* and the author of its Japanese preface. Although he died at the early age of thirty-seven, a personal poetry collection, the *Akishino Gessei Shū,* is extant. He has 319 poems in the *Senza-ishū* and later imperial anthologies, 78 of them in the *ShinKokinshū* alone—the most of any poet after Saigyō (Poem 86) and Jien. He is one of the Late Classical Thirty-Six Poetic Immortals.

Commentary

The debate around this poem has not been so much about the meaning of the poem itself as about the poem's sources. Ariyoshi states that Yoshitsune's verse is an allusive variation *(honka-dori)* of Poem 3 by Hitomaro and the following anonymous verse from the *Kokinshū* 14 (Love 4): 689:

sa-mushiro ni
koromo kata-shiki
koyoi mo ya
ware wo matsururamu
ujhi no hashi-hime

On the cold reed-mat
spreading out her robe just for one,
    this evening too
is she waiting for me—
the Goddess of Uji Bridge?

However, the *Minazuki Shō* suggests a poem by Saigyō (*SKKS* 5 [Autumn 2]: 472); the *Tenri-bon Kiki-gaki* and *Kaikan Shō* cite a poem from the *Tales of Ise* (Episode 63); and the *Uimanabi* and *Iken* identify a poem from the *Man'yō Shū* (9: 1692). Moreover, some of these commentaries suggest that the conception comes from a verse in the Chinese *Classic of Poetry (Shih Ching)*, the practical result of which is to change the location of the crying crickets from near the poet's bed to near the eaves of his house.

The Pictures

The Tan'yū album [**91–1**] is distinctive for portraying Yoshitsune at a writing desk in the midst of composing, presumably, the hundred-poem sequence from which the verse was taken. In the background is reed matting, though it appears to be serving as a fence. While the *Zōsanshō* print is hard to make out, the Kyoto version [**91–2**] makes it clear that the crickets are actually being depicted in the field—with rather frightening results. The bamboo plant would seem to be included to suggest the long night (an expression not actually part of Yoshitsune's poem but a major expression in the *honka* by Hitomaro). The inclusion of one cricket (on the far-right leaf) in the *Sugata-e* [**91–3**] is much more successful, and the pairing of figures transforms the poem from a lonely lament into a coy proposition. Another solution is found in the mid-nineteenth-century *Eiga Hyakunin Isshu* [**91–4**], with pictures by Utagawa Sadahide, where only the hut and grasses are depicted in the *uta-e* and the cricket is confined to the border decoration below the poet. Kimono design displays both extremes: the *Hyakushu Hinagata* book uses crickets and fans as the primary motif, while the *Shikishi Moyō* dispenses with the crickets altogether, showing instead a kind of fern with the words "frosty night" *(shimo-yo)*.

91-1

91-2

91-3

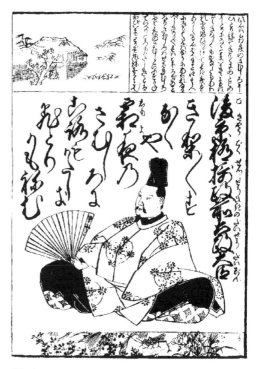

91-4

POEM 92

wa ga sode ha　　　　My sleeves are like
shihohi ni mienu　　　the rock in the offing that
oki no ishi no　　　　　can't be seen even at low tide,
hito koso shirane　　　unknown to anyone, but
kawaku ma mo nashi[37]　there's not a moment they are dry.

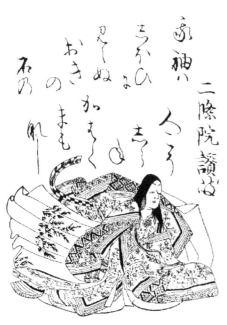

Sanuki of Nijō In

Nijō In no Sanuki was a daughter of Minamoto no Yorimasa. She lived from around 1141 to about 1217 and served first Retired Emperor Nijō (whence her sobriquet) and later GoToba's empress, Ninshi. Along with Shokushi (Poem 89), Sanuki was one of the leading female poets of her day and is counted among the Late Classical Thirty-Six Poetic Immortals. A collection of her early poetry is extant, and she has seventy-three poems in the *Senzaishū* and later imperial anthologies.

Commentary

The *Senzaishū* indicates that this poem was composed on the topic "love like a rock" *(ishi ni yosuru kohi),* and commentators have long been taken by Sanuki's preface *(jo)* "like a rock in the offing that cannot be seen even at low tide." The rock itself, however, has attracted a number of bizarre interpretations. The *Yūsai Shō* and others identify it with the "fertile burning rock" *(yokushōseki)* mentioned in a Chinese Taoist text, the *Chuang-tze.* The *Kamijō-bon* further identifies this rock as a lid on the furnace of hell, and the *Minō Shō* gives its dimensions as ten thousand leagues *(ri)* high and fifty thousand leagues wide. Kageki identifies the rock with one said to be in Wakasa province, where Sanuki's father was once posted.

The Pictures

The *Zōsanshō* pictorialization [**92–1**] is confusing: the poet is gazing out at a bay that includes birds, boats, and fishing nets (motifs that also appear in kimono designs), but it is unclear if the land with the nets is meant to represent the rock of the poem. The Kyoto artist [**92–2**] attempts to adjust things by replacing the nets with very definite (and rather Chinese) rocks and replacing the figure of the poet with her image from Moronobu's *kasen-e* [**92–1**]. The *Sugata-e*

[**92–3**] uses a different composition: water represents the unseen rock, and the poet, in a robe with a spiderweb motif, gazes at a young attendant. In this connection, note that the line *hito koso shirane* is ambiguous and can mean either that the man himself does not know of her love or that other people, that is, society, does not know of the woman's love. The former interpretation implies that the poem was one that would be sent to the man concerned (referring to him in the third person), while the latter suggests a soliloquy. The Tan'yū album typically shows the woman hiding her face behind a fan when the poem is actually being addressed to the man: while Sanuki does have a fan here, she is holding it closed, perhaps suggesting the ambiguity of interpretation. All other renditions, except the *Sugata-e*, show the poet alone. The *Kangyoku* [**92–4**] rendition represents the general solution to the problem of illustrating this poem: the poet is gazing at the offing, under which the rock is presumably hidden.

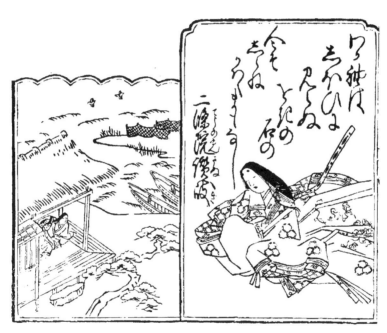

92-1

92-2

92-3

92-4

POEM 93

yo no naka ha
tsune ni mogamo na
nagisa kogu
ama no wo-bune no

tsunade kanashi mo[38]

If only this world
could always remain the same!
The sight of them towing
the small boats of the fishermen who row in
the tide
is touching indeed!

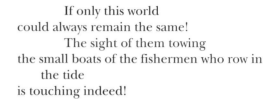

The Kamakura Minister of the Right
Kamakura no Udaijin was Minamoto no Sanetomo (1192–1219). He was the second son of Yoritomo, the founder of the Kamakura shogunate, and became shogun himself on the death of his older brother. He was assassinated at the age of twenty-eight. He studied poetry under Teika and received Teika's *Superior Poems of Our Times (Kindai Shūka)* as a manual of instruction. He was particularly fond of poetry in the *Man'yō* style. His personal poetry collection is entitled the *Kinkai Waka Shū,* and he has ninety-three poems in the *ShinChokusenshū* and later imperial anthologies.

Commentary
This poem was classified by Teika as a travel poem in the *ShinChokusenshū,* suggesting the topic "lodging on the seashore" *(kaihen ryohaku),* in contrast to its appearance in Sanetomo's collection under "boats" in a series that concentrates on the transcience of life. Medieval commentators focused on the poem as an expression of ephemerality, believing the famous poem by Sami Manzei (early eighth century), *SIS* 20 (Laments): 1327, to be a *honka:*

yo no naka wo
nani ni tatohen
asaborake
kogi-yuku fune no
ato no shira-nami

This world—
to what shall we compare it?
the white waves of the wake
of a boat being rowed out
at dawn.

Like the preceding poem (Poem 91) by Yoshitsune, Sanetomo's contribution is an allusive variation *(honka-dori)* on two earlier poems. The first two lines allude to a poem found in the *Man'yō Shū* 1:22:

kaha no he no	Just as the grasses
yutsu-iha-mura ni	do not grow on the sacred rocks
kusa musazu	near the river, if only she
tsune ni mogamo na	could always remain the same!
toko wotome nite	staying a maiden forever.[39]

The second half of Sanetomo's poem alludes to a "Northern Song" *(Michinoku no uta)* preserved as *Kokinshū* 20 (Court Poems): 1088:

michinoku ha	In Michinoku
idzuku ha aredo	the spots are various but
shiho-gama no	how touching the sight
ura kogu fune no	of them towing the boats that
tsunade kanashi mo	are rowed on Shiogama's bay.

Despite the allusions, many commentators insist that Sanetomo combined these earlier poems with an actual vista he had seen on the beach near Kamakura. For the later reader, of course, poignance is added by knowing that Sanetomo was assassinated in Kamakura at an early age.

The Pictures
The poet's mention of both "rowing" and "towing" has proved insurmountable for many artists. The scene described is one of rowboats being towed by ropes attached to their prows; nonetheless, the image of the boat being rowed is apparently overpowering, probably due to the Sami Mansei subtext. This is the case in the *Zōsanshō* picture [93–1]. The Kyoto artist [93–2] is apparently attempting to indicate the towing, but still no rope is visible. The *Sugata-e* [93–3] reduces the size of the boat so that the problem literally disappears. The *Sugata-e* is actually fairly close to the Tan'yū album version [93–4] and indeed appears to be a parody of it, offering in place of the formal robes and posture of Tan'yū's Sanetomo the poet at his leisure, with hat off, in informal robes, leaning on an armrest and receiving a massage from an attractive young woman—a situation far more likely to arouse thoughts of "if only this world could always remain the same!" Yūsai, however, makes no mention of *Man'yō Shū* 1:22 (the first reference appears to be in the *San'oku Shō*), so it is unlikely that the young woman represents any reference to the maiden of that poem.

93-1

世中は
つねに
もがもな
なぎさこ
ぐ
あまの
小ぶねの
つなで
かなしも

93-2

93-3

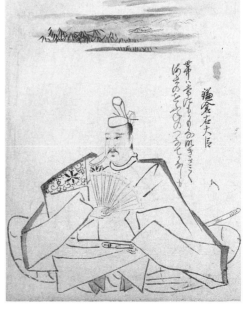

93-4

POEM 94

mi-yoshino no
yama no aki-kaze
sa-yo fukete
furu-sato samuku
koromo utsu nari[40]

Fair Yoshino,
the autumn wind in its mountains
    deepens the night and
in the former capital, cold
I hear the fulling of cloth.

Consultant Masatsune

Sangi Fujiwara no Masatsune (1170–1221) founded the Asukai house of poets and calligraphers. He studied poetry with Shunzei (Poem 83) and was one of the editors of the *ShinKokinshū*. His personal poetry collection is called the *Asukai Shū*, and he has 134 poems in the *ShinKokinshū* and later imperial anthologies. He is one of the Late Classical Thirty-Six Poetic Immortals.

Commentary

The *ShinKokinshū* indicates that this poem was composed "on the sentiment of 'fulling cloth'" *(tōi no kokoro)*, the practice of pounding fabric to bring out a glossy sheen. From the *Asukai Shū* we know that the poem comes from a hundred-poem sequence composed in 1202.

Masatsune's poem is based on an earlier verse by Korenori (Poem 31), *Kokinshū* (Winter): 325:

mi-yoshino no
yama no shira-yuki
tsumorurashi
furu-sato samuku
nari-masaru nari

Fair Yoshino,
the white snow in its mountains
    seems to be collecting,
for the former capital seems
to have become ever colder.

Here again, as Ariyoshi notes, the poet's perception of the sound of the fulling blocks is not an actual sensation but occurs "in the world of the foundation poem." There has been no disagreement about the interpretation of this poem and, unlike the case of Poem 93, the foundation poem was identified in texts as early as the *Ōei Shō*. In early modern commentaries, the *San'oku Shō* is the first to point out that the phrase *aki-kaze sa-yo fukete* can be understood to mean "autumn deepens, the wind blows, and the night deepens." The *Uimanabi* points out that whereas in Korenori's poem it is the former capital that is cold, in Masatsune's poem it is the sound of the fulling blocks.[41]

The Pictures

The *Zōsanshō* picture [**94–1**] shows both the poet and someone fulling cloth: the clouds between them suggest that the poet cannot see but only hear the fulling (as indicated by the poem's *utsu nari*). The Kyoto artist maintains this composition. The *Sugata-e* [**94–2**] shows only autumn hills with the foreground occupied by a man, a woman, and a small serving-boy—the woman's fist suggests that she is massaging the man's lower back by pounding it. The conspicuous earhole on the man seems to suggest he is hearing something. This basic conception of the poet in a listening posture becomes standard, as seen in the Porter illustration [**94–3**] and the *Kangyoku*. In the *Shikishi Moyō* kimono design [**94–4**], no fulling blocks appear either: only autumn maples, pampas, and the character for "robe" *(koromo)*.

94-1

94-2

94-3

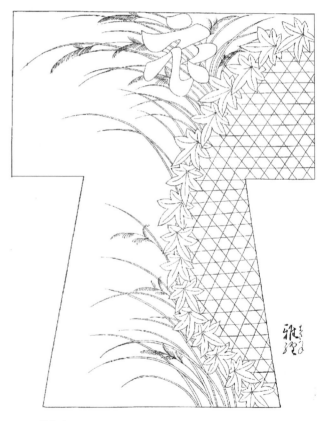

94-4

POEM 95

<table>
<tr><td>

ohoke naku
uki yo no tami ni
ohofu kana
wa ga tatsu soma ni
sumi-zome no sode[42]

</td><td>

Inadequate, but
they must shelter the folk
    of this wretched world—
my ink-black sleeves, having begun to live
"in this timber-forest that I enter."

</td></tr>
</table>

Former Major Archbishop Jien

Saki no DaiSōjō Jien (1155–1225) was a son of Tadamichi (Poem 76). He participated in many of the poetic events sponsored by GoToba and was a member of the poetic circle of his nephew Yoshitsune (Poem 91) and Teika. He has a personal poetry anthology, the *Shūgyoku Shū (Collection of Gathered Jewels),* and is the best-represented poet in the *ShinKokinshū* after Saigyō (Poem 86). He is perhaps best known today for his historiographic work, the *Gukan Shō (The Future and the Past;* 1219–1220). He is one of the Late Classical Thirty-Six Poetic Immortals and has 267 poems in the *Senzaishū* and later imperial anthologies.

Commentary

This poem quotes directly from a poem by Saichō (Dengyō Daishi, 767–822), who established the esoteric Buddhist Tendai sect in Japan and founded its headquarters on Mount Hiei above Kyoto. The poem is found in the *ShinKokinshū* 20 (Buddhist Verses), 1921:

When he had built the central hall on Mount Hiei

<table>
<tr><td>

anokutara
samiyaku sabojhi
hotoke-tachi
wa ga tatsu soma ni
miyauga arase-tamahe

</td><td>

Most omniscient
and supremely enlightened
    Buddha Hosts!
On this timber-forest that I enter,
bestow your divine protection!

</td></tr>
</table>

Due to this allusion, many commentaries, such as the *Keikō Shō* (1530), interpreted Jien's poem as a kind of vow he took when he became the chief abbot of Mount Hiei in 1192. But since this poem is included in the *Senzaishū* (under "topic unknown"), which was completed around 1188, this interpretation is untenable. Other commentaries, such as the *Ōei Shō* and the *Kamijō-bon,* find precedent for the idea of "sheltering the folk of this wretched world" in a story about Emperor Daigo, who was said to have taken off his robe one winter night to suffer the same cold as his subjects.

The Pictures

The *Zōsanshō* [**95–3**] presents a tranquil scene showing Jien in ecclesiastical garb looking out over the hills from a temple, which in fact conforms to Ariyoshi's interpretation of this poem as "not a resolution, but placid and composed." The Kyoto artist [**95–4**] attempts to give a sense of Hiei's mountain fastness by adding towering peaks all over, even in the foreground. Note also the trees he has introduced in the extreme right foreground: these suggest the cryptomeria used for timber mentioned in the poem. However, the artist also has Jien with his sleeve to his face, and tearlike shapes in the foliage. This would suggest a "tears on sleeves" interpretation analogous to Emperor Tenji's Poem 1 and following the *Ōei Shō* identification with Emperor Daigo. The *Kangyoku* artist [**95–2**] and the Porter artist use a different conception, showing the poet walking into a woods, and thus pictorializing the phrase *wa ga tatsu soma*, "the timber-forest which I enter." The *Sugata-e* [**95–1**] shows a very young Jien looking meaningfully at a young samurai, which encourages the reader to interpret *uki yo* as the "floating world" of Edo and to find an erotic nuance to the phrase "sleeves . . . that shelter." Finally, the *Shikishi Moyō* kimono design has inscribed the phrase *uki yo* but has superimposed it over a bridge with irises—a clear allusion to the Yatsuhashi episode and its poem in the *Tales of Ise*. The connection between Jien's poem and that episode is far from clear, however, except that both poems are about robes.

95-1

95-2

95-3

95-4

POEM 96

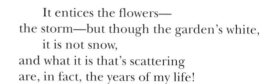

hana sasofu
arashi no niha no
yuki narade
furi-yuku mono ha
wa ga mi narikeri[43]

It entices the flowers—
the storm—but though the garden's white,
    it is not snow,
and what it is that's scattering
are, in fact, the years of my life!

The Former Chancellor and Lay Novice
Nyūdō Saki no Daijō Daijin, born Fuji-
wara no Kintsune (1171–1244), was
founder of the Sai'onji branch of the Fuji-
wara clan. He was married to a niece of
Minamoto no Yoritomo and eventually
became the grandfather of the shogun
Yoritsune. Teika was married to his older
sister and received his protection and
patronage. Kintsune was active in court
poetry circles and is the fourth best repre-
sented poet in the *ShinChokusenshū*,
which Teika edited. He has 114 poems in
the *ShinKokinshū* and later imperial
anthologies.

Commentary
Medieval commentaries concerned them-
selves with establishing what they under-
stood to be the implied contrast between the man and the falling flowers. For
instance, the *Keikō Shō* states that while cherry blossoms are appreciated even as
they scatter in decline, such is not the case for men. The *Yoritaka-bon* sees the
contrast as one between the flowers, which will return next year, and the man,
who will not. Later commentaries, such as the *Kaikan Shō*, reject this line of inter-
pretation entirely and argue for a simpler analogy centered on the one pun in
the poem (*furi*, meaning both "to fall" and "to grow old"): the blossoms are scat-
tering like falling (*furi*) snow, but they are not snow, therefore they are not falling
(*furi*); the only thing that is growing old (*furi*) is the poet himself. The *Kamijō-bon*
is unique in seeing this poem as an allusive variation (*honka-dori*) of one by Nari-
hira (*Tales of Ise*, Episode 17). In terms of placement in the collection, Kintsune's
poem follows the somber tone set by the previous poem and seems to be a
reprise of the sentiments found much earlier in Komachi's verse (Poem 9), com-
bined with the storm topos and rhetoric of Yasuhide's (Poem 22).

The Pictures

The *Zōsanshō* [**96–1**] shows the poet in secular dress watching cherry blossoms scatter; the Kyoto artist repeats this format but emphasizes the blossoms by making them bigger and more numerous. The *Sugata-e* [**96–2**] shows a courtier gazing down upon a young samurai and is most likely comparing the few remaining days of the young man's youth with the transience of the blossoms (see Poem 35). The transcription of the poem is done in two diagonals, suggesting "falling." The *Shikishi Moyō* kimono design [**96–4**] shows cherry blossoms; the character for "snow" *(yuki)* is superimposed on the upper part of the garment and that for "garden" *(niwa)* among the fallen blossoms below. Finally, the *Kangyoku* [**96–3**] is distinctive for depicting the poet as a monk—in fact, the sentiment of the poem suggests that it was written after Kintsune took vows, at the age of sixty-one, though only the Tan'yū album depicts Kintsune as an old man. The inclusion of bending grasses in the *Kangyoku* version also suggests the word "storm" *(arashi)*.

96-1   96-2

96-3

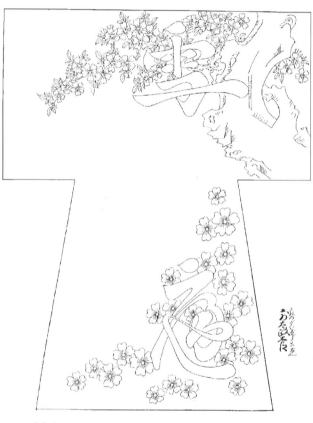

96-4

POEM 97

konu hito wo
matsuho no ura no
yufu-nagi ni
yaku ya mo-shiho no
mi mo kogaretsutsu[44]

For the man who doesn't come
I wait at the Bay of Matsuo—
    in the evening calm
where they boil seaweed for salt,
I, too, burn with longing!

Supernumerary Middle Counselor Teika

GonChūnagon Fujiwara no Teika (also read "Sada'ie"; 1162–1241) was the son of Shunzei (Poem 83). He was one of the editors of the *ShinKokinshū* and later edited the *ShinChokusenshū* by himself. He collated and edited many of the classics of Japanese literature, such as *The Tale of Genji*. His descendants exercised a near monopoly on Japanese court-style poetry for centuries after his death. His personal poetry collection is entitled the *Shūi Gusō* and he has 465 poems in the *Senzaishū* and later imperial anthologies. He is the compiler of the *One Hundred Poets*.

Commentary

This poem was written for a poetry contest that took place in the imperial palace in 1216.[45] The topic is "love" and the speaker of the poem is a woman. The poem is an allusive variation *(honka-dori)* of lines from a "long poem" *(chōka)* found in the *Man'yō Shū* 6: 935:

ahajhi-shima
matsuho no ura ni
asa-nagi ni
tama-mo karitsutsu
yufu-nagi ni
mo-shiho yakitsutsu
ama-wotome
ari to kikedo
mi ni yukamu . . .
yoshi no nakereba

Awaji Island
on the Bay of Matsuo
    in the morning calm
they reap jewelled seaweed,
    in the evening calm
they boil seaweed for salt,
    the fisher-maidens—
and though I hear they are there,
    since I have no way
to go to see them . . . [46]

In the manner of allusive variation, Teika has changed the speaker of the poem from a man to a woman and from someone who goes into someone who waits for one who does not come. Some commentaries, such as the *Kamijō-bon*, suggest that "months and years" have passed since the man visited, but this is an exaggeration; nonetheless, the verbal suffix *-tsutsu* indicates that the speaker of the poem has continued to wait night after night. Other commentaries, such as the *Komezawa-bon* (1452), noting that Matsuo Bay is on Awaji Island, suggest that the man must come from the other side of the bay, that is, from Honshū. Finally, some commentators attempt to motivate the phrase "in the evening calm," suggesting that the fires burn more strongly in the still night, as does the speaker's love. Interestingly, the *ho* of *matsuho* means "sail," yet no commentary suggests a relationship between it and the becalmed bay. In terms of placement in the collection, Teika's poem grammatically echoes Poem 1 and Poem 4 while also alluding to the poetry of the *Man'yō* era.

The Pictures
Almost all artists depict the speaker of the poem as a man, Teika, rather than as a woman. The *Zōsanshō* [**97–2**] shows the poet, waiting beside a pine tree (*matsu* means both "pine tree" and "to wait" and suggests the name "Matsuo"), looking out to the other side of the bay, where men are carrying buckets of seaweed and boiling them in cauldrons. (Note that the smoke is rising straight up, suggesting calm weather.) The Kyoto artist's version is virtually identical. The *Sugata-e* [**97–3**] shows a man looking past his young swordbearer, as if expecting someone. The *Kangyoku* [**97–1**] dispenses with the sea-folk but clearly indicates that the person the poet is waiting for must come from across the water; it also includes a setting moon, indicating that the night is late. This composition bears a resemblance to Tan'yū's pictorialization of Teika's famous "Miwataseba" poem, though that depiction of Teika is very different from the one in the Tan'yū albums.[47] Though hard to make out, the salt-burners and the smoke from their fire are also depicted in the *Kangyoku* print. The Porter artist [**97–4**] avoids the problem of the speaker's gender by eliminating him/her and showing only the sea-folk carrying pails and the hut from which smoke is emerging.

97-1

97-2

97-3

97-4

POEM 98

kaze soyogu
nara no wo-gaha no
yufu-gure ha
misogi zo natsu no
shirushi narikeru[48]

In the evening
when the wind rustles the oaks
   at Nara-no-Ogawa,
it is the ablutions that are
the only sign it's still summer!

Ietaka of the Junior Second Rank
JuNi'i Fujiwara no Ietaka (also read "Karyū"; 1158–1237) had the sobriquet "Mibu Nihon." He became son-in-law to Jakuren (Poem 87) and studied poetry with Shunzei (Poem 83). He was a member of GoToba's poetic circle and one of the editors of the *ShinKokinshū*. He has a personal poetry collection known both as the *Mini Shū* (after his sobriquet) and the *Gyokugin Shū (Collection of Jewelled Songs)*. He has 282 poems in the *Senzaishū* and later imperial anthologies.

Commentary
There is no real disagreement among commentators over this poem. As early as the *Keikō Shō*, Ietaka's verse was identified as an allusive variation of the following poem, found first in the *Kokin Roku-jō*:[49]

misogi suru
nara no wo-gaha no
kaha-kaze ni
inori zo wataru

shita ni taeji to

In the river's wind
at Nara-no-Ogawa where
   they purify themselves,
"May my love, unknown to others, never
   cease!"—
that is what *I* keep praying for!

Misogi was a form of ablution, and every summer people performed the *minazuki-barae*, or "Sixth Month Purification," to rid themselves of the evils and pollutions they had accumulated during the first half of the year. Illicit love affairs might be included among these evils—as seen in a well-known episode from *The Tales of Ise*, where a young man attempts to purify himself of his love for one of the emperor's consorts.[50] The *Kokin Roku-jō* poem just quoted reverses this idea: the speaker is secretly praying that his or her secret affair *will* continue. Although Ietaka's verse uses similar wording, the conception is quite different and has no apparent erotic meaning at all.

It is not until the early modern period that commentaries such as the *Kai-kan Shō* identify the following poem by Minamoto no Yoritsuna (d. 1097) as a foundation poem:

natsu-yama no	In the evening
nara no ha soyogu	when the leaves of the oaks rustle
yufu-gure ha	in the summer hills,
kotoshi mo aki no	this year too, one has indeed
kokochi koso sure[51]	the sensation of autumn.

As can be seen, this poem is much closer in conception to Ietaka's. Yet Ietaka's is distinctive in treating the phrase *nara no wo-gaha* as a pivot word indicating both a proper name (Nara-no-Ogawa) and "oaks" *(nara)*. In terms of the poem's placement in the collection, it is clearly meant to echo Poem 2 by Empress Jitō, as both represent the poets' surprise at the signs of seasonal change. In other words, in Poem 2 Jitō realizes from the robes on Mount Kagu that spring has already passed and summer has come; for Ietaka, the *misogi* shows that it is still summer despite the autumn chill in the wind.

The Pictures
The poem's headnote in the *ShinChokusenshū* indicates that this poem was written for a screen depicting activities of the twelve months *(tsukinami byōbu)* taken by Fujiwara no Michi'ie's daughter, Junshi, when she entered court as a consort to Emperor GoHorikawa in 1229. Despite this fact, unlike Poem 17, also written for a screen, only the Tan'yū album [98–2] pictorializes this poem with the poet actually in front of a screen. Instead the *Zōsanshō* [98–1] shows a courtier on a riverbank performing a purification with a sacred wand in his hand while another courtier with a swordbearer walks past him. It is this latter courtier, observing the ablutions, who is presumably the speaker of the poem. The *Shi-kishi Moyō* kimono design [98–4] shows the word "Ogawa" dividing fresh summer irises from banana-plant leaves. The Porter artist [98–3] eliminates the observing figure and, like the Tan'yū album, shows ritual papers set in the river. Here we can see how the Porter artist has included all of the *Zōsanshō* figures but has ignored or eliminated their literary function in relation to the poem— that is, the rear figure is now participating in the ritual, rather than simply observing it, and no longer represents the speaker of the poem.

98-1

98-2

98-3

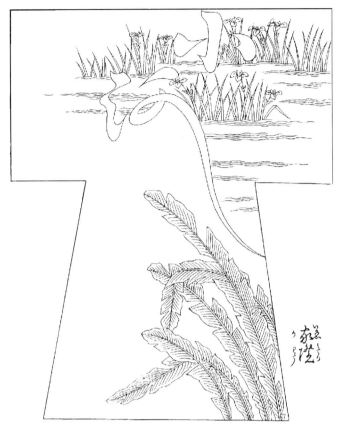

98-4

POEM 99

hito mo woshi
hito mo urameshi
ajhikinaku
yo wo omofu yuwe ni
mono-omofu mi ha[52]

    People seem dear and
people also seem hateful
    when vainly
I brood about the world—
this self who broods about things.

Retired Emperor GoToba

GoToba In (1180–1239; r. 1183–1198), the fourth son of Emperor Takakura, was counted as the eighty-second sovereign. He was placed on the throne at the age of four and abdicated at nineteen. A great patron of the arts, he was a dedicated poet who sponsored the compilation of the *ShinKokinshū* and worked closely with its editors. He and Teika eventually fell out over poetic matters. Politically he rebelled against the Kamakura military government in what is known as the Jōkyū Rebellion of 1221. GoToba's forces were defeated, and he was exiled to the island of Oki, where he lived another eighteen years. He has a personal poetry collection and one work on poetics. GoToba has 254 poems in the *ShinKokinshū* and later imperial anthologies.

Commentary

This poem is collected in the *ShokuGosenshū*, the thirteenth imperial anthology, edited by Nijō Tameyo (1250–1338) and completed in 1303, over one hundred years after Teika's death. Moreover, no poems by GoToba or Juntoku (Poem 100) are included in the *Hyakunin Shūka*. Accordingly, it had long been thought that the last two poems of the *Hyakunin Isshu* were added after Teika's death by someone such as his son, Tame'ie. However, a decorated paper poetry-cartouche *(shikishi)* of this poem, written in Teika's own hand, has been discovered, suggesting that he did indeed choose this poem. Shimazu suggests that the poem comes from those Teika had originally selected for inclusion in the *ShinChokusenshū* and then omitted for political reasons and that the private nature of the *One Hundred Poets* allowed their inclusion there. The poem is also collected in GoToba's own personal poetry anthology, where we learn that it was written as part of a group hundred-poem sequence in 1212 with four other poets, including Teika. GoToba contributed five poems on spring, ten on autumn, and five of "personal grievance" *(jukkai),* of which this was one.

Interpretations of this poem have divided into two camps: those, such as the *Ōei Shō,* that see the poet's complaint as directed against the tyranny of the Kamakura overlord; and those, such as the *Keikō Shō,* that see the poet dividing the world between the common folk, whom he regards as "dear," and subjects who opposed his rebellion, whom he detests. Given the date of the poem's composition, the latter interpretation is obviously anachronistic. Grammatically, "people" *(hito)* can refer to different groups or to the same people at different times; the translation offered above follows the latter interpretation.

The Pictures
The *Zōsanshō* [**99–3**] shows GoToba seated on ceremonial tatami, as befits his rank, talking with another courtier. The water in the background may be meant to suggest that he is in his place of exile, Oki Island; in any event, it is eliminated by the Kyoto artist, whose composition is otherwise identical. In the *Sugata-e* [**99–2**] the speaker could be interpreted as looking very preoccupied with thoughts characterized by the scene of the palace in the cloud inset—preoccupied to the point of ignoring even the young page who waits by his shoes—or the scene might be read as showing a capricious lord who runs hot and cold in his affections. The *Shikishi Moyō* kimono design [**99–4**] introduces the motif of Japanese chess pieces, which of course suggest both political machination and civil war. (The "king" pieces in Japanese chess are "generals" and not "kings" per se.) But this motif is especially appropriate to GoToba's verse since the Japanese game allows captured pieces to be returned to the board and used against their original side—thus the same piece can work both "for" and "against" a player. The waves may again suggest the emperor's exile. Finally, although the Porter artist [**99–1**] uses essentially the same elements in his composition as the *Zōsanshō,* the effect is very different: here it is a dark and brooding GoToba who surveys the residences below.

99-1

99-2

99-3

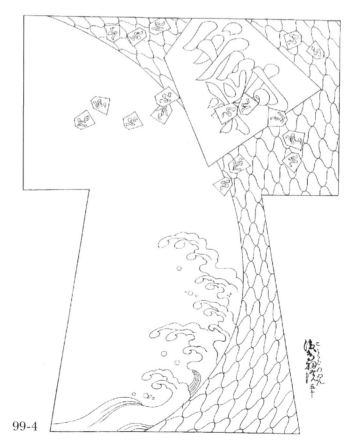

99-4

POEM 100

momoshiki ya
furuki noki-ba no
shinobu ni mo
naho amari aru
mukashi narikeri[53]

The hundredfold palace!
even in the *shinobu* grass
on its old eaves,
I find a past for which
I long yet ever more.

Retired Emperor Juntoku

Juntoku In (1197–1242; r. 1210–1221) was the third son of GoToba (Poem 99) and was numbered as the eighty-fourth sovereign of Japan. He joined his father's cause during the Jōkyū Rebellion of 1221 against the military power in Kamakura. He studied poetry under Teika and was a frequent participant in the poetry events sponsored by GoToba. After the defeat of the rebellion, he was exiled to Sado Island, where he lived for twenty years. He has a personal poetry collection and a poetic treatise, the *Yakumo MiShō*. He has 159 poems in the *ShokuGosenshū* and later imperial anthologies.

Commentary

From its inclusion in Juntoku's *Juntoku In GyoShū*, or the *Collected Poems of Retired Emperor Juntoku*, we know that this poem was composed in 1216, five years before the outbreak of military hostilities between the imperial family and the Kamakura shogunate. All commentators, from the *Ōei Commentary* to Ariyoshi, interpret this poem politically: Juntoku is deploring the decline of righteous government and the fortunes of the imperial house. As such, the poem is seen as the pendant to the first poem in the anthology, attributed to Emperor Tenji (Poem 1), also frequently interpreted as a lament over the decline of imperial authority. Note also that the collection ends, as it began, with a parent-child set of poems (Tenji/Jitō and GoToba/Juntoku). The political interpretation is not mandatory, however, and one can also imagine the poem to be representing Teika's own feelings, especially in regard to the poetry of the past, as he finishes his chronological review by means of the *One Hundred Poets* itself.

The Pictures

Unlike the relatively informal representation of GoToba in the previous poem [**99–3**], the *Zōsanshō* this time [**100–1**] presents the emperor as very much the ruler, partially hidden by blinds, with ministers arranged in an orderly fashion on either side. The cherry blossoms suggest the halcyon days of a munificent ruler. This interpretation is largely abandoned by the Kyoto artist [**100–2**]: it is not clear whether either of the male figures is meant to represent Juntoku (neither is sitting on tatami; see **99–3**], but the composition suggests a derelict palace much more strongly than does the *Zōsanshō* version. Or, rather than derelict, the setting could be seen as simply informal, with the lowered blinds across from Juntoku indicating the presence of a woman. This reading would suggest a more romantic interpretation, along the lines of the *Tenri-bon Kiki-gaki* and *Kamijō-bon*, neither of which mentions a political interpretation. In the *Sugata-e* [**100–3**] Moronobu also interprets the poem romantically, as the verb *shinobu* can also mean "to love secretly" (see Poem 40 among others); the roofs of the palace appear in the clouds above, the same motif used in the Tan'yū albums. The *Shikishi Moyō* kimono design [**100–4**] inscribes the characters *momoshiki* over *shinobu* ferns and the ceremonial blinds *(sudare)* characteristic of the palace.[54]

100-1   100-2

100-3

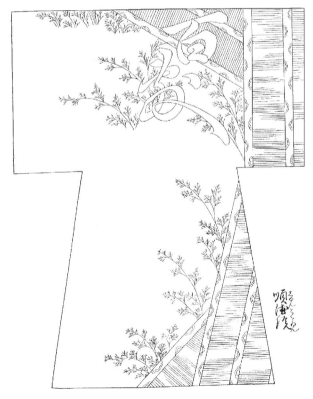

100-4

APPENDIXES

APPENDIX A
Imperial Anthologies and Exemplary Collections

Imperial Anthologies (to Teika's son, Tame'ie)

Man'yō Shū [*MYS*], final editing by Ōtomo no Yakamochi; last datable poem A.D. 759

Kokin (Waka) Shū [*KKS*], commissioned ca. 905 by Emperor Daigo; compiled by Ki no Tsurayuki, Ki no Tomonori, Ōshikōchi no Mitsune, and Mibu no Tadamine

Gosenshū [*GSS*], commissioned 951 by Emperor Murakami; compiled by Ōnakatomi no Yoshinobu, Kiyohara no Motosuke, Minamoto no Shitagō, Ki no Tokibumi, and Sakanoe no Mochiki (the "Five Men of the Pear Jar Room")

Shūishū [*SIS*], by Emperor Kazan; compiled ca. 1005 by Kazan and Fujiwara no Kintō

GoShūishū [*GSIS*], commissioned 1078 by Emperor Shirakawa; compiled by Fujiwara no Michitoshi

Kin'yōshū [*KYS*], commissioned by Emperor Shirakawa; compiled by Minamoto no Toshiyori (Shunrai); three drafts between 1124 and 1127

Shikashū [*SKS*], commissioned 1144 by Emperor Sutoku; edited by Fujiwara no Akisuke

Senzaishū [*SZS*], commissioned 1183 by Emperor GoShirakawa; edited by Fujiwara no Shunzei (Toshinari)

ShinKokinshū [*SKKS*], commissioned 1201 by Emperor GoToba; edited by GoToba, Fujiwara no Teika (Sada'ie), Jakuren, Fujiwara no Ari'ie, Fujiwara no Ietaka, Minamoto no Michitomo, and Fujiwara no Masatsune

ShinChokusenshū [*SCSS*], commissioned 1232 by Emperor GoHorikawa; compiled by Teika

ShokuGosenshū [*SGSS*], commissioned 1248 by Emperor GoSaga; compiled by Fujiwara no Tame'ie

Exemplary Collections
Pre-Teika

Shinsen Waka [*SSWK*], compiled by Tsurayuki, 930–934

Kokin Roku-jō [*KKRJ*], compiled by Kintō, 976–987

Kingyoku Shū [*KGS*], compiled by Kintō, ca. 1007

Shinsō Hishō [*SSHS*], compiled by Kintō, ca. 1008

Wakan Rōei Shū [*WKRES*], compiled by Kintō, ca. 1013–1018

Sanjūrokunin Sen [*SJRNS*], compiled by Kintō, date unknown

Shinsen Man'yō Shū [*SSMYS*], attributed to Sugawara no Michizane but dating from
    Kintō's time

GoRokuroku Sen [*GRRS*], compiled by Fujiwara no Norikane (1107–1165)

Kasen Ochi-gaki, anon., 1172

Korai Fūtei Shō [*KRFTS*], compiled by Shunzei, 1197

Teika

Teika Jittei [*TKJT*], 1207–1213

Kensō-bon (Kindai Shūka), 1209

(Jihitsu-bon) Kindai Shūka [*KDSK*], ca. 1215–1222

Eiga Taigai [*EGTG*] (also called *Shūka-tei Dairyaku*), 1222

Shūka no Daitai [*SKDT*], after 1226

Hyakunin Shūka [*HNSK*], 1229–1236

Nishidai Shū [*NSDS*] (also called *Hachidai(shū) Shō*), 1234–1235

Hachidaishū Shū'itsu [*HDSSI*], 1234

Hyakunin Isshu [*HNIS*], 1237

Post-Teika

Eiga no Ittei (also called *Yakumo Kuden*) [*EGIT*], by Fujiwara no Tame'ie, ca. 1274

APPENDIX B
One Hundred Poets: Selected Copies, Editions, and Commentaries

Ōei Shō. Colophon by Fujiwara no Michimoto, dated Ōei 13 (1406). Now the oldest extant commentary. Photographic reproduction by Kyōsojin Hitaku and Higuchi Yoshimaro, *Gosho-bon Hyakunin Isshu Shō* (Kasama Shoin, 1976), of copy owned by the Imperial Household Agency.

Sōgi Shō. Based on notes of lectures Sōgi (1421–1502) received from Tō no Tsuneyori (1402–1484), believed to represent the interpretations of Ton'a and the Nijō house. Two drafts: colophon dated 1478, reproduced by Yoshida Kōichi, *Ei'in-bon Hyakunin Isshu Shō* (Kasama Shoin, 1969), from an old printed edition *(ko-katsuji)*; colophon dated 1490, reprinted in Shimazu and Kamijō (1982). The latter is largely identical to the *Ōei Shō*.

Yoritsune-bon. Before 1478. Notes of Yoritsune, who inherited the commentaries of Tsuneyori. Owned by Ariyoshi.

Chōkyō Shō. Commentary dated Chōkyō 1 (1487). Thought to have been written by Gyōkō (1391–1455) or someone connected with him. Contents similar to the *Yoritsune-bon*. Both are representative of the exegetical tradition prior to the *Sōgi Shō*. Reproduced and transcribed by Yoshida Kōichi, *Hyakunin Isshu Kochū*, Koten Bunko 291 (Koten Bunko, 1971).

Komezawa-bon. Owned by Komezawa Municipal Library. A late Muromachi copy of a mid-Muromachi (dated 1452) manuscript. Perhaps representing the exegesis of Reizei no Tamehide (d. 1372). Reproduced by Komezawa Kobunsho Kenkyūkai, *Komezawa-bon Hyakunin Isshu Shō Kaidoku to Shūshaku* (Dōkenkyūkai, 1976).

Keikō Shō. 1530. Lecture notes of Cloistered Imperial Prince Sonchin with a colophon by Dharma-Seal Keikō. Teachings of Gyōkō, received from Gyōe by Keikō, representing a lineage distinct from that found in the *Sōgi Shō*. Reproduced in Shimazu and Kamijō.

Tenri-bon Kiki-gaki. 1564. Reizei teachings transmitted from Imagawa Ryōshun to Shōtetsu to Sōgi. Partially reproduced in Shimazu and Kamijō.

Yoritaka-bon. Muromachi period. Calligraphy attributed to Asukai no Yoritaka. Representing Asukai household traditions. Owned by Ariyoshi and reproduced by Ariyoshi and Kyūsojin, *Ogura Sansō Shikishi Waka (Hyakunin Isshu Kochū)* (Shintensha, 1975).

Kamijō-bon. Mid-Muromachi. A decidedly non-Nijō tradition, perhaps stemming from the Reizei house. Owned by Kamijō and reproduced in *Hyakunin Isshu KoChūshaku "Shikishi Waka" Honbun to Kenkyū* (Shintensha, 1981).

Minazuki Shō. Late Muromachi copy. Author and date unknown. Owned and reproduced by Yanase Kazuo as *Hyakunin Isshu Minazuki Shō* (privately published, 1968).

Minō Shō. Late Muromachi copy. Owned and reproduced by Yanase Kazuo as *Hyakunin Isshu Minō Shō* (privately published, 1962).

Hyakunin Isshu Kiki-gaki. Notes of lectures by Sanjōnishi no Kin'eda (1487–1563) with a colophon dated 1560. Two copies owned by Kyoto University.

Hyakunin Isshu Shō. Notes of lectures by Sanjōnishi no Saneki (1511–1579), Kin'eda's heir. Copies in Diet Library and Yōmei Bunko. Both this text and the previous one are based on the *Sōgi Shō* with amplifications of the Sanjōnishi house.

Yūsai Shō. 1596. While based on lectures by Sanjōnishi no Saneki, this commentary by Hosokawa Yūsai (1534–1610) discusses a number of interpretations. Holograph in Kitaoka Bunko. Many woodblock editions starting in 1631. Modern edition by Yoshikai Naoto (1988).

GoYōzei Tennō Hyakunin Isshu Shō. 1606. Sanjōnishi lineage. Reprinted in *Kōshitsu Bungaku Taikei*, vol. 1 (Meichō Kankōkai, 1979).

Soan-bon. Before 1632 (year of Soan's death). Poems and imaginary portraits. One copy in the Tōyō Bunko; reproduced in Shimazu Tadao, *Hyakunin Isshu* (1969). A virtually identical edition, attributed to Kōetsu (one volume, 21.8 × 18.8 cm, no publisher or date), is in the Atomi Gakuen Tanki Daigaku Toshokan.

Shisetsu Shō. 1658. Perhaps based on lectures by Sanjōnishi no Kin'eda. Copy in Naikaku Bunko.

GoMizuno'o Tennō Hyakunin Isshu Shō. 1661. Sanjōnishi lineage. Reprinted Mori Shōichi, *"Hankoku GoMizuno'o In Hyakunin Isshu GoKōshaku Kiki-gaki," Yashū KokuBungaku*, vols. 7–10 and 12–13 (1971–1974).

Tan'yū Gajō. Two versions: one on silk, formerly in the Date collection, produced between 1662 and 1669; the other a sketchbook produced sometime earlier. Silk work now in private collection; many pictures reproduced in *(Bessatsu) Taiyō* (Winter 1972). Sketchbook widely copied and disseminated; one in Tokyo National Museum; another reproduced in a limited edition, Miki Kōshin, ed., *(Tan'yū-hitsu) Hyakunin Isshu Kashin-chō* (Kyoto: Sūzandō, 1980).

Kisen Shō. Written by Inoue Shūsen in 1672, published 1673. Illustrated editions appear repeatedly after 1680. Reproduced by Kobayashi Yōjiro, *Hyakunin Isshu Kisen Shō* (Benseisha, 1978).

Zōsan Shō. *Hyakunin Isshu Zōsan Shō.* Edo: Urokogataya, 1678. 3 vols., 27 × 18.5 cm. Text of the *Yūsai Shō* with pictures by Hishikawa Moronobu. Reproduced and transcribed by Katagiri Yōichi, *"Hyakunin Isshu" to Mononobu no "Zōsan Shō,"* Hanpon Bunko 9 (Kokusho Kankōkai, 1975). Copies in Atomi Gakuen Tanki Daigaku Toshokan and Art Institute of Chicago.

Shūe Shō. 1681. Written by Kitamura Kigin (1624–1705). Reproduced as *Hyakunin Isshu Shūe Shō*, Kitamura Kigin KoChūshaku Shūsei 44 (Shintensha, 1977).

San'oku Shō. By Shimokōbe Chōryū (1627–1686); incomplete at the time of his death. Reprinted in *Chōryū Zenshū* in *Keichū Zenshū*, suppl. vol. 1 (Asahi Shinbunsha, 1927).

Kaikan Shō. 1688. By Keichū (1640–1701). Reprinted *Keichū Zenshū*, vol. 9 (Iwanami Shoten, 1974).

Hinagata Hyakushu. *Ogura Yama Hyakushu Hinagata.* Designs by Hakuyōken Gyōjō, published in Edo by Yezōshiya Hachiyemon and in Kyoto by Yezōshiya Kisayemon in

1688. 27.2 × 19 cm. Incomplete copy of vol. 1 in Art Institute of Chicago; incomplete copy of vol. 2 at Atomi Gakuen Tanki Daigaku Toshokan.

Shikishi Moyō. *Ogura Yama Shikishi Moyō.* Designs by Take Heiji, published in Edo by Hon'ya Seibei in 1689. Reprinted from new blocks in 1939 by Nihon Hanga Kyōkai; copy at Atomi Gakuen Tanki Daigaku Toshokan.

Zatsudan. 1692. Written by Toda Mosui (1629–1706). Reprinted in *Toda Mosui Zenshū* (Kokusho Kankōkai, 1914; rpt. 1969).

Sugata-e. *(Fūryū) Sugata-e Hyakunin Isshu.* Edo: Kinoshita Jin'emon, 1695. 3 vols., 27.5 × 18.5 cm. The poets in a Genroku-period setting; designs by Moronobu, published a year after his death by his son. Copies in Atomi Gakuen Tanki Daigaku Toshokan and Art Institute of Chicago. Reproduced with new blocks by Kurokawa Mamichi in *Nihon Fūzoku Zue* (1914) (copies in Atomi); reprinted (with transcriptions) by Kashiwa Shobō (1983).

Hyakunin Isshu Kosetsu. 1743. Kamo no Mabuchi. Reprinted *Kamo no Mabuchi Zenshū,* vol. 12.

(Ko-gata) Hyakunin Isshu Zōsan Shō. Kyoto: Kōto Shorin, 1746. 2 vols., 15.4 × 10.8 cm. Same as above but with different pictorializations of the poems. Copies in Atomi Gakuen Tanki Daigaku Toshoka and Mukogawa Gakuen Joshi Daigaku Toshokan.

Uchiwa. *Dansen Hyakunin Isshu Taisei.* Osaka: Ōsaka Shorin, 1755. 1 vol., 22.3 × 15.6 cm. Signed by Hasegawa Mitsunobu. Copy at Atomi Gakuen Tanki Daigaku Toshokan.

Uimanabi. 1765. Kamo no Mabuchi. Reprinted *Kamo no Mabuchi Zenshū,* vol. 12.

ShinShō. 1804. Ishihara Shōmei, a student of Motoori Norinaga. Modern edition by Yoshikai Naoto (1988).

Kangyoku. *Kangyoku Hyakunin Isshu Suishōsō.* No publisher, 1804. 1 vol., 25 × 17.8 cm. Pictures by Sōsekishi. Copies in Atomi Gakuen Tanki Daigaku Toshokan and Mukogawa collections.

Hyakushu Iken. Written 1815, published 1823. Kagawa Kageki (1768–1843). Reprinted Yoshida Kōichi and Kinsaku Kōichi, eds., *Hyakushu Iken,* Koten Bunko 353 (Koten Bunko, 1976).

Eiga. *Eiga Hyakushu Monjū Shō.* Edo: 1817; reprinted 1843, 1850, etc. 1 vol., 25.4 × 18 cm. Pictures by Utagawa Sadahide. Atomi Gakuen Tanki Daigaku Toshokan.

Azuma Kagami. *Jokyō Manpō Zensho Azuma Kagami.* First printed Edo: Sugiharaya, 1829; reprinted into the Meiji period. 1 vol., 25 × 18 cm.

Shūgyoku. *(Nichiyō Zatsuroku Fujin Shubunko) Shūgyoku Hyakunin Isshu-kan.* Edo: Hakkō Shorin, 1836; reprinted 1850. 1 vol., 25.4 × 18.2 cm. Pictures by Keisai Eisen (1790–1848). Atomi Gakuen Tanki Daigaku Toshokan.

Porter. *A Hundred Verses from Old Japan,* by William N. Porter (Oxford, 1909); reprinted 1979. This translation includes illustrations from a Japanese edition belonging to F. V. Dickins described as "probably dat[ing] from the end of the eighteenth century." Dickins left Japan in 1866, which can serve as the latest date for the pictures. The earliest edition I have found with identical pictures is the *Sensai Hyakunin Isshu Yamato Kotobuki,* published in 1829 by Bizenya Bunjirō in Nagoya and by Akitaya Ichigorō in Osaka, with a frontis picture by Katsushita Ōi. Copies in the Atomi collection.

Hyakunin Isshu Hitoyo-gatari. By Ozaki Masayoshi; illustrations by Ōishi Matora. Published 1833; reprinted Yūhōdō (1927).

NOTES

ABBREVIATIONS

EGIT	*Eiga no Ittei*	*NSDS*	*Nishidai Shū*
EGTG	*Eiga Taigai*	*SCSS*	*ShinChokusenshū*
GSIS	*GoShūishū*	*SGSS*	*ShokuGosenshū*
GSS	*Gosenshū*	*SIS*	*Shūishū*
HDSSI	*Hachidaishū Shū'itsu*	*SJRNS*	*Sanjūrokunin Sen*
JDFDUA	*Jidai Fudō Uta-awase*	*SKDT*	*Shūka no Daitai*
KDSK	*Kindai Shūka*	*SKKS*	*ShinKokinshū*
KGS	*Kingyoku Shū*	*SKS*	*Shikashū*
KKRJ	*Kokin Roku-jō*	*SSHS*	*Shinsōhō Hishō*
KKS	*Kokinshū*	*SSMYS*	*Shinsen Man'yō Shū*
KRFTS	*Korai Fūtei Shō*	*SSWK*	*Shinsen Waka*
KYS	*Kin'yōshū*	*STS*	*Shikashū Taisei*
MJ	*Modern Japanese*	*SZS*	*Senzaishū*
MYS	*Man'yō Shū*	*TKJT*	*Teika Jittei*
NKBT	Nihon Koten Bungaku Taikei	*TYZN*	*Toshiyori Zuinō*
NKBZ	Nihon Koten Bungaku Zenshū	*WKRS*	*Wakan Rōei Shū*

Chapter 1: Introduction

1. F. X. Šalda, quoted in Peter Steiner, ed., *The Prague School: Selected Writings, 1929–1946* (Austin: University of Texas Press, 1982), p. 105; emphasis in the original. All further Vodička quotes are from this translation.

2. There have been some notable exceptions. The first moves in this direction seem to have come from what might be called Japan's classical text par excellence, the *Tale of Genji,* as in the "World of Genji" conference at Indiana in 1982, the very same year that saw the appearance in English of Hans Robert Jauss' *Toward an Aesthetic of Reception.* It is in the *Genji* proceedings that we find papers on "Supplementary Narratives to *The Tale of Genji*" by Aileen Gatten; "Representation of *Genji Monogatari* in Edo Period Fiction" by Andrew Marcus; "*The Tale of Genji* as a Source of the Nō" by Janet

449

Goff; "*The Tale of Genji* and the Haikai Tradition" by Makoto Ueda; and Julia Meech-Pekarik's discussion of *Genji* illustrations through time, "Ukifune: Icon of Love." None of these scholars, however, seem to have seen themselves as doing *Rezeptiongeschichte*, or "reception history," and the published versions of their works generally minimize this aspect: for instance, the subtitle of Janet Goff's book speaks not of "reception" but of "The Art of *Allusion* in Fifteen Classical Plays" (emphasis added). More self-conscious reception histories have had to wait till the late 1980s and 1990s, with Thomas Harper's essay on the reception of the *Genji* in the eighteenth century, Royall Tyler's discussions of performance history in his recent anthology of *nō* plays, and, perhaps most notably, Richard Bowring's article on the "cultural history" of the *Tales of Ise*. All these English studies were preceded by work by Japanese scholars, largely in the 1970s, such as Ii Haruki's *Genji Monogatari no Densetsu* (1976) and Teramoto Naohiko's *Genji Monogatari Juyō Shi Ronkō* (1970).

3. René Wellek and Austin Warren, *Theory of Literature*, rev. ed. (Orlando: Harcourt Brace Jovanovich, 1977), p. 151.

4. See Helen McCullough's remarks on Tokugawa scholarship on the *Ise Monogatari* in her translation of the same, *Tales of Ise* (Stanford, Calif.: Stanford University Press, 1968), pp. 45–47.

5. On the mechanical and organic metaphors for literary works, see Peter Steiner, *Russian Formalism: A Metapoetics* (Ithaca: Cornell University Press, 1984), pp. 44–137.

6. Ariyoshi Tamotsu, *Hyakunin Isshu Zen Yakuchū* (Tokyo: Kōdansha, 1983).

7. Shimazu Tadao, ed., *Hyakunin Isshu* (Tokyo: Kadokawa Shoten, 1969).

8. See Steven Carter's translation in his *Traditional Japanese Poetry: An Anthology* (Stanford, Calif.: Stanford University Press, 1991), pp. 203–238.

9. Louis A. Montrose, "Professing the Renaissance: The Poetics and Politics of Culture," in H. Aram Veeser, ed., *The New Historicism* (London: Routledge, 1989), p. 20.

10. See my review of *Conversations with Shōtetsu*, trans. Robert H. Brower, in *Journal of the Association of Teachers of Japanese* 27(2) (November 1993): 265–269.

11. Komashaku Kimi, *Murasaki Shikibu no Messeeji* (Tokyo: Asahi Shinbunsha, 1991).

12. Ikeda Kikan et al., eds., *Makura no Sōshi, Murasaki Shikibu Nikki*, NKBT 19 (Iwanami Shoten, 1958), p. 462. See also Richard Bowring, trans., *Murasaki Shikibu*, p. 75.

13. Though, in fact, the issue of female homosexuality was earlier raised by Ivan Morris in *The World of the Shining Prince: Court Life in Ancient Japan* (Oxford: Oxford University Press, 1964), p. 232, n. 38.

14. Bonnie Zimmerman, "What Has Never Been: An Overview of Lesbian Feminist Criticism," in Elaine Showalter, ed., *The New Feminist Criticism: Essays of Women, Literature, and Theory* (New York: Pantheon, 1985), p. 202.

15. Edward Kamens, *The Buddhist Poetry of the Great Kamo Priestess: Daisaiin Senshi and Hosshin Wakashū*, Michigan Monograph Series in Japanese Studies, no. 5 (Ann Arbor: Center for Japanese Studies, University of Michigan, 1990), p. 32.

16. As evidenced in the *Wa ga Mi ni Tadoru Hime-gimi Monogatari;* see Donald Keene, "A Neglected Chapter: Courtly Fiction of the Kamakura Period," *Monumenta Nipponica* 44(1) (1989): 1–30.

17. Dorothy Ko, "Same-Sex Love Between Singing Girls and Gentry Wives in Seventeenth-Century Jiangnan," paper presented at "Women and Literature in Ming-Qing China" conference, Yale University, New Haven, 22–26 June 1993.

18. Rosemary M. Neilsen and Robert H. Solomon, "Aphra Behn and Pyrrha: Revealing Female Space in Horace, Odes I.5," paper presented at "Gender and the Construction of Culture and Knowledge" women's studies conference, University of British Columbia, Vancouver, 22–24 September 1989.

19. Adrienne Rich, "Compulsory Heterosexuality and Lesbian Existence," *Signs* 5 (Summer 1980): 648–649; quoted by Zimmerman, "What Has Never Been," p. 205.

20. For more on the relations between poetry and rank see Akiko Hirota, "Ex-Emperor Go-Toba: A Study in Personality, Politics and Poetry" (Ph.D. diss., UCLA, 1989), especially pp. 104–108.

21. Robert Graves, *The Greek Myths* (New York: Braziller, 1957), I:167.

22. There is a heated debate among scholars over the appropriateness of calling *ku* "lines"; see Hiroaki Sato, "Lineation of Tanka in English Translation," *Monumenta Nipponica* 42(3) (Summer 1987): 347–356; Mark Morris, "Waka and Form, Waka and History," *Harvard Journal of Asiatic Studies* 46(2) (December 1986): 551–610; and Earl Miner, "*Waka:* Features of Its Constitution and Development," *Harvard Journal of Asiatic Studies* 50(2) (December 1990): 669–706.

23. Morris, "Waka and Form," p. 571.

24. The terminology used by modern scholars to describe *waka* derives from a variety of historical periods. *Ji-amari* is first attested to in writings from the poetic descendants of the famous haiku poet Bashō in the early eighteenth century (*Nihon Kokugo Daijiten* [*NKDJ*] 9:343). *Uta-makura* appears in the *Kojidan* of 1212–1215; *honka* in Teika's *Maigetsu Shō (Iwanami Kogo Daijiten)*. Edwin Cranston notes that the term *makura-kotoba* first appears in the *Rakusho Roken* (ca. 1412) by the *waka* poet Ryōshun, while the term *jo (jo-kotoba)* appears in a work attributed, probably spuriously, to Teika, the *Sango Ki;* see Edwin A. Cranston, "The Ramifying Vein: An Impression of Leaves," *Journal of Japanese Studies* 9(1) (Winter 1983): 102–104, nn. 11–13. *Engo* appears in Shinkei's *Tokoro-dokoro Hentō* (1470) (*NKDJ* 3:267). *Mi-tate* appears in the *haikai Kefuki-gusa* of 1638 (*NKDJ* 18:582), while *kasane-kotoba* is attested to in the Portuguese *Vocabulario da Lingoa de Japam* ("Rodriguez's Dictionary") of 1604–1609 (*NKDJ* 4:516). *Gijinka* (or *-hō*) was imported from English aesthetics in the nineteenth century (*NKDJ* 5:581). The *NKDJ* gives no references in its entries on *taigen-dome* or *tōchi-hō*.

25. Uchiyama Masayoshi, *Yōshaku Hyakunin Isshu* (Bunsendō), p. 21. Curiously, Uchiyama does not comment on the extra syllable in the fourth line.

26. This discussion of techniques is drawn largely from the "Hyakunin Isshu Jiten, IV: Hyōgen," by Suzuki Yoshifuyu, in Kubota Jun, ed., *Hyakunin Isshu Hikkei* (Tokyo: Gakutōsha, 1982), pp. 189–192.

27. For another translation see Poem 3 in Part Two.

28. Prefaces are typically classified as either motivated at the level of the signified (*ushin,* or "with meaning") or motivated solely at the level of the signifier (*mushin,* or "without meaning"). Hitomaro's poem, with the metaphoric relationship between the preface and the rest of the poem, might be thought of as an example of the former sort (though see the Commentary in Poem 3), while a modification of the "ewe" example— "She runs through the woods, the [ewe] /yu/ [you] it is that I love"—is an example of the latter. For more on *ushin* and *mushin* see Poems 58 and 77.

29. See Helen Craig McCullough, *Brocade by Night: "Kokin Wakashū" and the Court Style in Japanese Classical Poetry* (Stanford, Calif.: Stanford University Press, 1985), p. 66. The term is also used by Robert H. Brower and Earl Miner in their *Japanese Court Poetry* (Stanford, Calif.: Stanford University Press, 1961). Both usages seem to derive from Konishi Jin'ichi, "*Kokinshū*-teki Hyōgen no Seiritsu," *Nihon Gakushi'In Kiyō,* 7(3) (November 1949): 163–198, trans. Helen C. McCullough, "The Genesis of the *Kokinshū* Style," *Harvard Journal of Asiatic Studies* 38(1) (June 1978): 61–170.

30. For another translation of this poem see Poem 30 in Part Two.

31. Kubota Jun, ed., *Koten Waka Hikkei* (Tokyo: Gakutōsha, 1986), p. 152; in English see Roselee Bundy, "The Uses of Literary Tradition: The Poetry and Poetics of the *Shinkokinshu*" (Ph.D. diss., University of Chicago, 1984), I:32–35.

Chapter 2: Historical Context

1. For a translation and discussion see Judith Rabinovitch, "Wasp Waists and Monkey Tails: A Study and Translation of Hamanari's *Uta no Shiki* (*The Code of Poetry,* 772), Also Known as *Kakyō Hyōshiki* (*A Formulary for Verse Based on the Canons of Poetry*)," *Harvard Journal of Asiatic Studies* 51(2) (December 1991): 471–560.

2. For complete translations of the *Kokinshū* and its prefaces see Laurel Rasplica Rodd with Mary Catherine Henkenius, *Kokinshū: A Collection of Poems Ancient and Modern* (Tokyo and Princeton: University of Tokyo Press/Princeton University Press, 1984); and Helen Craig McCullough, *Kokin Wakashū: The First Imperial Anthology of Japanese Poetry* (Stanford, Calif.: Stanford University Press, 1985). The quotation is from Rodd and Henkenius, *Kokinshū,* p. 36.

3. See Chia-ying Yeh and Jan Wall, "Theory, Standard, and Practice in Zhong Hong's *Shi pin,*" in Richard C. Miao, ed., *Studies in Chinese Poetry and Poetics* (San Francisco: Chinese Materials Center, 1978), vol. 1.

4. Rodd and Henkenius, *Kokinshū,* p. 44.

5. Poets who appear in both collections are typically represented by different poems.

6. Both are translated by Nicholas J. Teele in "Rules for Poetic Elegance," *Monumenta Nipponica* 31(2) (Summer 1976): 145–164.

7. Quoted in Clifton Wilson Royston, Jr., "The Poetics and Poetry of Fujiwara Shunzei (1114–1204)" (Ph.D. diss., University of Michigan, 1974), p. 371.

8. Much of the information on Teika's exemplary anthologies is taken from Robert H. Brower and Earl Miner, *Fujiwara Teika's Superior Poems of Our Time: A Thirteenth-Century Poetic Treatise and Sequence* (Stanford, Calif.: Stanford University Press, 1967), pp. 145–146.

9. See Hiroaki Sato, "From Format Composition of Tanka to the Creation of the Renga Form," *Journal of the Association of Teachers of Japanese* 21(2) (November 1987): 149–164.

10. Translated as "An Outline for Composing Tanka," in Hiroaki Sato and Burton Watson, *From the Country of Eight Islands* (New York: Doubleday, 1981), pp. 202–218.

11. Quoted in Ariyoshi Tamotsu, *Hyakunin Isshu ZenYakuchū* (Tokyo: Kodansha, 1983), pp. 416–417.

12. Higuchi Yoshimaro, "Hyakunin Shūka kara Hyakunin Isshu e," *Bungaku* 6 (June 1971): 784–802.

13. Ariyoshi, *Hyakunin Isshu ZenYakuchū,* pp. 416–422. Most recently, however, Ii Haruki has argued that it was the *Hyakunin Isshu* that preceded the *Hyakunin Shūka;* see his "Hyakunin Isshu no Seiritsu," in (Kikan) *Sumi,* Supesharu Hyakunin Isshu (Tokyo: Geijutsu Shinbunsha, 1990), pp. 49–54. For a good review of the history of the debates surrounding the genesis of the Hyakunin Isshu, see Tokuhara Shigemi, "Hyakunin Isshu Seiritsu Ron no Hensen," in Waka Bungaku Ronshū Henshū I'in Kai, eds., *Hyakunin Isshu to Shūka Sen,* pp. 165–194.

14. This is the title that appears on the oldest extant annotated copy, the *Ōei Commentary.* This manuscript is reproduced as Kyūsojin Hitaku and Higuchi Yoshimaro, eds., *GoShohon Hyakunin Isshu Shō Kunaichō Shoryōbu-zō* (Tokyo: Kasama Shoin, 1971).

15. Translated by Robert H. Brower, "Fujiwara Teika's *Maigetsushō,*" *Monumenta Nipponica* 40(4) (Winter 1985): 399–425.

16. Translated by Robert H. Brower, "The Foremost Style of Poetic Composition: Fujiwara Tameiei's *Eiga no Ittei,*" *Monumenta Nipponica* 42(4) (Winter 1987): 391–429.

17. Translated by Robert N. Huey and Susan Matisoff, "Lord Tamekane's Notes on Poetry," *Monumenta Nipponica* 40(2) (Summer 1985): 127–146.

18. Kamijō Shōji, "Hyakunin Isshu no Hon-dana," in Kubota, *Hyakunin Isshu Hikkei*, pp. 211–215.

19. Ibid.

20. Japan was involved in a military expedition against a Korean kingdom at the time.

21. This statement seems to refer to the following poem attributed to Tenji in *ShinKokinshū (SKKS)* 17 (Misc. 2), 1687:

asakura ya	Asakura!
ki no maro-dono ni	When I am in
wa ga woreba	the hall of unbarked logs,
na-nori wo shitsutsu	whose child is that,
yuku ha ta ga ko zo	who passes by, announcing his name?

22. Text in Ariyoshi, *ZenYakuchū*, pp. 17–18.

23. Ariyoshi Tamotsu and Kamisaku Kō'ichi, eds., *Ogura Sansō Shikishi Waka (Hyakunin Isshu Kochū)*, Ei'in Kōchū Koten Sōsho (Tokyo: Shintensha, 1975).

24. This poem is anthologized as *Man'yō Shū (MYS)* 10:2174, anon., and as *SKKS* 5 (Autumn 2): 454 (anon., topic unknown), with the first line as *akita moru*.

25. See *dan* 28 of Yoshida Kenkō's *Essays in Idleness*: "Nothing is more saddening than the year of imperial mourning. The very appearance of the temporary palace is forbidding: the wooden floor built close to the ground, the crudely fashioned reed-blinds, the coarse, grey cloth hung above the blinds, the utensils of rough workmanship, and the attendants all wearing strangely drab costumes, sword scabbards, and sword knots." See Donald Keene, trans., *Essays in Idleness* (New York: Columbia University Press, 1967), p. 29.

26. Yoshikai Naoto, "Hyakunin Isshu Shō Hanpon Nishu no Honkoku to Kaidai: Yūsai Shō to Shin Shō," *Kokubungaku Kenkyū Shiryōkan Kiyō* 14 (1988): 129.

27. The same technique, which was the norm, can be seen in *The New Rules of Linked Verse, with Kanera's New Ideas on the New Rules and Additional Comments by Shōhaku*, translated in Steven D. Carter, *The Road to Komatsubara: A Classical Reading of the* Renga Hyakuin (Cambridge, Mass.: Council on East Asian Studies, Harvard University, 1987).

28. Donald Keene, *World Within Walls: Japanese Literature of the Pre-Modern Era, 1600–1867* (New York: Holt, Rinehart, 1976), pp. 24–26.

29. The *Wamyō Shū*, usually called the *Wamyō Shō* (ca. 931–937), by Minamoto no Shitagō (911–983), is the first encyclopedic dictionary produced in Japan.

30. A work on economic and political policies, attributed to the famous minister Kuan Chung. See Burton Watson, trans., *The Tso Chuan: Selections from China's Oldest Narrative History* (New York: Columbia University Press, 1989), p. 19, n. 4.

31. *The Duke of Chou's Book of Changes*, an alternate title for the *I Ching*.

32. See James Legge, *The Original Chinese Texts of The Confucian Analects, The Great Learning, The Doctrine of the Mean, The Works of Mencius and the Work of Lao-tsze* (Taipei: Cave Books, n.d.), p. 987.

33. The translation is uncertain at this point and I have omitted one line.

34. Hisamatsu Sen'ichi et al., eds., *Keichū Zenshū* (Tokyo: Iwanami Shoten, 1973), 9:674–675.

35. See Peter Nosco: "Keichū (1640–1701): Forerunner of National Learning," *Asian Thought and Society: An International Review* 5 (1980): 237–252; "*Man'yōshū* Studies in Tokugawa Japan," *Transactions of the Asiatic Society of Japan*, 4th series, 1 (1986): 109–146; *Remembering Paradise: Nativism and Nostalgia in Eighteenth-Century Japan* (Cambridge, Mass.: Harvard University Press, 1990).

36. See Joseph J. Spae, *Itō Jinsai: A Philosopher, Educator and Sinologist of the Tokugawa Period* (New York: Paragon, 1967); Yoshikawa Kōjirō, *Jinsai, Sorai, Norinaga: Three Classical Philologists of Mid-Tokugawa Japan* (Tokyo: Tōhō Gakkai, 1983); Samuel Hideo Yamashita, "The Early Life and Thought of Itō Jinsai," *Harvard Journal of Asiatic Studies* 43(2) (1983): 245–280.

37. E. M. Satow, "The Revival of Pure Shiñ-tau," *Transactions of the Asiatic Society of Japan* (1882), p. 4.

38. *Gosenshū (GSS)* 6 (Autumn 2): 295 (anon.; topic unknown); the standard text has *aki no ta no / kariho no yado no / nihofu made.*

39. W. G. Aston, trans., *Nihongi: Chronicles of Japan from the Earliest Times to A.D. 697* (Tokyo: Tuttle, 1985), p. 272. I have added the romanization of the poem but have kept Aston's own lineation in his translation.

40. Minamoto no Sanetomo (1192–1219); see Poem 93.

41. Kamo Momoki, ed., *Kamo Mabuchi Zenshū* (Tokyo: Koshikawa Kōbunkan, 1927), 10:380–381.

42. Yoshikai, *Kokubungaku Kenkyū Shiryō Kan Kiyō* 14 (1988): 125–267.

43. R. P. Dore, *Education in Tokugawa Japan,* Michigan Classics in Japanese Studies, no. 8 (Ann Arbor: Center for Japanese Studies, University of Michigan, 1992), especially pp. 66 and 126.

44. Ibid., p. 253. For a translation of a related calligraphy book see Andrew J. Pekarik, *The Thirty-Six Immortal Women Poets: A Poetry Album with Illustrations by Chōbunsai Eishi* (New York: Braziller, 1991).

45. See Keene, *World Within Walls,* pp. 486–493.

46. Ozaki Masayoshi, *Hyakunin Isshu Hitoyo-gatari* (Tokyo: Yūhōdō, 1931).

47. For an English version see McCullough, *Tales of Ise.*

48. Translated in Helen McCullough's *Kokin Wakashū.*

49. "A poet who has not read the *Genji* is to be deplored"; *Roppyakuban Uta-awase,* "Winter I," 188; quoted by Konishi, *History of Japanese Literature,* III:58.

50. Brower and Miner, *Japanese Court Poetry,* p. 513.

51. Wayne P. Lammers, *The Tale of Matsura: Fujiwara Teika's Experiment in Fiction,* Michigan Monograph Series in Japanese Studies, no. 9 (Ann Arbor: Center for Japanese Studies, University of Michigan, 1992), p. 29 ff.

52. Konishi, *History of Japanese Literature,* III:216.

53. Ibid., pp. 214–216, with minor changes; the translations are by Gatten and Harbison. As in all other cases, I have changed the romanization.

54. Lammers, *Tale of Matsura,* pp. 42–43.

55. Kubota Jun, *Fujiwara Teika,* Ochō no Kajin 9 (Tokyo: Shūeisha, 1984), p. 115.

56. Minemura Fumihito, ed., *ShinKokin Waka Shū,* NKBZ 26 (Tokyo: Shōgakkan, 1974), p. 50.

57. Kubota Jun, ed., *Hyakunin Isshu Hikkei* (Tokyo: Gakutōsha, 1982), p. 35.

58. Higuchi Yoshimaro, "Hyakunin Shūka kara Hyakunin Isshu e," *Bungaku* 39(7) (1971): 792–793.

59. Earl Miner, *Japanese Linked Poetry* (Princeton, N.J.: Princeton University Press, 1979), pp. 9–11.

60. Carter, *Road to Komatsubara,* p. 11.

61. Ibid., p. 13; Carter is referring to Brower and Miner, *Japanese Court Poetry,* pp. 403–411.

62. *Harvard Journal of Asiatic Studies* 21 (1958): 67–127.

63. Review, *Harvard Journal of Asiatic Studies* 24 (1962–1963): 279.

64. W. Michael Kelsey, *Konjaku Monogatari-shū* (Boston: Twayne, 1982), especially pp. 107–108.

65. See, for instance, Bowring's translation and study, *Murasaki Shikibu.*

66. Brower and Miner, *Japanese Court Poetry,* p. 322.

67. Brower and Miner, *Fujiwara Teika's Superior Poems of Our Time,* p. 30.

68. Konishi, "Association and Progression," p. 96.

69. *Shōhaku's Renga Rulebook* of 1501; in Carter, *Road to Komatsubara,* p. 58.

70. Robert H. Brower, *Fujiwara Teika's* Hundred-Poem Sequence of the Shōji Era, *1200* (Tokyo: Sophia University, 1978), p. 27.

71. Stanley Fish, "What Makes an Interpretation Acceptable?" in his *Is There a Text in This Class? The Authority of Interpretive Communities* (Cambridge, Mass.: Harvard University Press, 1980), pp. 340 and 345.

72. See, for instance, Jack Stillinger, "The Order of Poems in Keats's First Volume," in his *The Hoodwinking of Madeline, and Other Essays on Keats's Poems* (Urbana: University of Illinois Press, 1971), pp. 1–13; Frances Ferguson, *Wordsworth: Language as Counter-Spirit* (New Haven: Yale University Press, 1977). This issue has been discussed more recently in Neil Fraistat, ed., *Poems in Their Place: The Intertextuality and Order of Poetic Collections* (Chapel Hill: University of North Carolina Press, 1986).

73. Brower describes Teika as "ever prone to identify his personal successes and reverses with the fortunes of the Art of Poetry"; see "Secret Teachings," p. 15.

74. The association between poetry and beneficent rule has a long history in East Asia; see, for instance, the following from Tsurayuki's preface to the *Kokinshū:*

> The four seasons have recurred nine times during His Majesty's reign. The wave of his all-encompassing benevolence flows beyond the outermost reaches of the Eight Islands; the shelter of his boundless mercy is more grateful than the shade at the foot of Mount Tsukuba. He concerns himself with many matters when his innumerable state duties allow him leisure. Thus it happened that, desirous of preserving the memory of the past and of renewing what had grown old, and also having in mind both a personal inspection and a transmission to prosperity . . . at his command, selections were made from among those poems. [Trans. McCullough, *Kokin Wakashū,* p. 7.]

75. *Man'yō-gana* refers to the use of Chinese characters in a combined phonetic and semantic fashion to record Japanese, as found in the *Kojiki* and *Man'yō Shū.* Owing to the peculiarities of this system, these texts were unreadable to the Japanese only decades after their composition.

76. *Koromo saraseri* is a variant reading of the *man'yō-gana,* rejected by modern scholars.

77. Ozaki Masayoshi, *Hyakunin Isshu Hitoyo-gatari* (Tokyo: Yūhōdō, 1931), pp. 27–28.

78. Katagiri Yōichi, *Uta-makura,* s.v. *"ama no kagu yama." "Kago"* is simply a variant form.

79. See Akimoto Shunkichi, "The Three Mountains of Yamato," *Japan Quarterly* 3 (1956): 356–363.

80. Ozaki, *Hyakunin Isshu Hitoyo-gatari,* pp. 27–28.

81. *ZenYakuchū,* p. 21.

82. This is a reading, as we shall see, suggested by Sōin. Contrarily one could argue that the "it is said" of Jitō's poem suggests that while others' robes may change and sleeves may dry, the poet's do not, implying that she is in mourning or retreat, which would again link up with the long, lonely night of Hitomaro's poem. No such reading of Jitō's poem has ever been suggested, however.

83. So described in the preface to the *Kokinshū.*

84. Ian Hideo Levy, trans., *The Ten Thousand Leaves* (Princeton, N.J.: Princeton University Press, 1981), I:178.

85. Katagiri Yōichi, *Uta-makura*, s.v. *"tago no ura."*

86. See Ozawa Masao, *Kokin Waka Shū*, NKBZ 7 (1971), p. 64, poem 3, n. 2.

87. T. S. Eliot, "Tradition and the Individual Talent," in *The Sacred Wood: Essays on Poetry and Criticism* (New York: University Paperbacks, 1966), p. 49.

88. *Fu shi* ("not dying").

89. This tradition was further reinforced by being combined with static paintings. See Joshua S. Mostow, *"E no Gotoshi:* The Picture Simile and the Feminine Re-Guard in Japanese Illustrated Romances," *Word & Image* 10(1) (April–June 1994): 10–27.

Chapter 3: *Waka* in Translation

1. Many are listed by Peter Morse in his *Hokusai: One Hundred Poets* (New York: Braziller, 1989), pp. 21–22 and 217–218. See also Nicholas J. Teele and Yoshikai Naoto, Eiyaku Hyakunin Isshu no Hikaku-teki Taishō Kenkyū (Shiryō-hen), *Sōgō Bunka Kenkyū-sho Kiyō* 11 (March 1994): 210–219.

2. Susan Bassnett-McGuire, *Translation Studies* (London: Methuen, 1980), p. 2.

3. The basic article on defamiliarization is Victor Shklovsky's "Art as Technique," translated in Lee T. Lemon and Marion J. Reis, *Russian Formalist Criticism: Four Essays* (Lincoln: University of Nebraska Press, 1965), pp. 3–24.

4. *Monumenta Nipponica* 41(3) (Fall 1986): 355.

5. John Dryden, *Dedication of the Aeneis* (1697), quoted by Bassnett-McGuire, *Translation Studies,* p. 60.

6. Henry Wadsworth Longfellow on his translation of Dante's *Commedia;* quoted by Bassnett-McGuire, *Translation Studies,* p. 70.

7. Ozawa Masao, ed., *Kokin Waka Shū*, NKBZ 7:97.

8. Ibid.

9. Helen C. McCullough, *Brocade by Night: "Kokin Wakashū" and the Court Style in Japanese Classical Poetry* (Stanford, Calif.: Stanford University Press, 1985), pp. 222–223.

10. See Konishi, "Genesis of the *Kokinshū* Style."

11. The *Hyakunin Isshu Mine no Kake-hashi* of Koromogawa Naga'aki (1806). See Tokuhara Shigemi, ed., *Mukogawa Joshi Daigaku Toshokan-zō Hyakunin Isshu Bunken Mokuroku* (1989), entry 75, where a copy of this text is cataloged.

12. This list of works is particularly flawed—for example, the *Genji Monogatari* is translated as the "History of Affairs of the Original Families."

13. Edward W. Said, *Orientalism* (New York: Vintage, 1978).

14. Bassnett-McGuire, *Translation Studies,* p. 65.

15. Roman Jakobson, "On the Translation of Verse," translated by Wendy and Peter Steiner, in Roman Jakoloson, *Selected Writings,* ed. Stephen Rudy and Martha Taylor (The Hague: Mouton, 1979), V:133–134. Jakobson continues: "I think that we approximate the art of the original when, to echo a foreign poetic work, a form is chosen which, in the sphere of forms of the given poetic language, corresponds *functionally,* not merely externally, to the form of the original."

16. Clay MacCauley, trans., *Hyakunin-Isshu and Nori no Hatsu-ne* (Yokohama: Kelly & Walsh, 1917), p. i.

17. Frederick Victor Dickins, *Primitive and Mediaeval Japanese Texts* (Oxford: Clarendon Press, 1906), p. v.

18. In fact, in the first paragraph of his general introduction Dickins prophetically defends future Japanese expansionism on racial grounds: "For the Japanese are Tartars; their kinsfolk in the West are the Huns and Turks; in the East the islanders of the Liukiu [Ryūkyū], the peninsulars of Korea, the nomads of Mongolia, and the farmers of Manchuria. In none of these lands and islands has the Chinaman or the Slav any

birthright of presence; among men who dwell outside their borders the Japanese can show the justest title to predominance" (p. xxv).

19. Cranston, "The Ramifying Vein," p. 98, n. 4.

20. Bassnett-McGuire, *Translation Studies,* p. 72.

21. William N. Porter, trans., *A Hundred Verses from Old Japan, Being a Translation from the Hyaku-Nin-Isshiu* (Oxford: Clarendon Press, 1909).

22. Bassnett-McGuire, *Translation Studies,* p. 71.

23. "Editorial Note," by L. Cranmer-Byng and S. A. Kapadia, in Clara A. Walsh, *The Master-Singers of Japan, Being Verse Translations from the Japanese Poets,* Wisdom of the East series (London: John Murray, 1910), p. 12. Walsh's translations were written with the assistance of the famous Zen popularizer D. T. Suzuki.

24. Arthur Waley, *Japanese Poetry: The "Uta"* (Oxford: Oxford University Press, 1919), p. 11.

25. The introduction to the 1940 translation stems from contemporary work on the *Kokutai no Hongi.* See Roy Andrew Miller, "The 'Spirit' of the Japanese Language," *Journal of Japanese Studies* 3(2) (Summer 1977): 251–298.

26. John Whitney Hall, *Japan from Prehistory to Modern Times* (Rutland, Vt.: Tuttle, 1976), p. 316.

27. Curtis Hidden Page, trans., *Japanese Poetry: An Historical Essay with Two Hundred and Thirty Translations* (Folcroft, PA: Folcroft Library Editions, 1976), p. 169.

28. K. Wadagaki, trans., *Gleanings from Japanese Literature* (Tokyo: Nampokusha, 1919), pp. 14–15.

29. He mentions Aston, Dickins, Porter, Noguchi, Waley, de Rosny, Revon, and Florenz.

30. Dickins, *Primitive and Mediaeval Japanese Texts,* I:xciii.

31. Ernest Fenollosa, *The Chinese Written Character as a Medium for Poetry,* ed. Ezra Pound (San Francisco: City Lights Books, 1936).

32. Miyamori Asatarō, *Masterpieces of Japanese Poetry Ancient and Modern* (Tokyo: Maruzen, 1936), I:i.

33. H. H. Honda, trans., *One Hundred Poems from One Hundred Poets* (Tokyo: Hokuseido Press, 1956), p. 9.

34. Kokusai Bunka Shinkōkai, ed., *Introduction to Classic Japanese Literature* (Tokyo, 1948), pp. 27–28.

35. Donald Keene, *Dawn to the West, Japanese Literature in the Modern Era: Poetry, Drama, Criticism* (New York: Holt, 1984), p. 75.

36. On Blunden see Miner, *The Japanese Tradition,* pp. 202–207.

37. Ken Yasuda, trans., *Poem Card (The* Hyakunin-isshu *in English)* (Tokyo: Kamakurabunko, 1948), p. 5.

38. Kenneth Rexroth, *One Hundred Poems from the Japanese* (New York: New Directions, 1955), p. xix.

39. *The Burning Heart,* trans. and ed. Kenneth Rexroth and Ikuko Atsumi (New York: Seabury Press, 1977), p. 16.

40. The NKDJ's earliest example are from the 1918–1919 *Ku no Sekai* by Uno Kōji (1891–1961).

41. Kenneth Rexroth, *One Hundred More Poems from the Japanese,* p. 39. In the notes (pp. 114–115) Marichiko is described as follows:

MARICHIKO is the pen name of a contemporary young woman who lives near the temple of Marishi-ben in Kyoto. Marishi-ben is an Indian, pre-Aryan, goddess of the dawn who is a bodhisattva in Buddhism and patron of geisha, prostitutes, women in childbirth and lovers. Few temples or shrines to her or even statues exist in Japan, but her presence is indicated by statues, often in avenues like sphinxes, of wild boars, who draw her chariot. She has three faces: the front of compassion; one side, a sow; the other a woman in orgasm. She is a popular, though hidden diety of tantric, Tachigawa Shingon, and as the Light of Lights, the *shakti,* the Power of Bliss of Vairocana (the primordial Buddha, Dainichi Nyorai), seated on his lap in sexual bliss.

42. Jane Hirshfeld with Mariko Aratani, trans., *The Ink Dark Moon: Love Poems by Ono no Komachi and Izumi Shikibu, Women of the Ancient Court of Japan* (New York: Scribner's, 1988), p. 33.

43. Roy Andrew Miller, *Nihongo: In Defence of Japanese* (London: Athlone Press, 1986), p. 218.

44. Keene, *Anthology of Japanese Literature,* p. 81.

45. The journal *Comparative Literature* was founded in 1949, the *Yearbook of Comparative and General Literature* in 1952, and *Comparative Literature Studies* in 1964.

46. Brower and Miner, *Japanese Court Poetry,* p. 217.

47. J. M. Cohen, "General Editor's Foreword" to Francis Scarfe, *Baudelaire* (Harmondsworth: Penguin, 1964), p. v.

48. *The Penguin Book of Japanese Verse,* trans. Geoffrey Bownas and Anthony Thwaite (Harmondsworth: Penguin, 1964), p. 84.

49. Helen C. McCullough, *Tales of Ise,* p. 167.

50. Rodd and Henkenius, *Kokinshū,* p. 80.

51. See Tejaswini Niranjana, *Siting Translation: History, Post-Structuralism, and the Colonial Context* (Berkeley: University of California Press, 1992).

52. Sato and Watson, *Eight Islands,* p. 116.

53. Ibid., p. 206.

54. See his "Translating Tanka in One-Line Form," *Montemora* 4 (1978), and his "Lineation of Tanka in English Translation," *Monumenta Nipponica* 42(3) (Winter 1987): 347–356.

55. William R. LaFleur, "Marginalia: The Expanse and the Limits of a New Anthology," *Monumenta Nipponica* 38(2) (Summer 1983): 199–200; quoted by Sato, "Lineation," p. 348.

56. Eric Rutledge, "The *Man'yōshū* in English," *Harvard Journal of Asiatic Studies* 43 (June 1983): 284–285.

57. Trans. Sato and Watson, *Eight Islands,* p. 81.

58. Steven Carter, *Traditional Japanese Poetry,* p. 208.

59. Roy E. Teele, Nicholas J. Teele, and H. Rebecca Teele, trans., *Ono no Komachi: Poems, Stories, Nō Plays* (New York: Garland, 1993).

60. Ibid., pp. 11–12.

61. Anne Birrell, trans., *New Songs from a Jade Terrace: An Anthology of Early Chinese Love Poetry* (Harmondsworth: Penguin, 1982), p. 50.

62. Morris, "Waka and Form; Waka and History," pp. 560–561 and 563.

Chapter 4: The Poem-Picture Tradition
1. The text is in Taniyama Shigeru and Higuchi Yoshimaro, eds., *Mikan Chūsei Uta-awase Shū* (Tokyo: Koten Bunko, 1959), pp. 47–48; trans., Maribeth Graybill, "*Kasen-e:* An Investigation into the Origins of the Tradition of Poet Pictures in Japan" (Ph.D. diss., University of Michigan, 1983), pp. 59–60, with emendations.

2. Graybill, *"Kasen-e,"* p. 66.

3. Itoh Toshiko, "Satake-bon Sanjūrokkasen Emaki no Kōsei to Seiritsu," in Mori

Tōru, ed., *Sanjūrokkasen-e* (Tokyo: Kadokawa Shoten, 1979), pp. 48–63; cited by Graybill, *"Kasen-e,"* p. 96. On Nobuzane's dates see most recently Inoue Muneo. On applications of the term *kasen-e* see Namiki Seishi, "Bunken Yori Mita Nise-e," *Kinko Sōsho* 9 (1981): 798–825.

4. Originally two handscrolls, the *Satake-bon Sanjūrokkasen-e* has been widely dispersed. It is illustrated in Mori, *Sanjūrokkasen-e,* vol. 19.

5. Fewer than half of the original thirty-six portraits, held in various collections, are extant. For illustrations see Suntory Bijutsukan, ed., *Sanjūrokkasen-e—Satake-bon o Chūshin ni.*

6. There are two roughly contemporaneous extant versions of the *Jidai Fudō Uta-Awase-e:* one is in the Tokyo National Museum; the other is a scroll formerly in the Yabumoto Collection that has since been cut up and sold to various collections. See Maribeth Graybill, "An Iconographic Approach to the Study of Poet Portraiture in Medieval Japan," *Transactions of the International Conference of Orientalists in Japan,* no. 25 (Tokyo: Tōhō Gakkai, 1980), pp. 74–91. Illustrations of both scrolls can be found in Mori, *Uta-Awase-e* or, by the same author, "Jidai Fudō Uta-Awase-e ni tsuite," *Kobijutsu* 8 (March 1965): 25–57.

7. Graybill, *"Kasen-e"* p. 76.

8. Ibid., p. 159.

9. Ibid., pp. 175–176.

10. Ibid., p. 183.

11. Tokyo National Museum; for illustrations see Minemura Fumihito, ed., *ShinKokin Waka Shū,* NKBZ 26 (Tokyo: Shōgakkan, 1974). See also Chino Kaori, "Jingoji-zō 'Senzui Byōbu' no Kōsei to Kaigashi-teki Ichi," *Bijutsu Shi* 28(2) (February 1979): 146–162.

12. See Joshua S. Mostow, "*Uta-e* and Interrelations Between Poetry and Painting in the Heian Era" (Ph.D. diss., University of Pennsylvania, 1988); and Joshua S. Mostow, "Painted Poems, Forgotten Words: Poem-Pictures and Classical Japanese Literature," *Monumenta Nipponica* 47(3) (Autumn 1992): 341–344.

13. *Mitsune Shū,* Naikaku Bunko-bon, *Shikashū Taisei,* I:130.

14. *Murasaki Shikibu Shū,* ed. Namba Hiroshi (Tokyo: Iwanami Bunko, 1973), p. 25. Who drew the picture, and to whom it was sent, are matters of some debate. Takeuchi Michiyo (*Murasaki Shikibu Shū Hyōshaku* [Tokyo: Ōfūsha, 1976], pp. 85–89) and Suzuki Hideo ("Murasaki Shikibu Shū ZenHyōshaku," *KokuBungaku—Kaishaku to Kyōzai no Kenkyū* 27 [1982] 14:107) interpret the passage as reading that someone sent the picture to Murasaki Shikibu and that she thereupon wrote a reponse and sent it back. However, Shimizu Yoshiko (*Murasaki Shikibu* [Tokyo: Iwanami Shoten, 1973], pp. 58–60), Namba Hiroshi (p. 25), and Kibune Shigeaki (*Murasaki Shikibu Shū no Kenkyū to Ronkō* [Tokyo: Kasama Shoin, 1981], pp. 54–59) take the subject for the two appearances of the verb *kakite* to be the same, thus making it Murasaki Shikibu herself who both drew the picture and wrote the poem. For further discussion see Mostow, *"Uta-e,"* pp. 34–37.

15. See also Willa J. Tanabe, *Paintings of the Lotus Sutra* (New York: Weatherhill, 1988), pp. 52–63.

16. Edward G. Seidensticker, tr., *The Tale of Genji* (New York: Knopf, 1981), pp. 856–857. *Genji Monogatari,* ed. Abe Akio, Akiyama Ken, and Imai Gen'e, NKBZ 16:293–294.

17. McCullough, *Tales of Ise,* p. 103; *Taketori Monogatari/Ise Monogatari/Yamato Monogatari/Heichū Monogatari,* ed. Katagiri Yōichi, Fukui Sadasuke, Takahashi Masaji, and Shimizu Yoshiko, NKBZ 8:175.

18. Fritz Vos, *A Study of the Ise-monogatari, with the Text According to the Den-Teika-Hippon and an Annotated Translation* (The Hague: Mouton, 1957), II:105.

19. McCullough, *Tales of Ise*, p. 222.

20. Katagiri Yōichi, *Ise Monogatari/Yamato Monogatari*, Kanshō Nihon Koten Bungaku (Tokyo: Kadokawa Shoten, 1975), V:128–131.

21. NKBZ 14:139–140.

22. I am alluding here to the work of Roman Jakobson; see especially "Closing Statement: Linguistics and Poetics," in T. Sebeok, ed., *Style in Language* (Cambridge, Mass.: MIT Press, 1960), pp. 350–377.

23. See Ikeda Shinobu, "Heian Jidai Monogatari Kaiga no Hōhō: Monogatari o Yobi-komu Kaiga no Dentō o Kangaeru," in Nakano Masaki et al., eds., *Ōchō Emaki to Sōshoku-kyō*, Heian no Kaiga/Kōgei II, Nihon Bijutsu Zenshū 8 (Tokyo: Kōdansha, 1990), pp. 168–175; and Ii Haruki, "Monogatari-e Kō," *Kokugo to KokuBungaku* 67(7) (July 1988): 17–31.

24. Yamanoue (or Yamanoe) Okura (660–ca. 733) was a major early poet whose verse is marked by a Confucian-inspired social consciousness and didacticism almost completely foreign to the poetry of the Heian era. The work referred to here is the *Classified Forest of Verse (Ruiju karin)*, an anthology of Japanese poetry compiled by Okura that survives only through fragmentary quotation in the *Man'yō Shū*.

25. Called "old" to distinguish it from the *Shinsen Man'yō Shū*, traditionally credited to Sugawara no Michizane (845–903).

26. *Uta-awase Shū*, ed. Hakitani Boku and Taniyama Shigeru, NKBT 74:166.

27. Reproduced in Tokugawa Bijutsukan, ed., *Meihin Zuroku* (Nagoya: Tokugawa Bijutsukan, 1987), pl. 67.

28. Shirahata Yoshi, *"Byōbu-e to Uta-e,"* Zusetsu Nihon Koten, vol. 4, *Kokinshū/ ShinKokinshū*, ed. Kubota Jun (Tokyo: Shūeisha, 1979), p. 94. The boldface letters indicate *ashi-de* script; see Mostow, *"Uta-e."*

29. Translated by McCullough, *Kokin Wakashū*, poem 1 (Spring 1): 27.

30. Trans. Graybill, *"Kasen-e,"* p. 184, from Mori, *Uta-awase-e*, p. 177, n. 6.

31. *Meigetsuki*, ed. Kokusho Kankōkai (1970), I:71; dated 1198. See also Mostow, *"Uta-e,"* pp. 159–161; and Mostow, "Minamoto no Shunrai and *Uta-e*," *Transactions of the International Conference of Orientalists in Japan* 32 (1987): 52–64.

32. Edward Kamens, "The Past in the Present: Fujiwara Teika and the Traditions of Japanese Poetry," in Wheelwright, *Word in Flower*, pp. 26–28.

33. While there is a historical range in Kintō's selection, from Hitomaro to his own day, the poets are matched against each other in two teams without regard to chronological order. Thus, for instance, Hitomaro is paired against Tsurayuki, Mitsune against Ise, and Yakamochi against Akahito. See Graybill, *"Kasen-e,"* pp. 200–211.

34. See on this topic Kendall Brown: "Shōkadō Shōjō as 'Tea Painter,'" *Chanoyu Quarterly* 49 (1987): 7–40; "Re-Presenting Teika's *Flowers and Birds*," in Wheelwright, *Word in Flower*, pp. 33–53; and "Fujiwara Teika—Kan'ei Cultural Hero," *Association for Asian Studies, Abstracts of the 1993 Annual Meeting*, p. 80. Lineage was also of great importance to the Tokugawa clan, who manufactured a genealogical connection between themselves and the Minamoto clan in order to claim the hereditary privilege of becoming shogun.

35. Mori Tōru, *Kasen-e—Hyakunin Isshu-e* (Tokyo: Kadokawa Shoten, 1981), pp. 80–83. One copy is extant in the Tōyō Bunko and is reproduced in Shimazu's *Hyakunin Isshu*. The copy is in one volume measuring 26.4 × 18.7 cm and missing any introduction or colophon (Mori, pp. 80–81).

36. E. S. Crawcour, "Changes in Japanese Commerce in the Tokugawa Period," in John W. Hall and Marius B. Jansen, eds., *Studies in the Institutional History of Early Modern Japan* (Princeton, N.J.: Princeton University Press, 1968), p. 191; cited by Charles Franklin Sayre, "Illustrations of the *Ise monogatari*: Survival and Revival of Heian Court Cul-

ture" (Ph.D. diss., Yale University, 1978), pp. 272. In Japanese see Hayashi Susumu, "Suminokura Soan-hitsu Sōshū-kō Heiji-dono Ate Shojō" [Letter from Suminokura Sōan to (Fujimoto) Sōshū and (Suminokura) Heiji], *Yamato Bunka* 87 (March 1992): 43–60.

37. On the Kanō school and its position in the early Edo period see Quitman E. Phillips, "*Honchō gashi* and the Kano Myth," *Archives of Asian Art* (forthcoming).

38. Mori notes that the album format was popular in the Edo period, and albums of the *One Hundred Poets* formed part of the bridal trousseaux in daimyo families (p. 75). It is not surprising, then, that the oldest examples should come from the painting school longest associated with warrior patronage.

39. Two volumes, pigment on silk, 31.4 × 27.5 cm, private collection.

40. Mori, *Kasen-e*, pp. 76–77.

41. One volume, 30 × 20 cm.

42. The Tokyo National Museum album deserves more analysis than can be offered here. See Joshua S. Mostow, "The *One Hundred Poets* album (Hyakunin Isshu Gajō) attributed to Kanō Tan'yū: Its Historical Significance and Reception" 40th International Conference of Eastern Studies (Tōhō Gakkai), May 1995. It should be noted, however, that unlike the Date version, poets appear on paired sides and this pairing had a definite influence on the pictorialization of some of the poets and some of their poems. The tendency toward pairing in Tan'yū's case may also have been influenced by the pairs of portraits of famous Chinese poets that he had painted earlier for Ishikawa Jōzan's Shisendō. See J. Thomas Rimer et al., *Shisendo: Hall of the Poetry Immortals* (New York: Weatherhill, 1991); and Ishikawa Takudo, ed., *Shisendō* (Kyoto: Benridō, 1971).

43. Tanaka Sōsaku, *Hyakunin Isshu KoChūshaku no Kenkyū* (Tokyo: Ōfūsha, 1966), p. 196.

44. The full title is *Ken'yō E-iri Uta to Kenzu Hyakunin Isshu Denki Keifu,* in three volumes (27 × 18.5 cm), published in Edo by Urokogataya. The colophon of this edition informs us that "Hishikawa Kichibei Moronobu, the Japanese-style painter *(yamato-eshi)* from Musashi, who has been in Edo a long time," was responsible for the pictures, which "corrected the court costumes [of the poets], together with indicating the heart of the poems in pictures." The book is reproduced from a copy owned by Nonaka Harumizu in Hanpon Bunko, vol. 9, Katagiri Yōichi, ed., *"Hyakunin Isshu" to Moronobu no "Zōsanshō."* The reading of the colophon is based on Ono Tadashige, *Ukiyo-e: Kinsei Minshū Hanga no Eshi-tachi* (Tokyo: Tōkai Daigaku Shuppankai, 1980), p. 49.

45. Mori Tōru, however, considers the *Soan-bon* and Moronobu's work separate lineages and notes that the *kasen-e* have various differences between them; Mori, *Kasen-e,* p. 82.

46. See Hishikawa Moronobu Kinen-kan Zuroku (1986), pl. 2, p. 21.

47. Kobayashi Tadashi, in Ishida Hisatoyo et al., eds., *Nihon Bijutsu Shi Jiten* (Tokyo: Heibonsha, 1987), s.v. "Hishikawa Moronobu."

48. Published by Nihon-bashi Kawasaki Shichirōhei. See Ono, *Ukiyo-e,* pp. 47–49.

49. Reproduced in *Hishikawa Moronobu E-hon,* ed. Tōyō Bunko and Nihon Koten Bungakkai (Tokyo: Kijū-bon Kankō-kai, 1974). Curiously, Ono believes the *Kongen* version was created *between* 1683 and 1684 (pp. 47–48).

50. *Taga-sode* ("whose sleeves?"), a compositional format found on screens, depicts colorful robes hung casually from clothes racks.

51. See Kengi Hamada, trans., *The Life of an Amorous Man* (Rutland, Vt.: Tuttle, 1964), pp. 19–21.

52. Reproduced in Tom Evans and Mary Anne Evans, *Shunga: The Art of Love in Japan* (New York: Paddington Press, 1975), fig. 5.63.

53. Reproduced in Evans and Evans, *Shunga,* fig. 5.51.

54. Reproduced in Evans and Evans, *Shunga,* fig. 5.6.

55. Three volumes, 27.5 × 18.5 cm; Edo: Kinoshita Jin'emon, publisher; published posthumously by his son, Morofusa, in Genroku 8 (1695), the year after Moronobu's death. A complete copy is owned by the Art Institute of Chicago (Toda, *Descriptive Catalogue,* p. 110); reproduced in Kurokawa Shindō, ed., *Nihon Fūzoku Zue,* vol. 2 (Tokyo: Nihon Fūzoku Zue Kankō-kai, 1914). Some scholars attribute this work to Morofusa rather than Moronobu. (See Miyatake Gaikotsu, *Moronobu Gafu;* and Tanaka Kōsaku, *Ukiyo-e no Kenkyū,* nos. 15–16.) I am not concerned here with the issue of attribution, however, and my argument does not depend on whether the *Sugata-e* is by Moronobu, Morofusa, both, or neither. My interest is in demonstrating that the images can be read to have meaningful associations with the poems they accompany. I believe this kind of association was widely practiced and understood, and I use the label "Moronobu" simply as a convenience.

56. Note the heavily outlined boulder reminiscent of Moronobu's *Yokei-zukuri Niha no Zu* (1680).

57. Philip Conisbee, *Soap Bubbles (Masterpiece in Focus)* (Los Angeles: County Museum of Art, 1991), p. 12.

58. An aim which Conisbee dismisses with the observation that "the more public [Chardin's] art became, first by exhibition at the Salon and then by dissemination through engravings, the more easily accessible and even trivial its meaning was rendered for wider consumption"; ibid., p. 12.

59. Ihara Saikaku, *The Great Mirror of Male Love,* trans. Paul Gordon Schalow (Stanford, Calif.: Stanford University Press, 1990), p. 13.

60. The complete title is *Chū-iri Kashira-zu Buke Hyakunin Isshu,* one volume, 27 × 19 cm; signed "Eshi Hishikawa Kichibei" (Edo: Tsuruya Kiemon, 1627); Art Institute of Chicago. See Toda, *Descriptive Catalogue,* pp. 93–94.

61. Prints, *ōban* format, *sumizuri-e,* ca. 1682; Art Institute of Chicago. Reproduced in Evans and Evans, *Shunga,* figs. 5.10 and 5.20. *Shunga,* or "spring pictures," is the term given erotic Japanese prints.

62. This interpretation is not mentioned in the *Yūsai shō* commentary that accompanies Moronobu's picture in the *Zōsanshō;* nor does it appear in the commentary appended to the *Sugata-e,* which quotes the *Kokinshū* headnote verbatim and adds a few appreciative comments.

63. Kigin was one of the most distinguished scholars of classical Japanese literature in the early Edo period. His annotated edition of the first eight imperial anthologies, the *Hachidaishū Shō,* was, until very recently, the standard edition of many of these anthologies.

64. Paul Gordon Schalow, "The Invention of a Literary Tradition of Male Love— Kitamura Kigin's *Iwatsutsuji,*" *Monumenta Nipponica* 48(1) (Spring 1993): 2. Kigin's text was not published until 1713, but it enjoyed many reprintings until 1849 (Schalow, p. 1). Moronobu's *Zōsanshō* was reissued in 1680 under the title *Hyakunin Isshu Kisen-shō* with a prefaced added by Kigin (Mori, *Kasen-e* p. 81).

65. Schalow, "Invention," p. 4. The Japanese text of Sōin's work can be found in Kaneko Kinjirō et al., eds., *Renga Haikai Shū,* NKBZ 32, Shōgakkan, 1974, pp. 309–332; for a partial translation see Carter, *Traditional Japanese Poetry,* pp. 342–343.

66. Mostow, "Painted Poems," pp. 341–344.

67. "*Kono Takasago ha, yama no sōmei. Meisho ni ha arazu*" (Katagiri, "Zōsanshō," p. 104).

68. Two volumes, 15.4 × 10.8 cm; Enkyō 3 (1746); Kyoto: Kōto Shorin Sakaiya Jinbei and Sakaiya Gihei; Atomi Gakuen Tanki Daigaku Toshokan. The frontispiece shows Teika inscribing the poems on hanging scrolls. The format is different from Moronobu's:

the family trees are inscribed above the *kasen-e,* while the poems are inscribed in the picture plane of the *uta-e,* and the two pictures are rarely on facing pages.

69. *Kangyoku Hyakunin Isshu Suishōsō,* one volume, 26.1 × 18 cm (1804); no publisher or place listed; the artist is listed as Sōsekishi; Atomi Gakuen Tanki Daigaku Toshokan.

70. Matsumura, *Eiga Monogatari ZenChūshaku,* VII:77; trans. Mostow, *Uta-e,* pp. 118–125.

71. Kawaguchi Hisao and Shida Nobuyoshi, eds., NKBT 73 (1965), p. 344.

72. Karen Brazell, trans., *The Confessions of Lady Nijō* (Stanford, Calif.: Stanford University Press, 1973), p. 93. Brazell gives the poem as from *The Tale of Genji* and quotes Waley's translation. Seidensticker's translation (p. 93) is:

> A wind strays down from the hills to end my dream,
> And tears well forth at these voices upon the waters.

73. Nagasaki Iwao, "Designs for a Thousand Ages: Printed Pattern Books and Kosode," trans. Amanda Mayer Stinchecum, in Dale Carolyn Gluckman and Sharon Sadako Takeda, eds., *When Art Became Fashion* (Los Angeles: County Museum of Art, 1992), p. 99.

74. Sharon Sadako Takeda, "Clothed in Words: Calligraphic Design on Kosode," in Gluckman and Takeda, *When Art Became Fashion,* p. 178, n. 10.

75. See Betty Y. Siffert, "*Hinagata Bon:* The Art Institute of Chicago Collection of Kimono Pattern Books," in *Five Centuries of Japanese Kimono,* Art Institute of Chicago Museum Studies, vol. 18, no. 1, pp. 86–87. For Lady Nijō see Brazell, *Confessions,* pp. 4 and 194.

76. Takeda, "Clothed in Words," p. 178, n. 12.

77. Suntory, *Moronobu,* p. 72. The *Kosode OnHinagata* of 1677 is also often attributed to Moronobu. For a reproduction and translation see Liza Crihfield Dalby, *Kimono: Fashioning Culture* (New Haven: Yale University Press, 1993), pp. 271–321. The *Ishō Hiinagata* (Suntory Museum) is probably earlier. See Suntory Bijutsukan, *Sanbyaku Kinen, Ukiyo-e Tanjō, Hishikawa Moronobu* (1994).

78. This theory was convincingly demonstrated in a recent lecture by Nagasaki Iwao, "Miyazaki Yūzen to Yūzen-zome, Ogata Kōrin to Kōrin-Moyō," Gakushūin Kasumi Kaikan Geijutsu Kōza, 21 September 1994, Gakushūin University, Tokyo. In fact, fans seem to have played a major role in the transmission of the *uta-e* tradition. See Wada, *Saga-bon Kō;* Katagiri Yayoi, "Ōgi-e to Waka—Muromachi Jidai ni okeru Ōgi-e Kyōju no Ichimen."

79. Two volumes, 27 × 19.2 cm; designs by Hakuyōken Gyōjō; Kyoto: Yezōshiya, Jōkyō 6 (1688). An incomplete copy of vol. 1 is in the Atomi collection (Poems 1 to 48); vol. 2 is in the Art Institute of Chicago (Poems 51 to 100). See Ueda Saeko, *Kosode Moyō* pp. 46–47.

80. *Ogura Yama Shikishi Moyō* (Pattern Book of Ogura Mountain Cartouche Designs; also called *Shikishi OnHinagata*); Edo: Hon'ya Seibei, 1689; two volumes; designs by Take Heiji; reprint Tokuryoku Tomiyoshirō, ed. (Nihon Hanga Kyōkai, 1938); copy in Atomi collection. Also reproduced in Ueda Saeko, *Kosode Moyō,* vol. 1.

81. Ueda, *Kosode Moyō,* pp. 49–50.

82. Private collection. One double-spread is reproduced in Kokuritsu Rekishi Minzoku Hakubutsukan, ed., *Kinsei Kimono Bankakyō,* fig. 222.

83. Nagasaki, "Designs," p. 104.

Chapter 5: Pictorialization as Reception

1. Akita Minoru and Watada Masaru, *Ochi no Hyōjō* (Tokyo: Bun'yūsha, 1978), pp. 98–99. I am grateful to Pat Welch for bringing this book to my attention.

2. Yūsai's text reads:

Kariho no iho to ha, issetsu ha kari-ho no iho, issetsu ha kari-iho no iho nari. Kari-ho toki mo, kariwo to yomu-beshi to zo. Tadashi, nawo, kari-iho no iho yoroshikaru-beki niya. Rei no kasane-kotoba nari. . . . Kariho ha, ho to ifu setsu mo aredomo, tada kariho to yomu-beshi. . . . Kariho ha, kari naru iho naru. Man'yō ni kari-iho to kakeri. [Katagiri, *Zōsanshō*, pp. 44–45]

"Kariho no iho": one explanation is "the hut of cut ears [of grain]," another explanation is "the hut, the temporary hut." It is said that even if it is taken to mean "cut ears [*kariho*]," it should be pronounced /*kariwo*/. However, still, mustn't "temporary hut" be correct? It is a typical case of word repetition. . . . As for "kariho," even though there is the explanation that it means "ears," it is to be read simply as /*kariho*/. . . . As for "kariho," it is a temporary hut. In the *Man'yō* it is written [with the characters] "to borrow" and "hut."

3. The "Porter illustrations," as I call them, appear in William N. Porter's translation, *A Hundred Verses from Old Japan* (Rutland, Vt.: Tuttle, 1979), originally published by the Clarendon Press in 1909. The introduction states that the "illustrations have been reproduced from a native edition of the *Hyaku-nin-isshiu*, which probably dates from the end of the eighteenth century, and which has been kindly lent to me by Mr. F. V. Dickins" (p. xiii). The earliest edition I have been able to find that has pictures identical to that in Porter is the *Sensai Hyakunin Isshu Yamato Kotobuki*, published in 1829 in Nagoya by Minoya Monjirō and in Osaka by Akitaya Ichigorō (Atomi collection). The artist of the frontispiece is Hokusai's daughter Ōi—whether she is also responsible for the other drawings is not clear. The possibility of the Porter pictures coming from some edition of this work was first pointed out by Teele and Yoshikai (1994), p. 210.

4. Though not related to the *nō* play, the idea that this poem refers to a heavenly maiden drying her robe can be seen as early as the *Komezawa Shō* (1452).

5. Indeed, Porter thanks "Mr. S. Uchigasaki, for his kind assistance toward the meaning of some of the more obscure passages" (p. xiii). Color woodblock print; publisher: Nishimuraya; signed "Zen Hokusai Manji"; British Museum; reproduced in Morse, *Hokusai*.

6. Drawing; signed "Zen Hokusai Manji"; Freer Gallery of Art; reproduced in Morse, *Hokusai*.

7. The *kanji* for "deer" is used for *shika* in the *Shikishi waka*, as well as in the *Kyōchōshō;* see Shimazu and Kamijō *Kochū Shō*.

8. Hagitani Boku, quoted by Shimazu, *Hyakunin Isshu*, pp. 214–215.

9. NKBZ 56:515. The modern editor states that much of the interest in the poem is lost if one does not see a contrast between *uma* (written 午) and *ushi* (牛).

10. Ariyoshi, *ZenYakuchū* pp. 36–37.

11. Reproduced in Shōgaku Tosho, ed., *Hyakunin Isshu no Techō* (Tokyo: Shōgakkan, 1989). See also Nakamachi Keiko, "Ogata Kōrin no Zōkeisei ni Kan suru Ichi Kōsatsu: Hyakunin Isshu-e Karuta o Chūshin to shite," *Kokka* 1027 (1979): 9–36.

12. The first edition so designed appears to have been the *Manpō Hyakunin Isshu Taisei*, published in 1707.

13. Anon., *Ogura Hyakunin Isshu* (Edo: Kinkadō, Suwaraya Sasuke, n.d.); collection of the author.

14. See, for example, Torii Kiyonaga (1752–1815), *Kodakara Gosetsu Asobi: Tanabata (Hoshi Matsuri)*, polychrome woodblock print, *ōban* format, Royal Museum of Art and History, Brussels; in Sadamura Tadashi, ed., *Sharaku Debyuu ni Hyakunen Kinen: Sharaku to Utamaro, Edo no Ukiyo-e-ten* (Tokyo: Kōdansha, 1994), fig. 40.

15. Color woodblock print; publisher: Iseya; signed "Zen Hokusai Manji"; British Museum; reproduced in Morse, *Hokusai*.

16. Nakagawa Tsuneki, ed., *Man'yō Hyakunin Isshu* (n.p.), printed 1700; one volume, 25.8 × 18.3 cm; Atomi Gakuen Tanki Daigaku Toshokan.

17. Ikeda Tōritei, ed., *Nichiyō Zatsuroku Fujin Shu-Bunko Shūgyoku Hyakunin Isshu Ogura Shiori;* pictures by Keisai Eisen (1790–1848); Edo (n.p.); Atomi Gakuen Tanki Daigaku Toshokan.

18. Sōsekishi, *Kangyoku Hyakunin Isshu Suishōsō,* "Tenji Tennō"; Edo, 1804; Atomi Gakuen Tanki Daigaku Toshokan.

19. In fact, Kuniyoshi seems to have had a special talent for stirring up political controversy, intentionally or not. In 1843 his triptych *The Earth Spider Generates Monsters at the Mansion of Lord Minamoto Yorimitsu* was banned and its blocks destroyed. But as Sarah Thompson writes, "Kuniyoshi escaped punishment, perhaps because it was unclear whether he had really intended any satire or whether the hidden political meanings had simply been imagined by a public that saw what it wanted to see." See Thompson and Harootunian, *Undercurrents in the Floating World: Censorship and Japanese Prints* (New York: Asia Society Galleries, 1991), p. 63. See also Melinda Takeuchi, "Kuniyoshi's *Minamoto Raikō and the Earth Spider:* Demons and Protest in Late Tokugawa Japan," *Ars Orientalis* 17 (1987): 5–38. Ten years later, he was fined for *The Miracle of Famous Paintings by Ukiyo Matabei* (Thompson and Hartoonian, *Undercurrents*, p. 65).

20. Reproduced in Julia Meech-Pekarik, *The World of the Meiji Print* (New York: Weatherhill, 1986), fig. 67.

21. Yoshihara Sachiko and Nakada Yumiko, *Manga Hyakunin Isshu* (Tokyo: Heibonsha, 1986), pp. 12–14.

Poems 1–25

1. Poem 1: *GSS* 6 (Autumn 2): 302; *TKJT* 12; *NSDS* 332; *EGTG* 34; *SKDT* 54; *HNSK* 1; *HDSSI* 1; *KDSK* 15; *KRFTS* 313

2. *Chōshū Eisō,* II, quoted by Kubota, *Hikkei,* p. 30.

3. Brower and Miner, *Japanese Court Poetry,* p. 507.

4. "Kariho no iho to ha, issetsu ha kari-ho no iho, issetsu ha kari-iho no iho nari. Kari-ho no toki mo, kari-wo to yomubeshi to zo. Tadashi, nawo, kari-iho no iho yoroshikaru-beki niya. Rei no kasane-kotoba nari. . . . Kariho ha, ho to ifu setsu aredomo, tada kari-ho to yomu-beshi. . . . Kariho ha, kari naru iho nari" (Katagiri, *Zōsanshō,* p. 44).

5. Poem 2: *SKKS* 3 (Summer): 175; *NSDS* 198; *EGTG* 32; *KRFTS* 16.

6. Kitamura Kigin, *Hachidaishū Shō* (rpt. Yūseidō), vol. 2.

7. See Akimoto Shunkichi, "The Three Mountains of Yamato," *Japan Quarterly* 3 (1956): 356–363.

8. Poem 3: *SIS* 13 (Love 3): 778; *NSDS* 1122; *EGTG* 97; *SKDT* 93; *HNSK* 3; *HDSSI* 26; *KDSK* 64; *KKRJ* 924; *WKRS* 238; *SJRNS* 8; *JDFDUA* 3.

9. F. Victor Dickins, "The Makura-Kotoba of Primitive Japanese Verse," *Asiatic Society of Japan,* vol. 35, pt. 4 (Yokohama, 1908), p. 14.

10. Ōno Susumu et al, eds., *Iwanami Kogo Jiten,* s.v. *"ashi-hiki."*

11. Brower and Miner, *Superior Poems,* pp. 141–142.

12. See Kubota, *Hikkei,* p. 32.

13. Teika himself composed the following "allusive variation" *(honka-dori)* based on this poem (*SKKS* [Autumn II]: 487):

hitori neru	Ah, the moonlight of Toko
yama-dori no wo no	as it shines like frost

shidari-wo ni	on the trailing tail
shimo oki-mayofu	of the mountain pheasant
toko no tsuki-kage	sleeping alone in its bed.

14. For a recent paper on Hitomaro iconography see Shimao Arata, "Kakinomoto no Hitomaro-zō ni okeru 'Katachi' to 'Imi,'" Tokyo National Research Institute of Cultural Properties, ed., *Human Figure in the Visual Arts of East Asia,* International Symposium on the Preservation of Cultural Property 1994, pp. 220–232.

15. Poem 4: *SKKS* 6 (Winter): 675; *NSDS* 563; *SKDT* 91.

16. Trans. Ian Hideo Levy, *The Ten Thousand Leaves* (Princeton, N.J.: Princeton University Press, 1981), p. 178.

17. Katagiri Yōichi, *Uta-makura Uta-kotoba Jiten* (Tokyo: Kadokawa Shoten, 1983), s.v. *"tago no ura."*

18. See "Teika and the 'Simultaneous Order'" in Chapter 2.

19. Poem 5: *KKS* 4 (Autumn 1): 215; *NSDS* 422; *EGTG* 46; *KDSK* 20; *SJRNS* 61; *KRFTS* 246.

20. Laurel Rodd, trans., *Kokinshū* (Princeton, N.J.: Princeton University Press, 1984), p. 383.

21. See, for instance, Rodd's translation: (*Kokinshū,* p. 109):

> treading through the
> autumn leaves in the deepest
> mountains   I hear the
> belling of the lonely deer—
> then it is that autumn is sad

22. The pose is similar to one seen at the end of the so-called *Genre Scenes of the Four Seasons* handscroll, signed by Moronobu, in the Idemitsu Collection. See Idemitsu Bijutsukan, ed., *Nihon no Kaiga Hyakusen* [One hundred masterpieces of Japanese painting], fig. 57; and Suntory Bijutsukan, ed., *Hishikawa Moronobu-ten,* fig. 4.

23. Poem 6: *SKKS* 6 (Winter): 620; *NSDS* 518; *SKDT* 85; *JDFDUA* 17.

24. For more on Yakamochi in English see Paula Doe, *A Warbler's Song in the Dusk: The Life and Work of Ōtomo no Yakamochi (718–785)* (Berkeley: University of California Press, 1982).

25. In Episode 125 of the *Tales of Yamato* we read:

One day the Major Captain of Izumi went to visit the late Minister of the Left. He had had some saké on his way there and was quite inebriated when he unexpectedly showed up in the middle of the night. Surprised by the late visit, the Minister asked: "Where have you come from?" When his servants, making a great deal of racket, raised the upper half of the lattice door, the Minister saw that the Major Captain had Mibu no Tadamine with him. Tadamine, holding aloft a burning pine torch at the foot of the stairs, knelt and said: "This is what my master wishes to say to you:

Kasasagi no	Over the frost
Wataseru hashi no	On the bridge formed by the magpies,
Shimo no ue o	Have I trod
Yowa ni fumiwake	In the hush of night
Kotosara ni koso	Especially to see you.

Trans. Mildred Tahara, *Tales of Yamato* (Honolulu: University of Hawai'i Press, 1980), pp. 76–77.

26. Ariyoshi cites the following two poems by Teika's contemporaries, Ietaka ("Kenpō 4 Palace Poetry Contest," topic: "Winter Mountain Frost"):

kasasagi no	Where is it that
watasu ya idzuko	the magpies spread their wings?
yufu-shimo no	The peak's hanging bridge,
kumowi ni shiroki	white above the clouds
mine no kake-hashi	of evening frost.

and GoToba *(Eigo Hyakushu Waka):*

kasasagi no	The hanging bridge,
kumo no kake-hashi	formed by magpies in the clouds,
sae-watari	is frozen over fast—
shimo woki-madofu	and filled with frost is
ariake no tsuki	the pale moon of daybreak.

27. Poem 7: *KKS* 9 (Travel): 406; *NSDS* 772; *SKDT* 111; *SSWK* 182; *KKRJ* 252; *WKRS* 258; *KRFTS* 267; *TYZN* 172.

28. A fantastic account of Kibi's stay in China is seen in the thirteenth-century *Kibi Dainagon Illustrated Scrolls,* Museum of Fine Arts, Boston, and reproduced in Nihon Emaki Taisei, vol. 3 (Chūō Kōronsha).

29. Trans. McCullough, *Kokin Wakashū,* p. 97.

30. McCullough, *Classical Japanese Prose,* p. 87.

31. The phrase reads "fuji no takane wo / ama no hara / furi-sake mireba;" translated by Levy as "Fuji's lofty peak / . . . As I gaze up to it / through the fields of heaven" (p. 178).

32. Poem 8: *KKS* 18 (Misc. 2): 983, "topic unknown"; *NSDS* 1648; *SKDT* 107; *KKRJ* 885.

33. Rodd, *Kokinshū,* p. 45.

34. *MJ: "to iu koto da."*

35. Poem 9: *KKS* 2 (Spring 2): 113; *TKJT* 44; *NSDS* 122; *EGTG* 13; *HNSSI* 1; *KDSK* 6; *SJRNS* 62; *JDFDUA* 37.

36. Poem 10: *GSS* 15 (Misc. 1): 1089; *NSDS* 1654; *HNSK* 16; *HDSSI* 20; *KDSK* 82.

37. This is the reading found also in Shunzei's *Korai Fūtei Shō.* The *-te ha* construction has an analogous function, indicating repeated action. Grammatically, however, it connects with the *afu* of *afusaka (wakarete . . . afu),* which might then be translated as "parting . . . to meet [again]."

38. Susan Matisoff, *The Legend of Semimaru, Blind Musician of Japan* (New York: Columbia University Press, 1978), pp. 56 and 57–58. This work is the most complete treatment of the Semimaru legend in English.

39. *GSS,* p. 323.

40. See Matisoff, *Legend,* pp. 165–168.

41. Morris, *Amorous Woman,* p. 220.

42. Poem 11: *KKS* 9 (Travel): 407; *TKJT* 223; *NSDS* 780; *SSWK* 186; *KGS* 56; *WKRS* 648; *JDFDUA* 19; *KRFTS* 268.

43. For translations see Ward Geddes, "Takamura Monogatari," *Monumenta Nipponica* 46(3) (Autumn 1991): 275–291; and Joshua S. Mostow et al., trans., "Tales of Takamura," *B.C. Asian Review* 3/4 (September 1990): 355–380.

44. Poem 12: *KKS* 17 (Misc. 1): 872; *NSDS* 1455; *KDSK* 77; *SSWK* 217; *KKRJ* 441; *WKRS* 718; *KRFTS* 287.

45. Poem 13: *GSS* 11 (Love 3): 776; *NSDS* 964; *KKRJ* 1549.

46. Rodd, *Kokinshū,* p. 46.

47. Poem 14: *KKS* 14 (Love 4): 724; *NSDS* 854; *KKRJ* 3312; *TYZN* 287; *KRFTS* 280.

48. *Jōkyō Manpō Zensho Azuma-kagami* (Edo: Suharaya Mohei, 1829).

49. Poem 15: *KKS* 1 (Spring 1): 21; *TKJT* 161; *NSDS* 19; *EGTG* 2; *SKDT* 11; *SSWK* 29; *KKRJ* 45; *JDFDUA* 43.

50. Poem 16: *KKS* 8 (Parting): 365; *TKJT* 54; *NSDS* 730; *EGTG* 72; *HDSSI* 5; *KDSK* 36; *SSWK* 181; *KKRJ* 1275; *JDFDUA* 25; *KRFTS* 264.

51. See Donald Keene, ed., *Twenty Plays of the Nō Theatre* (New York: Columbia University Press, 1970).

52. A large single print on this theme by Moronobu is also extant: the *Matsukaze Murasame Zu,* Hishikawa Moronobu Memorial Museum, Chiba prefecture.

53. Poem 17: *KKS* 5 (Autumn 2): 294; *NSDS* 465; *EGTG* 52; *KRFTS* 257.

54. Poem 18: *KKS* 12 (Love 2): 559; *NSDS* 1219; *KDSK* 66; *KKRJ* 2033.

55. Poem 19: *SKKS* 11 (Love 1): 1049; *NSDS* 909; *EGTG* 85; *KDSK* 47.

56. Howard A. Link, *Primitive Ukiyo-e* (Honolulu: University of Hawai'i Press, 1980), p. 6.

57. Poem 20: *GSS* 13 (Love 5): 960; *TKJT* 1; *NSDS* 1205; *EGTG* 98; *HDSSI* 25; *KDSK* 65; *KKRJ* 1960; *Kuhon Waka; JDFDUA* 65; *KRFTS* 330.

58. Poem 21: *KKS* 14 (Love 4): 691; *TKJT* 31; *NSDS* 1105; *KDSK* 62; *EGTG* 95; *KKRJ* 2827; *WKRS* 789; *KGS* 44; *SJRUS* 53; *JDFDUA* 71; *TYZN* 35; *KRFTS* 279.

59. Poem 22: *KKS* 5 (Autumn 2): 249, "A Poem from the Poetry Contest at the Residence of Prince Koresada"; *NSDS* 410; *EGTG* 44; *SSMYS* 372; *KKRJ* 431; *JDFDUA* 26; *Waka Kuhon.*

60. Poem 23: *KKS* 4 (Autumn 1): 193; *TKJT* 225; *NSDS* 306; *KDSK* 11; *EGTG* 27; *HNSK* 30.

61. See McCullough, *Brocade by Night,* pp. 254–261.

62. Kawaguchi Hisao, ed., *Wakan Rōei Shū* (Tokyo: Kōdansha, 1982), pp. 183–184.

63. Poem 24: *KKS* 9 (Travel): 420; *TKJT* 66; *NSDS* 806; *HDSSI; EGTG* 75; *SSWK* 192; *KKRJ* 2401; *KRFTS* 270.

64. For a discussion of this last attribution see Robert Borgen, *Sugawara no Michizane and the Early Heian Court* (Cambridge, Mass.: Harvard University Press, 1986), pp. 221–222.

65. Ibid., pp. 260–268.

66. Many modern textbooks suggest the additional meaning "for the time being," or "first of all," from the modern Japanese meaning for *tori-aezu,* but there is no evidence of such a reading in the premodern sources.

67. Borgen, *Sugawara no Michizane,* p. 304.

68. Poem 25: *GSS* 11 (Love 3): 700; *NSDS* 1108; *KKRJ* 3888.

Poems 26–50

1. Poem 26: *SIS* 17 (Misc./Autumn): 1128; *NSDS* 482; *HDSSI.*

2. McCullough and McCullough, *Flowering Fortunes,* I:364.

3. Tahara, *Yamato,* p. 57.

4. McCullough, *Ōkagami* p. 220.

5. Kamens, *Word in Flower,* p. 26.

6. Poem 27: *SKKS* 11 (Love 1): 996; *NSDS* 913; *KKRJ* 1572; *JDFDUA* 95.

7. Poem 28: *KKS* 6 (Winter): 315; *NSDS* 508; *KKRJ* 983; *WKRS* 564; *SJRNS* 97; *JDFDUA* 56.

8. See *KKS* 68, 205, 214, and 944.

9. Poem 29: *KKS* 5 (Autumn 2): 277; *SSWS* 100; *SJRNS; WKRS* 273; *KGS* 32; *NSDS* 435; *EGTG* 48; *KKRJ* 3744; *SJRNS* 28.

10. For a similar composition see Moronobu's *Genre Scenes of the Four Seasons* handscroll in the Idemitsu Museum of Art.

11. Poem 30: *KKS* 13 (Love 3): 625; *TKJT* 6; *NSDS* 1070; *EGTG* 93; *HDSSI* 7; *KDSK* 59; *KKRJ* 362; *JDFDUA* 119.

12. Poem 31: *KKS* 6 (Winter): 332, "Composed when he saw that snow had fallen, while he was traveling down to Yamato province"; *NSKS* 558; *KDSK* 27; *EGTG* 63; *HDSSI*; *KKRJ* 731; *JDFDUA* 135.

13. For more on Teika's search see Mostow, *"Uta-e,"* pp. 159–161.

14. Poem 32: *KKS* 5 (Autumn 2): 303, "Composed on the mountain pass of Shiga"; *NSDS* 467; *EGTG* 53; *KKRJ* 1636.

15. Poem 33: *KKS* 2 (Spring 2): 84; *NSDS* 150; *EGTG* 15; *SKDT* 24; *KDSK* 7; *KKRJ* 4196 and 4033.

16. Sunflowers belong to the same family as chrysanthemums; the term *hi-mawari* is attested to in Japanese sources from the very early 1700s. The motif of man and shamisen-playing courtesan can be seen in Moronobu's *Genre Scenes of the Four Seasons* handscroll in the Idemitsu Museum of Art.

17. Reproduced in Komatsu Shigemi, ed., *Nihon Emaki Taisei,* vol. 10 (Tokyo: Chūō Kōronsha, 1978).

18. Poem 34: *KKS* 17 (Misc. 1): 909; *SJRNS* 108; *NSDS* 1696; *SSWK* 205; *KKRJ* 4111; *WKRS* 740; *JDFDUA* 69; *KRFTS* 290.

19. Rodd, *Kokinshū,* pp. 40–41.

20. See Royall Tyler's translation and introduction to this play in his *Japanese Nō Dramas* (Harmondsworth: Penguin, 1992), pp. 277–292.

21. Poem 35: *KKS* 1 (Spring 1): 42; *NSDS* 53; *EGTG* 5.

22. Trans. Schalow, *Great Mirror,* p. 98.

23. Poem 36: *KKS* 3 (Summer): 166; *SSWK* 159; *KKRJ* 289; *KRFTS* 241; *NSDS* 252; *HNSK* 33; *KDSK* 8; *JDFDUA* 139.

24. See the similar figures in his *Genre Scenes of the Four Seasons* handscroll in the Idemitsu Museum of Art.

25. Poem 37: *GSS* 6 (Autumn 2): 308; *SSMYS; NSDS* 467; *EGTG* 35; *HDSSI* 12; *KDSK* 16.

26. Paul Schalow (*Great Mirror,* pp. 28–29) explains:

At the age of eleven or twelve the crown of a male child's head was shaved, symbolizing the first of three steps towards adulthood. The shaved crown drew attention to the forelocks *(maegami),* the boy's distinguishing feature. At the age of fourteen or fifteen the boy's natural hairline was reshaped by shaving the temples into right angles, but the forelocks remained as *sumi-maegami* (cornered forelocks). This process, called "putting in corners" *(kado o ireru),* was the second step towards adulthood. From being a maegami (boy with forelocks), the wakashu had now graduated to being a sumi-maegami (boy with cornered forelocks). The final step, completed at the age of eighteen or nineteen, involved cutting off the forelocks completely; the pate of his head was shaved smooth, leaving only the sidelocks *(bin).* Once he changed to a robe with rounded sleeves, the boy was recognized as an adult man *(yarō).* He was no longer available as a wakashu for sexual relations with adult men like himself but was now qualified to establish a relationship with a wakashu.

27. Poem 38: *SIS* 14 (Love 4): 870; *KKRJ* 2967; *NSDS* 1419; *HDSSI; KKRJ* 2967; *JDFDUA* 173.

28. Trans. Tahara, *Yamato,* p. 47.

29. Poem 39: *GSS* 9 (Love 1): 577; *NSDS* 869; *EGTG* 82; *HDSSI* 16; *KDSK* 44; *JDFDUA* 121.

30. Poem 40: *SIS* 11 (Love 1): 622; *KRFTS* 375; *NSDS* 885; *JDFDUA* 197; *TYZN* 177; *EGIT* 20.

31. Pictures of contests are mentioned as early as the *Musasaki Shikibu Nikki;* see Bowring's translation, pp. 86–87.

32. Poem 41: *SIS* 11 (Love 1): 621; *KRFTS* 374; *NSDS* 884; *EGIT.*

33. Poem 42: *GSIS* 14 (Love 4): 770; *NSDS* 1316; *EGTG* 102; *HDSSI* 37; *KDSK* 68; *JDFDUA* 217; *KRFTS* 468.

34. Trans. Rodd, *Kokinshū,* p. 372.

35. In the *Kokinshū,* poem 1093 is included among the "Eastern Songs" *(Azuma-uta),* including Michinoku, the "Far North." Norinaga argued that *suwe* was a place-name (and *matsu-yama* just generic "pine-clad mountains"), though its location is unclear. Some thought it to be near Matsushima, though in modern times a place near Tagajō City lays claim to the name. *Suwe* also means "tips," however, and commentaries by Kenshō provide a gloss of *tachi-nami no kano matsu-yama no uhe ni koyuru* ("the rising waves pass over the top of that pine-clad mountain); see Kubota, *Hikkai* pp. 71 and 188.

36. Poem 43: *SIS* 12 (Love 2): 710; *NSDS* 1073; *KKRJ* 2598; *SJRNS* 72.

37. Poem 44: *SIS* 11 (Love 1): 678; *NSDS* 1117; *KGS* 45; *SJRNS* 70.

38. Poem 45: *SIS* 15 (Love 5): 950; *NSDS* 1408; *HDSSI; JDFDUA* 187.

39. Poem 46: *SKKS* 11 (Love 1): 1071; *NSDS* 967; *KDSK* 51.

40. Poem 47: *SIS* 3 (Autumn): 140; *NSDS* 274; *EGTG* 24; *JDFDUA* 243; *HDSSI* 22; *KDSK* 9.

41. Poem 48: *SKS* 7 (Love 1): 211; *NSDS* 966; *HDSSI; SJRNS* 93; *JDFDUA* 225; *KRFTS* 550.

42. Poem 49: *SKS* 7 (Love 1): 225; *NSDS* 1010; *HDSSI; KKRJ* 781; *JDFDUA* 213.

43. Poem 50: *GSIS* 12 (Love 2): 669; *NSDS* 1050. Many texts have the last line as *omohikeru kana.*

Poems 51–75

1. Poem 51: *GSIS* 11 (Love 1): 612; *NSDS* 849; *KRFTS* 452; *EGIT* 53.

2. Poem 52: *GSIS* 12 (Love 2): 672; *NSDS* 1046; *HDSSI; JDFDUA* 275.

3. Poem 53: *SIS* 14 (Love 4): 912; *NSDS* 1087; *JDFDUA* 205; *KRFTS* 378.

4. Trans. McCullough, *Classical Japanese Prose,* p. 110.

5. Poem 54: *SKKS* 13 (Love 3): 1149; *NSDS* 1094; *JDFDUA* 233.

6. Trans. McCullough, *Ōkagami,* p. 170.

7. Poem 55: *SIS* 8 (Misc. 1): 449; *SZS* 16 (Misc. 1): 1035.

8. Poem 56: *GSIS* 13 (Love 3): 763; *NSDS* 1387; *HDSSI; KRFTS* 466. Many texts have the last line as *afu yoshi mogana.*

9. Trans. Edwin A. Cranston, *The Izumi Shikibu Diary: A Romance of the Heian Court* (Cambridge, Mass.: Harvard University Press, 1969).

10. Poem 57: *SKKS* 16 (Misc. 1): 1499; *NSDS* 1617.

11. Trans. Richard Bowring, *Murasaki Shikibu: Her Diary and Poetic Memoirs* (Princeton, N.J.: Princeton University Press, 1985), p. 217.

12. Komashaku Kimi, *Murasaki Shikibu no Messeeji* (Tokyo: Asahi Shinbunsha, 1991), pp. 11–25. See Chapter 1 "Introduction: A Poetics of Interpretation."

13. Poem 58: *GSIS* 12 (Love 2): 709; *NSDS* 1402.

14. Carter, *Traditional Japanese Poetry,* p. 224.

15. Poem 59: *GSIS* 12 (Love 2): 680; *KRFTS* 458; *NSDS* 1079.

16. Trans. McCullough and McCullough, *Flowering Fortunes.*

17. Trans. Bowring, *Murasaki Shikibu,* p. 131.

18. This case may indicate that the Japanese edition from which Porter took his illustrations actually postdates the publication of Kageki's *Iken* in 1823.

19. Poem 60: *KYS* 9 (Misc. 1): 550; *NSDS* 1656; *HDSSI; JDFDUA* 174; *TYZN.*

20. Poem 61: *SKS* 1 (Spring): 29; *NSDS* 134; *HDSSI.*

21. Poem 62: *GSIS* 16 (Misc. 2): 939; *NSDS* 1655; *KRFTS* 482.

22. Trans. Ivan Morris, *The Pillow Book of Sei Shōnagon* (New York: Columbia University Press, 1967), I:140–141; emphasis added. The romanization of the poem has been added from Tanaka Jūtarō, ed., *Makura no Sōshi*, Nihon Koten Bungaku Zensho (Tokyo: Asahi Shinbunsha, 1947), p. 244. "Ōsaka" (or *Afusaka*) can be translated as "Meeting Hill."

23. Poem 63: *GSIS* 13 (Love 3): 750; *NSDS* 1112; *HDSSI.*

24. See McCullough and McCullough, *Flowering Fortunes*, II:816.

25. For a translation see Francine Hérail, *Notes journalières de Fujiwara no Michinaga, ministre à la cour de Hei.an (995–1018),* 3 vols. (Geneva/Paris: Librairie Droz, 1988–1991).

26. McCullough and McCullough, *Flowering Fortunes*, II:451–452.

27. Poem 64: *SZS* 6 (Winter): 420; *NSDS* 390. The *Zōsanshō* gives *arahare-idzuru.*

28. *Gon* referred to the appointment of individuals to posts already filled by the maximum number of people allowed by the civil code. Thus, for example, while the position of Major Counselor *(Dainagon)* could be given to only two men, others could be appointed as "supernumerary" *(gon),* that is, "above the legal number." The term is often translated into English as "provisional," but it is not clear that there was anything particularly temporary about these appointments. I have, accordingly, followed Robert Borgen *(Sugawara no Michizane)* and translated the term as "supernumerary."

29. Trans. Levy, *Ten Thousand Leaves,* p. 162.

30. Poem 65: *GSIS* 14 (Love 4): 815; *NSDS* 1335; *HDSSI; JDFDUA* 162; *KRFTS* 471.

31. Poem 66: *KYS* 9 (Misc. 1): 21; *NSDS* 1512; *HDSSI; JDFDUA* 274.

32. Poem 67: *SZS* 16 (Misc. 1): 964; *NSDS* 955.

33. Poem 68: *GSIS* 15 (Misc. 1): 860; *KRFTS* 476; *NSDS* 1606.

34. McCullough and McCullough, *Flowering Fortunes*, II:439.

35. Note that the inscription uses the textual variant *kono yo* in place of *uki yo.*

36. Poem 69: *GSIS* 5 (Autumn 2): 366; *NSDS* 480.

37. Poem 70: *GSIS* 4 (Autumn 1): 333; *NSDS* 405; *HDSSI; JDFDUA* 100.

38. Poem 71: *KYS* 3 (Autumn): 173; *TKJT* 147; *KSB* 1; *NSDS* 402; *EGTG* 41; *HDSSI* 43; *KDSK* 18; *JDFDUA* 2; *KRFTS* 503.

39. Poem 72: *KYS* 8 (Love 2): 469; *NSDS* 987; *HDSSI* 47; *KDSK* 54; *JDFDUA* 126.

40. Poem 73: *GSIS* 1 (Spring 1): 120; *NSDS* 98; *HDSSI; JDFDUA* 248; *KRFTS* 414.

41. For a partial translation see Marian Ury, "The Ōe Conversations," *Monumenta Nipponica* 48(3) (Autumn 1993): 359–380.

42. Poem 74: *SZS* 12 (Love 2): 708; *TKJT* 179; *NSDS* 933; *EGTG* 86; *HNSSI* 67; *KDSK* 48; *EGIT* 37; *GoToba In Kuden.*

43. Poem 75: *SZS* 16 (Misc 1): 1026; *NSDS* 1489; *HDSSI; KDSK* 78.

44. On the history of this period see G. Cameron Hurst III, *Insei: Abdicated Sovereigns in the Politics of Late Heian Japan, 1086–1185* (New York: Columbia University Press, 1976).

Poems 76–100

1. Poem 76: *SKS* 10 (Misc. 2): 382; *KRFTS* 564; *NSDS* 1667; *HDSSI; JDFDUA* 12.

2. In fact, Teika's *Nishidai Shū* and Muromachi-period copies of the *One Hundred Poets* have the word *mayofu* instead of *magafu.*

3. The Shin Nihon Koten Bungaku Taikei edition of the *Shikashū* calls this poem a "likeness" *(omokage)* of Takamura's.

4. Poem 77: *SKS* 7 (Love 1): 229; *NSDS* 934; *EGTG* 87; *HDSSI; JDFDUA* 154; *KRFTS* 554; *TKJT* 254.

5. Poem 78: *KYS* 4 (Winter): 270; *NSDS* 533; *HDSSI.*

6. In the lower hemistich *(iku yo nezamenu / suma no seki-mori), nu* is understood as a perfective *(kanryō)* in the conclusive form *(shūshikei)*. However, the interrogative "how many" *(iku)* grammatically requires the following verb to be in the attributive form *(ren-taikei)*, that is, *ne-zamenuru*. While there are other examples of this rule being broken, the discrepancy led to a number of alternative explanations. Most commentaries assume that there has been some kind of abbreviation, either from *ne-zamenuru (Kaikan Shō, Iken)* or *ne-zamenuramu (Yūsai Shō, Shūishō, Mabuchi)*. Some replace *-nu* with *no (Ka-mijō-bon)* or *wo (Komezawa-bon)* and see the *su* of *suma* as a pivot word *(sa-hen dōshi)*.

7. Awaji served as a pivot word meaning "to meet" in the *Man'yō Shū* in conjunction with the pillow word *wagimoko ni* ("with my beloved," as in *MYS* 3627). There is no example of this usage in the imperial anthologies, however; when it is used as a pivot word there, it appears with "pale" *(ahashi)* or "pathetic" *(ahare)*.

8. Poem 79: *SKKS* 4 (Autumn 1): 413; *NSDS* 316. Grammatically this poem is one long verbal phrase modifying the final noun: "the clear brightness of the light of the moon that leaks out from the breaks in the clouds that trail on the autumn wind."

9. See McCullough and McCullough, *Flowering Fortunes,* II:816.

10. Poem 80: *SZS* 13 (Love 3): 802; *NSDS* 1053.

11. Poem 81: *SZS* 3 (Summer): 161; *NSDS* 242; *JDFDUA* 236.

12. Phillip Harries writes: "The hototogisu, a small bird of the cuckoo family *(Cuculus poliocephalus)*, was famous for its beautiful song. It first sang in the hills, where its song was considered to be at its freshest, and appeared in the city somewhat later, usually in the fifth month, when the song was thought to have passed its best. In any case, the song was eagerly awaited." See Harries, *The Poetic Memoirs of Lady Daibu* (Stanford, Calif.: Stanford University Press, 1980), p. 120. Traditionally the term "cuckoo" has been used in English, but this word calls to mind associations (such as cuckold) that have nothing to do with the Japanese image. I have opted for the Japanese term.

13. The *GoMizuno'o Shō* mentions the "Akashi" chapter of *The Tale of Genji,* but the reference is not clear.

14. Poem 82: *SZS* 13 (Love 3): 818.

15. See Harries, *Daibu,* p. 72.

16. From *tafu,* "to endure." The *Kamijō-bon* is unique in taking the verb to be *tayu,* "to cease," though this is the reading the *Sugata-e* pictorialization suggests, despite its transcription of the poem as *tahezu* (rather than *taezu*).

17. Porter writes that the "illustration shows the priest alone in his hut, lamenting over the sorrows of humanity"; see Porter, *Hundred Verses.*

18. Poem 83: *SZS* 17 (Misc. 2): 1151; *NSDS* 1710; *HDSSI* 70; *KDSK* 83; *JDFDUA* 30; *EGIT* 39.

19. This story is told, and refuted, in the *Yūsai Shō* and repeated in Kigin's widely circulated *Shūe Shō.*

20. For a discussion of the deer motif see Kubota, *Hikkei* p. 163. He notes that although poems on deer are usually placed in the seasonal books in imperial anthologies, many of these poems include a love motif.

21. Poem 84: *SKKS* 18 (Misc. 3): 1843; *TKJT* 94; *NSDS* 1559; *KDSK* 79.

22. Poem 85: *SZS* 12 (Love 2): 766; *NSDS* 958.

23. Trans. Hilda Katō, "The *Mumyōshō* of Kamo no Chōmei and Its Significance in Japanese Literature," *Monumenta Nipponica* 23(3–4) (1968): 321–430.

24. On this topic see Margaret H. Childs, "*Chigo Monogatari:* Love Stories or Buddhist Sermons?," *Monumenta Nipponica* 35(2) (Summer 1980): 127–151.

25. Poem 86: *SZS* 15 (Love 5): 929; *NSDS* 1365; *EGTG* 103; *HDSSI* 68; *KDSK* 73; *JDFDUA* 22.

26. Trans. H. H. Honda, *The Sanka Shū* (Hokuseido); selected translations by Bur-

ton Watson, *Saigyō: Poems of a Mountain Home* (New York: Columbia University Press, 1991); see also William R. LaFleur, trans., *Mirror for the Moon: A Selection of Poems by Saigyō (1118–1190)* (New York: New Directions, 1978).

27. Poem 87: *SKKS* 5 (Autumn 2): 491; *NSDS* 392; *TKJT* 167.

28. Poem 88: *SZS* 13 (Love 3): 807; *NSDS* 1071.

29. Poem 89: *SKKS* 11 (Love 1): 1034; *NSDS* 977; *TKJT* 86.

30. Her entire corpus has been translated by Hiroaki Sato, *String of Beads: Complete Poems of Princess Shikishi* (Honolulu: University of Hawai'i Press, 1993).

31. *Nagarafu* is a *shimo nidan* verb; hence *nagarahe-* is the "negative" *(mizen)* form of the verb, whereas the conditional *(izen)* form would be *nagafure-*.

32. Note that Porter's translation completely misses the romantic nature of the poem.

33. Poem 90: *SZS* 14 (Love 4): 886; *NSDS* 1326; *TKJT* 195.

34. Medieval commentaries are in general agreement, though a minority believe that it is the fishermen's sleeves that the poet wants to show. The *Yoritaka-bon* is unique in claiming that *iro kaharu* refers to "changing affections," an interpretation repeated by Porter.

35. See *KKS* 16 (Grief): 852.

36. Poem 91: *SKKS* 5 (Autumn 2): 518; *NSDS* 441; *HDSSI*.

37. Poem 92: *SZS* 12 (Love 2): 760; *NSDS* 957.

38. Poem 93: *SCSS* 8 (Travel): 525, "topic unknown."

39. "The Reign of Emperor Temmu, Who Ruled from the Kiyomihara Palace in Asuka (673–686): During Princess To'ochi's pilgrimage to the shrine at Ise, Fufuki Toji wrote this poem upon seeing the range of crags at Hata" (Levy, *Ten Thousand Leaves*, p. 49).

40. Poem 94: *SKKS* 5 (Autumn 2): 483; *NSDS* 381.

41. In fact, *samuku* functions in two ways: first, *furu-sato samuku*, "the former capital is cold and . . ."; second, *samuku koromo utsu*, "[the sound of them] striking the cloth coldly." While *furu-sato* in Korenari's poem refers to Nara, in Masatsune's it refers to Yoshino, the supposed site of detached palaces from as early as the reign of Emperor Ōjin (r. 270–310).

42. Poem 95: *SZS* 17 (Misc. 2): 1137; *NSDS* 1712; *JDFDUA* 34.

43. Poem 96: *SCSS* 16 (Misc. 1): 1052, "composed on falling blossoms."

44. Poem 97: *SCSS* 13 (Love 3): 849; Teika also included this poem in his *Teika-kyō Hyaku-ban Ji-Uta-awase*.

45. The headnote in the *SCSS* has Kenpō 6, but it is recorded in Teika's *Shūi Gusō* as Kenpō 4.

46. For a complete translation see Cranston, *Gem-Glistening Cup*, pp. 297–298.

47. This observation was pointed out by an anonymous reader. The famous poem (*SKKS* 363) is:

mi-wataseba	As I gaze out,
hana mo momijhi mo	of blossoms or autumn leaves
nakarikeri	there are neither:
ura no toma-ya no	the thatch-hut of the bay
aki no yufugure	in autumn twilight.

For a reproduction of the Tan'yū pictorialization see Wheelwright, *Word in Flower*, fig. 11.

48. Poem 98: *SCSS* 3 (Summer): 192.

49. Also anthologized as *SKKS* 15 (Love 5): 1375, misattributed to the *Man'yō*-period female poet Yashiro no Ōkimi.

50. Episode 65. The poem speaks of Mitarashi-gawa, an alternative name for

Nara-no-Ogawa. This was a small stream that flowed near the Upper Kamo Shrine on the outskirts of Kyoto and was used by pilgrims to purify themselves by washing their hands *(mi-t[e]-arashi)* and rinsing their mouths before entering the shrine.

51. *GSIS* 3 (Summer): 231: "Composed on the topic 'The evening is cool like autumn,' at the house of Lord Toshitsuna."

52. Poem 99: *SGSS* 17 (Misc. 2): 1202, topic unknown.

53. Poem 100: *SGSS* 18 (Misc. 3): 1205, topic unknown.

54. Perhaps influenced by the *nō* play *Ōmu Komachi,* which is based on the following poem, sent to an aged Komachi, retired from court:

kumo no uhe ha	The court above the clouds:
arishi mukashi ni	although it has not changed
kawarenedo	from the past that was,
mishi tama-dare no	are you curious about life behind
uchi ya yukashiki	the jewelled blinds that once you knew?

For a full translation of the play see Roy E. Teele, Nicholas J. Teele, and H. Rebecca Teele, trans., *Ono no Komachi: Poems, Stories, Nō Plays* (New York: Garland, 1993).

CHARACTER GLOSSARY

Abe no Nakamaro	阿部仲麿	Asukai no	飛鳥井
Abutsu Ni	阿仏尼	Masaari	雅有
afu	逢	Masachika	雅親
afu koto	逢事	Masahide	雅康
Agemaki	総角	Masa'ie	雅家
ahare	哀	Masatsune	雅経
ahazaru kohi	逢はざる恋	Masayo	雅世
ahite ahazaru kohi	逢ひて逢はざる恋	Masayori	雅縁
ai'oi	相生	Masayoshi	雅孝
Akazome	赤染	Yoritaka	頼孝
Emon	衛門	Atsumi Shinnō	敦実親王
Tokimochi	時用	Atsumichi Shinnō	敦道親王
Akiko (Shōshi)	秋子	Atsumori	敦盛
Akishino Gessei Shū	秋篠月清集	Awa	安房
ama	海人	Awaji-shima	淡路島
Amaterasu	天照	Bashō (Matsuo)	芭蕉（松尾）
Anpō Hōshi	安法法師	Benkei	弁慶
arashi	嵐	*biwa hōshi*	琵琶法師
ariake	有明	*Bokuyō Kyōka Shū*	卜養狂歌集
Arima-yama	有馬山	*botan*	牡丹
Ariwara no	有原	*Buke Hyakunin Isshu*	武家百人一首
Narihira	業平	*bushidō*	武士道
Yukihira	行平	*byōbu-uta*	屏風歌
asa	朝	*chi-jhi*	千々
ashi-de	芦手	*chōka*	長歌
Ashi-de Kokin Waka Shū-gire		*chokusen shū*	勅撰集
	芦手古今和歌集	*Chōkyō Shō*	長享抄
	切れ	*chōnin*	町人
ason	臣	*Chōshū Eisō*	長秋詠藻

475

Chōwa	長和	*esha jōri*	会者定離
Chuang-tze	荘子	*e-zōshi*	絵草子
chūko sanjūrokkasen	中古三十六歌仙	*Fuboku Waka Shū*	夫木和歌集
chūnagon	中納言	*Fuji-bakama*	藤袴
dai	題	Fujitsubo	藤壺
dai'ei	題詠	Fujiwara	藤原
Daigo Tennō	醍醐天皇	Akisuke	顕輔
Daikakuji	大覚寺	Asatada	朝忠
dainagon	大納言	Atsutada	敦忠
Daini no Sanmi	大弐三位	Atsuyori	敦頼
DaiSaiin GyoShū	大斎院御集	Hamanari	浜成
dai shirazu	題知らず	Hōshi	褒子
DaiSōjō	大僧正	Ietaka	家隆
Dansen Hyakunin Isshu Taisei		Junshi	遵子
	団扇百人一首	Kane'ie	兼家
	大成	Kanesuke	兼輔
Daruma	達磨	Kanezane	兼実
Date	伊達	Kinnori	公教
Dengyō Daishi	伝教大師	Kintō	公任
Dōin Hōshi	道因法師	Kintsune	公経
Dōjo Hōshinnō	道助法親王	Kiyokawa	清河
doku'eika	独詠歌	Kiyosuke	清輔
dōsei'ai	同性愛	Kiyotaka	清孝
ebi	海老	Korechika	伊周
Edo	江戸	Koremasa	伊尹
Egyō Hōshi	恵慶法師	Kōshi (Takaiko)	高子
e-hon	絵本	Masatsune	雅経
Eiga Hyakunin Isshu Monjū Shō		Michi'ie	道家
	永花百人一首文	Michimasa	道雅
	十抄	Michinaga	道長
Eiga Monogatari	栄華物語	Michimoto	満基
Eiga no Ittei	詠歌一体	Michinobu	道信
Eiga(no) Taigai	詠歌大概	Michitaka	道隆
E-iri Genji Monogatari	絵入り源氏物語	Michitoshi	道俊
Eiryaku	永暦	Moromichi	師通
Eishō Gonen Shigatsu Nijūroku-nichi Saki no		Morosuke	師輔
Reikeiden no Nyōgo Enshi no Uta-e-awase		Mototoshi	基俊
	永承五年四月二十	Mototsune	基経
	六日先麗景殿	Nagakiyo	長清
	女御延子歌絵合	Nagatō	長能
e-monogatari	絵物語	Nakahira	仲平
en	艶	Narikane	業兼
engo	縁語	Nobunari	信成

Nobutaka	宣孝	*gajō*	画帖
Nobuzane	信実	Genbō	玄肪
Okikaze	興風	*Gengen Shū*	玄々集
Sadakata	定方	*Genji Monogatari*	源氏物語
Sadako (Teishi)	定子	Gidōsanshi no Haha	儀同三司母
Sadanaga	定長	*gijinka*	擬人歌
Sadayori	定頼	*Gōdan Shō*	江談抄
Sanekata	実方	GoHorikawa In	後堀川院
Sanesada	実定	GoIchijō Tennō	後一条天皇
Saneyoshi	実能	GoKyōgoku Sesshō Saki no Daijōdaijin	
Seika	惺窩		後京極摂政前太政
Shunzei (Toshinari)			大臣
	俊成	GoMizuno'o Tennō	後水尾天皇
Suenawa	季縄	*GoMizuno'o Tennō Hyakunin Isshu Shō*	
Tadahira	忠平		後水尾天皇百人
Tadamichi	忠通		一首抄
Tadazane	忠実	*gon*	権
Takanobu	隆信	Gonnō-hon	厳王品
Tame'ie	為家	*Gō no Sochi Shū*	江帥集
Tametoki	為時	GoReizei Tennō	後冷泉天皇
Tame'uji	為氏	*GoRokuroku Sen*	後六々撰
Teika (Sada'ie)	定家	Gosechi	五節
Tokihira	時平	*Gosen (Waka) Shū*	後撰(和歌)集
Tōshi	当子	*GoShūi (Waka) Shū*	後拾遺(和歌)拾
Toshitada	俊忠	GoSuzaku Tennō	後朱雀天皇
Toshiyuki	敏行	GoToba In	後鳥羽院
Tsugukage	継蔭	GoTokudaiji Sadaijin	
Yasumasa	保昌		後徳大寺左大臣
Yorinaga	頼長	GoYōzei Tennō	後陽成天皇
Yoshifusa	良房	*GoYōzei Tennō Hyakunin Isshu Shō*	
Yoshitaka	義孝		後陽成天皇百人
Yoshitsune	良経		一首抄
Yukinari	行成	*Gukan Shō*	愚管抄
Fujiwara no Miya	藤原の宮	Gyō'e	尭恵
Fukuro-zōshi	袋草子	Gyōjin	尭尋
fūkyō shitaru katachi	風狂したるかたち	Gyōkō	尭孝
fumidzuki	文月	*Gyokugin Shū*	玉吟集
Fun'ya	文屋	Gyōson	行尊
Asayasu	朝康	*Hachidaishū Shūitsu*	八代集秀逸
Yasuhide	康秀	*haikai*	俳諧
Furuta Oribe	古田織部	Hakuyōken Gyōjō	柏葉軒　暁嶷
fūryū	風流	Hanamichi no Tsurane	
fushimono renga	賦物連歌		花道のつらね

hanka	反歌
Harumichi no Tsuraki	
	春通列樹
Hasegawa Mitsunobu	
	長谷川光信
Hatsune	初音
hatsu-shimo	初霜
Heian	平安
Heian-kyō	平安京
Heike Nōkyō	平家納経
hengaku kasen-e	扁額歌仙絵
hentai-gana	変体仮名
hi-mawari	日周り
hinagata-bon	雛形本
hisakata	久方
hisetsu	秘説
Hishikawa	菱川
Moronobu	師宣
Yoshisa'eimon	吉左衛門
hito-yo	一夜
Hōgen no Ran	保元乱
Hōjō Ki	方丈記
Hon'ami Kōetsu	本阿弥光悦
hon'i	本意
honka-dori	本歌取り
Hon'ya Seibei	本屋清兵衛
Horikawa Hyakushu	堀川百首
Horikawa In	堀川院
Hosokawa Yūsai	細川幽斎
Hosshōji Nyūdō Saki no Kanpaku Daijō-	
daijin	法性寺入道前関白
	太政大臣
hyakuin	百韻
Hyakunin Isshu	百人一首
Hyakunin Isshu Hitoyo-gatari	
	百人一首一夕語
Hyakunin Isshu Iken	百人一首異見
Hyakunin Isshu Kenzu	百人一首顕図
Hyakunin Isshu Kiki-gaki	
	百人一首聞書
Hyakunin Isshu Kosetsu	
	百人一首古説
Hyakunin Isshu Shō	百人一首抄

Hyakunin Isshu Zōsan Shō	
	百人一首像讃抄
Hyakunin Shūka	百人秀歌
hyakushu	百首
Ichijō Sesshō GyoShū	一条摂政御集
Ichijō Tennō	一条天皇
Ichikawa Danjūrō	市川団十郎
Ichi-no-Miya no Kii Shū	
	一宮紀伊集
ichiya-setsu	一夜説
idzumi	泉
ie no shū	家集
Ihara Saikaku	井原西鶴
Ikuno	生野
imada ahazaru kohi	未だ逢はざる恋
Imagawa Ryōshun	今川了峻
imayō	今様
Ina no Hara	猪名原
Inoue Shūsen	井上秋扇
Inpumon In no Tayū	
	殷富門院大輔
Insei	院政
Ise	伊勢
Ise Monogatari	伊勢物語
Ise no Go	伊勢御
Ise no Miyasu-dokoro	
	伊勢御息所
Ise no Tayū	伊勢大輔
Ishihara Shōmei	石原正明
ishi ni yosuru kohi	寄石恋
Ishō Hinagata	衣裳雛形
Itō Jinsai	伊藤仁斎
Izumi Shikibu	和泉式部
Izumi Shikibu Nikki	和泉式部日記
Jakuren Hōshi	寂蓮法師
jhōya	長夜
ji-amari	字余り
Jidai Fudō Uta-awase	時代不同歌合
Jihitsu-bon Kindai Shūka	
	自筆本近代秀歌
Jingoji Senzui Byōbu	神護寺山水屏風
Jinshin no Ran	壬申乱
Jishō Sanjūrokunin Uta-awase	
	治承三十六人歌合

ji-tarazu	字足らず	Kanke	菅家
Jitō Tennō	持統天皇	*Kanke Bunsō*	菅家文章
jo	序	*Kanke Kōshū*	菅家後集
Jōben	浄弁	Kannon	観音
jokeika	叙景歌	Kanō	狩野
Jokyō Manpō Zensho Azuma Kagami		Masanobu	益信
	女教万宝全書東鏡	Tan'yū	探幽
Jōkyū no Ran	承久乱	Tsunenobu	常信
Jōmei Tennō	舒明天皇	Yasunobu	安信
joryū bunshi	女流文師	kanpaku	関白
jukkai	述懐	*Kanpyō Ōn Toki Kisai no Miya no Uta-awase*	
JuNi-i	従二位		寛平御時后宮歌合
Juntoku In	順徳院	*kanshi*	漢詩
ka	香	Kanze	観世
kachō-ga	花鳥画	*Kao-t'ang Fu*	高唐賦
kadō	歌道	Karigane-ya	雁金屋
kado-ta	門田	Karin'en	歌林苑
Kagari-bi	篝火	*kasane-kotoba*	重詞
Kagawa Kageki	香川景樹	*kasen-e*	歌仙絵
Kagerō Nikki	蜻蛉日記	Katsuragi Shinnō	葛城親王
kaiga-ka	絵画化	Katsushika	葛飾
kaihen ryohaku	海辺旅泊	Hokusai	北斎
kaijō enbō	海上遠望	Ōi	応為
Kaikan Shō	改観抄	Kawara Sadaijin	河原左大臣
kake-kotoba	掛言葉	Kazan In Nagachika	
Kakinomoto no Hitomaro			花山院長親
	柿本人麿	*kaze*	風
Kamakura	鎌倉	Keichū	契沖
Kamijō-bon	上条本	Kei'en-ryū	桂園流
kami no ku	上の句	*Keikō Shō*	経厚抄
Kamochi Masazumi	鹿持雅澄	Keisai Eisen	渓斎英泉
Kamo no Chōmei	鴨長明	Kei'un	慶運
Kamo no	賀茂	*Kenchū Mikkan*	顕注密勘
Mabuchi	真淵	Kenkō	兼好
Shigeyasu	重保	Kenshi (Empress)	妍子
kamuro (kaburo)	禿	Kenshō	顕昭
Kan'ei	寛永	*Kensō-bon Kindai Shūka*	
Kanfugen-kyō Sasshi-e	観普賢経冊子絵		遣送本近代秀歌
Kangyoku Hyakunin Isshu Suishōsō		Kentokukō	謙徳公
	冠玉百人一首	*kesa*	今朝
	水精箱	*kesō-bumi-awase*	懸想文合
kanji	漢字	Kibi no Makibi	吉備真備
Kanjinchō	勧進帳	*kibutsu chinshika*	寄物陳思歌

kichō	几帳	Konoe Tennō	近衛天皇
kin	琴	*Korai Fūtei Shō*	古来風体抄
Kindai Shūka	近代秀歌	Koresada Shinnō	是貞親王
Kingyoku Shū	金玉集	*Koresada Shinnō no Ie no Uta-awase*	
Kinoshita Jin'emon	木下甚右門		是貞親王家歌合
Ki no	紀	*koromo*	衣
Tomonori	友則	*koromo-gahe*	衣替へ
Tsurayuki	貫之	KoShikibu no Naishi	
kinshin	近臣		小式部内侍
Kintada (Minamoto no)		*Kōshoku Ichidai Otoko*	好色一代男
	公忠(源)	KoShōshō	小少々
kinu-ginu no uta	衣衣/後朝 歌	*kosode*	小袖
Kin'yō (Waka) Shū	金葉(和歌)集	Kōtaikō-gū no Daibu	皇太后宮大夫
Kisen Hōshi	喜撰法師	*kotoba-gaki*	詞書
Kisen Shō	喜撰抄	*ku*	句
Kitamura Kigin	北村季吟	*Kudai Waka*	句題和歌
Kitano Tenjin Engi	北野天神縁起	Kudara	百済
Kiyohara no	清原	*kumo*	雲
Fukayabu	深養父	*kuni-mi*	国見
Motosuke	元輔	Kunisada (Utagawa)	国貞(歌川)
Kiyotada (Fujiwara no)		Kuniyoshi (Utagawa)	
	清正(藤原)		国芳(歌川)
Kodai no Kimi	小大君	*kusari-renga*	鎖連歌
(Ko-gata) Hyakunin Isshu Zōsan Shō		Kyōgoku	京極
	(小型)百人一首	*kyōka*	狂歌
	像讃抄	*kyōka e-hon*	狂歌絵本
Kōgyoku Tennō	皇極天皇	Kyōken	経賢
kohi	恋	*kyū-kana-zukai*	旧仮名遣い
Kōkaku	光覚	Li Po	李白
Kōkamon In no Bettō	皇嘉門院別当	*maki*	巻
Kokin (Waka) Rokujō	古今(和歌)六帖	*maki-e*	蒔絵
Kokin (Waka) Shū	古今(和歌)集	*makura-kotoba*	枕詞
Kokin Waka Shū Uchi-giki		*Makura no Sōshi*	枕草子
	古今和歌集打聴	*Manpō Hyakunin Isshu Taisei*	
Kōkō Tennō	光孝天皇		万宝百人一首大成
kokugaku	国学	*man'yō-gana*	万葉仮名
kokugakusha	国学者	*Man'yō Shū*	万葉集
Koma	高麗	*Man'yō Shū Kogi Chūshaku*	
Komachi Shū	小町集		万葉集古義注釈
Komezawa-bon	米沢本	Masahito Shinnō	雅仁親王
Kongō	金剛	*Matsukaze*	松風
Kōnin Tennō	光仁天皇	Matsunaga Teitoku	松永貞徳
Konjaku Monogatari Shū		*Matsura no Miya Monogatari*	
	今昔物語集		松浦宮物語

Meigetsu Ki	明月記	Miyazaki Yūzen	宮崎友禅
Meiji	明治	*mi-yuki*	行幸
Meiji Eimei Hyakunin Isshu		*momoshiki*	百敷
	明治英明百人一首	Momoyama	桃山
Meireki	明暦	Monmu Tennō	文武天皇
meisho-e	名所絵	*monogatari-chū no jinbutsu*	
Meng-ch'ang	孟嘗		物語中の人物
Mibu Nihon	壬生二品	*monogatari-e*	物語絵
Mibu no	壬生	*monogatari-teki*	物語的
Tadami	忠見	*mōsō*	盲僧
Tadamine	忠峯	Motoori Norinaga	本居宣長
Michitsuna no Haha	道綱母	Motoyoshi Shinnō	元良親王
Midō Kanpaku Ki	御堂関白記	Motozane (Fujiwara no)	
Mikohidari	御子左		基実〔藤原〕
Mimuro	三室	Mujū	無住
minadzuki-barae	六月祓	*mukashi*	昔
Minamoto no	源	*Mumyō Shō*	無名抄
Akinaka	顕仲	Munenaga Shinnō	宗良親王
Hitoshi	等	Murakami Tennō	村上天皇
Kanemasa	兼昌	Murasaki Shikibu	紫式部
Morokata	師堅	*Murasaki Shikibu Nikki*	
Motohira	基平		紫式部日記
Muneyuki	宗干	*Murasaki Shikibu Shū*	紫式部集
Sadakata	定方	Muromachi	室町
Sanetomo	実朝	*mushin*	無心
Shigeyuki	重之	*naga-uta*	長歌
Shitagō	順	*nashi-tsubo no gonin*	梨壺の五人
Taka'akira	高明	Nakafumi (Fujiwara no)	
Tōru	融		仲文〔藤原〕
Toshitaka	俊高	Nakanoin Michikatsu	中院通勝
Toshiyori	俊頼	Naka no Kanpaku	中関白
Tsunenobu	経信	Naka no Ōe Shinnō	中大兄親王
Yorimasa	頼政	Nakatomi no Kamatari	
Yorimitsu	頼光		中臣鎌足
Yoritomo	頼朝	Nakatsukasa	中司
Yoritsuna	頼綱	*Nanshoku Ōkagami*	男色大鏡
Yoritsune	頼常	Narikane	業兼
Yoshi'uji	義氏	*nenjū gyōji*	年中行事
Minazuki Shō	水無月抄	*nihofu*	匂
Mini Shū	壬二集	Nijō	二条
minori	稔	Tame'akira	為明
Minō Shō	美濃抄	Tamefuji	為藤
mi-tate	見立て	Tamemichi	為道

Tamesada	為定	*Ogura Yama Shikishi Moyō*	
Tameyo	為世		小倉山色紙模様
Nijō In	二条院	Ōishi Matora	大石真虎
Nijō In no Sanuki	二条院讃岐	*Ōkagami*	大鏡
ni-ku-gire	二句切れ	Okumura Masanobu	
Ninmyō Tennō	仁明天皇		奥村政信
Ninna GyoShū	仁和御集	*oku shimo*	置霜
Ninshi	任子	*Ōmi-ryō*	近江令
Niou no Miya	匂宮	*omohi-someshika*	思ひ初しか
nise-e	似絵	*omohi-wabi*	思詫
Nishidaishū	二十代集	Ōnakatomi no	大中臣
Nishi Honganji Sanjūrokkasen Shū		Sukechika	輔親
	西本願寺三十六歌	Yoshinobu	能宣
	仙集	*OnE-chō*	御絵帖
Nishiyama Sōin	西山宗因	*Onna Imagawa*	女今川
niwa	庭	*Onna Shorei Shū*	女諸礼集
nō	能	Onshi	穏子
Nōin Hōshi	能因法師	Ono no	小野
Nōin Uta-Makura	能因歌枕	Komachi	小町
Nonoguchi Ryūho	野々口立圃	Takamura	篁
nushi aru kotoba	主有る詞	O-ō no Kimi	小大君
Nyūdō Saki no Daijōdaijin		Ōsawa no Ike	大沢の池
	入道前太政大臣	Ōshikōchi no Mitsune	
Nyūdō Sesshō	入道摂政		凡河内躬恒
ōchō joryū bungaku	王朝女流文学	*oto kiku*	音聞
Ōei Shō	応永抄	*Otome*	少女
Ōe no	大江	Ōtomo no	大伴
Chisato	千里	Kuronushi	黒主
Kin'yori	公資	Yakamochi	家持
Masafusa	匡房	Ozaki Masayoshi	尾崎雅喜
Masahira	匡衡	Po Chü-i	白居易
Masamune	雅致	*raigo zu*	来迎図
Ogata	尾形	Reizei	冷泉
Kenzan	乾山	Mochitame	持為
Kōrin	光琳	Tamehide	為秀
Sōken	宗謙	Tamehiro	為広
ōgi	扇	Tamekuni	為邦
Ōgi Shō	奥儀抄	Tamemasa	為尹
Ogura Sansō Shikishi Waka		Tamesuke	為相
	小倉山荘色紙和歌	Reizei In	冷泉院
Ogura Yama	小倉山	*rekishi-teki kana-zukai*	歴史的仮名使い
Ogura Yama Hyakushu Hinagata		*renga*	連歌
	小倉山百首雛形	*ri'ai shi*	理合詩

Rimpa	琳派	*San'oku Shō*	三奥抄
Rinshi	倫子	*Sarashina Nikki*	更級日記
Rin'yō Shū	林葉集	Sarumaru-Dayū	猿丸大夫
risshun	立春	*Sarumaru Shū*	猿丸集
rokkasen	六歌仙	*sashi-e*	挿絵
Rokujō	六条	Satake-bon	佐竹本
Rokujō Tennō	六条天皇	Satō no Norikiyo	佐藤義清
Ryōjin Hishō	梁塵秘抄	*sayo fukete*	小夜更
Ryōshi Naishinnō	亮子内親王	*seijutsu shincho*	正述心緒
Ryōzen Hōshi	良暹法師	Seishi	聖子
Sagami	相模	Sei Shōnagon	清小納言
Saga Tennō	嵯峨天皇	Seiwa Tennō	清和天皇
Sagoromo Monogatari	狭衣物語	Semimaru	蝉丸
Saichō	最澄	*Senzai (Waka) Shū*	千載(和歌)集
Saifukuji-bon	最福寺本	*sesshō*	摂政
Saigū no Nyōgo	斎宮女御	*Shaseki Shū*	沙石集
Saigyō Hōshi	西行法師	*shidare-zakura*	枝垂れ桜
Saimei Tennō	斉明天皇	*Shih Ching*	詩経
Sai'onji	西園寺	*Shih P'ing*	詩品
Saishō Shitennō In	最勝四天王院	*shika*	鹿
Sakae-gusa Tōsei Musume		*shikaku-teki kake-kotoba*	
	栄草当世娘		視覚的掛詞
Saka-no-ue no Korenori		*Shika (Waka) Shū*	詞花(和歌)集
	坂上是則	*shikishi*	色紙
Saki no DaiSōjō Jien		*shi-ku-gire*	四句切れ
	前大僧正慈円	Shimokōbe Chōryu	下河辺長流
sakka bamen no zu	作歌場面の図	*shimo no ku*	下の句
Sakyō no Daibu	左京大夫	*shimo-yo*	霜夜
Sami Manzei	沙弥満誓	*ShinChokusen (Waka) Shū*	
Sanboku Kika Shū	散木奇歌集		新勅撰(和歌)集
Sane'akira (Minamoto no)		Shinkei	心敬
	信明(源)	*ShinKokin (Waka) Shū*	
sangi	参議		新古今(和歌)集
Sanjō In	三条院	*shinobi*	忍
Sanjōnishi	三条西	*shinobu kohi*	忍恋
Kin'eda	公条	*Shinsen Man'yō Shū*	新撰万葉集
Saneki	実枝	*Shinsen Waka*	新撰和歌
Sanetaka	実隆	*Shinsen Zuinō*	新撰髄脳
Sanjō no Udaijin	三条の右大臣	*ShinShō*	新抄
sanjūrokkasen-e	三十六歌仙絵	*Shinsō Hishō*	深窓秘抄
Sanjūrokunin Sen	三十六人選	Shirakawa In	白河院
Sanka Shū	山家集	*shira-tsuyu*	白露
san-ku-gire	三句切れ	*shisen shū*	私選集

Shisetsu Shō	師説抄	Sosei Hōshi	素性法師
shishō	師承	Sōsekishi	漱石子
Shitagō (Minamoto no)		*Sotan Shū*	曽丹集
	順(源)	*sudare*	簾
Shōhaku	肖柏	*(Fūryū) Sugata-e Hyakunin Isshu*	
Shōji Hyakushu	正治百首		(風流)姿絵百人
shoku-gire	初句切れ		一首
ShokuGosen (Waka) Shū		*Sugawara Jikki*	菅原実記
	続後撰(和歌)集	Sugawara no Michizane	
Shokushi Naishinnō	式子内親王		菅原道真
Shōmu Tennō	聖武天皇	Sugimura Jihei	杉村治兵衛
Shōshi (Akiko)	秋子	*suhama*	洲浜
Shōtetsu	正徹	*Sui'a Ganmoku*	水蛙眼目
Shūe Shō	拾穂抄	Suishi (Yasuko)	綏子
(Nichiyō Zatsuroku Fujin Shubunko) Shūgyoku Hyakunin Isshu Ogura Shiori		Suminokura Soan	角倉素庵
		Sumiyoshi Monogatari	住吉物語
	(日用雑録婦人珠	Suō no Naishi	周防内侍
	文匣)秀玉百人	Sutoku In	宗徳院
	一首小倉栞	Tachibana no	橘
Shūgyoku Shū	拾玉集	Michisada	道貞
Shūi Gusō	拾遺愚草	Nagayasu	永愷
Shūi Shō	拾遺抄	Tada'ie (Fujiwara no)	
Shūi (Waka) Shū	拾遺(和歌)集		忠家(藤原)
Shūka-tei no Dairyaku	秀歌体大略	*Tadamine Jittei*	忠岑十体
Shūka no Daitai	秀歌大体	Tadatoshi (Fujiwara no)	
shūka shū	秀歌集		忠俊(藤原)
Shun'e Hōshi	俊恵法師	*ta ga sode*	誰が袖
shunga	春画	Taga Taisha	多賀大社
Shunshi Naishinnō	佝子内親王	*taigen-dome*	体言止め
Shūshi Naishinnō	修子内親王	Taika no Kaishin	大化改新
Soan-bon	素庵本	Taikenmon In no Horikawa	
sobiki mono	簪物		待賢門院堀河
Sōchō	宗長	Taira no	平
Soga no	蘇我	Kanemori	兼盛
Iruka	入鹿	Munenaka	棟仲
Ochi	遠智	Nakako	仲子
Sōgi	宗祇	Tsunekata	経方
Sōgi Shō	宗祇抄	Yasuhira	保衡
Sōjō Henjō	僧正遍昭	*Takafusa-kyō Tsuya-kotoba Emaki*	
Sonchin Hōshinnō	尊鎮法親王		隆房卿艶詞絵巻
Sone no Yoshitada	曽禰好忠	Takakura Tennō	高倉天皇
Sonkai Nyūdō Shinnō		Takamitsu (Fujiwara no)	
	尊快入道親王		高光(藤原)

Takasago	高砂	*Toyokage Shū*	豊陰集
Takashina no	高階	Toyokuni	豊国
Nari'akira	成章	Toyotomi Hideyoshi	
Nariyori	成順		豊臣秀吉
Naritada	成忠	*Towazu-gatari*	問はず語り
Takako (Kishi)	貴子	*tsuke-ku*	付句
Take Heiji	武平次	*tsuki*	月
Taketori Monogatari	竹取物語	*tsukigoro-setsu*	月頃説
taki	滝	*Tsuki Mōde Waka Shū*	
Tamekane-kyō Waka Shō			月詣和歌集
	為兼卿和歌抄	*tsukinami-byōbu*	月次屏風
Tametaka Shinnō	為尊親王	Tsutsumi Chūnagon	
T'ang Hsüan-tsung	唐玄宗		堤中納言
tanka	短歌	*udaijin*	右大臣
Tan'yū Gajō	探幽画帖	Uda In	宇多院
Tatsuta	龍田	*udaishō*	右大将
Teika Jittei	定家十体	*Uimanabi*	宇比麻奈備
Teishi (Sadako)	定子	Ujitada	氏忠
Teishinkō	貞信公	*uki yo*	憂き世
Tendai	天台	*ukiyo-e*	浮世絵
tengu	天狗	Ukon	右近
Tenji Tennō	天智天皇	*ukon'e no shōshō*	右近衛小将
Tenmu Tennō	天武天皇	*Uma no Naishi Shū*	馬内侍集
Tenpō	天保	Urokogataya	鱗形屋
Tenri-bon Kiki-gaki	天理本聞書	*ushin*	有心
Tentoku Yonen Dairi Uta-awase		*uta*	歌
	天徳四年内裏歌合	*uta-awase*	歌合
Toba In	鳥羽院	*uta-e*	歌絵
tōchi-hō	倒置法	Utagawa Sadahide	歌川貞秀
Toda Mosui	戸田茂睡	*uta-makura*	歌枕
tōi no kokoro	擣衣の心	Utamaro	歌麿
Tōji Senzui Byōbu	東寺山水屏風	*Uta no Shiki*	歌の式
Tōkan Kikō	東関紀行	Utsunomiya no Yoritsuna	
Tokugawa Ieyasu	徳川家康		宇都宮頼綱
Ton'a	頓阿	*wa ga na*	我が名
Tō no Tsuneyori	東常縁	*waka*	和歌
Tosa Nikki	土佐日記	*Waka Kuhon*	和歌九品
Tōsei Hinagata Enpitsu Yae-mugura		*Wakan Rōei Shū*	倭漢朗詠集
	当世雛形艶筆	*Wamyō Shō*	和名抄
	八重律	Wang Wei	王威
Toshiyori Zuinō	俊頼髄脳	*wo-gaha*	小河
Toyohara Kunichika		*wonohe*	尾の上
	豊原国周	Wu Shan	巫山

Yakumo Kuden	八雲口伝	*Yoritsune-bon*	頼常本
Yakumo MiShō	八雲御抄	Yoshimine no	良岑
yama	山	Harutoshi	玄利
Yamabe no Akahito	山辺赤人	Munesada	宗貞
yamabushi	山伏	Yoshishige no Yasuaki	
Yamamoto Shunshō (Harumasa)			慶滋保章
	山本春正	*Yoshitada Hyakushu*	好忠百首
yamato-e	やまと絵	Yōzei In	陽成院
Yamato-e no Kongen	大和絵のこんげん	*Yūgao*	夕顔
yamato eshi	大和絵師	Yūjinsai Kiyochika	友尽斎清親
yamato jō-eshi	大和上絵師	*yuki*	雪
yamato kotoba	やまと言葉	*yuku-suwe*	行末
Yamato Monogatari	大和物語	*yume*	夢
Yezōshiya	ゑさうしや	*Yūsai Shō*	幽斎抄
Hachiyemon	八右衛門	*Yūshi Naishinnō-ke Meisho Uta-awase*	
Kisayemon	卉左衛門		祐子内親王家名所
yōen	妖艶		歌合
yoha	夜半	Yūshi Naishinnō-ke no Kii	
yojō	余情		祐子内親王家紀伊
yokushōseki	沃焦石	*Yūzen Hiinakata*	友禅雛形
yomi-bito shirazu	読み人知らず	*Zatsudan*	雑談
yomu	詠む	Zeami	世阿弥
Yorimoto (Ōnakatomi no)		*zokkai*	俗解
	頼基（大内臣）	*zōtōka*	贈答歌
Yoritaka-bon	頼孝本		

BIBLIOGRAPHY

Akimoto Shunkichi. "The Three Mountains of Yamato." *Japan Quarterly* 3 (1956): 356–363.

Ariyoshi Tamotsu. *Waka Bungaku Jiten*. Tokyo: Ōfūsha, 1982.

———. "Hyakunin Isshu E-iri Chūsaku-bon ni tsuite—Shinshutsu Shiryō 'San'oku Shō' o Chūshin ni." KokuBungaku Kenkyū Shiryōkan Bunken Shiryōbu. *Chōsa Kenkyū Hōkoku* 9 (March 1988): 1–17.

———, ed. *Hyakunin Isshu ZenYakuchū*. Tokyo: Kōdansha, 1983.

Ariyoshi Tamotsu and Kamisaku Kōichi, eds. *Ogura Sansō Shikishi Waka (Hyakunin Isshu Kochū)*. Ei'in Kōchū Koten Sōsho. Tokyo: Shintensha, 1975.

Ariyoshi Tamotsu et al. *Hyakunin Isshu (Kensai-pitsu)*. Ei'in Kōchū Koten Sōsho 2. Tokyo: Shintensha, 1971.

Art Institute of Chicago. *Five Centuries of Japanese Kimono*. Art Institute of Chicago Museum Studies, vol. 18, no. 1. Chicago: Art Institute of Chicago, 1992.

Aston, W. G., trans. *Nihongi: Chronicles of Japan from the Earliest Times to A.D. 697*. Tokyo: Tuttle, 1985. Originally published in 1896.

Atomi Gakuen Tanki Daigaku Toshokan. *Atomi Gakuen Tanki Daigaku Toshokan-zō Hyakunin Isshu Mokurokukō*. 4 vols. 1986–1988.

———. *Hyakunin Isshu-ten Zuroku*. 1990.

Bassnett-McGuire, Susan. *Translation Studies*. London: Methuen, 1980.

Birrell, Anne, trans. *New Songs from a Jade Terrace: An Anthology of Early Chinese Love Poetry*. Harmondsworth: Penguin, 1982.

Borgen, Robert. *Sugawara no Michizane and the Early Heian Court*. Cambridge, Mass.: Harvard University Press, 1986.

Bownas, Geoffrey, and Anthony Thwaite, trans. *The Penguin Book of Japanese Verse*. Harmondsworth: Penguin, 1964.

Bowring, Richard, trans. *Murasaki Shikibu: Her Diary and Poetic Memoirs*. Princeton, N.J.: Princeton University Press, 1985.

———. "The *Ise monogatari*: A Short Cultural History." *Harvard Journal of Asiatic Studies* 52 (1992): 401–480.

Brazell, Karen, trans. *The Confessions of Lady Nijō*. Stanford, Calif.: Stanford University Press, 1973.

Brower, Robert H., trans. "The Secret Teachings of Ex-Emperor Go-Toba: *Go-Toba no In Gokuden*." *Harvard Journal of Asiatic Studies* 32 (1972): 5–70.

———. *Fujiwara Teika's Hundred-Poem Sequence of the Shōji Era, 1200*. Tokyo: Sophia University, 1978.

———. "Fujiwara Teika's *Maigetsushō*." *Monumenta Nipponica* 40(4) (Winter 1985): 399–425.

———. "The Foremost Style of Poetic Composition: Fujiwara Tameie's *Eiga no Ittei*." *Monumenta Nipponica* 42(4) (Winter 1987): 391–429.

Brower, Robert H., and Earl Miner. *Japanese Court Poetry*. Stanford, Calif.: Stanford University Press, 1961.

———, trans. *Fujiwara Teika's Superior Poems of Our Time: A Thirteenth-Century Poetic Treatise and Sequence*. Stanford, Calif.: Stanford University Press, 1967.

Brown, Delmer M., and Ichirō Ishida, trans. *The Future and the Past: A Translation and Study of the* Gukanshō, *an Interpretive History of Japan Written in 1219*. Berkeley: University of California Press, 1979.

Brown, Kendall. "Shōkadō Shōjō as 'Tea Painter,'" *Chanoyu Quarterly* 49 (1987): 7–40.

———. "Re-Presenting Teika's *Flowers and Birds*." In Carolyn Wheelwright, ed., *Word in Flower*. New Haven: Yale University Art Gallery, 1989.

———. "Fujiwara Teika—Kan'ei Cultural Hero." *Abstracts of the 1993 Annual Meeting*. Ann Arbor: Association for Asian Studies, 1993.

Bundy, Roselee. "The Uses of Literary Tradition: The Poetry and Poetics of the *Shinkokinshu*." Ph.D. dissertation, University of Chicago, 1984.

———. "Poetic Apprenticeship: Fujiwara Teika's *Shogaku Hyakushu*." *Monumenta Nipponica* 45(2) (Summer 1990): 157–188.

Carter, Steven D. *The Road to Komatsubara: A Classical Reading of the* Renga Hyakuin. Cambridge, Mass.: Council on East Asian Studies, Harvard University, 1987.

———, trans. *Waiting for the Wind: Thirty-Six Poets of Japan's Late Medieval Age*. New York: Columbia University Press, 1989.

———, trans. *Traditional Japanese Poetry: An Anthology*. Stanford, Calif.: Stanford University Press, 1991.

Chibbett, David. *The History of Japanese Printing and Book Illustrations*. Tokyo: Kodansha International, 1977.

Childs, Margaret H. "*Chigo Monogatari:* Love Stories or Buddhist Sermons?" *Monumenta Nipponica* 35(2) (Summer 1980): 127–151.

Chino Kaori. "Jingoji-zo 'Senzui Byōbu' no Kōsei to Kaigashi-teki Ichi." *Bijutsu Shi* 28(2) (February 1979): 146–162.

Conisbee, Philip. *Soap Bubbles (Masterpiece in Focus)*. Los Angeles: County Museum of Art, 1991.

Cranston, Edwin A. "The Ramifying Vein: An Impression of Leaves." *Journal of Japanese Studies* 9(1) (Winter 1983): 97–138.

———, trans. *The Izumi Shikibu Diary: A Romance of the Heian Court*. Cambridge, Mass.: Harvard University Press, 1969.

———, trans. *A Waka Anthology, Volume One: The Gem-Glistening Cup*. Stanford: Stanford University Press, 1993.

Crawcour, E. S. "Changes in Japanese Commerce in the Tokugawa Period." In John Whitney Hall and Marius B. Jansen, eds., *Studies in the Institutional History of Early Modern Japan*. Princeton, N.J.: Princeton University Press, 1968.

Dalby, Liza Crihfield. *Kimono: Fashioning Culture*. New Haven: Yale University Press, 1993.

De Bruijn, R. "The One Hundred Poems Explained by the Nurse." In H. M. Kempfer and Jhr. W. O. G. Sideinghe, eds., *The Fascinating World of the Japanese Artist: A Collection of Essays on Japanese Art by the Members of the Society for Japanese Arts and Crafts, The Hague, Netherlands*. Los Angeles: Dawson's Books, 1971.

Dickins, Frederick Victor, trans. *Hyak Nin Is'shiu, or Stanzas by a Century of Poets, Being Japanese Lyrical Odes, Translated into English, with Explanatory Notes, the Text in Japanese and Roman Characters, and a Full Index*. London: Smith, Elder and Co., 1866.

———, trans. *Primitive and Mediaeval Japanese Texts*. Oxford: Clarendon Press, 1906.

———. "The Makura-Kotoba of Primitive Japanese Verse." *Asiatic Society of Japan,* vol. 35, pt. 4. Yokohama, 1908.

Doe, Paula. *A Warbler's Song in the Dusk: The Life and Work of Ōtomo no Yakamochi (718–785)*. Berkeley: University of California Press, 1982.

Dore, R. P. *Education in Tokugawa Japan*. Michigan Classics in Japanese Studies, no. 8. Ann Arbor: Center for Japanese Studies, University of Michgan, 1992. Originally published in 1965.

Eliot, T. S. "Tradition and the Individual Talent." In *The Sacred Wood: Essays on Poetry and Criticism.* New York: University Paperbacks, Barnes and Noble, 1966. Originally published in 1917.

Evans, Tom, and Mary Anne Evans. *Shunga: The Art of Love in Japan*. New York: Paddington Press, 1975.

Fenollosa, Ernest. *The Chinese Written Character as a Medium for Poetry*. Edited by Ezra Pound. San Francisco: City Lights Books, 1968. Originally published in 1936.

Ferguson, Frances. *Wordsworth: Language as Counter-Spirit*. New Haven: Yale University Press, 1977.

Fish, Stanley. *Is There a Text in This Class? The Authority of Interpretive Communities*. Cambridge, Mass.: Harvard University Press, 1980.

Fraistat, Neil, ed. *Poems in Their Place: The Intertextuality and Order of Poetic Collections*. Chapel Hill: University of North Carolina Press, 1986.

Gatten, Aileen. "Supplementary Narratives to *The Tale of Genji*." In *The World of Genji*.

Geddes, Ward, trans. "Takamura Monogatari." *Monumenta Nipponica* 46(3) (Autumn 1991): 275–291.

Gluckman, Dale Carolyn, and Sharon Sadako Takeda. *When Art Became Fashion: Kosode in Edo-Period Japan*. Los Angeles: County Museum of Art, 1992.

Goff, Janet. "*The Tale of Genji* as a Source of the Nō." In *The World of Genji*.

———. *Noh Drama and* The Tale of Genji: *The Art of Allusion in Fifteen Classical Plays*. Princeton, N.J.: Princeton University Press, 1991.

Graves, Robert. *The Greek Myths*. New York: Braziller, 1957.

Graybill, Maribeth. "An Iconographic Approach to the Study of Poet Portraiture in Medieval Japan." *Transactions of the International Conference of Orientalists in Japan,* no. 25. Tokyo: Tōhō Gakkai, 1980.

———. "*Kasen-e:* An Investigation into the Origins of the Tradition of Poet Pictures in Japan." Ph.D. dissertation, University of Michigan, 1983.

Hall, John Whitney. *Japan from Prehistory to Modern Times*. Rutland, Vt.: Tuttle, 1976.

Hall, John Whitney, and Marius B. Jansen, eds. *Studies in the Institutional History of Early Modern Japan*. Princeton, N.J.: Princeton University Press, 1968.

Hamada Gi'ichirō et al., eds. *Kibyōshi, Senryū, Kyōka*. Nihon Koten Bungaku Zenshū 46. Tokyo: Shōgakkan, 1974.

Hamada, Kengi, trans. *The Life of an Amorous Man*. Rutland, Vt.: Tuttle, 1964.

Harper, Thomas. "*The Tale of Genji* in the Eighteenth Century: Keichū, Mabuchi and Norinaga." In C. Andrew Gerstle, ed., *Eighteenth Century Japan*. Sydney: Allen & Unwin Australia, 1989.

Harries, Phillip Tudor, trans. *The Poetic Memoirs of Lady Daibu*. Stanford, Calif.: Stanford University Press, 1980.

Hayashi Susumu. "Suminokura Soan-hitsu Sōshū-kō Heiji-dono Ate Shojō" [Letter from Suminokura Sōan to (Fujimoto) Sōshū and (Suminokura) Heiji]. *Yamato Bunka* 87 (March 1992): 43–60.

Hibbett, Howard S. "The Role of the Ukiyo-zōshi Illustrator." *Monumenta Nipponica* 13 (1957): 67–82.

————. *The Floating World in Japanese Fiction.* Rutland, Vt.: Tuttle, 1975. Originally published in 1959.

Higuchi Yoshimaro. "Hyakunin Shūka kara Hyakunin Isshu e." *Bungaku* 39(7) (July 1971): 784–802.

Hillier, Jack R. *The Japanese Picture Book: A Selection from the Ravicz Collection.* New York: Abrams, 1991.

Hirota, Akiko. "Ex-Emperor Go-Toba: A Study in Personality, Politics and Poetry." Ph.D. dissertation, UCLA, 1989.

Hirshfeld, Jane, with Mariko Aratani, trans. *The Ink Dark Moon: Love Poems by Ono no Komachi and Izumi Shikibu, Women of the Ancient Court of Japan.* New York: Scribner's, 1988.

Hisamatsu Sen'ichi et al., eds. *Keichū Zenshū.* Tokyo: Iwanami Shoten, 1973.

Hishikawa Moronobu Kinenkan, ed. *Hishikawa Moronobu Kinenkan Zuroku.* Tokyo: Gabundō, 1986.

Honda, H. H., trans. *One Hundred Poems from One Hundred Poets.* Tokyo: Hokuseido Press, 1956. Originally, published in 1938.

————. *The Sanka Shū.* Tokyo: Hokuseido Press, 1971.

Huey, Robert N., and Susan Matisoff, trans. "Lord Tamekane's Notes on Poetry." *Monumenta Nipponica* 40(2) (Summer 1985): 127–146.

Hurst, G. Cameron III. *Insei: Abdicated Sovereigns in the Politics of Late Heian Japan, 1086–1185.* New York: Columbia University Press, 1976.

Idemitsu Bijutsukan, ed. *Nihon no Kaiga Hyakusen* [One hundred masterpieces of Japanese painting]. Tokyo: Idemitsu Museum of Art, 1983.

Ii Haruki. *Genji Monogatari no Densetsu.* Tokyo: Shōwa Shuppan, 1976.

————. "Monogatari-e Kō." *Kokugo to KokuBungaku* 67(7) (July 1988): 17–31.

————. "Hyakuni Isshu no Seiritsu." In *(Kikan) Sumi,* Supesharu Hyakunin Isshu. Tokyo: Geijutsu Shinbunsha, 1990.

Ikeda Kikan et al., eds. *Makura no Sōshi, Murasaki Shikibu Nikki.* NKBT 19. Tokyo: Iwanami Shoten, 1958.

Ikeda Shinobu. "Heian Jidai Monogatari Kaiga no Hōhō: Monogatari o Yobi-komu Kaiga no Dentō o Kangaeru." In Nakano Masaki et al., eds., *Ōchō Emaki to Sōshoku-kyō.* Heian no Kaiga/Kōgei II, Nihon Bijutsu Zenshū 8. Tokyo: Kodansha, 1990.

Inoue Muneo. *Heian Kōki Kajin-den no Kenkyū.* Tokyo: Kasama Shoin, 1978.

————. "Fujiwara Nobuzane Nenpu Kōshō—Shokyū made." In Morimoto Motoko, ed., *Waka Bungaku ShinRon.* Tokyo: Meiji Shoin, 1982.

————. "Fujiwara Nobuzane Nenpu Kōshō—Kangen kara Bun'ei made." *Nihon Bungaku* 59. Tokyo: Rikkyō Daigaku, 1987.

————. "Fujiwara Nobuzane Nenpu Kōshō—Tei'ō kara Ninji made." In *Chūsei Setsuwa to Sono Shūhen.* Tokyo: Meiji Shoin, 1987.

Ishida Hisatoyo et al., eds. *Nihon Bijutsu Shi Jiten.* Tokyo: Heibonsha, 1987.

Ishikawa Takudo, ed. *Shisendō.* Kyoto: Benridō, 1971.

Itoh Toshiko. "Satake-bon Sanjūrokkasen Emaki no Kōsei to Seiritsu." In Mori Tōru, ed., *Sanjūrokkasen-e.* Tokyo: Kadokawa Shoten, 1979.

Jakobson, Roman. "Closing Statement: Linguistics and Poetics." In T. Sebeok, ed., *Style in Language.* Cambridge, Mass.: MIT Press, 1960.

————. "On the Translation of Verse." Translated by Wendy and Peter Steiner. In Roman Jakobson, *Selected Writings,* ed. Stephen Rudy and Martha Taylor. Vol. 5. The Hague: Mouton, 1979.

Jauss, Hans Robert. *Toward an Aesthetic of Reception.* Translated by Timothy Bahti. Minneapolis: University of Minnesota Press, 1982.

Kamens, Edward. "The Past in the Present: Fujiwara Teika and the Traditions of Japanese Poetry." In Carolyn Wheelwright, ed., *Word in Flower*. New Haven: Yale University Art Gallery, 1989.

———, trans. "Translation of Teika's *Poems on Flowers and Birds of the Twelve Months*." In Carolyn Wheelwright, ed., *Word in Flower*. New Haven: Yale University Art Gallery, 1989.

———. *The Buddhist Poetry of the Great Kamo Priestess: Daisaiin Senshi and* Hosshin Wakashū. Michigan Monograph Series in Japanese Studies, no. 5. Ann Arbor: Center for Japanese Studies, University of Michigan, 1990.

Kamijō Shōji. "Hyakunin Isshu no Hon-dana." In Kubota Jun, ed., *Hyakunin Isshu Hikkei*. Tokyo: Gakutōsha, 1985.

Kamo Momoki, ed. *Kamo Mabuchi Zenshū*. Vol. 10. Tokyo: Koshikawa Kōbunkan, 1927.

Kaneko Kinjirō et al., eds. *Renga Haikai Shū*. Nihon Koten Bungaku Zenshū 32. Tokyo: Shōgakkan, 1974.

Katagiri Yayoi. "Ōgi-e to Waka—Muromachi Jidai ni okeru Ōgi-e Kyōju no Ichimen." In *Sesshū to Yamato-e Byōbu*. Nihon Bijutsu Zenshū, vol. 13. Tokyo: Kōdansha, 1993.

Katagiri Yōichi. *Uta-makura Uta-kotoba Jiten*. Tokyo: Kadokawa, 1983.

———, ed. *Hyakunin Isshu to Moronobu no Zōsanshō*. Tokyo: Kokusho Kankō-kai, 1975.

Katō, Hilda. "The *Mumyōshō* of Kamo no Chōmei and Its Significance in Japanese Literature." *Monumenta Nipponica* 23(3–4) (1968): 321–430.

Kawaguchi Hisao, ed. *Wakan Rōei Shū*. Tokyo: Kōdansha, 1982.

Kawaguchi Hisao and Shida Nobuyoshi, eds. *Waka Rōei Shū, Ryōjin Hisshō*. Nihon Koten Bungaku Taikei 73. Tokyo: Iwanami Shoten, 1965.

Kawamura Teruo et al., eds. *Kin'yō Waka Shū, Shika Waka Shū*. Shin Nihon Koten Bungaku Taikei 9. Tokyo: Iwanami Shoten, 1989.

Keene, Donald. *World Within Walls: Japanese Literature of the Pre-Modern Era, 1600–1867*. New York: Holt, 1976.

———. *Dawn to the West, Japanese Literature in the Modern Era: Poetry, Drama, Criticism*. New York: Holt, Rinehart and Winston, 1984.

———. "Review of Brower and Miner, *Japanese Court Poetry*." *Harvard Journal of Asiatic Studies* 29 (1962–1963): 279.

———. "A Neglected Chapter: Courtly Fiction of the Kamakura Period." *Monumenta Nipponica* 44(1) (1989): 1–30.

———, ed. *Twenty Plays of the Nō Theatre*. New York: Columbia University Press, 1970.

———, ed. *Anthology of Japanese Literature, from the Earliest Era to the Mid-Nineteenth Century*. New York: Grove Press, 1995. Originally published in 1955.

———, trans. *Essays in Idleness*. New York: Columbia University Press, 1967.

Kelsey, W. Michael. *Konjaku Monogatari-shū*. Twayne's World Authors Series, no. 621. Boston: Twayne, 1982.

Keyes, Roger. "Hokusai's Illustrations for the *100 Poems*." In *The Art Institute of Chicago Centennial Lectures: Museum Studies 10*. Chicago: Contemporary Books, 1983.

Kibune Shigeaki. *Murasaki Shikibu Shū no Kenkyū to Ronkō*. Tokyo: Kasama Shoin, 1981.

Ko, Dorothy. "Same-Sex Love Between Singing Girls and Gentry Wives in Seventeenth-Century Jiangnan." Paper presented at "Women and Literature in Ming-Qing China" Conference, Yale University, New Haven, 22–26 June 1993.

Kokuritsu Rekishi Minzoku Hakubutsukan, ed. *Kinsei Kimono to Bankakyō—Kosode-ten Byōbu—Zuroku* [A kaleidoscope of Japanese early modern kimono—an exhibition of *Kosode Byōbu*]. Tokyo: Asahi Shinbunsha, 1994.

Kokusai Bunka Shinkōkai, ed. *Introduction to Classic Japanese Literature*. Tokyo: Kokusai Bunka Shinkōkai, 1948.

Kokusho Kankōkai, ed. *Meigetsu Ki*. 3 vols. Tokyo: Kokusho Kankōkai, 1970.

Komashaku Kimi. *Murasaki Shikibu no Messeeji*. Tokyo: Asahi Shinbunsha, 1991.

Komatsu Shigemi. *Heike Nōkyō no Kenkyū.* 2 vols. Tokyo: Kōdansha, 1976.

Konishi Jin'ichi. "Kokinshū-*teki Hyōgen no Seiritsu.*" *Nihon Gakushi In Kiyō,* 7(3) (November 1949): 163–198. Translated by Helen C. McCullough, "The Genesis of the *Kokinshū* Style," *Harvard Journal of Asiatic Studies* 38(1) (June 1978): 61–170.

————. "Association and Progression: Principles of Integration in Anthologies and Sequences of Japanese Court Poetry, A.D. 900–1350." Translated and adapted by Robert H. Brower and Earl Miner. *Harvard Journal of Asiatic Studies* 21 (1958): 67–127.

————. *A History of Japanese Literature,* vol. 3: *The High Middle Ages.* Translated by Aileen Gatten and Mark Harbison; edited by Earl Miner. Princeton, N.J.: Princeton University Press, 1991.

Kubota Jun, ed. *Hyakunin Isshu Hikkei.* Tokyo: Gakutōsha, 1982.

————. *Fujiwara Teika.* Ōchō no Kajin 9. Tokyo: Shūeisha, 1984.

————, ed. *Koten Waka Hikkei.* Tokyo: Gakutōsha, 1986.

Kurokawa Shindō, ed. *Nihon Fūzoku Zue.* Vol. 2. Tokyo: Nihon Fūzoku Zue Kankō-kai, 1914.

Kyūsojin Hitaku and Higuchi Yoshimaro, eds. *GoShohon Hyakunin Isshu Shō Kunaichō Shoryōbu-zō.* Tokyo: Kasama Shoin, 1971.

LaFleur, William R. "Marginalia: The Expanse and the Limits of a New Anthology." *Monumenta Nipponica* 38(2) (Summer 1983): 199–200.

————, trans. *Mirror for the Moon: A Selection of Poems by Saigyō (1118–1190).* New York: New Directions, 1978.

Lammers, Wayne P. *The Tale of Matsura: Fujiwara Teika's Experiment in Fiction.* Michigan Monograph Series in Japanese Studies, no. 9. Ann Arbor: Center for Japanese Studies, University of Michigan, 1992.

Lane, Richard. *Images of the Floating World.* New York: Konecky & Konecky, 1978.

Legge, James. *The Original Chinese Texts of The Confucian Analects, The Great Learning, The Doctrine of the Mean, The Works of Mencius and the Work of Lao-tsze.* Taipei: Cave Books, n.d. Originally published in 1861.

Levy, Ian Hideo, trans. *The Ten Thousand Leaves.* Vol. 1. Princeton, N.J.: Princeton University Press, 1981.

Link, Howard A. *Primitive Ukiyo-e.* Honolulu: University of Hawai'i Press, 1980.

MacCauley, Clay. *Hyakunin-Isshu and Nori no Hatsu-Ne.* Yokohama: Kelly & Walsh, 1917. *Hyakunin-Isshu* originally published in 1899.

Marcus, Andrew. "Representation of *Genji Monogatari* in Edo Period Fiction." In *The World of Genji.*

Matisoff, Susan. *The Legend of Semimaru, Blind Musician of Japan.* New York: Columbia University Press, 1978.

Matsumura Sei'ichi, ed. *Eiga Monogatari ZenChūshaku.* 8 vols. Tokyo: Kadokawa Shoten, 1975.

McCullough, Helen Craig. *Brocade by Night: "Kokin Wakashū" and the Court Style in Japanese Classical Poetry.* Stanford, Calif.: Stanford University Press, 1985.

————, trans. *Tales of Ise: Lyrical Episodes from Tenth-Century Japan.* Stanford, Calif.: Stanford University Press, 1968.

————, trans. *Ōkagami: The Great Mirror.* Princeton, N.J.: Princeton University Press, 1980.

————, trans. *Kokin Wakashū: The First Imperial Anthology of Japanese Poetry.* Stanford, Calif.: Stanford University Press, 1985.

————, trans. *Classical Japanese Prose.* Stanford, Calif.: Stanford University Press, 1990.

McCullough, William H., and Helen Craig McCullough, trans. *A Tale of Flowering Fortunes: Annals of Japanese Aristocratic Life in the Heian Period.* 2 vols. Stanford, Calif.: Stanford University Press, 1980.

Meech-Pekarik, Julia. "Ukifune: Icon of Love." In *The World of Genji*.

———. *The World of the Meiji Print*. New York: Weatherhill, 1986.

Miller, Roy Andrew. "The 'Spirit' of the Japanese Language." *Journal of Japanese Studies* 3(2) (Summer 1977): 251–298.

———. *Nihongo: In Defence of Japanese*. London: Athlone Press, 1986.

Minemura Fumihito, ed. *Shin Kokin Waka Shū*. Nihon Koten Bungaku Zenshū 26. Tokyo: Shōgakkan, 1974.

Miner, Earl. *The Japanese Tradition in British and American Literature*. Princeton, N.J.: Princeton University Press, 1958.

———. *Japanese Linked Poetry*. Princeton, N.J.: Princeton University Press, 1979.

———. "Waka: Features of Its Constitution and Development." *Harvard Journal of Asiatic Studies* 50(2) (December 1990): 669–706.

Miner, Earl, Hiroko Odagiri, and Robert E. Morrell. *The Princeton Companion to Classical Japanese Literature*. Princeton, N.J.: Princeton University Press, 1985.

Miyamori Asatarō, trans. *Masterpieces of Japanese Poetry Ancient and Modern*. 2 vols. Tokyo: Maruzen, 1936.

Miyata, Haruo, trans. *The Ogura Anthology of Japanese Waka: A Hundred Pieces from a Hundred Poets*. Osaka: Kyoiku Tosho, 1981.

Montrose, Louis A. "Professing the Renaissance: The Poetics and Politics of Culture." In H. Aram Veeser, ed., *The New Historicism*. London: Routledge, 1989.

Mori Tōru. *Uta-awase-e no Kenkyū: Kasen-e*. Tokyo: Kadokawa Shoten, 1970.

———. *Kasen-e—Hyakunin Isshu-e*. Tokyo: Kadokawa Shoten, 1981.

———, ed. *Sanjūrokkasen-e*. Tokyo: Kadokawa Shoten, 1979.

———. "Jidai Fudō Uta-Awase-e ni tsuite." *Kobijutsu* 8 (March 1965): 25–57.

Morris, Ivan. *The World of the Shining Prince: Court Life in Ancient Japan*. Oxford: Oxford University Press, 1964.

———, trans. *The Pillow Book of Sei Shōnagon*. 2 vols. New York: Columbia University Press, 1967.

———, trans. *The Life of an Amorous Woman, and Other Writings*. New York: New Directions, 1969.

Morris, Mark. "Waka and Form, Waka and History." *Harvard Journal of Asiatic Studies* 46(2) (December 1986): 551–610.

Morse, Peter. *Hokusai: One Hundred Poets*. New York: Braziller, 1989.

Mostow, Joshua S. "*E no Gotoshi:* The Picture Simile and the Feminine Re-Guard in Japanese Illustrated Romances." *Word & Image* 10(1) (April–June 1994): 10–27.

———. "Minamoto no Shunrai and *Uta-e*." *Transactions of the International Conference of Orientalists in Japan* 32 (1987): 52–64.

———. "*Uta-e* and Interrelations Between Poetry and Painting in the Heian Era." Ph.D. dissertation, University of Pennsylvania, 1988.

———. "Painted Poems, Forgotten Words: Poem-Pictures and Classical Japanese Literature." *Monumenta Nipponica* 47(3) (Autumn 1992): 341–344.

———. "Review of *Conversations with Shōtetsu*, trans. Robert H. Brower." *Journal of the Association of Teachers of Japanese* 27(2) (November 1993): 265–269.

——— et al., trans. "Tales of Takamura." *B.C. Asian Review* 3/4 (September 1990): 355–380.

Nagasaki Iwao. "Designs for a Thousand Ages: Printed Pattern Books and Kosode." Translated by Amanda Mayer Stinchecum. In Dale C. Gluckman and Sharon S. Takeda, eds., *When Art Became Fashion*. Los Angeles: County Museum of Art, 1992.

———. "Miyazaki Yūzen to Yūzen-zome, Ogata Kōrin to Kōrin-Moyō." Gakushūin Kasumi Kaikan Geijutsu Kōza, 21 September 1994, Gakushūin University, Tokyo.

Nakada Yumiko and Yoshihara Sachiko. *Manga Hyakunin Isshu.* Tokyo: Heibonsha, 1986.

Nakamachi Keiko. "Ogata Kōrin no Zōkeisei ni Kan suru Ichi Kōsatsu: Hyakunin Isshu Karuta o Chūshin to shite." *Kokka* 1027 (1979): 9–36.

Nakano Masaki et al., eds. *Ōchō Emaki to Sōshoku-kyō.* Heian no Kaiga/Kōgei II, Nihon Bijutsu Zenshū 8. Tokyo: Kōdansha, 1990.

Namiki Seishi. "Bunken Yori Mita Nise-e." *Kinko Sōsho* 9 (1981): 798–825.

Neilsen, Rosemary M., and Robert H. Solomon. "Aphra Behn and Pyrrha: Revealing Female Space in Horace, Odes I.5." Paper presented at the "Gender and the Construction of Culture and Knowledge" Women's Studies Conference, University of British Columbia, Vancouver, 22–24 September 1989.

Nihon Kokugo Daijiten Kankō-kai, ed. *Nihon Kokugo Daijiten.* 20 vols. Tokyo: Shōgakkan, 1972.

Niranjana, Tejaswini. *Siting Translation: History, Post-Structuralism, and the Colonial Context.* Berkeley: University of California Press, 1992.

Nosco, Peter. "Keichū (1640–1701): Forerunner of National Learning." *Asian Thought and Society: An International Review* 5 (1980): 237–252.

———. "*Man'yōshū* Studies in Tokugawa Japan." *Transactions of the Asiatic Society of Japan,* 4th series, 1 (1986): 109–146.

———. *Remembering Paradise: Nativism and Nostalgia in Eighteenth-Century Japan.* Cambridge, Mass.: Harvard University Press, 1990.

Ono Tadashige. *Ukiyo-e: Kinsei Minshū Hanga no Eshi-tachi.* Tokyo: Tōkai Daigaku Shuppankai, 1980.

Ōno Susumu et al. *Iwanami Kogo Daijiten.* Tokyo: Ōfūsha, 1974.

Ozaki Masayoshi. *Hyakunin Isshu Hitoyo-gatari.* Tokyo: Yūhōdō, 1931. Originally published in 1833.

Ozawa Masao, ed. *Kokin Waka Shū.* Nihon Koten Bungaku Zenshū 7. Tokyo: Shōgakkan, 1971.

Page, Curtis Hidden, trans. *Japanese Poetry: An Historical Essay with Two Hundred and Thirty Translations.* Folcroft, Pa.: Folcroft Library Editions, 1976. Originally published in 1923.

Papinot, E. *Historical and Geographical Dictionary of Japan.* Rutland, Vt.: Tuttle, 1972. Originally published in 1910.

Pekarik, Andrew J. *The Thirty-Six Immortal Women Poets: A Poetry Album with Illustrations by Chōbunsai Eishi.* New York: Braziller, 1991.

Phillips, Quitman E. "*Honchō gashi* and the Kano Myth." *Archives of Asian Art.* Forthcoming.

Porter, William N., trans. *A Hundred Verses from Old Japan, Being a Translation from the Hyaku-Nin-Isshiu.* Rutland, Vt.: Tuttle, 1979. Originally published in 1909.

Rabinovitch, Judith. "Wasp Waists and Monkey Tails: A Study and Translation of Hamanari's *Uta no Shiki* (*The Code of Poetry,* 772), Also Known as *Kakyō Hyōshiki* (*A Formulary for Verse Based on the Canons of Poetry*)." *Harvard Journal of Asiatic Studies* 51(2) (December 1991): 471–560.

Reischauer, Edwin O., and Joseph K. Yamagiwa. *Translations from Early Japanese Literature.* 2nd ed., abridged. Cambridge, Mass.: Harvard University Press, 1972.

Rexroth, Kenneth, trans. *One Hundred Poems from the Japanese.* New York: New Directions, 1955.

———, trans. *One Hundred More Poems from the Japanese.* New York: New Directions, 1976.

Rexroth, Kenneth, and Ikuko Atsumi, trans. *The Burning Heart: Women Poets of Japan.* New York: Seabury Press, 1977.

Rich, Adrienne. "Compulsory Heterosexuality and Lesbian Existence." *Signs* 5 (Summer 1980): 648–649.

Rimer, J. Thomas, Jonathan Chaves, Stephen Addiss, and Hiroyuki Suzuki. *Shisendo: Hall of the Poetry Immortals.* New York: Weatherhill, 1991.

Robinson, B. W. *Kuniyoshi: The Warrior-Prints.* Oxford: Phaidon, 1982.

Rodd, Laurel Rasplica, with Mary Catherine Henkenius. *Kokinshū: A Collection of Poems Ancient and Modern.* Tokyo and Princeton: University of Tokyo Press/Princeton University Press, 1984.

Royston, Clifton Wilson, Jr. "The Poetics and Poetry of Fujiwara Shunzei (1114–1204)." Ph.D. dissertation, University of Michigan, 1974.

Rutledge, Eric. "The *Man'yōshū* in English." *Harvard Journal of Asiatic Studies* 43 (June 1983): 263–290.

Sadamura Tadashi, ed. *Sharaku Debyuu Ni Hyaku-nen Kinen: Sharaku to Utamaro, Edo no Ukiyo-e-ten.* Tokyo: Kōdansha, 1994.

Said, Edward W. *Orientalism.* New York: Vintage, 1978.

Sasaki Nobutsuna, ed. *Nihon Kagaku Taikei.* Vols. 1–3. Tokyo: Kasama Shobō, 1963.

Sato, Hiroaki. *String of Beads: Complete Poems of Princess Shikishi.* Honolulu: University of Hawai'i Press, 1993.

———. "Translating Tanka in One-Line Form." *Montemora* 4 (1978).

———. "Lineation of Tanka in English Translation." *Monumenta Nipponica* 42(3) (Summer 1987): 347–356.

———. "From Format Composition of Tanka to the Creation of the Renga Form." *JATJ Journal of the Association of Teachers of Japanese* 21(2) (November 1987): 149–164.

Sato, Hiroaki, and Burton Watson, trans. *From the Country of Eight Islands.* New York: Doubleday, 1981.

Satow, E. M. "The Revival of Pure Shiñ-tau." *Transactions of the Asiatic Society of Japan.* 1882.

Sayre, Charles Franklin. "Illustrations of the *Ise monogatari:* Survival and Revival of Heian Court Culture." Ph.D. dissertation, Yale University, 1978.

Scarfe, Francis. *Baudelaire.* Harmondsworth: Penguin, 1964.

Schalow, Paul Gordon. "The Invention of a Literary Tradition of Male Love—Kitamura Kigin's *Iwatsutsuji.*" *Monumenta Nipponica* 48(1) (Spring 1993): 1–31.

———, trans. *The Great Mirror of Male Love.* Stanford, Calif.: Stanford University Press, 1990.

Sebeok, T., ed. *Style in Language.* Cambridge, Mass.: MIT Press, 1960.

Seidensticker, Edward G., trans. *The Tale of Genji.* New York: Knopf, 1981.

Shikashū Taisei. 7 vols. Tokyo: Meiji Shoin, 1973.

Shimao Arata. "Kakinomoto no Hitomaro-zō ni okeru 'Katachi' to 'Imi.'" In Tokyo National Research Institute of Cultural Properties, ed., *Human Figure in the Visual Arts of East Asia.* Tokyo: International Symposium on the Preservation of Cultural Property, 1994.

Shimazu Tadao, ed. *Hyakunin Isshu.* Tokyo: Kadokawa Shoten, 1969.

Shimazu Tadao and Kamijō Shōji, eds. *Hyakunin Isshu Kochū Shō.* Osaka: Izumi Shoin, 1982.

Shimizu Yoshiko. *Murasaki Shikibu.* Tokyo: Iwanami Shoten, 1973.

Shklovsky, Victor. "Art as Technique." Translated in Lee T. Lemon and Marion J. Reis, *Russian Formalist Criticism: Four Essays.* Lincoln: University of Nebraska Press, 1965.

Shōgaku Tosho, ed. *Hyakunin Ishhu no Techō.* Tokyo: Shōgakkan, 1989.

Showalter, Elaine, ed. *The New Feminist Criticism: Essays of Women, Literature, and Theory.* New York: Pantheon, 1985.

Siffert, Betty Y. "*Hinagata Bon:* The Art Institute of Chicago Collection of Kimono Pattern Books." In Art Institute of Chicago, *Five Centuries of Japanese Kimono.* Chicago: Art Institute of Chicago, 1992.

Spae, Joseph J. *Itō Jinsai: A Philosopher, Educator and Sinologist of the Tokugawa Period.* New York: Paragon, 1967. Originally published in 1948.

Steiner, Peter, ed. *The Prague School: Selected Writings, 1929–1946.* Austin: University of Texas Press, 1982.

————. *Russian Formalism: A Metapoetics.* Ithaca: Cornell University Press, 1984.

Stillinger, Jack. *The Hoodwinking of Madeline, and Other Essays on Keats's Poems.* Urbana: University of Illinois Press, 1971.

Suntory Bijutsukan, ed. *Sanjūrokkasen-e—Satake-bon o Chūshin ni.* Tokyo: Suntory Bijutsukan, 1986.

————. *Sanbyaku Kinen, Ukyo-e Tanjō, Hishikawa Moronobu.* Tokyo: Suntory Bijutsukan 1994.

Suzuki Hideo. "Murasaki Shikibu Shū Zen Hyōshaku." *KokuBungaku—Kaishaku to Kyōzai no Kenkyū* 27 (1982) 14: 107.

Suzuki Yoshifuyu. "Hyakunin Isshu Jiten, IV: Hyōgen." In Kubota Jun, ed., *Hyakunin Isshu Hikkei.* Tokyo: Gakutōsha, 1982.

Tahara, Mildred, trans. *Tales of Yamato.* Honolulu: University of Hawai'i Press, 1980.

Takeda, Sharon Sadako. "Clothed in Words: Calligraphic Design on Kosode." In Dale C. Gluckman and Sharon S. Takeda, *When Art Became Fashion.* Los Angeles: County Museum of Art, 1992.

Takeuchi, Melinda. "Kuniyoshi's *Minamoto Raikō and the Earth Spider:* Demons and Protest in Late Tokugawa Japan." *Ars Orientalis* 17 (1987): 5–38.

Takeuchi Michiyo. *Murasaki Shikibu Shū Hyōshaku.* Tokyo: Ōfūsha, 1976.

Tanabe, Willa J. *Paintings of the Lotus Sutra.* New York: Weatherhill, 1988.

Tanaka Jūtarō, ed. *Makura no Sōshi.* Nihon Koten Bungaku Zensho. Tokyo: Asahi Shinbunsha, 1947.

Tanaka Sōsaku. *Hyakunin Isshu KoChūshaku no Kenkyū.* Tokyo: Ōfūsha, 1966.

Taniyama Shigeru, and Higuchi Yoshimaro, eds. *Mikan Chūsei Uta-awase Shū.* Tokyo: Koten Bunko, 1959.

Teele, Nicholas J. "Rules for Poetic Elegance." *Monumenta Nipponica* 31(2) (Summer 1976): 145–164.

Teele, Nicholas J., and Yoshikai Naoto. "Eiyaku Hyakunin Isshu no Hikaku-teki Taishō Kenkyū (Shiryō-hen)." *Sōgō Bunka Kenkyū-sho Kiyō* 11 (March 1994): 210–219.

Teele, Roy E., Nicholas J. Teele, and H. Rebecca Teele, trans. *Ono no Komachi: Poems, Stories, Nō Plays.* New York: Garland, 1993.

Teramoto Naohiko. *Genji Monogatari Juyō Shi Ronkō.* Tokyo: Kazamu Shobō, 1970.

Thompson, Sarah, and H. D. Harootunian. *Undercurrents in the Floating World: Censorship and Japanese Prints.* New York: Asia Society Galleries, 1991.

Tōbu Bijutsukan et al., ed. *Ukiyo-e no Kodomo-tachi: Zuroku* [Children depicted in *ukiyo-e*]. Tokyo: Kumon Shuppan, 1994.

Toda, Kenji. *Descriptive Catalogue of Japanese and Chinese Illustrated Books in the Ryerson Library of the Art Institute of Chicago.* Chicago: Art Institute of Chicago, 1931.

Tokugawa Bijutsukan, ed. *Meihin Zuroku.* Nagoya: Tokugawa Bijutsukan, 1987.

Tokuhara Shigemi. "Hyakunin Isshu Seritsu Ron no Hensen." In Waka Bungaku Ronshū Henshu I'in Kai, eds., *Hyakunin Isshu to Shūka Sen.* Tokyo: Kazama Shobō, 1994.

————, ed. *Mukogawa Joshi Daigaku Toshokan-zō Hyakunin Isshu Bunken Mokuroku.* Nishinomiya: Mukugawa Joshi Daigaku, 1989.

Tōyō Bunko and Nihon Koten Bungakkai, eds. *Hishikawa Moronobu E-hon.* Tokyo: Kijūbon Kankō-kai, 1974.

Tsukamoto Tetsuzō, ed. *Hyakunin Isshu Hitoyo-gatari.* Tokyo: Yūseidō, 1948.

Tyler, Royall. *Japanese Nō Dramas.* Harmondsworth: Penguin, 1992.

Uchiyama Masayoshi. *Yōshaku Hyakunin Isshu.* Tokyo: Bunsendō, n.d.

Ueda Makoto. "*The Tale of Genji* and the Haikai Tradition." In *The World of Genji.*

———. *Bashō and His Interpreters: Selected Hokku with Commentary.* Stanford, Calif.: Stanford University Press, 1991.

Ueno Saeko. "Kosode Moyō Hinagata-bon Shūsei Kaidai." In *Kosode Moyō Hinagata-bon Shūsei.* 4 vols. Tokyo: Gakushū Kenkyūsha, 1974.

Ury, Marian, trans. "The Ōe Conversations." *Monumenta Nipponica* 48(3) (Autumn 1993): 359–380.

Veeser, H. Aram, ed. *The New Historicism.* London: Routledge, 1989.

Vodička, Felix. "The Concretization of the Literary Work: Problems of the Reception of Neruda's Works." In Peter Steiner, ed., *The Prague School.* Austin: University of Texas Press, 1982.

Vos, Fritz. *A Study of the Ise-monogatari, with the Text According to the Den-Teika-Hippon and an Annotated Translation.* 2 vols. The Hague: Mouton, 1957.

Wada Ijirō. *Saga-bon Kō.* Tokyo: Shinbi Shoin, 1916.

Wadagaki, K., trans. *Gleanings from Japanese Literature.* Tokyo: Nampokusha, 1919.

Wakameda, T. *Early Japanese Poets: Complete Translation of the Kokinshiu.* London: Eastern Press, 1922.

Waley, Arthur. *Japanese Poetry: The "Uta."* Oxford: Oxford University Press, 1919.

Walsh, Clara A., trans. *The Master-Singers of Japan, Being Verse Translations from the Japanese Poets.* Wisdom of the East. London: John Murray, 1910.

Watanabe, Tsuneo, and Jun'ichi Iwata. *The Love of the Samurai: A Thousand Years of Japanese Homosexuality.* London: GMP, 1989.

Watson, Burton, trans. *The* Tso Chuan*: Selections from China's Oldest Narrative History.* New York: Columbia University Press, 1989.

———. *Saigyō: Poems of a Mountain Home.* New York: Columbia University Press, 1991.

Wellek, René, and Austin Warren. *Theory of Literature.* Rev. ed. Orlando: Harcourt Brace Jovanovich, 1977.

Wheelwright, Carolyn, ed. *Word in Flower: The Visualization of Classical Literature in Seventeenth-Century Japan.* New Haven: Yale University Art Gallery, 1989.

The World of Genji: Perspectives on the Genji Monogatari. Papers presented at the 8th Conference on Oriental-Western Literary Cultural Relations: Japan, 17–21 August 1982, at Indiana University, Bloomington.

Yamagishi Tokuhei, ed. *Hachidaishū Zenchū.* 3 vols. Tokyo: Yūseidō, 1960.

Yamashita, Samuel Hideo. "The Early Life and Thought of Itō Jinsai." *Harvard Journal of Asiatic Studies* 43(2) (1983): 245–280.

Yasuda, Ken, trans. *Poem Card (The* Hyakunin-isshu *in English).* Tokyo: Kamakurabunko, 1948.

Yeh Chia-ying and Jan Wall. "Theory, Standard, and Practice in Zhong Hong's *Shi pin.*" In Richard C. Miao, ed., *Studies in Chinese Poetry and Poetics,* vol 1. San Francisco: Chinese Materials Center, 1978.

Yiu, Angela. "The Category of Metaphorical Poems *(Hiyuka)* in the *Man'yōshū:* Its Characteristics and Chinese Origins." *Journal of the Association of Teachers of Japanese* 24(1) (April 1990): 7–33.

Yoshida Teruji. *Ukiyo-e Jiten.* 3 vols. Tokyo: Kakubundō, 1971.

Yoshihara Sachiko and Nakada Yumiko. *Manga Hyakunin Isshu.* Tokyo: Heibonsha, 1986.

Yoshikai Naoto. *Hyakunin Isshu no ShinKōsatsu: Teika no Senka Ishiki o Saguru.* Kyoto: Sekai Shisōsha, 1993.

Yoshikai Naoto. "Hyakunin Isshu Ruisho Kankō Mokuroku-Kō." *Chōsa Kenkyū Hōkoku* (KokuBungaku Kenkyū Shiryōkan) 8 (1987): 91–157.

———. "Hyakunin Isshu Shō Hanpon Nishu no Honkoku to Kaidai: Yūsai Shō to Shin Shō." *Kokubungaku Kenkyū Shiryōkan Kiyō* 14 (1988): 125–267.

———. "Hyakunin Isshu Kiso Shiryō Kō." *Chōsa Kenkyū Hōkoku* (KokuBungaku Kenkyū Shiryōkan) 10 (March 1989): 245–334.

———. "Hyakunin Isshu Kenkyū no Genzai." *Kokugaku In Zasshi* 92–1 (January 1992): 177–191.

———. "Hyakunin Isshu Shōha Shō' no Honkoku to Kaidai." *Dōshisha Joshi Daigaku Nihongo Nihon Bungaku* 4 (1992): 31–61.

———. "Ihon 'Hyakunin Isshu Sōgi Shō' no Honkoku to Kaidai." *Dōshisha Joshi Daigaku Nihongo Nihon Bungaku* 5 (1993): 13–47.

———. " 'Sugata-e Hyakunin Isshu' no Honkoku to Kaidai." *Dōshisha Joshi Daigaku Nihongo Nihon Bungaku* 6 (1994): 12–49.

Yoshikawa Kōjirō. *Jinsai, Sorai, Norinaga: Three Classical Philologists of Mid-Tokugawa Japan.* Tokyo: Tōhō Gakkai, 1983.

Zimmerman, Bonnie. "What Has Never Been: An Overview of Lesbian Feminist Criticism." In Elaine Showalter, ed., *The New Feminist Criticism: Essays of Women, Literature, and Theory.* New York: Pantheon, 1985.

PICTURE CREDITS

Part One
Figures

Figure 1. From Steven D. Carter, *Waiting for the Wind: Thirty-Six Poets of Japan's Late Medieval Age* (New York: Columbia University Press, 1989), with additions.

Figure 2. Reproduction from Imperial Household Agency Collection. Kyūsojin Hitaku and Higuchi Yoshimaro, eds. *GoShohon Hyakunin Isshu Shō Kunaichō Shoryōbu-zō* (Kasama Shoin, 1971).

Figure 3. Rpt. ed. Tsukamoto Tetsuzō (Tokyo: Yūhōdō, 1931).

Figure 4. Ozawa Masao, ed., NKBZ 7 (1971), p. 97.

Figure 5. Rpt. *Hyakunin-Isshu and Nori no Hatsu-Ne* (Yokohama: Kelly & Walsh, 1917); photocopy Univ. of British Columbia.

Figure 6. Gotō Museum of Art, Tokyo.

Figure 7. Tokugawa Art Museum, Nagoya.

Figure 8. Tokyo National Museum.

Figure 9. Tokyo National Museum.

Figure 10. Atomi Gakuen Tanki Daigaku Toshokan.

Figure 11. Atomi Gakuen Tanki Daigaku Toshokan.

Figure 12. Atomi Gakuen Tanki Daigaku Toshokan.

Figure 13. Atomi Gakuen Tanki Daigaku Toshokan.

Figure 14. Atomi Gakuen Tanki Daigaku Toshokan.

Figure 15. Osaka: Aratogiya, 1682. KokuBungaku Kenkyū Shiryōkan.

Figure 16. Edo: Nihon-bashi Kawasaki Shichirōhei, 1684. Tenri Daigaku Tenri Toshokan.

Figure 17. Edo: Iwasaki Bunko, n.d. Reproduced in *Hishikawa Moronobu E-hon*, ed. Tōyō Bunko and Nihon Koten Bungakkai (Tokyo: Kijō-bon Kankō-kai, 1974).

Figure 18. Photograph © 1994. The Art Institute of Chicago. All rights reserved.

Figure 19. Former D. Caplan Collection. Reproduced in Tom Evans and Mary Anne Evans, *Shunga: The Art of Love in Japan* (New York: Paddington Press, 1975), fig. 5.63.

Figure 20. Former Vergez Collection. Reproduced in Evans and Evans, fig. 5.51.

Figure 21. Courtesy, Museum of Fine Arts, Boston.

Figure 22. Los Angeles County Museum of Art. Gift of the Ahmanson Foundation.

Figure 23. Photograph © 1994. The Art Institute of Chicago. All rights reserved.

Figure 24. Photograph © 1994. The Art Institute of Chicago. All rights reserved.

Figure 25. Photograph © 1994. The Art Institute of Chicago. All rights reserved.

Figure 26. Atomi Gakuen Tanki Daigaku Toshokan.

Figure 27. Atomi Gakuen Tanki Daigaku Toshokan.
Figure 28. Atomi Gakuen Tanki Daigaku Toshokan.
Figure 29. Atomi Gakuen Tanki Daigaku Toshokan.
Figure 30. Atomi Gakuen Tanki Daigaku Toshokan
Figure 31. Tokyo National Museum.
Figure 32. Tokyo National Museum.
Figure 33. Itsukushima Shrine.
Figure 34. Komatsu Shigemi, *Heike Nōkyō no Kenkyū*, vol. II (Tokyo: Kōdansha, 1976), p. 829.
Figure 35. Osaka Municipal Museum of Art.
Figure 36. From Dale Carolyn Gluckman and Sharon Sadako Takeda, *When Art Became Fashion: Kosode in Edo-Period Japan* (Los Angeles: County Museum of Art, 1992), fig. 29a.
Figure 37. Atomi Gakuen Tanki Daigaku Toshokan.
Figure 38. British Museum.
Figure 39. Courtesy of the Freer Gallery of Art, Smithsonian Institution, Washington, D.C. 07.548.
Figure 40. Atomi Gakuen Tanki Daigaku Toshokan.
Figure 41. Atomi Gakuen Tanki Daigaku Toshokan.
Figure 42. Tokyo National Museum.
Figure 43. Collection of the author.
Figure 44. Collection of the author.
Figure 45. Collection of the author.
Figure 46. Collection of the author.
Figure 47. Atomi Gakuen Tanki Daigaku Toshokan.
Figure 48. Atomi Gakuen Tanki Daigaku Toshokan.
Figure 49. Atomi Gakuen Tanki Daigaku Toshokan.
Figure 50. Atomi Gakuen Tanki Daigaku Toshokan.
Figure 51. Kanagawa Prefectural Museum of History, Yokohama.
Figure 52. Yoshihara Sachiko and Nakada Yumiko, *Manga Hyakunin Isshu* (Tokyo: Heibonsha, 1986).

Color Plates

Plate 1. Tōyama Memorial Museum, Saitama Prefecture.
Plate 2. Kanebo, Ltd.
Plate 3. Mukogawa Joshi Daigaku Toshokan.
Plate 4. Kumon Kodomo Kenkyūjo.
Plate 5. British Museum.
Plate 6. Mukogawa Joshi Daigaku Toshokan.
Plate 7. Atomi Gakuen Tanki Daigaku Toshokan.

Part Two
Atomi Gakuen Tanki Daigaku Toshokan

Hyakunin Isshu Soan-bon (Hyakunin Isshu Kōetsu-hitsu), Poems 1–100.

Hishikawa Moronobu, *(Ken'yō E-iri Uta to Kenzu) Hyakunin Isshu Zōsan Shō Denki Keifu).* Edo: Urokogataya, 1678.
        2–4, 3–1, 4–2, 5–1, 6–2, 7–2, 8–1, 9–2, 10–1, 11–2, 12–1, 13–1, 14–2, 15–1, 16–1, 18–2, 19–1, 20–2, 21–2, 22–4, 23–1, 24–2, 27–1, 28–1, 29–1, 30–1, 31–1, 32–1, 33–1, 34–1, 35–1, 36–1, 39–1, 40–1, 42–1, 43–2, 44–1, 45–1, 46–1, 47–1, 48–1, 49–4, 50–1, 51–1, 52–1, 53–1, 54–1, 55–1, 56–1, 57–1, 58–1, 59–1, 60–1, 61–1, 62–2, 63–1, 64–1,

65–1, 66–1, 67–2, 68–1, 69–1, 70–1, 71–1, 72–1, 73–1, 74–1, 75–2, 76–3, 77–1, 78–1, 79–1, 80–1, 81–1, 82–2, 83–1, 84–1, 85–1, 86–1, 87–1, 88–1, 89–1, 90–3, 92–1, 93–1, 94–1, 95–3, 96–1, 97–2, 98–1, 99–3, 100–1

Hishikawa Moronobu, *Hyakunin Isshu Zōsan Shō.* 3 vols. 27.5 x 18.5 cm. Edo: Kinoshita Jin'emon, 1695.
    4–4, 5–2, 9–3, 10–2, 11–3, 13–3, 16–2, 18–1, 19–2, 20–3, 21–3, 23–2, 25–2, 26–4, 28–2, 29–2, 31–3, 32–4, 33–3, 38–2, 39–3, 40–4, 41–1, 42–2, 43–1, 44–4, 45–2, 46–4, 47–3, 48–3, 49–1, 50–3, 51–2, 52–2, 53–4, 54–3, 56–4, 57–2, 60–3, 61–3, 62–1, 63–4, 64–2, 65–4, 66–3, 67–3, 68–2, 69–2, 70–3, 71–2, 73–3, 74–4, 75–4, 76–2, 77–4, 79–3, 80–4, 81–3, 82–1, 83–2, 84–3, 85–3, 86–3, 87–3, 88–2, 89–3, 91–3, 92–3, 93–3, 94–2, 95–1, 96–2, 97–3, 99–2, 100–3

Anon., *(Ko-gata) Hyakunin Isshu Zōsan Shō.* Kyoto: Kōto Shorin, 1746.
    1–1, 3–2, 4–3, 7–3, 8–2, 11–4, 12–3, 13–2, 17–4, 18–4, 19–3, 20–4, 22–1, 24–4, 25–1, 26–1, 27–2, 28–3, 32–2, 33–1, 37–1, 38–1, 39–2, 41–2, 43–3, 46–2, 47–2, 48–2, 49–3, 50–2, 55–2, 59–2, 61–2, 62–4, 70–2, 72–2, 73–2, 74–2, 75–3, 76–4, 77–2, 78–2, 79–2, 81–2, 84–2, 85–2, 86–2, 87–2, 89–2, 91–2, 92–2, 93–2, 95–4, 100–2

Hakuyōken Gyōjō, *Ogura Yama Hyakushu Hinagata.* Kyoto: Yezōshiya Kisaemon, 1688.
    2–5, 6–3, 8–4, 9–3, 10–3, 26–2, 27–3, 31–4, 41–3

Take Heiji, *Ogura Yama Shikishi Moyō.* Edo: Hon'ya Seibei, 1689.
    1–3, 6–4, 8–4, 9–4, 13–4, 15–4, 17–3, 18–3, 19–4, 21–4, 22–3, 23–4, 27–4, 28–4, 29–4, 33–4, 34–3, 35–3, 36–2, 37–3, 38–4, 40–3, 41–4, 42–4, 43–4, 44–3, 45–4, 48–4, 53–3, 54–2, 55–3, 57–4, 58–4, 64–4, 66–4, 68–4, 69–3, 72–4, 77–3, 78–3, 79–4, 80–3, 82–4, 83–4, 84–4, 85–4, 88–3, 90–4, 94–4, 96–4, 98–4, 99–4, 100–4

Kangyoku Hyakunin Isshu Suishōsō. Pictures by Sōsekishi. 1804.
    3–4, 8–3, 15–2, 20–1, 22–2, 24–1, 25–4, 26–3, 30–2, 34–2, 35–2, 36–3, 42–3, 44–2, 50–4, 51–4, 52–3, 53–2, 55–4, 56–2, 60–2, 66–2, 67–1, 68–3, 70–4, 74–3, 76–1, 81–4, 83–3, 87–4, 92–4, 95–2, 96–3, 97–1

Anon., *A Hundred Verses from Old Japan,* trans. William N. Porter (Oxford, 1909).
    1–2, 2–2, 5–3, 6–1, 7–1, 12–2, 16–4, 17–1, 21–1, 30–4, 33–2, 38–3, 39–4, 46–5, 47–4, 52–4, 54–4, 58–2, 59–4, 60–4, 61–4, 67–4, 71–4, 73–4, 88–4, 89–4, 94–3, 97–4, 98–3, 99–1

Hasegawa Mitsunobu, *Dansen Hyakunin Isshu Taisei.* Osaka: Osaka Shorin, 1755.
    2–1, 4–1, 9–1, 11–1, 12–4, 14–1, 15–3, 16–3, 17–2, 23–3, 29–3, 30–3, 31–2, 32–3, 40–2, 45–3, 46–3, 51–3, 56–3, 57–3, 63–3, 64–3, 69–4, 72–3, 75–1, 80–2, 86–4

(Nichiyō Zatsuroku Fujin Shubunko) Shūgyoku Hyakunin Isshu-kan. Pictures by Keisei Eisen. Edo: Hakkō Shorin, 1836; rpt. 1850.
    2–3, 5–4, 14–4, 65–2

Kuniyoshi, *Hyakunin Isshu no Uchi.*
    6–4

The Art Institute of Chicago

Kimono Designs, vol. 2 (Edo: Yezōshiya Hachiyemon; Kyoto: Yezōshiya Kisayemon, 1688), plate I. Photograph © 1994. The Art Institute of Chicago. All rights reserved.
    58–3

Kimono Designs, vol. 2 (Edo: Yezōshiya Hachiyemon; Kyoto: Yezōshiya Kisayemon, 1688), plate III. Photograph © 1994. The Art Institute of Chicago. All rights reserved.
    59–3

Kimono Designs, vol. 2, (Edo: Yezōshiya Hachiyemon; Kyoto: Yezōshiya Kisayemon, 1688),

Tokyo National Museum

Kanō Tan'yū (attrib.), *Hyakunin Isshu Gazō, Tan'yū-hitsu, Kan,* undated (17th century?). Ink and colors on paper, remounted as an album, 1 vol. 30 x 20 cm.
90–1, 91–1, 93–4, 98–2

Dazaifu Temmangū

Kose Hidenobu, *Ehon Sugawara Jikki.* 1810; rpt. 1842.
24–3

Tokyo Daigaku Toshokan

Saga-bon Ise Monogatari: "Kutakake" (*dan* 14)
62–3

Collection of the author

Eiga Hyakushu Monshū Shō. Pictures by Utagawa Sadahide. Edo: 1817; rpt. 1843, 1850.
3–3, 10–4, 91–4

E-iri Genji Monogatari. Pictures by Yamamoto Shunshō. Edo: 1652; rpt. Yūhōdō, 1927.
49–2, 90–2

INDEX OF POETS AND
FIRST LINES

SUBJECT INDEX

ABOUT THE AUTHOR

Joshua S. Mostow received his doctorate from the Comparative Literature and Literary Theory Program of the University of Pennsylvania. He is currently an associate professor in the Department of Asian Studies at the University of British Columbia.